ROMANTICISM AND THE HERITAGE OF ROUSSEAU

ROMANTICISM AND THE HERITAGE OF ROUSSEAU

THOMAS McFARLAND

CLARENDON PRESS · OXFORD
1995

Oxford University Press, Walton Street, Oxford OX2 6DP
Oxford   New York
Athens   Auckland   Bangkok   Bombay
Calcutta   Cape Town   Dar es Salaam   Delhi
Florence   Hong Kong   Istanbul   Karachi
Kuala Lumpur   Madras   Madrid   Melbourne
Mexico City   Nairobi   Paris   Singapore
Taipei   Tokyo   Toronto
and associated companies in
Berlin Ibadan

Oxford is a trade mark of Oxford University Press

Published in the United States
by Oxford University Press Inc., New York

British Library Cataloguing in Publication Data
Data available

Library of Congress Cataloging in Publication Data
McFarland, Thomas, 1926–
Romanticism and the heritage of Rousseau/Thomas McFarland.
Includes bibliographical references.
1. Rousseau, Jean-Jacques, 1712–1778—Influence.   2. Literature,
Modern—History and criticism—Theory, etc.   3. Influence (Literary,
artistic, etc.)   4. Romanticism.   I. Title.
PQ2057.A2M28   1995
809'.9145—dc20   94-29775
ISBN 0 19 818287 2

Typeset by Cotswold Typesetting Ltd., Gloucester
Printed in Great Britain on acid-free paper by
Biddles Ltd.,
Guildford and King's Lynn

For
my teacher and friend
Albert B. Friedman

Preface

THE arguments of this book issue from a conviction that Romantic studies in the last quarter of the twentieth century have gone significantly astray. Very striking editorial successes have been achieved—no scholar can be unaware of the magnificence of the *Collected Coleridge* or of the *Cornell Wordsworth*. The new edition of De Quincey, now in progress under the general editorship of Grevel Lindop, promises to revolutionize De Quincey studies. But such unarguable achievement in editing hardly finds a parallel in interpretational studies. A great, and indeed, ever-augmenting number of books and articles appears. Many of these, however, are redundant; many more are devoted to quasi-sociological endeavours—ethnic studies, feminist studies—that however important they may be thought to be in a larger social context, are hardly more than ancillary to what is already known about Romanticism.

A small but significant number of interpretational and theoretical studies, however, bears directly upon the main reality of Romantic culture. Produced by important scholars, these studies warrant, and have received, the most serious attention. Working in synergy, they have tended to direct attention away from the consideration of the personal and the qualitative, and rebestow it upon the socio-historical and the political. Though they are by no means identical, and even in some instances not compatible, in their combined effect they have nevertheless managed to result in what has become a reigning orthodoxy of attitudes and approaches.

The present volume attempts to shake the foundations of that new orthodoxy. On the one hand, it mounts a polemic against certain works that figure importantly, now and in recent years, in the reconceiving of Romanticism. On the other, by attempting to consider in renewed depth certain central collocations of Romanticism, it attempts to hear once more the plangency of Romantic activity. It brings to bear, in the latter endeavour, an unusually dense incidence of quotation. To whatever extent so much quotation might make it difficult to read the book rapidly, that extent, it is hoped, will prove justified by providing a sense of the variety, complexity, and resonance of Romantic phenomena.

A briefer and less ramified version of Chapter 3 was delivered as the inaugural paper for the Oxford Interfaculty Seminar: Restoration to Reform 1660–1832, at All Souls College in the University of Oxford; and it was published in 1989 by the Ohio State University Press, in a volume edited by Frederick Burwick and called *Coleridge's* Biographia Literaria: *Text and Meaning*.

I have no adequate words to express how important the following circle of friends has been to me: Barbara Bauer, Alan Berk, Haskell Block, Marcus Boggs, Drummond Bone, Frederick Burwick, M. Donald Coleman, Albert Cook, Robert Crawford, Christopher Drummond, Richard Gravil, Noyes Keller Grovier, Norma Hurlburt, Darr Kartychak, Robert Langbaum, Molly Lefebure, Alice Lentz, Samuel R. Levin, Grevel Lindop, James McFarland, Daniel Miller, Stuart Miller, Robert Morrison, Joseph Moses, and Nicholas Roe.

T.M.

Contents

Key to Brief Titles Cited

BRIEF titles that appear in the notes refer either to full citations occurring shortly before or to the editions listed below.

Abrams
: M. H. Abrams, *The Correspondent Breeze: Essays on English Romanticism* (New York: W. W. Norton, 1984).

Addison
: Joseph Addison, Richard Steele, *et al.*, *The Spectator*, ed. Gregory Smith, Everyman's Library (London: J. M. Dent; New York: E. P. Dutton, 1961–3). 4 vols.

Aids to Reflection
: S. T. Coleridge, *Aids to Reflections in the Formation of a Manly Character, on the Several Grounds of Prudence, and Religion* ... (London: Taylor and Hessey, 1825).

Allsop
: *Letters, Conversations, and Recollections of S. T. Coleridge* [ed. Thomas Allsop] (New York: Harper and Brothers, 1836).

Argument
: Thomas McFarland, 'A Coleridgean Criticism of the Work of M. H. Abrams', in *High Romantic Argument: Essays for M. H. Abrams*, ed. Lawrence Lipking (Ithaca, NY: Cornell University Press, 1981).

Arnold
: Matthew Arnold, *Essays in Criticism, Second Series* (London: Macmillan, 1905 [1888])

Aulard, *Christianity*
: A. Aulard, *Christianity and the French Revolution*, trans. Lady Frazer (Boston: Little, Brown, and Company, 1927).

Aulard, *Revolution*
: A. Aulard, *The French Revolution: A Political History 1789–1804*, trans. Bernard Miall (New York: Charles Scribner's Sons, 1910). 4 vols.

Aulard, *Taine*
: A. Aulard, *Taine: Historien de la révolution française* (Paris: Librairie Armand Colin, 1907).

Barron Field
: *Barron Field's Memoirs of Wordsworth*, ed. Geoffrey Little (Sydney: Sydney University Press, 1975).

Barth
: J. Robert Barth, SJ, *The Symbolic Imagination: Coleridge and the Romantic Tradition* (Princeton, NJ: Princeton University Press, 1977).

Bate
: Walter Jackson Bate, *Coleridge* (New York: The Macmillan Co., 1968).

Baudelaire   Baudelaire, *Œuvres complètes*, ed. Claude Pichois,
                      Bibliothèque de la Pléiade (Paris: Gallimard,
                      1975–6). 2 vols.
Beck   Immanuel Kant, *Critique of Practical Reason and Other
                      Writings in Moral Philosophy*, trans. and ed. with an
                      introduction by Lewis White Beck (Chicago: Uni-
                      versity of Chicago Press, 1950).
Benjamin   Walter Benjamin, *The Origins of the German Tragic
                      Drama*, trans. John Osborne (London: NLB, 1977).
Benjamin, *Reflections*   Walter Benjamin, *Reflections, Essays, Aphorisms, Auto-
                      biographical Writings*, ed. Peter Demetz, trans.
                      Edmund Jephcott (New York: Harcourt Brace
                      Jovanovich, 1978).
Besterman   Theodore Besterman, *Voltaire* (Chicago: University of
                      Chicago Press, 1976).
Biographia   Samuel Taylor Coleridge, *Biographia Literaria*, ed.
                      James Engell and W. Jackson Bate, 2 vols. (The
                      Collected Works of Samuel Taylor Coleridge, vii;
                      London: Routledge & Kegan Paul; Princeton, NJ:
                      Princeton University Press, 1983).
Blake   *The Complete Poetry and Prose of William Blake*, ed.
                      David V. Erdman (Berkeley and Los Angeles:
                      University of California Press, 1982).
Blake, *Life*   Mona Wilson, *The Life of William Blake* (1927, rev.
                      1948; repr. New York: Cooper Square, 1969).
Brinkley   *Coleridge on the Seventeenth Century*, ed. Roberta
                      Florence Brinkley (New York: Greenwood Press,
                      1968).
Brinton   Clarence Crane Brinton, *The Jacobins: An Essay in the
                      New History* (New York: The Macmillan Co.,
                      1930).
Buonarotti   Philippe Buonarotti, *Babeuf's Conspiracy for Equality*,
                      trans. Bronterre O'Brien (New York: August M.
                      Kelley, 1965 [1836]).
Carlyle   *The Works of Thomas Carlyle in Thirty Volumes*, ed.
                      H. D. Traill, centenary edition (London: Chapman
                      & Hall, 1896–9). 30 vols.
Church and State   Samuel Taylor Coleridge, *Constitution of the Church
                      and State*, ed. John Colmer (The Collected Works of
                      Samuel Taylor Coleridge, x; London: Routledge &
                      Kegan Paul; Princeton, NJ: Princeton University
                      Press, 1976).
Cobb   Richard Cobb, *The People's Armies, the armées révolu-
                      tionnaires, Instrument of the Terror in the Depart-

ments in April 1793 to Floréal Year II, trans. Marianne Elliott (New Haven, Conn.: Yale University Press, 1987 [1961–3]).

Cobban   *The Debate on the French Revolution*, ed. Alfred Cobban (London: Nicholas Kaye, 1950).

Coleridge, *Marginalia*   Samuel Taylor Coleridge, *Marginalia*, ed. George Whalley *et al.* 3 vols. to date (The Collected Works of Samuel Taylor Coleridge, xii; London: Routledge & Kegan Paul, Princeton: Princeton University Press, 1980–).

Coleridge, *Poems*   *The Complete Poetical Works of Samuel Taylor Coleridge*, ed. Ernest Hartley Coleridge (Oxford: Clarendon Press, 1912). 2 vols.

Collected Letters   *Collected Letters of Samuel Taylor Coleridge*, ed. Earl Leslie Griggs (Oxford: Clarendon Press, 1956–71). 6 vols.

Condillac   [Etienne Bonnot, Abbé de] Condillac, *Traité des sensations, Traité des animaux*, Corpus des œuvres de philosophie en langue Française (Paris: Librairie de Arthème Fayard, 1984).

Cone   Carl B. Cone, *The English Jacobins: Reformers in Late 18th Century England* (New York: Charles Scribner's Sons, 1968).

Conquest   Robert Conquest, *The Harvest of Sorrow: Soviet Collectivization and the Terror-Famine* (New York: Oxford University Press, 1986).

CPT   Thomas McFarland, *Coleridge and the Pantheist Tradition* (Oxford: Clarendon Press, 1969).

De Man   Paul De Man, 'The Rhetoric of Temporality', in *Interpretation: Theory and Practice*, ed. Charles Singleton (Baltimore: Johns Hopkins University Press, 1969).

De Man, *Allegories*   Paul De Man, *Allegories of Reading: Figural Language in Rousseau, Nietzsche, Rilke, and Proust* (New Haven, Conn.: Yale University Press, 1979).

De Man, *Writings*   Paul De Man, *Critical Writings, 1953–78*, ed. Lindsay Waters (Minneapolis: University of Minnesota Press, 1989).

De Quincey   *The Collected Writings of Thomas De Quincey*, ed. David Masson (Edinburgh: Adam and Charles Black, 1889–90). 14 vols.

Descartes   *The Philosophical Works of Descartes*, trans. Elizabeth S. Haldane and G. R. T. Ross (Cambridge: Cambridge University Press, 1967). 2 vols.

Descartes, *Œuvres*   *Œuvres de Descartes*, ed. Charles Adam and Paul Tannery, vi (Paris: Léopold Cerf, 1902).

De Vleeschauwer   Herman-J. De Vleeschauwer, *The Development of Kantian Thought: The History of a Doctrine*, trans. A. R. C. Duncan (London: Thomas Nelson and Sons Ltd., 1962).

De Vleeschauwer, *Déduction*   H. J. de Vleeschauwer, *La Déduction transcendentale dans l'œuvre de Kant* (Paris: Edouard Champion; 's-Gravenhage: Martinus Nijhoff; Antwerp: 'De Sikkel', 1934–7). 3 vols.

Diderot   Denis Diderot, *Œuvres philosophiques*, ed. Paul Vernière (Paris: Éditions Garnier Frères, 1956).

Doyle   William Doyle, *The Oxford History of the French Revolution* (Oxford and New York: Oxford University Press, 1989).

Early Years   *The Letters of William and Dorothy Wordsworth: The Early Years, 1787–1805*, ed. Ernest de Selincourt, revised by Chester L. Shaver (Oxford: Clarendon Press, 1967).

Eichner   Hans Eichner, *Friedrich Schlegel* (New York: Twayne, 1970).

Emerson   *The Complete Works of Ralph Waldo Emerson*, ed. E. W. Emerson, centenary edition (Boston: Houghton Mifflin & Co., 1903–12). 12 vols.

Emerson, *Journals*   *The Journals and Miscellaneous Notebooks of Ralph Waldo Emerson*, ii. *1822–26*, ed. William H. Gilman, Alfred R. Ferguson, Merrell P. Davis (Cambridge, Mass.: Harvard University Press, 1961).

Engell   James Engell, *The Creative Imagination: Enlightenment to Romanticism* (Cambridge, Mass.: Harvard University Press, 1981).

Erdman   David V. Erdman, *Commerce des Lumières: John Oswald and the British in Paris, 1790–1793* (Columbia: University of Missouri Press, 1986).

Essays   Samuel Taylor Coleridge, *Essays on His Times, in* The Morning Post *and* The Courier, ed. David V. Erdman, 3 vols. (The Collected Works of Samuel Taylor Coleridge, iii; London: Routledge & Kegan Paul; Princeton, NJ: Princeton University Press, 1978).

Fairchild   Hoxie Neale Fairchild, *The Romantic Quest* (New York: Columbia University Press, 1931).

Feher   Ferenc Feher, *The Frozen Revolution: An Essay on Jacobinism* (Cambridge: Cambridge University

	Press; Paris: Éditions de la Maison des Sciences de l'Homme, 1987).
Fletcher	Angus Fletcher, *Allegory: The Theory of a Symbolic Mode* (Ithaca, NY: Cornell University Press, 1964).
Friend	Samuel Taylor Coleridge, *The Friend*, ed. Barbara E. Rooke, 2 vols. (The Collected Works of Samuel Taylor Coleridge, iv; London: Routledge & Kegan Paul; Princeton, NJ: Princeton University Press, 1969).
Froissart	Froissart, *Chronicles*, trans. and ed. Geoffrey Brereton (Harmondsworth, Middlesex: Penguin Books, 1978).
Fuhrmans	*F. W. J. Schelling Briefe und Dokumente*, iii. *1803–1809*, ed. Horst Fuhrmans (Bonn: Bouvier Verlag Herbert Grundmann, 1975).
Furet	François Furet, *Marx and the French Revolution*, trans. Deborah Kan Furet, with Selections from Karl Marx edited and introduced by Lucien Calvié (Chicago: University of Chicago Press, 1988).
Furet and Ozouf	François Furet and Mona Ozouf, *Dictionnaire Critique de la Révolution française* (Paris: Flammarion, 1988).
Gadamer	Hans-Georg Gadamer, *Truth and Method* (New York: Seabury Press, 1975).
Gaxotte	Pierre Gaxotte, *La Révolution française*, nouvelle édition (Paris: Fayard, 1970).
Godwin	William Godwin, *An Enquiry Concerning Political Justice, and its Influence on General Virtue and Happiness* (London: G. G. J. and J. Robinson, 1793). 2 vols. Facsimile edn. published by Woodstock Books, Oxford and New York, 1992.
Goethe	Johann Wolfgang Goethe, *Gedenkausgabe der Werke, Briefe und Gespräche*, ed. Ernst Beutler (Zurich: Artemis Verlag, 1948–71). 27 vols.
Goethes Werke	*Goethes sämtliche Werke*, ed. Eduard von der Hellen, Jubilee edn. (Stuttgart and Berlin: Cotta, 1902–12). 41 vols.
Goodwin	Albert Goodwin, *The Friends of Liberty: The English Democratic Movement in the Age of the French Revolution* (London: Hutchinson & Co. (Publishers) Ltd., 1979).
Gravil	*Coleridge's Imagination: Essays in Memory of Pete Laver*, ed. Richard Gravil, Lucy Newlyn, and Nicholas Roe (Cambridge: Cambridge University Press, 1985).

Hallam Tennyson   [Hallam Tennyson], *Alfred Lord Tennyson: A Memoir*,
                       by his son (New York: Greenwood Press, 1969
                       [1897]). 2 vols.

Hanson   Lawrence Hanson, *The Life of S. T. Coleridge*
                       (London: George Allen & Unwin Ltd., 1938).

Harper   George McLean Harper, *William Wordsworth: His
                       Life, Works, and Influence* (New York: Charles
                       Scribner's Sons, 1916). 2 vols.

Hartley   David Hartley, *Observations on Man, His Frame, His
                       Duty, and His Expectations* (London: S. Richardson,
                       for James Leake and Wm. Frederick, 1749).
                       Scholars' Facsimiles and Reprints, Delmar, New
                       York, 1976. 2 vols. in 1.

Hartman   Geoffrey Hartman, *Wordsworth's Poetry 1787–1814*
                       (New Haven, Conn.: Yale University Press, 1964).

Hazlitt   *The Complete Works of William Hazlitt*, ed. P. P.
                       Howe, after the edition by A. R. Waller and Arnold
                       Glover (London: J. M. Dent & Sons, 1930–4). 21
                       vols.

Heine   *Heinrich Heine: Historisch-kritische Gesamtausgabe der
                       Werke*, Dusseldorf edn., ed. Manfred Windfuhr
                       (Hamburg: Hoffman and Campe, 1973–). 15 vols.

Holmes   Richard Holmes, *Shelley: The Pursuit* (New York:
                       E. P. Dutton, 1975).

Holmes, *Coleridge*   Richard Holmes, *Coleridge: Early Visions* (New York:
                       Viking, 1990).

Hume   David Hume, *An Enquiry Concerning Human Under-
                       standing*, reprinted from the posthumous edition of
                       1777 and edited . . . by L. A. Selby-Bigge, second
                       edition (Oxford: Clarendon Press, 1961).

Husserl   Edmund Husserl, *Cartesianische Meditationen und
                       Pariser Vorträge*, second edition (The Hague:
                       Martinus Nijhoff, 1963).

Idler   *The Yale Edition of The Works of Samuel Johnson*, ii.
                       The Idler *and* The Adventurer (New Haven, Conn.:
                       Yale University Press, 1963).

Inquiring Spirit   *Inquiring Spirit: A New Presentation of Coleridge from
                       his Published and Unpublished Writings*, ed. Kathleen
                       Coburn (New York: Pantheon Books, 1951).

Jackson   J. R. de J. Jackson, *Method and Imagination in
                       Coleridge's Criticism* (Cambridge, Mass.: Harvard
                       University Press, 1969).

Jacobi   *Friedrich Heinrich Jacobi's Werke*, ed. Friedrich Roth and Friedrich Köppen (Leipzig: Gerhard Fleischer. 1812–25). 7 vols. in 6.

James — William James, *The Principles of Psychology*, ed. George A. Miller (Cambridge, Mass.: Harvard University Press, 1983).

J. M. Thompson — J. M. Thompson, *Robespierre* (Oxford: Basil Blackwell, 1988 [1935]).

Jonathan Bate — Jonathan Bate, *Romantic Ecology: Wordsworth and the Environmental Tradition* (London and New York: Routledge, 1991).

Jordan — David P. Jordan, *The Revolutionary Career of Maximilien Robespierre* (New York: Free Press, 1975).

Kant — *Kants gesammelte Schriften*, ed. by the Royal Prussian Academy of Sciences (Berlin: Druck und Verlag von Georg Reimer; continued to the present by Walter de Gruyter & Co., 1902–). 31 vols. to date.

Keats, *Letters* — *The Letters of John Keats, 1814–1821*, ed. Hyder E. Rollins (Cambridge, Mass.: Harvard University Press, 1972). 2 vols.

Kelly — J. N. D. Kelly, *Early Christian Creeds*, third edition (London: Longman, 1972).

Kitson — Peter Kitson, '"The Electric Fluid of Truth": The Ideology of the Commonwealthsman in Coleridge's The Plot Discovered', *Coleridge and the Armoury of the Human Mind: Essays on his Prose Writings*, ed. Peter J. Kitson and Thomas N. Carns (London: Franklin Cass, 1991).

Knight — G. Wilson Knight, *Lord Byron: Christian Virtues* (London: Routledge & Kegan Paul, 1952).

Kolakowski — Leszek Kolakowski, *Main Currents of Marxism: Its Origin, Growth, and Dissolution*, trans. P. S. Falla (Oxford: Clarendon Press, 1978). 3 vols.

Korngold — Ralph Korngold, *Robespierre: First Modern Dictator* (London: Macmillan, 1937).

Kritische Schriften — *Friedrich Schlegel: Kritische Schriften*, ed. Wolfdietrich Rasch, second, enlarged edition (Munich: Carl Hanser Verlag, 1964).

Kurtz — Benjamin P. Kurtz, 'Coleridge on Swedenborg with Unpublished Marginalia on the "Prodromus"', in *Essays and Studies: University of California Publications in English*, xiv (Berkeley and Los Angeles: University of California Press, 1943).

Lamartine — Alphonse de Lamartine, *Histoire des Girondins*, ed.

	Tradition (London: Oxford University Press, 1951 [1936]).
Liu	Alan Liu, *Wordsworth: The Sense of History* (Stanford, Calif.: Stanford University Press, 1989).
Locke	John Locke, *An Essay Concerning Human Understanding*, ed. Peter H. Nidditch (Oxford: Clarendon Press, 1975).
McElderry	*Shelley's Critical Prose*, ed. Bruce R. McElderry, Jr., Regents Critical Series (Lincoln: University of Nebraska Press, 1967).
McFarland, *Romanticism*	Thomas McFarland, *Romanticism and the Forms of Ruin: Wordsworth, Coleridge, and Modalities of Fragmentation* (Princeton, NJ: Princeton University Press, 1981).
McFarland, *Wordsworth*	Thomas McFarland, *William Wordsworth: Intensity and Achievement* (Oxford: Clarendon Press, 1992).
McGann	Jerome J. McGann, *The Romantic Ideology: A Critical Investigation* (Chicago: The University of Chicago Press, 1983).
Madelin	Louis Madelin, *The French Revolution*, trans. from the French (New York: G. P. Putnam's Sons, 1928).
Manning	Peter Manning, *Reading Romantics: Text and Context* (New York and Oxford: Oxford University Press, 1990).
Marxist Reader	*The Marxist Reader: The Most Significant and Enduring Works of Marxism*, ed. Emile Burns (New York: Avenel Books, 1982).
Matrat	Jean Matrat, *Robespierre; or the Tyranny of the Majority*, trans. Alan Kendall and Felix Brenner (New York: Charles Scribner's Sons, 1971).
Mayne	[Zachary Mayne], *Two Dissertations Concerning Sense, and the Imagination. With an Essay on Consciousness* (London: Printed for J. Tonson in the Strand, 1728).
Michelet	[Jules] Michelet, *Histoire de la Révolution française*, ed. Gérard Walter, Bibliothèque de la Pléiade (Paris: Gallimard, 1952). 2 vols.
Miscellaneous Criticism	*Coleridge's Miscellaneous Criticism*, ed. T. M. Raysor (London: Constable, 1936).
Monk	Ray Monk, *Ludwig Wittgenstein: The Duty of Genius* (London: Vintage, 1991).
Montaigne	Michel de Montaigne, *Œuvres complètes*, ed. Albert Thibaudet and Maurice Rat, Bibliothèque de la Pléiade (Paris: Gallimard, 1962).

Nettleship   Richard Lewis Nettleship, *Lectures on the Republic of Plato* (London: Macmillan, 1963).

Notebooks   *The Notebooks of Samuel Taylor Coleridge*, ed. Kathleen Coburn *et al.*, 4 vols. in 8 to date (London: Routledge & Kegan Paul; Princeton, NJ: Princeton University Press, 1957–).

Originality   Thomas McFarland, *Originality and Imagination* (Baltimore: Johns Hopkins University Press, 1985).

Packe   Michael St. John Packe, *The Life of John Stuart Mill* (New York: The Macmillan Co., 1954).

Paine   Thomas Paine, *Political Writings*, ed. Bruce Kuklick (Cambridge: Cambridge University Press, 1989).

Paley   Morton D. Paley, *The Continuing City: William Blake's* Jerusalem (Oxford: Clarendon Press, 1983).

Pascal   Blaise Pascal, *Œuvres complètes.* ed. Louis Lafuma (Paris: Éditions Seuil, 1963).

Pearsall Smith   *Donne's Sermons: Selected Passages with an Essay by Logan Pearsall Smith* (Oxford: Clarendon Press, 1951 [1919]).

Philosophical Lectures   *The Philosophical Lectures of Samuel Taylor Coleridge, Hitherto Unpublished*, ed. Kathleen Coburn (London: Pilot Press, 1949).

Piper   H. W. Piper, *The Singing of Mount Abora: Coleridge's Use of Biblical Imagery and Natural Symbolism in Poetry and Philosophy* (Rutherford, NJ: Fairleigh Dickinson University Press, 1987).

Pollin   Burton R. Pollin, assisted by Redmond Burke, 'John Thelwall's Marginalia in a Copy of Coleridge's *Biographia Literaria*', *Bulletin of the New York Public Library*, 74 (1970).

Prose   *The Prose Works of William Wordsworth*, ed. W. J. B. Owen and Jane Worthington Smyser (Oxford: Clarendon Press, 1974). 3 vols.

Rabelais   François Rabelais, *Œuvres complètes.* ed. Jacques Boulenger and Lucien Scheler, Bibliothèque de la Pléiade (Paris: Gallimard, 1955).

Rambler   *The Yale Edition of the Works of Samuel Johnson*, iii–v. The Rambler (New Haven, Conn.: Yale University Press, 1969).

Randall   John Herman Randall, Jr., *The Career of Philosophy*, ii. *From the German Enlightenment to the Age of Darwin* (New York: Columbia University Press, 1965).

Ransom   John Crowe Ransom, *The New Criticism* (Norwalk, Conn.: New Directions, 1941).

Review	E. P. Thompson, Review of David Erdman (ed.), *Essays on His Times*, 3 vols., in *The Collected Works of Samuel Taylor Coleridge*, iii (London: Routledge & Kegan Paul; Princeton, NJ: Princeton University Press, 1970), in *The Wordsworth Circle*, 10 (Summer 1979).
Robespierre	*Robespierre: Textes choisis*, ed. Jean Poperen (Paris: Editions Sociales, 1956–8). 3 vols.
Robinson	*Henry Crabb Robinson on Books and their Writers*, ed. Edith J. Morley (London: J. M. Dent, 1938). 3 vols.
Roe, *Politics*	Nicholas Roe, *The Politics of Nature: Wordsworth and Some Contemporaries* (Basingstoke and London: Macmillan, 1992).
Roe, *Wordsworth*	Nicholas Roe, *Wordsworth and Coleridge: The Radical Years* (Oxford: Clarendon Press, 1988).
Romantic Cruxes	Thomas McFarland, *Romantic Cruxes: The English Essayists and the Spirit of the Age* (Oxford: Clarendon Press, 1987).
Rose	R. B. Rose, *Gracchus Babeuf: The First Revolutionary Communist* (London: Edward Arnold, 1978).
Rousseau	Jean-Jacques Rousseau, *Œuvres complètes*, ed. Bernard Gagnebin and Marcel Raymond, Bibliothèque de la Pléiade (Paris: Gallimard, 1959–69). 4 vols.
Salvesen	Christopher Salvesen, *The Landscape of Memory: A Study of Wordsworth's Poetry* (Lincoln: University of Nebraska Press, 1965).
Schama	Simon Schama, *Citizens: A Chronicle of the French Revolution* (London: Viking, 1989).
Schelling	*Friedrich Wilhelm Joseph von Schellings sämmtliche Werke*, ed. K. F. A. Schelling (Stutgart: J. G. Cotta'scher Verlag, 1856–61). 14 vols.
Schiller	*Friedrich Schiller: Werke in drei Bänden*, ed. Herbert G. Göpfel, with the assistance of Gerhard Fricke (Munich: Carl Hanser Verlag, 1981). 3 vols.
Schiller, *Letters*	Friedrich Schiller, *Briefe*, ed. Gerhard Fricke (Munich: Carl Hanser Verlag, 1955).
Schleiermacher	*Friedrich Schleiermacher's sämmtliche Werke* . . . (Berlin: Georg Reimer, 1835–64). 30 vols.
Schopenhauer	Arthur Schopenhauer, *Sämtliche Werke*, ed. Arthur Hübscher (Wiesbaden: F. A. Brockhaus, 1972). 7 vols.
Shakespearean Criticism	Samuel Taylor Coleridge, *Shakespearean Criticism*, ed. T. M. Raysor, Everyman's Library (London: Dent; New York: Dutton, 1964 [1960]). 2 vols.

Shapes of Culture	Thomas McFarland, *Shapes of Culture* (Iowa City: University of Iowa Press, 1987).
Shelley	*The Complete Works of Percy Bysshe Shelley*, ed. Roger Ingpen and Walter E. Peck (New York: Gordian Press, 1965). 10 vols.
Shelley, *Letters*	*The Letters of Percy Bysshe Shelley*, ed. Frederick L. Jones (Oxford: Clarendon Press, 1964). 2 vols.
Sime	James Sime, *Schiller* (Edinburgh and London: William Blackwood and Sons, 1882).
Simmel	*Georg Simmel on Individuality and Social Forms*, ed. Donald N. Levine (Chicago: University of Chicago Press, 1971).
Smith	Norman Kemp Smith, *A Commentary to Kant's 'Critique of Pure Reason'*, second edition (New York: Humanities Press, 1950).
Snyder	Alice D. Snyder, *Coleridge on Logic and Learning, with Selections from the Unpublished Manuscripts* (New Haven, Conn.: Yale University Press, 1929).
Sørensen	Bengt Sørensen, *Symbol und Symbolismus in den ästhetischen Theorien des 18. Jahrhunderts und der deutschen Romantik* (Copenhagen: Munksgaard, 1963).
Southey	Robert Southey, *Poetical Works* (London: Longman, 1840). 10 vols.
Southey, *New Letters*	*New Letters of Robert Southey*, ed. Kenneth Curry (New York: Columbia University Press, 1965). 2 vols.
Spinoza	*Spinoza Opera*, commissioned by the Heidelberg Academy of Sciences, ed. Carl Gebhardt (Heidelberg: Carl Winters Universitaetsbuchhandlung, 1972). 4 vols.
Starobinski	Jean Starobinski, *Jean-Jacques Rousseau: Transparency and Obstruction*, trans. Arthur Goldhammer (Chicago: University of Chicago Press, 1988).
Steffens	Henrich Steffens, *Grundzüge der philosophischen Naturwissenschaft* (Berlin: Im Verlage der Realschulbuchhandlung, 1806).
Stephen	Leslie Stephen, *Hours in a Library* (London: Smith, Elder & Co., 1909). 3 vols.
Stevens	Wallace Stevens, *The Necessary Angel: Essays on Reality and the Imagination* (New York: Vintage Books, 1951).
Stone	I. F. Stone, *The Trial of Socrates* (New York: Doubleday Anchor Books, 1989).

Taine   Hippolyte Taine, *Les Origines de la France contempor-*
                           aine (Paris: Librairie Hachette et Cie, 1875–93). 6
                           vols.

Thelwall   *The Life of John Thelwall*, by his widow [Mrs Cecil
                           Boyle Thelwall] (London: John Macrone, St James
                           Square, 1837).

Todorov   Tzvetan Todorov, *Theories of the Symbol*, trans.
                           Catherine Porter (Ithaca, NY: Cornell University
                           Press, 1982).

Tolstoy   Leo Tolstoy, *What is Art? and Essays on Art*, trans.
                           Aylmer Maude (London: Oxford University Press,
                           1956).

Thompson   E. P. Thompson, 'Disenchantment or Default? A Lay
                           Sermon', in *Power and Consciousness*, ed. Conor
                           Cruise O'Brien and William Dean Vanech (London:
                           London University Press, 1969).

Trelawny   Edward John Trelawny, *Records of Shelley, Byron, and*
                           the Author, ed. David Wright, The Penguin English
                           Library (Harmondsworth, Middlesex: Penguin
                           Books, 1973).

TT   *The Table Talk and Omniana of Samuel Taylor*
                           Coleridge, ed. T. Ashe (London: George Bell &
                           Sons, 1888).

Watchman   Samuel Taylor Coleridge, *The Watchman*, ed. Lewis
                           Patton (The Collected Works of Samuel Taylor
                           Coleridge, ii; London: Routledge & Kegan Paul;
                           Princeton, NJ: Princeton University Press, 1970).

White   Newman Ivey White, *Shelley* (New York: Alfred A.
                           Knopf, 1940). 2 vols.

Wiedmann   Franz Wiedmann, *Hegel*, trans. Joachim Neugröschel
                           (New York: Pegasus, 1968).

Wiese   Benno von Wiese, *Friedrich Schiller* (Stuttgart:
                           Metzler, 1959).

Wilson   Arthur M. Wilson, *Diderot* (New York: Oxford
                           University Press, 1972).

Woloch   Isser Woloch, *Jacobin Legacy: The Democratic Move-*
                           ment under the Directory (Princeton, NJ: Princeton
                           University Press, 1970).

Wordsworth, *Poems*   *The Poetical Works of William Wordsworth*, ed. Ernest
                           de Selincourt and Helen Darbishire (Oxford:
                           Clarendon Press, 1940–9). 5 vols.

Wordsworth, *Prelude*   William Wordsworth, *The Prelude 1799, 1805, 1850:*
                           Authoritative Texts, Context, and Reception; Recent

Critical Essays, ed. Jonathan Wordsworth, M. H. Abrams, Stephen Gill (New York and London: W. W. Norton & Company, 1979).

Wu   Duncan Wu, *Wordsworth's Reading 1770–1799* (Cambridge: Cambridge University Press, 1993).

Introduction: Texture and Text

THE word 'texture' is encountered as first and foremost a tactile richness. One stresses its primary appeal to the sense of touch, though the co-inherence—to use a term favoured by Coleridge—of richness also invokes visual vividness. Visualization, however, is always secondary in the consideration of texture. For to use the word texture is to present ourselves with the trope of fingers touching a fabric. If we run our fingers over a pattern of rich brocade, we are by that sole action aware of pattern and texture, but we can thereby only assume that such richness involves colour as well. Even apart from awareness of texture, touch, when involved in a primary configuration, suggests a depression of the visual. We think of touch as the arena and enabling function of the blind. The more touch is foregrounded, the less is sight at issue; the greater the hegemony of sight, the less the appeal to touch. To confront texture is to elevate the reality of touch and lessen the reality of sight.

That defining situation urges another aspect of texture. When we touch a fabric, what we learn is qualitative: the closeness of a weave and the softness or hardness, the smoothness or roughness, of the strands that compose it. We also learn configuration. We do not learn colour, however, and we do not learn form. If it were possible to reach out and touch one of the Unicorn tapestries at The Cloisters in Manhattan, we should simultaneously both learn from that touching the texture of the tapestry, and occlude its larger form. We should be aware of both the quality of the fabric and the configuration of its pattern, but we should not simply by touching be aware of the dimensions of the tapestry itself. Yet at the very moment we realized the limitation of our touch, we would necessarily be aware that the suppressed entity of the tapestry was implied by the texture we apprehended. We would not be aware of form, but we would be aware of entity.

To be sure, we might by another application of touching to some extent cognize the form, or at least the shape, of the tapestry. We might, standing on ladders, run our fingers around its edges, and we might by counting come to some reasonable cognizance of its dimensions—after all, before the era of satellites, that, *mutatis mutandis*, was what geographers did in making their maps. None the less, by diverting the sense of touch to an awareness of shape, we should occlude the awareness of tactile quality. We should lose the awareness of texture. In order to apprehend quality, on the one hand, and form, on the other, we should still be forced to employ two distinct and separate operations; and in that event, we would be better off reverting to common sense and common usage, and fully to apprehend the tapestry simply combine touch and sight.

It is by combining the functions of touch and sight that we seek fully to cognize those cultural episodes that we refer to as works of literature. Broadly speaking, the apprehension of the episodes as works is a function of sight, and renders us what we generically call texts. The apprehension of the episodes as literature, that is, as literature with the significance of art, is a function of touch, and renders us what we may generically call textures. Every text has a texture, and every texture is presumed to relate to a text.

'Avez vous un texte?' The question was the watchword of Fustel de Coulanges, and it incorporated his scorn for airy hypothesis, random conjecture, and unsupported speculation. At the same time it summoned up a palpable entity, one whose function was to be inspected. More recently, through the agency of Derrida, 'text' has been elevated to supreme position as the generic name for literary entity. Text is the focusing moment for the entire continuum of *écriture*. Where earlier theoretical placements had identified literary entity as shapes—sestinas and Spenserian stanzas, rime royale and heroic couplets—and kinds—ode and sonnet, novel and drama, epic and elegy: the full panoply of 'tragedy, comedy, history, pastoral, pastoral-comical, historical-pastoral, tragical-historical, tragical-comical-historical-pastoral'—such lineaments were now erased and replaced by the single term 'text.'

For deconstructive purposes, nothing was sacrificed by collapsing all forms into 'text', for such surface features would be obliterated in any case by the dismantling of the apparent entity. One way of describing the deconstructive action might be by an illustration that is increasingly familiar as computers gain ever greater cultural sway. As those who use such computers for literary composition are aware, some software has what may be called an 'expanded display' mode that replaces the on-screen text—the 'received text', as it were, of literature as it is culturally presented—by an altered text, one that indicates all orthographic features, as well as all footnotes, as components in the text itself. The purpose of 'expanded display' is to see exactly what all the components of the text are, even those nominally not present; when this is seen, and possibly worked on, the computer then is instructed to switch back to normal display, and it is in that more conventional form, even when altered by the recourse to expanded display mode, that the text is then printed.

Deconstruction converts normal texts into something somewhat analogous to expanded display texts. That is to say, it does not dismantle texts arbitrarily: it simply changes an assumed surface into a depth awareness that is also fully responsible to the conception of 'text', though quite different from the text as culturally presented. In its method of close examination, it comes near to the tactile reality of 'texture'; indeed, one method of asserting the aim of deconstruction is to use the metaphor of a fabric. 'The deconstructive critic', Hillis Miller has said, 'seeks to find, by a process of retracing, the element in the system studied which is alogical, the thread in the text in question which will unravel it all.' Again, he notes that 'One feature of Derrida's criticism is a patient and minutely philological "explication de texte." Nevertheless, the thread of logic' that the deconstructive critic isolates leads 'into regions which are alogical, absurd'.

Both by customarily reducing 'text' to a single passage to be examined, and by attention to the 'threads' of that text, deconstruction thus tends to move from a larger conception of text to magnified instances of 'texture'. After all, etymologically speaking, 'texture' seems to occupy a position that slightly precedes 'text'. Texture arises from Latin *textura*, which derives from *texere*, to weave. Text comes via Old French *texte* from Latin *textus*, which is the past participle of *texere*, to weave. In both words, the underlying reality is a fabric, not a form. As a dictionary picked up at random (it is *Webster's New World Dictionary*) says for the first two meanings of 'texture':

1. originally, a woven fabric; textile. 2. the character of a woven fabric resulting from the arrangement, size, quality, etc. of the fabric's threads: as, a fine or coarse *texture*, a ribbed or twilled *texture*.

Yet, despite its characteristic tendency to move from text to texture, to darken the one and to magnify the other, deconstructive activity, though it deals with texture, does not render texture. Rather, by seeking to find 'the thread in the text in question which will unravel it all', such activity actually does violence to texture. The threads of the fabric are woven into harmony with other threads; to prise up a single thread and then start a process of unravelling is wholly opposed to the ontology of texture. The process raises a question that has haunted deconstruction from the beginning: to what end other than nihilism does the method tend? Derrida, doubtless stung by such charges of nihilism—repeated again as often as he denies them—has recently said that deconstruction does not seek to annul or cancel the subject, and that after the deconstructive operation a reconstructive process must occur. Yet it is not clear that the fabric of texture can be very satisfactorily restored after being yanked on so summarily. Specifically, the unravellings of deconstruction completely bypass the conception of quality, and it is the qualitative that texture itself so ineluctably renders.

One is led to the surmise that it is not by pulling on the threads of texture, but by patiently touching the fabric—descrying it—that the critical assessment might be most fully useful; if, that is, one feels that the apprehension of quality is the compelling reason for critical assessment in the first place. Coleridge, in writing to a correspondent and discussing what a great poet does, beautifully enlists the conception of a touch that does not disturb; and such a descrying touch, as opposed to the prising touch of deconstruction, is what this book endorses:

a great Poet must be, implicitè if not explicitè, a profound Metaphysician. He may not have it in logical coherence, in his Brain & Tongue; but he must have it by *Tact* / for all sounds, & forms of human nature he must have the *ear* of a wild Arab listening in the silent Desart, the eye of a North American Indian tracing the footsteps of an Enemy upon the Leaves that strew the Forest—; the *Touch* of a Blind Man feeling the face of a darling Child—

The apotheosis of tactile descrying, of course, places a heavy burden on the conception of touch. It is sight, not touch, that has generally been most honoured among human faculties. The desire of human beings to know, says Aristotle, makes them prefer sight to all other senses (*Metaphysics* 980^{a}22–8). Nevertheless, though not nominated in such a ranking, touch is surely as important. That it is not hailed in the same terms as sight is almost certainly a result of the fact that though humans can see or not see, can have the function of sight or be without that function, it is impossible to be human and not have the sense of touch. Sight can be lost; touch cannot. As an unperceived background in all human possibility, therefore, touch tends to be taken for granted, while sight is properly hailed as a miraculous gift.

Nevertheless, in the most intense sense of life known to humans, touch is always more ultimate than sight. For in the realm and act of love, though sight is important, touch is the final realization. To be sure, the verb 'know', which is used in the King James Bible to indicate the grandest realization of all, that of man's relation to God, is subsumed there under the faculty of sight: 'For now we see through a glass, darkly; but then face to face: now I know in part; but then shall I know even as also I am known.' Nevertheless, the greatest of all purely human consummations, that of sexual love, is rendered in that same Bible under the repeated use of 'know' in the sense of an ultimate touching: for in purely human encounters touch reigns supreme. As Donne says,

> So must pure lovers soules descend
> T'affections, and to faculties,
> Which sense may reach and apprehend,
> Else a great Prince in prison lies.
> To'our bodies turne wee then, that so
> Weake men on love reveal'd may looke;
> Loves mysteries in soules doe grow,
> But yet the body is his booke.

Notable in Donne's formulation is that a full seeing ('that so | Weake men on love reveal'd may looke') can in love only occur through a full touching.

To resort to body is to resort to touch. And 'the world's body', which in the view of John Crowe Ransom is what poetry presents, is apprehended also by the touching that reveals texture. Indeed, it is quite in accord with this truth that one of Ransom's key theoretical terms is precisely 'texture'.

It is touch that connects itself metaphorically with feeling, which is the most distinctive qualitative component of that literature known as art, even taking literature, in its largest signification, to encompass music and the other arts. Wherever feeling is present, present also is the possibility of being 'touched'. But sight seems to have no such primary relation to feeling. One is touched by Cordelia's choking statement, 'No cause, no cause', which is an apex of the representation of feeling in literature; one does not 'see' that feeling. One may 'see' a mathematical proof; but one does not 'see' Wordsworth's 'Knowing my heart's best treasure was no more'. One 'feels' the poignancy of that statement, and thereby is 'touched' by it. One would not say that he 'saw' an exquisite melody by Mozart—say in the third movement of the thirteenth piano concerto—but rather that he was 'touched' by it.

Even certain theorists of sight itself elevate touch to high and indispensable position. Berkeley, in his *A New Theory of Vision*, argues that 'the objects of sight and touch are two distinct things'. Unexpectedly, however, he maintains that by sight we cannot determine the distance, size, or 'situation' of anything. 'That which I see is only variety of light and colours.' It is only by the extrapolation of touch that 'seeing' actually occurs:

I say, neither distance nor things placed at a distance are themselves, or their ideas, truly perceived by sight. This I am persuaded of, as to what concerns my self: and I believe whoever will look narrowly into his own thoughts and examine what he means by saying he sees this or that thing at a distance, will agree with me that what he sees only suggests to his understanding that after having passed a certain distance, to be measured by the motion of his body, which is perceivable by touch, he shall come to perceive such and such tangible ideas which have been usually connected with such and such visible ideas.

In extended and subtle argumentation, Berkeley urges that we must consider 'the difference there is betwixt the extension and figure which is the proper object of touch, and that other which is termed visible; and how the former is principally, though not immediately taken notice of, when we look at any object'. And he speaks of 'the customary and close connexion that has grown up in our minds between the objects of sight and touch; whereby the very different and distinct ideas are so blended and confounded together as to be mistaken for one and the same thing; out of which prejudice we cannot easily extricate ourselves'.

If it is thus conceded that touch occupies a co-ordinate plane of importance with sight, one is justified in recognizing two discrete concatenations, one the mutual implication of sight-text-form, the other the mutual implication of touch-texture-quality. Both concatenations are present in any satisfactory contemplation of the literary work of art.

At the present moment in cultural history, however, it is desirable to emphasize the second concatenation, touch-texture-quality. For as emphasized above, the methodology of deconstruction cannot approach at all the consideration of quality, and there is, in consequence, at present a cultural lacuna in qualitative determination. Indeed, deconstruction does not theoretically restrict itself to literary art, but regards any text whatever as a proper subject for deconstructive analysis. A political manifesto, a newspaper editorial, a politician's speech, a philosopher's argument, a historian's description—these and other texts disclose themselves at least as richly to deconstructive examination as does a poem. In sum, many of the texts available as focus of deconstruction do not in any aspect involve the idea of quality. Only the textual formation known as art intrinsically involves the idea of quality. But the work of literary art requires the adjudication of quality for its very definition; and this deconstruction can neither supply nor reveal.

What is true of deconstruction is true also of its popular offshoot, New Historicism. New Historicism combines the lesson of deconstruction with the political legacy of Marx; but it too cannot approach the idea of quality. The idea of quality must be already assumed in the poem that receives New Historical analysis; there is nothing in that analysis that can in any way demonstrate—except by a jejune and irrelevant appeal to assumptions of political or sociological desirability—whether a poem has value or not.

To be sure, the New Criticism, which reigned at the end of the first half of the twentieth century, characteristically occupied itself with quality, and its analyses, by insisting on coherence and on such structural elements as paradox, irony, and ambiguity, could emphatically conclude whether a poem was good or bad. Some of its theoretical formulations, too, such as Robert Penn Warren's brilliant essay on pure and impure poetry, most satisfyingly engaged the conception of quality. But New Criticism's outstanding success with textures and their related realm of quality was accompanied by an almost total disengagement with larger textual forms. Texts such as *Paradise Lost* or *The Faerie Queene* or *The Prelude* were grossly misconceived, indeed, were mangled, by the New Critical approach. All that movement's virtuosity of touch with regard to poetic textures evaporated as soon as the poems lengthened to thousands of lines and hundreds of pages. New Criticism simply could not see texts.

It remained for the immediately supervening lucubrations of Northrop Frye to restore the sight of larger forms, and his elucidation of the structure of romance was and will always stand as a critical achievement of first importance. But despite the richness and depth of Frye's perceptions, he in his turn lost something; and what he lost was the sureness of touch with texture that had characterized the New Criticism.

In any event, both New Criticism and the contribution of Frye have long been, as the Germans say, *vorbei*. Both movements have been decisively supplanted by the deconstructive revolution. Of course no voice is wholly lost, and the lessons of both New Criticism and Frye have been incorporated into what we all assume about literature; but few indeed actually now read the writers who established this universal groundwork of assumption.

It is quite otherwise with deconstruction. Unlike the two previous revolutions in criticism, deconstruction was evolved in another language and had to filter through more slowly to the English-speaking *cognoscenti*. This impedance, however, served to make deconstruction mysterious, and its darkness seemed actually to guarantee profundity. Moreover, where an important factor in the rise of New Criticism was the characteristic American thinness in foreign languages and in European cultural attainment—one could set up quite respectably as a New Critic simply by learning a method, without any appeal whatever to a large body of historical or cultural knowledge—deconstruction, on the other hand, was virtually impenetrable without a substantial investment in such difficult matters as the thought of Saussure, the thought of Husserl, and the thought of Heidegger. But this daunting demand only increased the numinous effect of the first emergence of deconstruction into Anglo-Saxon awareness.

The upshot of the foreignness and contextual difficulty of deconstruction was that the conquering of the theory itself became a formidable cultural task. It was one that quickly became vested with high intellectual excitement. Simply theory itself, not the use of that theory, more and more became the preoccupation of the more advanced participants on the American critical scene. Actually to have read the volumes of Derrida—especially before translation made them more accessible—gave the American academic something of the same self-assurance and certain sense of importance that used to characterize 'made' members of the old Mafia. The Paul of this new movement of faith, De Man, shared, in his mediating importance, the prestige of Derrida himself.

But the high intellectual excitement that characterized the deconstructive revolution for the decade and a half between about 1975 and 1990 tended to obscure an important truth: the primacy of value. Value is a dividend of quality. Deconstruction does not address quality; yet the apprehension of quality is the first task of criticism. That truth must be emphasized: the apprehension of quality is the first, and the final, task of criticism.

The apprehension of quality requires the sense of touch. To bring the statement more in line with common usage, one may say that it requires 'touch'. Pascal made a distinction between the *esprit géométrique* and the *esprit de finesse*. Through a long descent, the *esprit de finesse* resurfaces as the semi-slang word 'touch'. We speak of a tennis player's 'touch' on his volley, of a football player's 'touch' on his passes, of a diplomat's 'touch' in his negotiations. There is never a need to define what we mean by 'touch'. The same may be said of the co-ordinate usage based on sight: we speak of a connoisseur's 'eye' for painting, of a recruiter's 'eye' for prospects.

Interestingly, both 'eye' and 'touch' in these usages do not oppose one another but are virtually interchangeable in their appeal to the *esprit de finesse*. Their easy co-ordination validates what was said above about the necessity of both sight-text-form and touch-texture-quality in the apprehension of a literary work. The two concatenations mesh so smoothly that in unexamined contexts they may seem the same thing. But they are not the same, and on the current intellectual scene touch-texture-quality is sorely in need of theoretical and practical rehabilitation.

Criticism, as opposed to games of critical play with texts already in place, is at present at a virtual standstill.

It is the hope of this volume somewhat to redress the balance on the side of touch-texture-quality. By touching some textures in the great text of Romanticism, the following chapters strive to bring back to the awareness of the intellectual public the richness and variety of the vast Romantic tapestry, and with such presentation to claim an enhanced value for that intricately woven cultural fabric.

The statement requires elucidation and commentary. On the surface it may seem that the ensuing discussions actually weave their textures out of parti-coloured Romantic threads, rather than revealing those textures as patterns already inherent in the tapestry. Secondly, one does not actually touch the textures here presented: touch is a physical act, and the touch invoked here is purely a mentalization. Neither objection, however, even though both may to an extent be conceded, actually dissipates the pertinence of the appeal to touch. To address the second objection first, the 'touch' here enlisted is indeed a mentalization, but it relates to 'touch' as a physical act with exactly the same propriety as 'see' meaning to 'understand' relates to 'see' as actual sight. In both cases the metaphorical extensions function with as much linguistic richness as do the primary, physically located meanings.

The parallelism of function is not mere coincidence. In each instance the richness of the metaphorical extension is guaranteed by the foundational strength of the physical act. If the physical act were less essential in the human economy, the metaphorical extension would not have so much strength. But 'see' meaning to understand is fully as frequent, and fully as emphatic, in linguistic usage as 'see' meaning the actual use of sight. By the same token, 'touch' meaning an engagement in terms of nuance and quality is no less valid than 'touch' meaning a physical meeting. For touch in its primary signification, it must be reiterated, is as humanly essential as sight.

Indeed, modern psychoanalytic theory and observation have elevated touch to a unique role in the actual founding of the human being. The psychoanalyst D. W. Winnicott speaks of a 'holding' environment ('Holding includes especially the physical holding of the infant, which is a form of loving') that is necessary for the development of ego strength. The psychoanalyst Hans Loewald, again, emphasizes that

The child, by internalizing aspects of the parent, also internalizes the parent's image of the child—an image which is mediated to the child in the thousand different ways of being handled, bodily and emotionally.... Part of what is introjected is the image of the child as seen, felt, smelled, heard, touched by the mother. The bodily handling of and concern with the child, the manner in which the child is fed, touched, cleaned, the way it is looked at, talked to, called by name, recognized and re-recognized—all these and many other ways of communicating with the child, and communicating to him his identity, sameness, unity, and individuality, shape and mould him so that he can begin to identify himself, to feel and recognize himself as one and separate yet with others.

With proleptic psychoanalytical acumen, Coleridge too understood the role of touch in the founding of the human being. He speaks of 'the three years child' that 'has awoke during the dark night' in the crib by the mother's bed, and can be heard to

entreat in piteous tones 'touch me, only touch me with your finger.' A child of that age under the same circumstances I myself heard using these very words. . . . 'I am not here, touch me Mother, that I may be here!' The witness of its own being has been suspended in the loss of the mother's presence by sight or sound or feeling.

For Winnicott, also, it is precisely touch that guarantees the sense of being:

Anxiety in these early stages of the parent–infant relationship relates to the threat of annihilation and it is necessary to explain what is meant by this term. . . . Being and annihilation are the two alternatives. The holding environment therefore has as its main function the reduction to a minimum of impingements to which the infant must react with resultant annihilation of personal being.

Indeed, the relation of touch to the foundation of the human being receives sublime expression in Michelangelo's painting on the ceiling of the Sistine Chapel, for there God creates Adam, and the creation is rendered unforgettably by God's finger reaching out to touch Adam's hand. It is one of the most profound moments in the entire history of art.

But even here the indispensable reciprocity, simultaneously with the absolute difference, of touch and sight are honoured; for the apotheosis of touch in this great moment takes place in a painting which by its uniquely elevated placement can never be itself the object of touch; it can only be apprehended by sight.

So too with the psychoanalytical understanding of the origins and development of the human being. To the apotheosis of touch indicated by Loewald and Winnicott may be added the emphasis on sight by the psychoanalyst René Spitz. In his classic treatise, *The First Year of Life*, Spitz notes that

In the course of the first six weeks of life a mnemonic trace of the human face is laid down in the infantile memory as the first signal of the need-gratifier; the infant will follow all the movements of this signal with his eyes.

On the same page of the treatise, Spitz reproduces a photograph of a nursing child with the caption: 'During Nursing the Breast-Fed Baby Stares Unwaveringly at His Mother's Face.'

Here too Coleridge achieved proleptic psychoanalytical understanding. He asserts that the 'first dawnings' of the baby's 'humanity will break forth in the Eye that connects the mother's face with the warmth of the mother's bosom, the support of the mother's Arms'.

So touch and sight, though absolutely opposed, repeatedly coalesce in their important functioning, both physically and metaphorically. They constitute a true *coincidentia oppositorum*. In terms of the cognizance of literary episodes in the stream of culture, both are necessary. Both are present in any address to a work of art. But both need not be equally present. The touching that is criticism seeks to discern quality and from there to assess value. Seeing, on the other hand, does not primarily assess value but discerns form.

For a homely instance, when one takes a university 'survey' course in French literature, the literary activity is not one of discerning quality or assessing value. On the contrary, both value and quality are absolutely presumed at the outset—are already fully assigned in cultural hierarchy—and the faith that value has already been established underlies the decision to offer the course in the first place. The course itself is a 'seeing' of forms—or to use the proffered description, a 'survey' of forms. One learns something of the works of Rabelais, of Molière, of Rousseau, of Victor Hugo. Those works are cognized as 'texts' of differing dimension and differing configuration. Each has, of course, its 'texture', and some attempt is usually made to acquaint the students with samples of such texture, though no value-establishing activity is undertaken, and the textures actually remain, in this apprehension, merely ancillary and more or less inert features of textual sighting as such.

It was said above, as the first of the possible objections against this volume's conception of texture and its relation to the critical task, that the ensuing discussions may as validly be describing as a weaving of textures as they may be described as discerning of textures. The objection is to some extent conceded, but it does not therefore impeach the procedure of the book. When one reads a poem, one must retrace the special linguistic configuration of the poem and reconstruct the meaning conveyed by the author of the poem. In that sense, the reader of the poem 'writes' the poem a second time. That he or she does not thereby quite totally comprehend the initial creation of the poem is true: every act of reading is merely an approximation, as is every act of criticism. On the other hand, the very author of the poem does not fully comprehend his or her own conception of the poem either. Shelley speaks for all poets when he says that 'The most glorious poetry that has been communicated to the world is probably a feeble shadow of the original conception of the Poet'.

In truth, every transaction concerned with poetry—its authoring, its reading, its criticism—occupies a kind of infinitesimal calculus of achievements and awareness, where an absolute congruence of idea and artefact is constantly, even infinitely approached, but never, ever, absolutely attained. That it is not absolutely attained is, one can hardly doubt, why critics constantly return to the examination of great poems; why poets continually write still other poems; why readers reread poems rehearsed many times before.

Every act of intellectual engagement, in short, is an activity, not a passivity. The poet does not perfectly write a poem that is then unchangingly inscribed on the *tabula rasa* of a reader's awareness. Rather, the poet tries, is engaged in activity; the reader tries, is engaged in activity; the critic tries, is engaged in activity. One must agree with Barthes's dictum that '*the text is experienced only as an activity, a production*'.

With such understanding, the ensuing discussions reveal themselves not as *creatio ex nihilo*, even though they weave, or perhaps more precisely, retrace the weaving, of complex ideational or historical textures. Rather they touch the fabric of Romanticism to animate figurations increasingly absent from cultural contemplation. They touch not merely the fabric of text, but the quality and configuration of texture. The touching and the resultant animation are the chapters that follow. But as with any true awareness of texture, the localizations are preceded by many other cultural activities: the conditions, possibilities, and varieties of weaving must be learned if touch is to reveal with authority; the colouring of similar textures must be known from previous encounters; the valuation of similar tapestries must be at the call of the touching critical fingers. In brief, the textures of the following chapters are engaged only because much previous learning and experience have been devoted to the conception of the fabric in which they occur, and specifically to its realization as the text called Romanticism. The text called Romanticism ineluctably underlies and supplies the thread for each texture addressed.

The text called Romanticism, though it underlies everything in this book, cannot itself be the focus of the book. As suggested above, to touch texture is necessarily, at least as long as the touching takes place, to occlude the sight of text as such, no matter how necessarily text as such is presumed. The text of Romanticism that is only touched, not viewed here, can, however, be viewed in multitudinous sightings elsewhere. Two only need be nominated to document that sight-text-form can as readily dominate our sense of the Romantic essence as can the touch-texture-quality concatenation that is awarded hegemony here. The two sightings, brought forward almost at random, are the present author's discussion called 'The Spirit of the Age', in his book named *Romantic Cruxes*, and René Wellek's 'The Concept of Romanticism in Literary History' and 'Romanticism Re-Examined' in his *Concepts of Criticism*.

Even in those firmly positive descriptions of the Romantic text, however, dimensions are problematic. If fully to exploit the touching of texture, sight must be occluded and the entity of text be only presumed, and not descried, the text called Romanticism lends itself ideally to such a distribution of awareness. Indeed, such have been the vicissitudes in recent years of the text called Romanticism, that its dimensions have become so indeterminate as sometimes to seem to recede into absolute negation. Along with such occlusions of the awarenesses that constitute the text called Romanticism, however, a parallel indeterminacy of the conception of text itself allows the text called Romanticism to retain viability.

Earlier understandings of text were firmly determinate. One spoke of an epic with a counted number of lines, in a book of such and such dimension and pagination. Or one spoke of a drama with so many acts and scenes and lines, also in a book of palpable dimension and explicit pagination. That was what the term 'text' implied in common speech. With the advent of Derrida, however, a new and hugely indeterminate conception of 'text' was offered instead. In the understandings of Derrida, while the text under examination may frequently be as small as a paragraph, the text as such may be almost infinitely large, or at least incommensurably ragged in dimension. '*Il n'y a pas de hors-texte*'—'there is nothing outside the text', says Derrida in a formulation made more emphatic by printing it in italics. Such an enlargement received sardonic notice by Foucault as 'the invention of voices behind texts in order not to have to analyse the modes of implication of the subject in discourse'; and deconstruction itself, said Foucault, was 'a pedagogy that tells the pupil that there is nothing outside of the text, but that within it, in its interstices, in its white spaces and unspokenness, the reserve of the origin reigns; it is not at all necessary to search elsewhere, for exactly here, to be sure not in the words, but in words as erasures, in their grill, "the meaning of being" speaks itself.'

From the standpoint of Derrida's reconstitution of the significance of text, therefore, the text called Romanticism can be seen as a text not merely occluded by the touching of textures, but indeed as in its inner reality virtually a self-occluding entity. As such, though it is everywhere present in the following textures, it is also everywhere absent.

Such play of presence and absence cures the text called Romanticism of flaws in its title posited by the equivocal approaches of recent years. Not only has the text called Romanticism not been clearly seen, but recent approaches seem to assume that it is not clearly seeable. Indeed, Marilyn Butler in 1981, in a volume called *Romantics, Rebels and Reactionaries: English Literature and its Background 1760–1830*, counselled abandoning the conception of Romanticism altogether:

Perhaps the best of all reasons for shedding preconceptions about Romanticism is not the point of principle—that they may be untrue—but the point of pragmatism—that they interfere with so much good reading. How many students have puzzled themselves into antipathy, trying to fathom what the *Lyrical Ballads* initiated; or what the common denominator may be in various writers' attitudes to the self, to God, or to Nature; or precisely why Shelley, Scott and Byron must be said to be Romantic?

But the Romantics, even though at least in England they had not settled on that name, were, contrary to Butler's position, quite aware that they participated in what might be called the 'spirit of the age'. 'The only remark', comments Shelley with respect to a review:

worth notice in this piece is the assertion that I imitate Wordsworth. It may as well be said that Lord Byron imitates Wordsworth, or that Wordsworth imitates Lord Byron, both being great poets, and deriving from the new springs of thought and feeling, which the great events of our age have exposed to view, a similar tone of sentiment, imagery, and expression. A certain similarity all the best writers of any particular age are marked with, from the spirit of that age working in all.

Butler's animadversions may seem to be based on the not very pressing urgency of making things easy for students; but a still more formidable scholar has also expressed an equivocal attitude towards the concept of Romanticism. M. H. Abrams, in a notable article called 'English Romanticism: The Spirit of the Age', says that

I hope to avoid easy and empty generalizations about the *Zeitgeist*, and I do not propose the electrifying proposition that 'le romantisme, c'est la révolution.'

Romanticism is no one thing. It is many very individual poets, who wrote poems manifesting a greater diversity of qualities, it seems to me, than those of any preceding age. But some prominent qualities a number of these poems share, and certain of these shared qualities form a distinctive complex which may, with a high degree of probability, be related to the events and ideas of the cataclysmic coming-into-being of the world to which we are by now becoming fairly accustomed.

One notes that Abrams at one and the same time seems to deny the text called Romanticism ('easy and empty generalizations about the *Zeitgeist*') and to rely wholly on the existence of such a text ('a distinctive complex'). One might mildly remonstrate that the issue is not 'easy and empty' generalization—which doubtless would never at any time find sponsors—but valid and responsible generalization, which is an entirely different matter, and a matter of the greatest importance.

In any event, Abrams both sees and does not see the text called Romanticism. This recent tendency perhaps arises from an ambiguity in the use of the term Romanticism as such. Though Coleridge said that 'the true genuine modern poetry' is 'the romantic; and the works of Shakespeare are romantic poetry revealing itself in the drama', the English Romantics for the most part did not call themselves Romantics, and when they were considered as a group, they were usually referred to as 'The Lake Poets' (otherwise, they were not customarily referred to in large groupings except, as Shelley urged, in the common consideration that they participated in the 'spirit of the age'). The French Romantics initially used the term only to designate the small group so memorably depicted by Gautier as being clustered in 1830 around Victor Hugo's *Hernani* (and somewhat earlier those who attended the salon of Charles Nodier). The German Romantics were thought of as only a small band, focused on the activities of the Schlegel brothers, and specifically excluding Goethe and Schiller, who were honoured as 'classic'.

Romanticism as it constitutes the great text is something quite different: it enscribes virtually all English cultural figures from Chatterton and Percy to Carlyle (and even Jane Austen can be seen as touched, if not defined, by Romanticism), virtually all French authors from Rousseau and Chateaubriand to Baudelaire, virtually all German authors—and most especially Goethe and Schiller—from Leibniz's *Nouveaux essais* of 1765 to Nietzsche a hundred years later. As I have urged in my book, *Shapes of Culture*:

What the great poet Hölderlin signifies in the language of his art is apprehended too in the language of criticism by his Romantic contemporaries. Actually

Romantic is a misnomer for those intense circles at Jena and Berlin that labored to define the nature of poetry and philosophy, for what they were actually attempting to grasp was nothing less than the essence of culture itself. Romanticism as an epoch in sensibility had been flourishing in Germany for decades. Such products of so-called 'Sturm und Drang' as *Werther* in 1774 or *Die Räuber* in 1781 are in fact the purest Romanticism. On the other hand, what the brothers Schlegel were trying to formulate around the turn of the nineteenth century, though they termed it 'Romantic poetry,' was, more deeply, the evacuated presence and pregnant absence that actually constitutes the subject matter and moving force of culture.

Thus the great text of Romanticism only gradually came to be described by that specific name, even though the reality of its cultural design had existed from the first. Heine's *Die romantische Schule* of 1833 (though the book was not called by that name until 1836), along with Gautier's later *Histoire du romantisme* were only two of the mileposts along the way that led to the gradual identification of an entire cultural fabric as Romanticism. Paradoxically, however, though this fabric was not universally designated Romanticism until the later nineteenth century, important textures of the undiscerned text had been available very early. Rousseau, who is often thought of as the founder of Romanticism, though he is usually—no doubt mistakenly—not considered an actual Romantic, repeatedly uses the term 'romantic' with the full textural valence that later critics ascribed to it. The adjective he employs is 'romanesque', which, according to the *Concise Oxford French Dictionary*, means 'Romantic, quixotic, imaginative, passionate'. Thus, in less than a hundred pages of the *Confessions*, Rousseau refers to 'une autre folie romanesque' (another romantic folly); says that 'ce tems fut celui de ma vie où sans projets romanesques je pouvois le plus raisonnablement me livrer à l'espoir de parvenir'—'this was the time of my life where without romantic schemes I might most reasonably have allowed myself hope for the future'; observes that 'L'expérience que je commençois d'avoir modéroit peu à peu mes projets romanesques'—'the experience that I was beginning to have was little by little beginning to moderate my romantic plans'.

A similar situation obtained with others beside Rousseau. Coleridge, for a single additional instance, in 1794, well before the name 'Romantic' had come into use to designate an intellectual movement, uses the word accurately, with a substantial if not entire part of its later meaning. 'At Denbigh is the finest ruined Castle in the Kingdom,' he writes: 'I wandered there two hours in a still Evening, feeding upon melancholy.— Two well drest young Men were roaming there—"I will play my Flute here"—said the first—"it will have a *romantic* effect".'

By the turn of the twentieth century, however, the text called Romanticism was being repeatedly discerned and measured. Indeed, the dimensions of the text were more often addressed than the touch of its textures. Since no one reads it today, modern critics have no means of knowing how clearly the Romantic text was delineated in a work such as Henry A. Beers's *A History of English Romanticism in the Eighteenth Century*, published in 1898, or its sequel on English Romanticism in the nineteenth century. What students tend to read today is Jerome McGann's *The Romantic Ideology*, published in 1983, which 'proposes a new, *critical* view of Romanticism and its literary products'.

It might be instructive to examine the argument of McGann's book in some detail, because in a notable—and lamentably influential—way, it manages both to diminish the text called Romanticism and to reduce the richness and variety of its textures. Though the volume is slight, it is densely compacted and requires careful reading. Briefly, McGann's argument is that 'the scholarship and criticism of Romanticism and its works are dominated by a Romantic Ideology, by an uncritical absorption in Romanticism's own self-representation'. In a later work, *The Beauty of Inflections*, McGann supplies a fuller description of what he was trying to do:

In the *Romantic Ideology* I tried to graph the characteristic patterns of Romantic displacement in poetry. The object of this exercise was twofold: first, to expose the tragic and/or self-critical aspects of Romantic poetry, and especially of Romantic poetry carried out under utopian or transcendental signs; and second, to persuade scholars that criticism ought to be trying not to reify, or recuperate, or repeat Romantic interests and experience, but to use them for clarifying and criticizing our own immediate interests and experiences. In both cases—whether I was facing the past or the present—the project might fairly be called, as it has since in fact been called by a demurring colleague, a 'project in radical unbelief'.

McGann's acceptance of the description of his book as a 'project in radical unbelief' exhibits on its face *The Romantic Ideology*'s tendency to occultate the sight of the text called Romanticism. The tendency to occultation is augmented by characteristics of McGann's use of language and his techniques of formulation. Most readers will probably feel that neither of the two descriptions of the work just quoted clarifies matters very successfully; both are, however, typical of McGann's presentation. What McGann is doing is both logical and coherent, but neither logic nor coherence presents itself very vividly to a first-time reader. Take the phrase 'a Romantic Ideology' in the first statement. The reader at the outset might well suppose that McGann is talking about some widely

accepted ideational description of Romanticism. Actually, he is adapting
Marx's term from *The German Ideology*, with the specific intent of taking
over Marx's characterization of such a mind-set as a 'false consciousness'.

   To that instance of self-occluding formulation, we may add instances of
self-occluding rhetoric. McGann repeatedly makes statements that cause a
blank reaction in the reader: they are so far removed from any examination
of the data that might support or invalidate them, that while the reader
may suspect them to be invalid—or, conversely, suspect them to be
correct—in the event he or she simply cannot engage with them. Still
further, McGann promotes a radical simplicity of Romantic conceiving
that one must judge to be hyperbolic at its outset.

   For instance, McGann begins his fourteenth chapter with these words:
'This idea that poetry, or even consciousness, can set one free of the ruins
of history and culture is the grand illusion of every Romantic poet. The
idea has been inherited and reproduced in the cultural support systems—
principally the academy—which have followed in the wake of the
Romantic Movement.' The assertion cries out for specifications that
McGann's book cannot provide—nor could even so vast a study as Rudolf
Haym's—for the bold enlisting of 'every' Romantic poet, and the
vagueness of 'the cultural support systems—principally the academy',
reach out to such various and intractable data that scepticism flares
immediately and intensely.

   And yet the statement, despite its manifest hyperbole, is very important
in the economy of *The Romantic Ideology*. So important, indeed, that it
occurs again in its exact wording at the end of chapter 8. It is invoked in a
passage that begins with a quotation from Macherey: 'Like a planet
revolving around an absent sun, an ideology is made out of what it does not
mention; it exists because there are things which must not be spoken of'
(one notes without comment that the validating metaphor asserts a
physical impossibility: a planet cannot, ever, revolve around an absent
sun). McGann then collapses the intricately elaborated meaning of
Wordsworth's Immortality Ode into a vehicle for his reduced conception:

These remarks are a latter-day version of a recurrent truth. From Wordsworth's
vantage, an ideology is born out of things which (literally) *cannot* be spoken of. So
the 'Immortality Ode' is crucial for us because it speaks about ideology from the
point of view and in the context of its origins. If Wordsworth's poetry elides
history, we observe in this 'escapist' or 'reactionary' move its own self-revelation.
It is a rare, original, and comprehensive record of the birth and character of a
particular ideology—in this case, one that has been incorporated into our academic
programs. The idea that poetry, or even consciousness, can set one free of the ruins

of history and culture is the grand illusion of every Romantic poet. This idea continues as one of the most important shibboleths of our culture especially—and naturally—at its higher levels.

But these important statements are not the only ones that lose more to obfuscation than they gain in clarification. 'Between 1793 and 1798', says McGann, 'Wordsworth lost the world merely to gain his own immortal soul.' The grasping for the biblical paradox of loss and gain overbalances any applicable truth that the statement might claim. One supposes that the statement might refer to Wordsworth's social disillusionment after the French Revolution, of which he speaks so memorably in *The Prelude*, and his regaining of peace and perspective through the triple agency of Dorothy, Coleridge, and Nature. But the attempt to assert moral paradox by rhetorical manipulation does not aid the assertion's comprehensibility or applicability.

Still again, one might consider a semi-opaque statement that is puzzling in both detail and conclusion:

Coleridge's entire Kantian-based theory of poetry, as is well known, depends upon analogous notions of the autonomy of the poetic event (*not* the poetic object, which is a post-Romantic conception). For Coleridge the poetic experience involved an encounter with 'the One Life', with the essential and non-contingent 'Ideas' of human nature. The polemic of Romantic poetry, therefore, is that it will not be polemical; its doctrine, that it is non-doctrinal; and its ideology, that it transcends ideology.

In that statement it is not easy to know—despite McGann's confident claim that it 'is well known'—what 'Coleridge's entire Kantian-based theory of poetry' is, or even that his theory of poetry is in fact 'Kantian-based'. The paradoxes asserted in the final sentence sound intriguing, but here too it is difficult to know just what is meant. Does Romantic poetry really mount a polemic, or does McGann just say that it does?

One final example of arbitrarily reduced conceiving—for the point is very important in assessing *The Romantic Ideology*—might be adduced. This example too indulges in paradoxical formulation; it too employs the hyperbolical emphasis of 'all' and 'entire' and 'fundamental'; it too is intrinsically important for McGann's argument even as it monotonizes the intricate fabric of Romanticism:

Ideas and ideology therefore lie at the heart of all Romantic poetry. Its entire emotional structure depends upon the credit and fidelity it gives to its own fundamental illusions. And its greatest moments usually occur when it pursues its last and final illusion: that it can expose or even that it has uncovered its illusions and false consciousness, that it has finally arrived at the Truth. The need to believe in such an achievement, either immediate or eventual, is deeply Romantic (and therefore illusive) because it locates the goal of human pursuits, needs, and desires in Ideal space. When Manfred, at the opening of his play, condemns his entire life's pursuit with the maxim 'The tree of knowledge is not that of life,' he lays open the heart of Romantic darkness. His manner of doing so remains, however, profoundly Romantic, as we see clearly in the drama's patterns of absolutes and ultimatums. Manfred's last cherished illusion is that he has no illusions left, that he has cleared his mind of cant and finally knows the whole truth: 'that nothing could be known' (*Don Juan* VII, st. 5).

In that passage, one applauds the neat paradox that 'Manfred's last cherished illusion is that he has no illusions left'.

The passage on its surface, however, does not invoke its Marxist inframeaning, which derives from Marx's turning of Hegel's absolute idealism upside down as absolute materialism, and which loads the dice before play has even begun. To say that the characteristic of Romantic effort is to 'locate the goal of human pursuits, needs, and desires in Ideal space' (leaving aside the question of whether that is in fact 'the' characteristic) is to open the sluice-gate to a subterranean current of eroding Marxist contempt for such Ideal space. As Marx says:

We shall, of course, not take the trouble to explain to our wise philosophers that the 'liberation' of 'man' is not advanced a single step by reducing philosophy, theology, substance and all the rubbish to 'self-consciousness' and by liberating 'man' from the domination of these phrases, which have never held him in thrall. Nor shall we explain to them that it is possible to achieve real liberation only in the real world and by real means, that slavery cannot be abolished without the steam-engine and the mule jenny, serfdom cannot be abolished without improved agriculture, and that, in general, people cannot be liberated as long as they are unable to obtain food and drink, housing and clothing in adequate quality and quantity. 'Liberation' is a historical and not a mental act.

Indeed, though it is perhaps one of *The Romantic Ideology*'s own illusions that it is not doing so, the book exactly parallels Marx's own programme of substituting dialectical materialism for dialectical ideationalism. The real situation described by Marx in the passage above—what Keats called 'the giant agony of the world'—was, insists McGann, typically converted into an ideological transcendence. 'The grand illusion of Romantic *ideology* is that one may escape such a world through imagination and poetry. The great truth of Romantic *work* is that there is no such escape.' In other words, for McGann—as against L. J. Swingle, whom he cogently refutes—Romantic poetry should be considered in both its ideological and its historical matrices. What McGann argues, however, is that it was a tendency for the Romantic poets themselves to displace historical factors into ideological ones; the critic, working against the grain, should attempt to resurrect the displaced historical and material circumstances in which the poem was formed. Of Wordsworth's 'Immortality Ode', for instance, McGann says that

The poem annihilates its history, biographical and socio-historical alike, and replaces these particulars with a record of pure consciousness. The paradox of the work is that it embodies an immediate and concrete experience of that most secret and impalpable of all human acts: the transformation of fact into idea, and of experience into ideology.

McGann's insistence on the displacement of concrete experience into ideological formation in Romantic poetry leads him to a new critical agenda, one that resituates the ideological structures of the poem within a recovered matrix of historical circumstance.

On all fronts the critic will move to enlarge the concept of the poetic work beyond that of a special kind of linguistic system, beyond even a certain type of semiological structure. The critic will be asked to expand the concept of the poem-as-text to the poem as more broadly based cultural product: in short, to the poem as poetical work. This hardly means that we cease being interested in linguistic and semiological aspects of poems; rather, it simply entails that those matters will be taken up in a cultural context which is at once more comprehensive (theoretically) and more particular (socially and historically).

The agenda, in sum, reflects Marx's insistence that ideational superstructures must be seen as historical formations dictated by materialist, especially economic, infrastructures. That, in fact, is what McGann has said virtually from the outset: 'This work assumes that poems are social and historical products and that the critical study of such products must be grounded in a socio-historical analytic.'

Such funnelling down of Romantic activity into a single mechanism: the displacement of the historical into the ideological ('the ideology represented through Romantic works is *a fortiori* seen as a body of illusions'), and the consequent critical call for the reprocessing of the ideological back into the socio-historical, are the strengths of McGann's book. But they are at the same time the reason it so radically bedims our sight of the great Romantic text, which is, to enlist a previous metaphor, a tapestry of intricate weave and varied design. What is needed in any general theory of Romanticism is a recognition both of the unity of the tapestry and of the variety of its design.

The present author has tried to indicate the outlines of such a theory in his discussion in *Romantic Cruxes*. In the book at hand an attempt shall be made to trace certain disparate patterns, located in distinct removal from one another, in that tapestry. It is this book's specific intent, by the topical discreteness of its seven chapters, to indicate—not exhaustively, to be sure, but it is hoped symbolically—the complex variety of Romantic textures. Three of the chapters take their focus from the consideration of individual figures and their involvement in cultural activity; three more deal primarily with intellectual collocations rather than cultural creators. The six interweave their concerns, whether looking from cultural figures to their works, or from ideational formations back to the people involved in them. A seventh chapter is devoted to rendering a texture that employs both modes simultaneously: it coalesces a major historical and ideational configuration—the French Revolution—and the ideational activity of a single figure—Coleridge. All seven chapters, whatever their nominal points of departure, devote themselves to a twin concern: to witness the complexity of their topics, and to present an interweaving of activities and thoughts. But the interweaving is undertaken in the interests of textural richness, not as an attempt to collapse data into *a priori* categories. McGann's approach tends to sacrifice the discreteness of Romantic phenomena to his own unitary theory of Romantic ideology. The present book attempts at all costs to 'save the phenomena.'

In its opposition to what has established itself as a reigning orthodoxy, the present book accordingly takes on something of a polemical character. Its underlying commitment to opposition, however, is not undertaken so much to try to dislodge McGann, on the one hand, or deconstruction and New Historicism, on the other, as to present vividly and unmistakably a widely diverse and even brutally separated variety—though woven all of the same threads—of Romantic textures.

It is the implied standpoint of the present volume, however, that McGann's agenda, when put into practice, tends to distort and encumber particular understandings. In other words, it is the contention of this book, often unspoken, that his theory of Romantic ideology not only tends to occlude, or at all events to diminish, the text called Romanticism, but that its praxis disrupts the textures it touches. In another place (in a volume called *William Wordsworth: Intensity and Achievement*) the present author takes detailed issue with Marjorie Levinson's reading of 'Tintern Abbey', which is a well-known embodiment of McGann's critical agenda for the examination of Romantic works. But that agenda and its new approach are so immediately beguiling, and at the same time ultimately so unsatisfactory in their promise of larger understanding, that a second polemical investigation has seemed to be necessitated.

To that end, this book places first among its ensuing textures a discussion called 'Drowning in Contexts'. In this initial chapter, criticism is directed against one of the most learned and powerful of recent studies of Wordsworth, one that incorporates the new requirement of historical recovery in the consideration of poetic matrix. In this first texture also, discourse is deliberately restricted to a work that is not 'Romantic' itself but is, in McGann's terminology, part of the 'cultural support systems' of Romanticism. These systems, which have grown up in the years that have elapsed since the high efflorescence of Romanticism itself (and especially cluster in the academy), are—one supposes McGann would insist, and the present discourse would agree—as undeniably features of the text called Romanticism as are the works of the original Romantics.

Before the reader embarks on the sequential and interlinked chapters that are now to follow, perhaps a word about the special narrative structure of this volume will prove helpful. The book does not offer a contract in terms of customary strategies of sight. It does not look towards, glimpse, hold in view a grand conclusion of argument, a far horizon towards which each paragraph is designed triumphantly to progress. On the contrary, the continuing argument as much as possible eschews sight in favour of touch. It provides no conspectus of its whole plan, no survey of the measured dimensions of its tapestry, no prediction as to the demarcated distance that will be traversed, or as to when, or even if, the end of the fabric might be reached.

Instead, it feels its way, as it were, by a patient touching of textures. At any specific point the argument aspires, in Coleridge's words earlier adduced, to be like 'the *Touch* of a Blind Man feeling the face of a darling Child'. Each texture, it is hoped, will seem to be woven into its succeeding texture as such succession occurs; but the book specifically abrogates those conventions that involve a looking forward, now or later, to a putative end. The book in that sense does not commit itself to conclude, but rather simply to cease. Its meanings are intended to be separated as much as possible from the kind of structural contract that arises from sight. They inhere, rather, in the experience of each thickening, each felt variation of the threads and patterns that constitute texture. That, indeed, is why so many and such diverse accumulations of quoted material are put forward.

The book bears as part of its title the rubric, 'The Heritage of Rousseau'. The words are not intended to suggest a source-and-influence approach, nor, indeed, any sort of one-to-one correspondence between

Rousseau and later Romantic figures and manifestations. Rousseau's presence, on the contrary, is conceived much in the way Friedrich Schlegel described Spinoza's presence in the Romantic epoch: 'Spinoza is everywhere in the background, like Fate in ancient tragedy.' To that end, Rousseau is sometimes found at the very centre of discussion, at other times in a secondary placement, and still elsewhere he is felt so faintly as almost to be impalpable.

A concluding point. There are secondary works of interpretation and scholarship, sometimes many of them, on almost every topic broached in this volume. To the utmost extent that it has seemed feasible, however, the book tries to avoid summoning this extensive publication—though in some few circumstances it is nevertheless forced to do so. For a single major instance, the bibliography of commentary and other secondary literature on Rousseau is inconceivably vast; here it is almost entirely absent. For a single minor instance, there are full-length studies of the relation of Shelley to Coleridge, of Wordsworth to Shelley, of Shelley to Rousseau; but this book, when discussing those realities, confines itself to primary texts and the author's idiosyncratic emphasis.

The present book, in these and other instances, shuns secondary reference; and it does so for two intertwined reasons. First, the volume aspires to touch its topics, as far as possible, in their original textures. To embark on extensive secondary citation would be to compromise the integrity of the patternings. Secondly, and even more urgently, this book seeks to recover the life and freshness of the collocations it touches. It has seemed essential, with that primary goal in view, not to allow actions and thoughts, once compelling and even now still vivid, to be lacquered over, and thereby embalmed, by successive coatings of secondary opinion.

I

Drowning in Contexts

A SEA change has occurred in recent Wordsworthian criticism. Conditioned by the deconstructionist upheaval, and owing fealty specifically to the rise of New Historicism, conditioned also by the critical agenda of Jerome McGann just discussed, this change has virtually abandoned qualitative and personal considerations in the assessment of poetry. There is substituted instead a preoccupation with social and political backgrounds, especially backgrounds so far in the background as to be invisible in the *prima facie* structure of the poem. The poem now is seen not as a formalist artefact, but as a hieroglyph that masks absent relevance. In Jonathan Bate's words, this changed criticism 'is interested in the ways in which literature is not "about" the things it says it is about, is interested in what literature suppresses (e.g. women, history) or in the proposition that literature cannot really be "about" anything since to "decode" a text is to "re-encode" it.'[1]

The sea change is interesting in many ways, one of which is certainly that it provides new topics and new possibilities of originality for the accumulating hordes of late-coming critics. The graduate schools pump out ever larger numbers of newly trained scholars eager to make their impress, but they find a situation in which almost everything that can be said about the intended statements of great poetry has already been said—and said, and said. No more elucidation seems to be needed; only endless redundancy is the prospect for further criticism. So a search for new possibilities must be mounted, and it leads in two primary directions: one is to make new additions to the canon, either by adding on large amounts of contemporary work or upgrading earlier uncanonical work, thereby enabling the critical farmer to plant a new field not exhausted by repeated harvesting. The other is to see the poem not as it is but as it is not. After all, in any silhouette, the inner colour is no more valid than the outer colour, and no more necessary. So the changed criticism has poured out of the central figure into its surrounding field. It has poured out of the focusing domain of presence into the domain of absence.

In this way new things are seen, new relevances are proposed, new

[1] Jonathan Bate, 5.

judgements are implied. Indeed, one of the most striking features of the sea change is that topics of critical attention characteristically are supplied by a canon erected on the conception of qualitative merit, and then those topics are re-evaluated in a way that tends to deny or qualify that merit. Thus 'Tintern Abbey', in the new reading by Marjorie Levinson, becomes not a great poem but 'a document of sociological bad faith.'[2] But all the new sightings, new relevances, and implied new judgements generated by the sea change of criticism, as too all the sightings, relevances, and judgements generated by the older canonical criticism, are functions of point of view. All criticism whatever is necessarily a function of point of view. The poem exists in itself as an artefact, or to use the newer vocabulary, a text. Its critical inspection, however, is produced by another entity, the critic, and the relation of the critic to the text is necessarily still a third entity, a point of view.

Though point of view will no doubt readily be conceded as a component of the critical act, its importance and complexity are less apparent. To examine a fruitful example, let us consider Schopenhauer's statement, in his *Parerga and Paralipomena*, that Byron, England's

greatest poet after the incomparable Shakespeare, was not allowed to be set up in Westminster Abbey, her national Pantheon, with other great men. This was simply because Byron had been honest enough not to make any concessions to Anglican parsondom, but went his own way unhampered by them; whereas the mediocre Wordsworth, the frequent target of his ridicule, had his statue suitably installed in Westminster Abbey in 1854.[3]

The statement is remarkable on a number of levels, and to examine them will be to make ourselves aware of what multi-layered complications can be subsumed by the simple phrase 'point of view'.

First of all, we note that the critical judgement emanates from a most unusual source, not an English critic but a German philosopher. Secondly, we note that not only does it lay claim to a knowledge of Wordsworth, but to a knowledge of Byron as well, and that it presents its judgement as a mode of comparison between the two. Thirdly, we note the self-confidence of the statement; it not only judges Wordsworth and Byron, but does so with an implicit claim to ranking the whole of English literature. Fourthly, and perhaps most strikingly, it astonishingly judges Wordsworth to be 'mediocre'.

That is a heterodox judgement indeed. Contrast it with the judgement of Matthew Arnold: 'I firmly believe that the poetical performance of

² McFarland, *Wordsworth*, 16–17.   ³ Schopenhauer, v. 288.

Wordsworth is, after that of Shakespeare and Milton, of which all the world now recognises the worth, undoubtedly the most considerable in our language from the Elizabethan age to the present time.'[4] 'We shall recognise him in his place, as we recognise Shakespeare and Milton; and not only we ourselves shall recognise him, but he will be recognised by Europe also.'[5] Contrast it too with the point of view of Coleridge, which led to the judgement that 'in imaginative power, [Wordsworth] stands nearest of all modern writers to Shakespear and Milton; and yet in a kind perfectly unborrowed and his own.'[6] Contrast it again to the point of view of Keats, which generated the judgement that 'Wordsworth is deeper than Milton',[7] that Milton 'did not think into the human heart, as Wordsworth has done'.[8]

And yet one should not be too hasty in dismissing 'the mediocre Wordsworth' as simply the misconception of a non-poetical foreigner who did not know English perfectly. On the contrary, it was the judgement of one of the greatest intellects in the history of culture, an intellect fortified, moreover, by voracious reading in seven languages. Though Schopenhauer did not know all the things that other Wordsworthian judges may have known, he certainly knew many other things that they did not, and these things worked to condition his judgements and the reasons for them.

It would be of great interest to know exactly what part of Wordsworthian production Schopenhauer had in his purview. One hopes that he was not speaking of *The Prelude*, which had appeared in 1850 and so was available before the publication of the first volume of the *Parerga* in 1851. The statement about Wordsworth, however, mentions the date of 1854, so at least that issue was clearly the result of a later address by Schopenhauer to his text. On the other hand, the essays were written over a period of years, mostly in the period following the second edition of *Die Welt als Wille und Vorstellung* in 1844, and Schopenhauer's preface to the first volume of the *Parerga* is dated December 1850. So it perhaps seems unlikely, though it may be possible, that Schopenhauer produced his phrase 'der mediocre Poët Wordsworth' with *The Prelude* in mind.

But even if he were indeed thinking of *The Prelude*—which the present author has on several occasions called 'the greatest poem of the nineteenth century'[9]—he was at least not alone in his judgment. The poem, when it was published, was for the most part not greeted with the acclaim it now elicits, and Macaulay, who was both a native speaker of English and a poet

[4] Arnold, 132.   [5] Ibid. 134.
[6] *Biographia*, ii. 151.   [7] Keats, *Letters*, i. 281.
[8] Ibid. 282.   [9] e.g. McFarland, *Wordsworth*, 104.

himself, recorded in his journal for 28 July 1850 a distinct verdict of 'mediocre':

I brought home, and read, the 'Prelude.' It is a poorer 'Excursion'; the same sort of faults and beauties; but the faults greater and the beauties fainter, both in themselves and because faults are made more offensive, and beauties less pleasing, by repetition. The story is the old story. There are the old raptures about mountains and cataracts; the old flimsy philosophy about the effect of scenery on the mind; the old, crazy mystical metaphysics; the endless wilderness of dull, flat, prosaic twaddle, and here and there fine descriptions and energetic declamations interspersed.[10]

Much later, John Crowe Ransom, a figure highly esteemed both as poet and critic, delivered an essentially similar verdict of 'mediocre'. Referring in 1941 to *The Prelude*, he says:

The poet became a little paralyzed, we may imagine, when he took pen in hand to write a poem; or got that way after going a certain distance in the writing of a long one. I go beyond the direct evidence here, but I assume that making distinguished metrical discourse was such a job, and consisted in his own mind with so much corruption of the sense at best, that he fell into the habit of choosing the most resounding words, and stringing them together as the meter dictated. This is not unusual in Romantic poetry. The point to make about Romantic poetry now is not the one about its noble words, but a negative and nasty one: the noble words are almost absurdly incoherent.[11]

So even if Schopenhauer were in fact thinking of *The Prelude*, his opinion, though not in the critical mainstream, would not have been without its analogues either. One hopes it is more likely though, that he might have been thinking about Wordsworth's volume of 1835 called *Yarrow Revisited*, which could most satisfactorily be described as 'mediocre'. As the present author has said:

I happen to own Wordsworth's volume of 1835 called *Yarrow Revisited*, and in its more than three hundred and twenty pages of verse there are hardly as many *lines* of what might, even by the most liberal standards, be called poetry. The entire volume, when perused as an entity, is a sombre spectacle of poetic desiccation.[12]

But here, too, matters remain complex. Despite my own emphatic judgement of 'mediocre' for this volume, not all critics agree. For instance, Peter Manning has recently mounted a circumspect defence of the quality of the late poetry contained in *Yarrow Revisited*.[13]

---

[10] Wordsworth, *Prelude*, 560.   [11] Ransom, 305–6.
[12] McFarland, *Romanticism*, 217.   [13] See Manning, 291–5.

If we return to the passage from Schopenhauer, we see evidences of vigorous judgement. The assertion that Byron is second only to Shakespeare in English literature, while bold indeed, is precisely the same judgement rendered by G. Wilson Knight, who was one of the most sensitive and passionate interpreters of both Byron and Shakespeare. Knight wrote numerous and important books on both figures, and his considered opinion was that 'Byron appears to me our greatest poet in the widest sense of this term since Shakespeare'.[14] Again, Schopenhauer's astute reference to 'Anglican parsondom' brilliantly compresses what, beginning with *The Excursion* and proceeding to the end of his life, became an increasing preoccupation of Wordsworth. One perhaps can do no better by way of illustration than to recall the contest between Tennyson and Fitzgerald to coin 'the weakest Wordsworthian line imaginable'. The delicious winning line, 'A Mr Wilkinson, a clergyman', is a *ne plus ultra* of 'Anglican parsondom'.[15]

So what instruction do we draw from Schopenhauer's judgement? What light does it shed on our present address to the sea change in Wordsworthian criticism? First of all, it suggests that point of view is not a simple but a complex factor in the critical equation. Secondly, it suggests that a point of view may be rich with interest in itself but nevertheless generate false judgement. Thirdly, it implies that though different points of view render different conclusions, there is nevertheless a true perspective on a poem, a Platonic idea so to speak, that either validates or invalidates the varied judgements generated by varied points of view. It is simply not the case that Wordsworth, judged as every poet has a right to be judged, that is, by his highest moments, can validly be judged to be 'mediocre'. Schopenhauer, profound intelligence that he was, is absolutely, though interestingly, wrong in that final assessment, as are Macaulay and Ransom in their allied assessments.

None of us truly believes in critical relativism. In the final analysis, the opinions of Schopenhauer, of Macaulay, and of Ransom recoil upon themselves and reveal themselves as adverse judgements, not upon Wordsworth, but upon the understandings of their promulgators. The poem—we intuitively know this or we simply cannot proceed with criticism—is a complex of true meanings, not of arbitrary meanings, and each critical act is valid only to the extent that it uncovers the authentic structure of the poem or other aesthetic object's meaning. To be sure, that authentic structure looks different since the rise of deconstruction from

[14] Knight, 3.
[15] Hallam Tennyson, i. 153.

the way it did in the heyday of New Criticism. Yet the uncovering of authentic structures of meaning remains the perennial task of critical interpretation, just as the assessing of value remains the perennial task of critical touching. Those things are true no matter what vicissitudes the apparent text encounters from the onslaught of Derridean deconstruction or De Manian nihilism. After all, Derrida has recently felt obliged to say that 'Deconstruction has no ambition to destroy or cancel the subject. Deconstruction and reconstruction go together.'[16] The reconstructed text will necessarily look somewhat different from the text as it initially appears, but in the wake of all the changes wrought by deconstructive processing, there must still emerge a text that is once again a vector of true meanings, otherwise the poem simply disappears.

The matter is so vital that perhaps an example or two should be adduced to show that an individual critical judgement must conform to the successive judgements that, as I have elsewhere described the situation, are necessary to establish a work as canonical.[17] If the individual judgement does not conform to the collective judgement, then it simply cannot stand: it sounds ludicrous; it becomes a cultural curiosity, derided by all, accepted by none. And it sounds ludicrous no matter how great the cultural credentials of the critic who promulgates it. Tolstoy, for instance, is universally recognized as one of the greatest figures in the entire history of literature. He was extremely well-informed about past and contemporary literatures and artistic theories in England, France, Germany, America, and classical antiquity. He thought long and hard about the nature of art and the value of literature. But when he rendered the judgement that the later works of Beethoven are poor, because Beethoven 'could not hear, could not perfect his work, and consequently published productions which are artistic ravings',[18] and that Beethoven's Ninth Symphony is 'not a good work of art',[19] he invited, and received, derision. There are many things that are simply a matter of opinion; but judgements of the quality of great art are not among them. If one says, 'I do not think coffee is as good as tea', the judgement, as a matter of taste, falls outside objective imputations of value. But if one says, 'I do not think *War and Peace* a great novel', an answer is implied, and that answer is always a form of 'you don't know what you're talking about'.

Again, Wittgenstein is regarded as one of the most profound of philosophical minds, but he was 'troubled by his inability to appreciate the greatness of Shakespeare', and that inability at length led to an

---

[16] *Times Literary Supplement*, 3 Apr. 1992, 13.   [17] *Argument*, 106–27.
[18] Tolstoy, 197.   [19] Ibid. 248.

impermissible judgement, one that precisely elicits the eternal answer, 'you don't know what you're talking about'. Wittgenstein's impermissible judgement is contained in a jotting: ' "Beethoven's great heart"—nobody could speak of "Shakespeare's great heart" '.[20] The very highest intellectual attainments do not insulate their possessor against formulating critical opinions that are simply wrong. But to say that critical judgements are simply wrong is at the same time to say that there must be a critical judgement that is right—not relatively or contingently right, but absolutely right. Wittgenstein's opinion is not a vagary of taste, but an imperfection in understanding. For taste resides on the surface; it implies no antecedent understanding or realization in depth. The differing structure of opinion that is called judgement, on the contrary, implies both antecedent understanding and knowledge. That is why, despite its surface similarity, it is not interchangeable with taste.

To extrapolate such inferences for a consideration of the sea change in Wordsworthian criticism is to reveal serious flaws in the new approaches. First of all, it is perhaps ungenerous but for all that necessary, in the polemic implied throughout this book, to point out that the new approaches almost all, either explicitly or implicitly, base themselves upon the validity of the Marxist analysis of the human situation; and that basing has become violently de-based by the collapse of Marxist governments throughout the world. The critics of the sea change have tried to insulate themselves from this colossal judgement by history; they would have done better had they, several years ago, for their own journeyman knowledges of Marx substituted the learned and destabilizing analysis contained in the three volumes of Kolakowski's *Main Currents of Marxism*. As it is, all their *theoria* has been contradicted by the massive *praxis* of communism's collapse. Their discomfort has been further compounded by the spectacular self-annihilation of their most eminent and doctrinally austere theorist, Althusser, who has left behind as his final intellectual testament a denunciation of all he stood for and a contemptuous dismissal of Marxism itself.

The critical adherents of Marxist theory in the Anglo-Saxon literary world thus find themselves in a quandary. The foundation has been washed from under their feet; but there is an understandable tendency on their parts to be reluctant to give up positions won only through substantial investments of learning and consideration. Though one frequently hears in their defence, at least for the time being, that the

[20] Monk, 568-9.

communist enterprise was a false understanding of Marx, and that they alone possess the true understanding, the claim hardly warrants serious consideration. Though few of these critics seem to realize it, or perhaps can allow themselves to realize it, Joseph Stalin, like Lenin, adhered closely and theoretically to Marxist doctrine and murdered millions of his countrymen in specific furtherance of its dogma.[21] In truth, Stalin was early on described by Trotsky himself, in the years of his exile, as in the very 'centre' of the Russian political spectrum.[22]

The second major flaw in the new approaches is that they are unable to confront or account for the quality of the poems they approach. If the poems were not already presented by the canon as masterpieces, there is nothing in these approaches, either by statement or by implication, that could demonstrate or conceive that greatness. As noted in the introduction, I have elsewhere, in a chapter called 'The Clamour of Absence: Reading and Misreading in Wordsworthian Criticism', attempted to point to this defect with reference to the criticism of Marjorie Levinson, so for further discussion those interested are referred to that chapter.[23]

Little additional mention of the first two flaws shall be undertaken here. What I shall try to do in the remainder of this discussion is rather to address what I take to be the third major flaw in the new approaches. That flaw appears as a by-product of the flow of critical attention from the inner figure of the poem to its surrounding outer field. The domain of presence is now characteristically compromised by the rush to the domain of absence, with the result that the new discourses of absence tend to forfeit the validations of relevance. A discourse of absence that locates itself just outside the defining line of the aesthetic silhouette can depend on that line for the structure we call relevance. As it strikes farther out into the field of absence, however, it loses sight of the configuration and substitutes instead a self-referential structure of its own. In doing so it runs the gravest risks of becoming either historically wrong or simply nugatory.

To try to expand upon and further specify this phenomenon, I shall select for discussion a single recent avatar of the new approach, Alan Liu's

[21] See below, Ch. 3, n. 231.
[22] Kolakowski, iii. 190. Kolakowski points out that Stalin attempted no innovations in Marxist doctrine—'Everyone knew that Stalin's articles, pamphlets, and speeches contained nothing original and showed no sign that they were intended to' (iii. 16)—and that, paradoxically, 'since, during his years of power, there was scarcely any other brand of Marxism than his, and since the Marxism of those days can hardly be defined except in relation to his authority, it is not only true but is actually a tautology to say that for a quarter of a century he was the greatest Marxist theoretician' (ibid.).
[23] McFarland, *Wordsworth*, 1–33.

Wordsworth: The Sense of History. I choose this work both because it is a learned and challenging book in its own right, and because it handles the discourse of absence with skill and subtlety.

Liu eagerly enrols himself among the proponents of the new approach. He speaks of

the regrounding of reference that Jerome McGann, David Simpson, and Marjorie Levinson have also applied to Romantic poetry in their discussion of literary displacement and that I would pursue, if possible, with even more force: the literary text is not just the displacement but the overdetermined and agonic *denial* of historical reference.[24]

Here, at the outset, an embarrassing question presents itself. If the literary text is a denial of historical reference, that is, when viewed by our own superior critical intelligences the text clearly reveals that when it does not talk about history it is really talking about history, does it follow that when it does overtly link itself to history—say, Byron's invocation of Waterloo in *Childe Harold*—it is by the same equation really not talking about history? And if it is not talking about history, what then is the subject of its discourse? One supposes that the new approach would have to fudge a bit at this point and say that the historical discourse about Waterloo is actually denying some further historical discourse that does not appear in the intended statement of the poem. Yet even this could not fully satisfy the equation; for if literary statement leaps and at the same time turns to a different domain, that is, to historical denial, historical statement could not properly stay within the historical domain, even by way of denial, and be true to the formula. It could not be true, for though there would be a leap there would be no turn, and leap and turn are both necessary to furnish the structure of the formula.

Liu, however, boldly commits himself to the hegemony of absence and negation. Much as Saussure's *parole* emerges from the sea of *langue*, Liu's texts are hypothesized to emerge from a vast ocean of historical context:

Literary texts emerge, I posit, precisely through a critical or second-order negation: the arbitrary but nevertheless determined differentiation by which they do not articulate historical contexts (the latter, of course, themselves constructed as arbitrary differentiation). Or put more empirically: it is not the case that contexts cue texts in the way the stick imparts spin and direction to the billiard ball. Rather, contexts are themselves constituted as masses of difference—as collisions or discontinuities with other contexts or with aspects of themselves. And it is this dynamic mass of marked breaks and shaped absences that determines the text by

spelling out in advance the shaped *absence* of context—negative yet determinate—
that is the defamiliarized text. I draw here in particular from Pierre Macherey who
defines the literary text as a sheaf of absences and dissonances stitched together by
that which is never on the page: the history not there.[25]

Despite the sophistication of his discussion of contexts, Liu is
continually forced to resort to radical denials of his own:

To make my own opening difference from 'Wordsworthianism' as wide as
possible, therefore, I nail on the church door a litany of broken faiths.
    There is no nature. Since I have already begun upon this refutation, I tender here
a brief, Berkleian argument. . . .
    A full list of corollaries to the above tenet can be unfolded as follows, where the
sequence traces the turns we have yet to take in tracking Wordsworth's
development, but counteracts any lingering idealism, Berkleian or otherwise:
    There is no time.
    There is no affection.
    There is no self or mind.
    Therefore, there is no Imagination.[26]

All these radical, these heroic denials are necessitated by a single
affirmation, deriving from Paul De Man: 'What there "is"', says Liu, 'is
history.'[27]

Alas, if one thinks about the matter, it becomes clear that if nature, time,
affection, self or mind, and imagination all disappear, their loss erodes so
many contextual connections that no viable conception of 'history' can
remain. Liu's placing all his eggs in the basket of history, indeed, reminds
one of a place in Coleridge's *Opus Maximum* where, in arguing against a
theoretical opponent who will 'admit of no mathematical or ideal
possibility, of no truth in Reason, or the Idea, which is not the reflex or
direct expression of some fact in experience', Coleridge says:

I really know of no other reply but one of condolence with the moral or intellectual
state of the objector. For what would it avail to make such a man see, that on such a
plan there could be no science, no philosophy, no religion, as distinct from history?
. . . Yes! the objector would reply, that is just what I mean. There is nothing but
history.[28]

That, of course, may not entirely be Liu's position; but the boldness of
Liu's statements masks an anxiety that leads him to a straining of evidence
that eventually compromises the validity of his entire position. Let us take
the single example of the proposition 'There is no nature'. Hidden behind

---

[25] Liu, 46.   [26] Ibid. 38–9.
[27] Ibid. 39.   [28] MS of the *Opus Maximum*.

this statement are historical claims by Harold Bloom and Geoffrey Hartman rejecting the role of nature in the Wordsworthian spectrum, claims that seem to me plainly wrong—or, to enlist the concerns just elucidated, 'simply wrong'—and that I have attacked on more than one occasion.[29] Liu does not allow these claims to emerge in his own overt statement, however, but substitutes instead his Berkleian argument

—in Berkleian personal voice—merely as a transition to an ongoing critique. Having lived for some years in a part of Connecticut not unlike the Lake District in its reservoirs, brooks, grasslands, and deep forest dells, I would go so far as to acknowledge the existence of a reservoir, brook, field, and possibly even forest (more certainly, trees). But 'nature' I have never set axe too.[30]

Liu's concession that there may be such an entity as 'forest' and not just 'trees', while clearly the whole thrust of his Berkleian argument is that there is no forest, provides a good example of his winning sophistication throughout his book. But that sophistication certainly masks anxiety. He does not really believe in forests, indeed, he can hardly see trees, if he thinks that the area around New Haven, Connecticut can be considered as in some meaningful way like the glories of the Lake District! I too have lived in Connecticut, and to regard it as comparable to the paradise in which Wordsworth was reared is to occlude vision and reject discrimination. The denial of 'nature' subtends an inadequate cognizance of those particularities that led historically to the emergence of the abstraction in the first place.

It is important to note this tiny but pregnant example of occluded vision in the practicality of Liu's approach to context. Seen without practicality, that approach is bathed in theoretical sophistication:

Historical context is not a massively stable totality but a domain of collective knowledge (world-view, folklore, kinship system, ideology, *longue durée*, discursive formation). Knowledge or reference of this sort is organized on the basis of arbitrary rifts of internal differentiation, of clashes, divisions, prejudices, and other living negativities of social experience; and as such is always both capricious and determinate, free as *jouissance* and bound as history.[31]

---

[29] See Thomas McFarland, 'Romantic Imagination, Nature, and the Pastoral Ideal', in *Coleridge's Imagination: Essays in Memory of Pete Laver*, ed. Richard Gravil, Lucy Newlyn, and Nicholas Roe (Cambridge: Cambridge University Press, 1985), 9–11; 'Involute and Symbol in the Romantic Imagination', in *Coleridge, Keats, and the Imagination; Romanticism and Adam's Dream: Essays in Honor of Walter Jackson Bate* (Columbia: University of Missouri Press, 1990), 30–7.

[30] Liu, 38.

[31] Ibid. 45.

Liu stresses the need for care in invoking even a conception of context fortified by as much literary, social, and anthropological theory as he brings to it. As he says:

We need to be careful here with degrees of certainty. An adequate reading of Wordsworth's texts in their historical context, I will suggest, requires not so much positivistic method as a deflected or denied positivism able to discriminate absence.[32]

Why, then, in the realm of context does Liu take such radical chances as the Berkleian example represents? Why does his argument, despite its skill and its learning, scarcely ever seem to see, that while contexts necessarily recede into an uncharted ocean, relevances are sharply circumscribed by the configuration of the text itself? At least part of the answer is that he runs great risk to achieve great reward. That reward is one we would all give much to attain: having it both ways. If one can have it both ways, then one must surely be right in any point he advances: 'Both these propositions are true: first that Wordsworth's largest, most sustained theme is the realization of history; and, second, that his largest theme is the denial of history.'[33]

Assured by the totalizing effect of history, Liu can proceed with his reassessing march—his tour—through Wordsworth:

Where we have come in our tour, then, is to the annunciation of the argument of this book. The true apocalypse for Wordsworth is reference. What now shocks us most about Wordsworth's poetry, after all, is its indelible stain of referentiality, its insistent mundanity. . . . But reference to history, I assert, is the only 'power' of Wordsworth's Imagination (as I will at last call it with unexamined significance); this power is as unstable, surprising, and full of hidden lights as any figure Mind can conceive; and its hold over Mind is not less but *more* persistent, when, as in *The Prelude*, it is manifest only in a poetics of denial, of reference lost.

Where we now have to go in our tour, as is characteristic of Wordsworth's own tours, is *back* from *The Prelude* to retrace the entire itinerary by which the poet learned to create his crowning denial of history: autobiography.[34]

The centre-piece, the validating instance, for Liu's substitution of denied history for nature, mind, and imagination in Wordsworth's text, is his finding of Napoleon's passage through the Alps embedded in the Simplon episode of the sixth book of *The Prelude*. The demonstration has already achieved notoriety in Wordsworthian studies, even where its specifics have not been examined. It is not only notorious, however, but of

[32] Liu. 24.   [33] Ibid. 39.   [34] Ibid. 35.

greatest importance in the underpinning of Liu's whole approach, and it accordingly must be examined more closely here.

One notes at the outset that the demonstration's virtuoso manipulations themselves constitute a kind of denial, an erasure almost, of another virtuoso moment in the history of criticism: Geoffrey Hartman's enormously influential discussion of that same episode.[35] Though both critics have in common an emphasis on the central importance of the Simplon episode, even here I find a slight deflection of what I myself take to be the true point of view towards Wordsworth. The most germane passage in the Simplon episode runs this way, as it appears in the 1805 version:

> Imagination! lifting up itself
> Before the eye and progress of my song
> Like an unfathered vapour—here that Power,
> In all the might of its endowments, came
> Athwart me; I was lost as in a cloud,
> Halted without a struggle to break through;
> And now recovering, to my soul I say—
> 'I recognize thy glory': in such strength
> Of usurpation, in such visitings
> Of awful promise, when the light of sense
> Goes out in flashes that have shown to us
> The invisible world, doth greatness make abode,
> There harbours whether we be young or old.
> Our destiny, our nature, and our home
> Is with infinitude, and only there;
> With hope it is, hope that can never die,
> Effort, and expectation, and desire,
> And something evermore about to be.
> The mind beneath such banners militant
> Thinks not of spoils or trophies, nor of aught
> That may attest its prowess, blest in thoughts
> That are their own perfection and reward,
> Strong in itself, and in the access of joy
> Which hides it like the overflowing Nile.

(bk. vi, ll. 525–48)

The Simplon Pass episode, asserts Liu, is 'Wordsworth at the peak of experience'.[36] He goes on to say that the readings 'we now have of the

---

[35] Hartman, 39–48.
[36] Liu, 4.

Simplon Pass episode, among which Geoffrey Hartman's is in the vanguard, are so powerful that the episode has become one of a handful of paradigms capable by itself of representing the poet's work'.[37] He says that he himself seeks 'to reimagine Wordsworth's 1790 trip and *The Prelude*'s insertion of Imagination into that trip'.[38]

But these statements reveal what I call above 'a slight deflection' of what I myself consider the true point of view towards Wordsworth. To me, the emphasis on the Simplon Pass episode seems an over-emphasis. Indeed, it seems to me that the mighty Wordsworthian current divides itself into two majestic rivers, the one running from the 1790 trip and the Simplon Pass and the residence in France to the ascent of Snowdon, and the other proceeding from 'Tintern Abbey', through *Home at Grasmere* into the 'Immortality Ode' and 'the supreme intensity of the first two books of *The Prelude*'.[39] To me, only the second flows into the vast sea of Wordsworthian greatness; the other loses itself in marshes of mystical evocation.

I adduce this disagreement not to assert a simple preference, but rather as affecting an entire conception of Wordsworth. Liu's whole point of view ultimately rests on the happenings and meanings of Wordsworth's 1790 tour in France:

The Prelude organizes the 1790 tour so that 'nature' is precipitated in Book 6 only as a denial of the history behind any tour, and the goal of the denial—not fully effective until the purge of Books 9 and 10—is to carve the 'self' out of history. The theory of denial is Imagination.[40]

But the happenings and meanings of the 1790 tour, important though they are, and linking together books vi, ix, and x of *The Prelude*, and generating the powerful poetry of the Simplon Pass episode and other great moments, still do not emanate from the deepest and purest depths of Wordsworth's experience of life. Those deepest and purest depths well up, rather, in his memories of early childhood, in his inspired recollections of the fair seed-time of his soul, and later in the paradisal reachings of *Home at Grasmere*. There is an absolute divagation between those memories and reachings and the matter of the Simplon Pass (which, indeed, looks not backward towards childhood, but forward towards 'something evermore about to be'). The memories of the seed-time of Wordsworth's soul, on the contrary, look not towards history, explicit or denied, but towards the 'depth' from which man's honours proceed:

[37] Liu, 4.
[38] Ibid.
[39] McFarland, *Wordsworth*, 79.
[40] Liu, 4–5.

Oh! mystery of man, from what a depth
Proceed thy honours. I am lost, but see
In simple childhood something of the base
On which thy greatness stands

.   .   .   .

                           The days gone by
Return upon me almost from the dawn
Of life: the hiding-places of man's power
Open; I would approach them, but they close.
I see by glimpses now; when age comes on,
May scarcely see at all; and I would give,
While yet we may, as far as words can give,
Substance and life to what I feel, enshrining,
Such is my hope, the spirit of the Past
For future restoration.

                     (*Prelude* (1850), bk. xii, ll. 272–86)

That passage, in my own view, is a truer paradigm representing the significant body of Wordsworth's work than is the Simplon Pass episode, even if one adds to it the wonderful apocalyptic passage in Gondo Gorge. It is a truer paradigm, and also one that works against the implications of Simplon and Snowdon.

Leaving aside, but not dismissing, my belief that the Simplon Pass episode is *not* the most compelling paradigm for contemplation of Wordsworth, it will be instructive to return to Liu's discourse on Napoleon with reference to that episode.

In Liu's analysis of the Simplon passage quoted above, 'Imagination cavitates nature to show the protruding bones of the historical world of 1804.'[41] It

sees in nature not just its own reflection but that of a firmly *historical* genius of imagination—of the Imaginer who, in a manner of speaking, wrote the book on crossing the Alps. I believe that if we look into 6b [the Simplon episode], we will see through the self and mind in the foreground, through even the nature in the middle ground, to a frightening skeleton in the background. Whatever else it is, Imagination is the haunt of Napoleon, the great Bone of the time (a standard play on words in the early 1800s; see below). More precisely, if Imagination reflects upon nature as a mirror, the mirror is of magistrates and shows Imagination to itself as a canny double for uncanny Napoleon. Imagination at once mimics and effaces Napoleon.[42]

---

[41] Ibid. 24.   [42] Ibid.

Though such a claim, taken as it is here with minimal context, can at first glance seem preposterous, Liu's support of it is brilliant. Even without Liu's full argument, if we return to the Simplon passage quoted above, we note Napoleonic matter: 'banners militant', 'spoils and trophies', 'prowess'. We note a Napoleonically pregnant word, 'usurpation' ('After 18 Brumaire, "usurper" was applied to Bonaparte in English parliamentary speeches, pamphlets, and newspapers with the consistency of a technical term').[43] We note, of all unexpected and exotic things, 'the overflowing Nile', which has little to do with the Alps or Switzerland, but much to do with Napoleon:

Wordsworth's stress in 1804 that the Imagination is its own reward, and so eschews spoils and trophies, should be seen to reject precisely Napoleon's famed spoliations. His homage to the overflowing Nile—which enriches, rather than, like the 'torrent' of Napoleon's armies, robs—then speaks the final 'no' to tyranny. Even as French forces occupied Switzerland in 1798, Bonaparte was preparing to sail for Egypt in an effort to disrupt British commerce with the Far East. Despite great successes on land, victory was robbed from him by Nelson, who destroyed the French fleet at Aboukir on the mouth of the Nile and so left Bonaparte's forces suddenly stranded in Egypt.[44]

These and other Napoleonic relevances and suggestions, both in the poetic text and in germane background materials of the time, are skilfully marshalled by Liu to suggest the congruence of Imagination with Napoleon, and the congruence of Wordsworth's Alpine situation with Napoleon's Alpine situation:

Recall the diversionary force that Napoleon sent to demonstrate in Simplon Pass. If my presentation has even the barest plausibility, it will appear that Wordsworthian nature is precisely such an imaginary antagonist against which the self battles in feint, in a ploy to divert attention from the real battle to be joined between *history* and self. Whatever the outcome of the skirmish (called dialectic) between nature and self, history, the real antagonist, is thus momentarily denied so that when it debouches at last, it will be recognized with shock by the feinting mind as the greatest power of the Wordsworthian defile. As envisioned in the framework of the total *Prelude*—where the books of unnatural history then come at the point of climax rather than, as in *Paradise Lost*, of denouement—denial is the threshold of Wordsworth's most truly shocking act of Imagination: the sense of history. The true apocalypse will come when history crosses the zone of nature to occupy the self directly, when the sense of history and Imagination thus become one, and nature, the mediating figure, is no more.[45]

[43] Liu, 26.   [44] Ibid. 29.   [45] Ibid. 31.

As to how nature is a mediating figure, Liu's earlier argument presents the rationale:

Imagine this composite painting of a tour: nature dominates the foreground; toward the back of the foreground, there is a mark composed of historical synopses, a mark like Brueghel's Icarus that seems ornamental because it points to no signified in the foreground; but the mark is crucial because its conventionality establishes the very perspective system, the social history or overall conventionality of vision within which foreground nature can be seen as a 'delightful' beauty in the first place. No jewel without its setting: without history in the background, after all, a landscape is not a landscape; it is wilderness. . . . I suggest that in the threefold 'painting' of a tour, the middle ground of nature is merely a mediation within the real antithesis of the time between background historical convention and foreground self.[46]

But a jewel can be a jewel without its setting; and though history is indeed always in the background, 'landscape' is no more privileged as an abstraction than 'wilderness'. Neither is given in the simple intuition of a prospect; both are supplied by an entire complex of background considerations, of which history is only one.

Though Liu's virtuoso excavation of the Napoleonic and revolutionary backgrounds of Wordsworth's poetic awareness, as related to his 1790 trip, does, in my judgement, add richness and resonance to our understanding of the Simplon Pass episode, it does not do anything more. The defining dialectic of Wordsworth's greatness works with self and nature first and foremost, self and history only secondarily. Though a great sonnet like 'To Toussaint L'Ouverture' emerges from the dialectic of self and history, a great sonnet like 'The World is Too Much With Us' relates only to a dialectic of self and nature.

But since the specific purpose of Liu's discussion is to discredit the validity of 'nature' and apotheosize the validity of 'history', the sentence above can hardly be considered an adequate resolution of the issue. The vastness of Liu's book makes any adjudication seem only partial; indeed, his discursiveness is both his strength and his weakness. It is his strength in that he discusses topic after interesting topic with copious leisure, often wandering so far afield that he must re-enter the main argument with a palpable break.

Yet the discursiveness is Liu's weakness in that his volume defies consecutive reading. Very few will ever finish this book, which consists of what are in effect many small essays that inevitably say more about most of

[46] Ibid. 10–11.

their topics than even the most committed Wordsworthian will stay to
hear. The coherence is purely schematic, the progression one of rhetorical
fittings rather than intrinsic urgency. So leisurely is the author's pace than
he can devote an entire section ('The Well Wrought Ruin') to a rehearsal
of Cleanth Brooks's essay on 'The Ruined Cottage'. He wanders into topic
after topic: the picturesque tradition in painting, the economics of
weaving in the late 1780s, the punishment of children in the Lake District,
Coleridge's political essays in *The Morning Post*, the organization of
households, the French Ideologues, the Russian Formalists, the relation of
New Criticism to Deconstruction, the doctrine of the Logos, the history of
the Terror in France, Napoleon's tactics in battle. These and many other
excursions have interest taken singly but much less interest taken in
tandem. More severely, one might observe that the essays are too copious
if Wordsworth is the topic, too sparse if history itself is the topic.

They impair the book as a critical approach to Wordsworth; they defer
any climax or point so long that one is finally forced to realize that as a play
of contexts they themselves are the point. To be sure, Liu is willing to state
the final cause of his effort:

To arrive upon Snowdon is to finish our tour of poetic beginnings. In this tour, I
have tried to reconstruct the very possibility of poetic beginning: the ideology of
originality that emerges from, but denies, the collective agon of absence—of the
loss, dispossession, becoming that is history. Denying the collective story of
absence, I have argued, Wordsworth's poetry produces by inversion a private lyric
of absence: imagination. Imagination is the refugee consciousness that—cut off by
history from its referential ground in nation, family, and riches—crosses its
mountain pass, climbs its cloud-veiled peak, to enter a new land where collective
loss can be imagined the gain of the individual.[47]

Liu's finishing the tour from the Simplon Pass by arriving upon Snowdon
is a re-emergence of Hartman's text upon the palimpsest scrubbed clean
by history, for in Hartman's own schematism the 'ascent of Snowdon, a
great moment in poetry, stands in a place of honor'; 'VI (abc) [the Alpine
passages of *The Prelude*] and XIV (abc) [the Snowdon episode] are two
rival highpoints of *The Prelude*. In one, imagination breaks through to
obscure the light of nature; in the other, the poet sees imagination directly
via the light of nature.'[48] Liu, by identifying imagination with Napoleon,
changes the content subsumed in Hartman's schematism by substituting
historical for abstractive data.

---

[47] Liu, 455.
[48] Hartman, 60, 63.

But unlike its suppressed paradigm, Liu's book effectively redirects its focus away from poetry and on to history:

This book has been about the elsewhereness of history, the gap in present being where the self stands in exchange with an absence or infinitude urgent with the ghosts of past selves, past presents, whole other worlds. Infinite absence can wear many names, many ideological vestments or ideas of history doomed always to be after-the-fact. Originating in a sense of alienated sourcehood that in its very moment of discovery—like the Nile flowing from undiscovered sources —evacuates the notions of sourcehood and origination, an idea of history, it seems can only emerge with a certain air of unreality. The moment when an individual— poet or critic—seeks to explain the reality of absent history, or first recognizes the existence of such a reality in need of historical account, is also the moment when he discovers that he cannot by himself originate a fully sufficient explanation. The very forms of his explanation are unreal. They evade the agon, the raw story of contest between the same and the other, the here and the not-here, the present and the past. Poet's description and critic's account, poet's lyric and critic's schema: all these forms cover as much as they recover.[49]

No doubt they do. But Liu's commitment to the welter of considerations just adduced characteristically keeps him so far from the text, and so deep in contexts, that the conclusions he presents move not towards illumination and relevance but, to a dismaying extent, towards a kind of contextual intoxication:

In short, we might hear the following as the poet's essential statement in the closing books of *The Prelude*: 'My public, I stand before you *already* corrected. Spots of time have *already* taught me the doctrine that makes my Imagination a mere stand-in between God and Nature. And so it is that I can now without open imperialism crown myself Poet in this, my world-cathedral at Snowdon, *my* Notre Dame in which the moon breaks through clouds to dim the revelation of that other ambitious mind across the Channel.'[50]

Whatever else those words may represent, they will not be accepted by many readers of Wordsworth as 'the poet's essential statement in the closing books of *The Prelude*'.

Liu disarmingly confesses, with reference to the eight-year travail of composing his work, that 'there were many moments of falling off, and they are recorded here in spots of contrivance or mere bridgework'.[51] But the spots of contrivance or mere bridgework in the particular ultimately compromise the book less, I believe, than does its accumulating contextual self-indulgence. As was pointed out at the beginning of this discussion, the

[49] Liu, 497.   [50] Ibid. 449.   [51] Ibid. 500.

third flaw in the new approaches to Wordsworth is that the pouring out from the presence of the text into the surrounding domain tends ultimately to lose cultural relevance in a receding ocean of absence. The inchoate vastness of Liu's endeavour seems a prime example of this tendency.

Certainly it is a tendency reinforced by Liu's commitment to having things both ways. He plunges both hands, so to speak, into the gigantic cornucopia of context:

Historical context and literary text, I have said, pursue each other in highly specific arabesques of denial and counter-denial, in precise patterns of overdetermined and agonic no-saying to lived experience; and one of the names identifying the specificity or precision of such denial, we now see, is 'I.' 'I,' in my internal rifts and faults, am the exact denial of the rifts and faults composing the nuclear family. 'I' am the figure of a family that is not just wholeness but also brokenness, not just presence but also representation or—in the most real, fatal sense possible—absence. And in my criminal fantasy life of Oedipal love and death, 'I' closet within myself the lingering drama of originary absence: the history of family rupture which is also the tragedy of my own breaking into self-consciousness.[52]

The philosophical, psychological, and sociological understandings contracted for in such a passage, far from presenting themselves as usable clarities, drift rapidly away into the receding ocean of absence.

Everywhere the submerged tides in the receding ocean of absence tend to draw matter away from the configured shore of a text. They are the element that destabilizes the conception of 'history'. Indeed, everything that is ultimately unsatisfactory in Liu's approach results from its unquestioning stand upon two shifting and unstable pedestals: the ocean of 'history', and the quicksand of 'genius'. 'Wordsworth's genius, we now see,' says Liu, 'is a given.'[53] Liu must say that, for he, like the other proponents of the new approach, can in no way ascertain or illuminate the actual fact of genius. The concession of Wordsworth's genius is the counterpart of an inability actually to confront quality. Liu *has* to beg the question, for his preoccupation with historical background, especially social and political historical background, occludes the view of cultural greatness. He must always talk about what is of lesser importance in the cultural reality of Wordsworth, because he cannot talk of what is of greater importance. Matthew Arnold can talk of what is greatly important; Liu cannot. It is not a failure of intelligence, but an encumberment by the extraneous. It is scarcely an accident that two of Liu's richest hunting-grounds prove to be lesser Wordsworthian statements like *Descriptive Sketches* and *The Borderers*, for in the strivings of the new approach lesser works serve as well as greater works, or perhaps better.

If the invocation of 'genius' begs the critical question, the invocation of 'history' leads to problems in another way. What is history? It is certainly not an easy conception to formulate, as countless theoretical discussions have witnessed. At the outset there must be a distinction between history and reality; for one aspect of reality is that it must be everything that has happened—or, to coin a phrase, everything that is the case. History, on the other hand, is not what has happened, but what is thought to have happened. Thought by whom? By the historian, one might idly answer. But a moment's reflection reveals that a fuller answer is: by everyone. But what is thought to have happened differs inconceivably from person to person: what Ranke thought to have happened has few points of congruence with what Billy the Kid thought to have happened. What Billy the Kid thought to have happened, however, though but an infinitesimal fraction of what Ranke thought to have happened, is still much closer to Ranke, in its extent, than what Ranke thought to have happened was to what actually happened. Ranke's works occupy more than sixty volumes and utilize many languages in their investigations, but for all that his life's effort is a pathetically, a ludicrously attenuated version of what actually happened. Scant wonder that Ranke's watchword, *wie es eigentlich gewesen*—'as it really was'—which described the goal of his study, was invoked sardonically, if affectionately, by Mommsen at a celebration honouring the old historian, for no illusion could be more absolute. Every 'history' is necessarily not a complete presentation but in part a formalized denial, to use Liu's terminology, of what actually happened. That is not its contingent but its eternal nature. And what happened in one part of the world—we are seeing this ever more readily as world population tends towards the homogenous—may not have happened at all, historically speaking, for another part of the world.

There are no boundaries whatever for history. And, because there are no inherent demarcations, there is no intrinsic form. Like the play of contexts—and that is certainly one definition that could be offered for 'history'—history is an incommensurable ocean. The farther out Liu swims into it, the more irrelevant his discourse becomes. Though his learning continues to accumulate, its relevance becomes ever more vitiated, until at times Liu almost seems to be playing games, designed and given rules by himself alone. His mixing of tiered abstractions, references to secondary works, titbits of history, and materials of absence results in a texture of argument not unfairly represented by a paragraph such as this:

At this point, I join company with other recent inquirers into Romanticism by taking the second road signed in the phrase, ideology of logos. What we must finally see is that Wordsworth's logos is ideologically determined in the full historical sense—a sense cognate, in fact, with what McGann (*Romantic Ideology*, pp. 7–8, 10), James Chandler (pp. 217–23), and Donald R. Kelley (pp. 14–17) have pointed out was the very notion of 'ideology' during our period in the friction between the French Ideologues and Napoleon. To criticize Wordsworth's autobiographical correctness historically is to recognize that autobiography is the most powerful ideological form the Romantics ever achieved. In particular, it is to recognize that the spots of time in *The Prelude* project Imagination as a highly specific, if denied, historical ideology. Some rough beast of history, its time come round again, slouched—if not toward Bethlehem—then towards Snowdon to be born again. It was this beast, antithetical to the poet's ideology of self and yet monstrously implicated in it, that forced the issue of correctness in the first place.[54]

It is not possible, within reasonable confines of space, to deal with the full panoply of Liu's enormous study, nor to take adequate notice of its admirable learning. But one point should be pressed home: Liu's commitment to historical absence tends by its very structure to compromise relevance. To restrict ourselves to a single illustration, we may take the figure of Napoleon, who provided Liu his strongest initiating example. The arguments for the submerged presence of the absent Napoleon in the Simplon Pass passage, as indicated above, are brilliant; and though the book wanders into many subsidiary evocations, Napoleon remains on tap, so to speak, throughout its course. He occupies centre stage for approximately fifty pages at about page 400. Such sonnets as 'I grieved for Buonaparte' of course overtly link Wordsworth and Napoleon, and Liu in general can use the manifestly political sonnets as good illustration for the hegemony of history.

But despite the insistence of Liu's insertion of Napoleon into the Wordsworthian picture, when that contextual sluice-gate is opened, other and possibly less tractable historical material flows in. The ocean of contexts does not allow itself to be bound or formalized. When Liu first mentions Napoleon, he calls him 'a firmly *historical* genius of imagination'; he calls him 'the Imaginer who, in a manner of speaking, wrote the book on crossing the Alps'.[55] But from the standpoint of even a provisional view of the firmly historical, the statement is not accurate. It was Hannibal, not Napoleon, who 'wrote the book on crossing the Alps'.

[54] Liu, 394.   [55] Ibid. 24.

That book was well known to any intellectual in an age when education still meant classical education. Thus when Rousseau, who himself lived much in the context of the Alps, like Napoleon set out towards Italy from the Alps, he said:

I looked forward to the prospect of crossing the mountains while still so young, and rising superior to my comrades by the full height of the Alps.[56]

The exhilaration of the trip itself elicited—it seems to have been almost *de rigueur*—a specific invocation of Hannibal:

I walked gaily on my way with my pious guide and his lively companion. . . . In fact nothing struck my eyes without bringing some thrill of pleasure to my heart. The grandeur, the variety, and real beauty of the landscape amply justified my pleasure, and vanity had a hand in it. To be traveling to Italy so young, to have seen so many countries already, to be following in Hannibal's footsteps across the mountains, seemed to me a glory beyond my years.[57]

To be sure, Liu himself is amply aware that priority in the paradigm of Alp-crosser devolved on Hannibal; he simply cannot allow himself to do anything with the knowledge:

Imagination's progress in 6b reflects Napoleon's most astonishing stroke to date: his 1800 passage through the Swiss Alps leading to the Battle of Marengo. . . . While part of his army crossed at Mount Cenis, Little St. Bernard, and Mount St. Gotthard, and a demibrigade of approximately 1000 would be at Simplon, Napoleon himself accompanied the main army through Great St. Bernard Pass (about 50 miles southwest of Simplon). In an action comparable to Hannibal's crossing by elephant, he broke down his artillery and sledded it through the snow-blocked defile.[58]

Despite this momentary acknowledgement of Hannibal's priority and pertinence, Liu cannot allow the contextual intrusion of Hannibal into his argument: 'In the context of 1804, then, any imagination of an Alpine pass would remember the military "genius" of Bonaparte. It seems natural that Wordsworth's "halt without a struggle to break through" at the beginning of 6b should lead to the "banners militant" toward the close.'[59] And yet, wherever Napoleon goes in the Alps, from the point of view of 'history', he follows in the footsteps of Hannibal. Indeed, Coleridge specifically refers to Napoleon as 'the modern Hannibal'.[60]

Liu knows and adduces the Coleridgean phrase; but again he does nothing with it. Though the phrase clearly shows that in the context of the

---

[56] Rousseau, i. 54. [57] Ibid. 59. [58] Liu, 28.
[59] Ibid. [60] *Essays*, ii. 138.

1800s to speak of Napoleon and the Alps is necessarily to speak of Hannibal and the Alps, Liu again does nothing with the proffered linkage. Why not? Because, one surmises, to allow the context of Napoleon to recede into the context of Hannibal would necessitate an expansion of argument, a refocusing of evidence, and a reworking of conclusions.

And yet, one must remember, Napoleon is not in the surface statement of the Simplon Pass episode at all; it is only Liu's invocation of absence that places him there. Once the statement of the episode is rewritten so that the absent Napoleon enters as presence, Hannibal enters too. From the point of view of 'history', the context of Napoleon includes the context of Hannibal. The ocean of history cannot be divided unless arbitrarily and schematically; connections of history flow into one another and eventually disperse themselves by their own interactions. But when they flow in the same channel, their oneness can only by arbitrary and disfiguring intervention be ignored. To invoke Napoleon alone in the military context of Alpine movement is to divide history arbitrarily, and at the same time to distort history. If Napoleon, then Hannibal.

Of course, one could legitimately focus on Napoleon alone were some historical argument of presence to be declared and delimited. It is only Liu's opening of the sluice-gates of historical absence that shifts perspective to the receding ocean of context. Liu on some level presumably is aware of this, for he summons quite a bit of data about Hannibal. But instead of feeding it into his theoretical categories, he sweeps it, if not under the rug, at least into a long footnote that effectively serves to remove such intriguing material—which from its inert resting place seems to plead its pertinence—from active consideration:

Turner's *Snowstorm: Hannibal and His Army Crossing the Alps*, exhibited in 1812, provides an analogue of the combined mimesis and effacement of Napoleon I indicate here. Napoleon is nowhere to be seen in Turner's celebrated landscape of human diminishment—no more so than Hannibal himself. But as Lynn R. Matteson shows, such invisibility is not simple absence. Relevant are Turner's earlier sketches on the Hannibal theme and the link between *Hannibal and His Army Crossing the Alps* and ancient British, as well as contemporary French, history (made more pointed, perhaps, by Turner's private viewing of David's *Napoleon at the St. Bernard Pass* in Paris in 1802 . . .).

and so on.[61]

What, then, should one conclude about Liu's challenging book and the point of view it asserts? Only this. Like Schopenhauer, Liu assumes a

[61] Liu, 519 n.

perspective on Wordsworth that leads to an unsatisfactory understanding about the poet and his work, even though the point of view, as such, involves matters of intrinsic interest. Schopenhauer's unsatisfactory understanding is signified by the formulation, 'the mediocre Wordsworth', which, despite its author's high intellectual credentials, cannot be allowed to stand by the common pursuit of true judgement. Somewhat the same may be said of Liu's point of view and the cultural discourse it generates. Though it does not eventuate in a critical ranking, as Schopenhauer's does, the point of view adopted by Liu provides us, in a different way, with a 'mediocre Wordsworth', with the focus and meaning of his great poetry deflected into an encumbering obfuscation of Napoleonic social and historical considerations.

So much for this intricate texture located in the support structures of Romanticism. The name of Rousseau having necessarily arisen in the latter part of the foregoing discussion, that thread will be followed, in closer examination, as it leads into a different texture, this one a consideration of the purport of Rousseau as that name figures in the origins of Romanticism itself. To the ardent Shelley, Rousseau was 'a mighty Genius',[62] and he hails the 'sacred name of Rousseau; the contemplation of whose imperishable creations had left no vacancy in my heart for mortal things'.[63] 'Rousseau is indeed in my mind the greatest man the world has produced since Milton.'[64] What Shelley felt was echoed by Romantic sensibilities all over Europe, and in simple truth one can go neither far nor deep in the comprehension of Romanticism without taking Rousseau into account. Rousseau of course has also constituted a favourite hunting-ground for deconstructionist theory, in Derrida himself and in his annunciator, De Man. The examination of the texture that follows, however, will reveal a patterning quite different from theirs.

---

[62] Shelley, *Letters*, i. 493.
[63] Ibid. 488.
[64] Ibid. 494.

2

The Sea of Unhappiness

ROUSSEAU may well have been the most important single cultural figure of the last quarter millennium. Not the most brilliant, not the greatest benefactor of human life, certainly not the finest character, but possibly the most important figure in intellectual history nevertheless. For he figured at the very centre of the profound shift of sensibility that eventuated in the world as we know it today. Though not specifically a political proponent of revolution, he was taken both by the French Revolutionists themselves, and by their arch-enemy Burke, as the chief instigator of that Revolution. So, too, though he is often thought of as a product of the Enlightenment rather than a Romantic as such, he may be seen as the most important and influential progenitor of Romanticism's enormous shift in the way of viewing reality. Babbitt's *Rousseau and Romanticism*, though too tendentious to have much modern authority, identifies him as the father of all that Babbitt despised. Less polemically, we may say that just as the *Social Contract* was the most important single formative document for the French Revolution,[1] so too the *Confessions* is probably the most important single antecedent for the development of the Romantic sensibility. But so complex and intertwined was Rousseau's texture of origins that perhaps *The New Héloïse* equals, or possibly even surpasses, each of those mighty originants in its effect both on the Revolutionary sensibility and on the emerging Romantic sensibility. After all, the raptures of Shelley noted at the end of the preceding chapter were elicited by that work, not by the *Social Contract* or the *Confessions*.

It is perhaps inevitable that a cultural presence of such lambent vitality as Rousseau's should pulsate with electrical polarity. The unique and

---

[1] This truth persists despite a recent tendency to challenge the dissemination of the *Social Contract* in comparison to other works of Rousseau: 'les études les plus récentes sur la diffusion du *Contrat social* montrent que sans être ignoré, l'ouvrage avait eu bien moins de succès que l'*Émile* et, surtout, *La Nouvelle Héloïse*, un des plus grands succès de librairie du siècle. Le *Contrat social* avait été édité treize fois, de façon séparée, avant 1789, l'*Émile* vingt-deux fois et *La Nouvelle Héloïse* cinquante fois. De surcroît, les rééditions de ces deux ouvrages furent régulières. Les éditions du *Contrat social* ont été, au contraire, concentrées autour de sa première publication, ce qui suggère un succès de lancement suivi d'une indifférence relative. Il y a donc de solides raisons pour affirmer qu'avant 1789 l'influence et la notoriété de Rousseau tenaient plus à *La Nouvelle Héloïse* et à l'*Émile* qu'au *Contrat social*' (Furet and Ozouf, 873–4).

unprecedented individualism brought into being by the *Confessions* stands—and it is a bemusing thought—as the very antipode of the submission to the general will espoused by the *Social Contract*. It is almost equally striking that the enormous charge of Rousseauist thought should reappear, in undiminished though transformed intensity, in other and later vehicles. The gloomy portrait of modern society painted by Freud's great treatise, *Civilization and its Discontents*, is the same portrait, though composed in different colours and effectuated with different brush strokes, offered by Rousseau in the *Discourse on Inequality* and the *Social Contract*.

But the *Confessions*, or at least the first six books, which appeared in 1781, may be thought of as the inaugurating text of Romanticism. There are, of course, still other claimants to the title of originating text: Leibniz's *Nouveaux essais*, or Goethe's *Werther*, are just two of the works that spring to mind. Yet the *Confessions*, both from the universality of its dissemination in the European reading public, and from its inexhaustible suggestive power, would seem to take the palm. Neither De Quincey's *Confessions of an English Opium Eater*, nor Lamb's *Confessions of a Drunkard*, nor Hazlitt's *Liber Amoris*, nor Wordsworth's *Prelude* is thinkable without the *Confessions*, though each of these entirely different creations is some way along from that source, which has been refracted so often as hardly to be heard in the later works. But it nevertheless is heard—for a single instance, one thinks of the weight of the modifier 'English' in the rubric *Confessions of an English Opium Eater*. It seems likely that Fichte's location of all reality in the ego was made possible only by the precursorship of Rousseau's dauntless insistence on self. It seems equally likely that neither Byron's self-dramatization nor his Byronic heroes would have been thought of, or if thought of would have found a validating audience, without the prior saturation of European culture in Rousseau's shocking self-revelation. Max Stirner's *Der Einzige und sein Eigenthum*, appearing near the mid-point of the nineteenth century, and bizarre in its radical egotism, still is in the final analysis hardly more than the lesson of the *Confessions* writ large. And both Dostoevsky's wormlike Underground Man and Nietzsche's apocalyptic Superman take their impetus from Rousseau's epoch-making turn to the examination of the individual self.

The *Confessions* is of course pertinent to the text called Romanticism in many ways—its rejection of the city, for instance, or its apotheosis of solitude, or in many statements such as this: 'Never does a plain, however beautiful it may be, seem so in my eyes. I need torrents, rocks, firs, dark woods, mountains, steep roads to climb or descend, abysses beside me to make me afraid.'[2] But it is in its placing of subjectivity front and centre that the book seems most important, an importance that the texture here descried shall attempt to reveal, in essential outline if not in ultimate ramification.

How did Rousseau manage to figure so cataclysmically in the annals of posterity, and how specifically did the *Confessions* manage to shift the path of literature permanently into the mode of self-revelation? The answer to those questions assuredly involves factors of *milieu, moment,* and *race.* It was decisive that Rousseau wrote in the chief European intellectual language, that he was at the centre of the philosophical ferment of the Enlightenment, that he lived just as the feudal social and intellectual synthesis was preparing to come crashing down in ruins. But to those factors must be added one personal to Rousseau himself: the simplicity of genius. He saw something different from the prevailing approach in intellectual matters; equally important, what he saw was very large, not localized or particularized; entirely accessible, not recondite or guarded by educational requirements; and unequivocally universal, not the province of a select and privileged few. Rousseau himself, at least by modern standards, was a cultivated man, proficient in several languages and adept in music (I happen to own a recording of his opera, *Le Devin du village*, and can attest to its merit). But the door to reality that he now opened needed no such cultural refinements to enter: anyone from stable boy or shop girl on up, if only he or she knew how to read and write, could stride confidently through to partake of the new cornucopia of possibilities. For where strategies of literature before had presupposed sophisticated commitments to objectification—genres, classical imitations, social placements—Rousseau turned and looked the other way: into himself.

It was the simplicity of genius. A huge and inexhaustible range of topics was opened, and opened to all regardless of high training or profound knowledge. At one sweep the entire world of cultural attainment—the kind of savant world that so much impressed Rabelais—was rendered nugatory; at one sweep an intoxicating alternate world invited everyone. Before Rousseau, the common culture of Europe had, in its received moralities and civilities, been saturated by the self-abnegation preached by the Christian religion (for a single random example from among the myriads possible, Thomas Hooker's treatise of 1640 called *The Christian's Two Chiefe Lessons*, had a first chapter of one hundred pages entitled 'The Christian's Lesson of Selfe-Deniall'). 'The ego is hateful', had said the super-intellectual Pascal;[3] and all decorums had heretofore existed to

---

[2] Rousseau, i. 172.   [3] Pascal, 584.

proscribe the ego. But Rousseau, with the audacity of the bounder, broke through the taboo. 'I have resolved on an enterprise,' said the shabby genius, and said it as the very first words of his masterpiece, 'which has no precedent, and which, once complete, will have no imitator. My purpose is to display to my kind a portrait in every way true to nature, and the man I shall portray will be myself.'[4]

It was truly the simplicity of genius. At one turn the tradition of cultural labour that had produced a Scaliger or a Casaubon was rendered irrelevant. No scholar could even be considered alongside the author of the topic of 'myself'. That author was the sole arbiter, the only authority, the unique savant. No library was needed or would have been pertinent. No philosophy need be read. No history need be studied.

The shabby genius understood from the first the inexhaustible nature of his subject-matter and the absolute authority it conferred. 'Simply myself,' he continues,

I know my own heart and understand my fellow man. But I am made unlike anyone I ever met; I will even venture to say I am like no one in the whole world. I may be no better, but at least I am different. Whether Nature did well or ill in breaking the mould in which she formed me, is a question which can only be resolved after the reading of my book.[5]

As to how that question should be resolved, Rousseau, his egotism enormously enlarged by the exercise of writing, said at the conclusion of the book that

I have told the truth. If anyone knows anything contrary to what I have here recorded, though he prove it a thousand times, his knowledge is a lie and an imposture; and if he refuses to investigate and inquire into it during my lifetime he is no lover of justice or of truth. For my part, I publicly and fearlessly declare that anyone, even if he has not read my writings, who will examine my nature, my character, my morals, my likings, my pleasures, and my habits with his own eyes and can still believe me a dishonorable man, is a man who deserves to be throttled.[6]

The illusion of originary firstness was, of course, a cherished shibboleth of Romanticism, and Rousseau as a founding father can be forgiven for saying that his enterprise has no precedent. But the claim is actually no more accurate than its yoked prediction that it will have no imitator. The enterprise not only has a precedent, but a titanic precedent, one, indeed,

---

[4] Rousseau, i. 5. For the *Confessions*, the English is for the most part that of J. M. Cohen's Penguin edition.
[5] Ibid.
[6] Ibid. 656.

that not only undoubtedly played a role in the subliminal genesis of the *Confessions* but also conditioned its audience to accept Rousseau's revelations of self. I refer not to Augustine's *Confessions*, that fabled false lead that is actually only tangentially pertinent to Rousseau. I refer instead to Montaigne's *Essais*, which was its direct precursor. After all, Montaigne's cultural effect was so powerful and so widely disseminated that the *Essais* had gone into four editions before Montaigne himself, in 1588, prepared a fifth; had gone into twelve editions by the time John Florio began his English translation in 1599; and by the later seventeenth century was so popular that, as the polymath Daniel Huet said, there was no gentleman in France who had a few books and had not Montaigne for one of them.

Montaigne, like Rousseau, turned to his own self for subject-matter:

I turne my sight inward, there I fix it, there I ammuse it. Every man lookes before himselfe, I looke within my selfe: I have no busines but with my selfe. I uncessantly consider, controle and taste my selfe; other men goe ever else-where if they thinke well on it: they go ever foreward . . . as for me, I roule me unto my selfe.[7]

Like Rousseau, Montaigne understood how completely sufficing the subject-matter of his turning inward was. 'I have nothing that is mine own but myself,' he says: 'finding myselfe afterward wholy unprovided of subject, and void of other matter, I have presented myself unto myselfe for a subject to write and argument to descant upon.'[8]

Yet Montaigne, despite his towering stature—he too was not of an age but for all time—despite the enormous dissemination of his work, despite his prior discovery of the vast domain of self, did not permanently change things the way Rousseau did; he did not precipitate a political revolution, or an entirely different way of culturally seeing the world. The discrepancy in the effects of the otherwise similar figures is doubtless explained in large part by differences in the political and cultural situations of their times, as well as by fundamental differences in the approach of the two authors.

One of those cultural differences, the only one, indeed, to which attention will be directed here, was in the situation of religion in the respective eras of the two giants. Montaigne lived at the time of the St Bartholomew's Day massacre, so it can hardly be said that all was quiet on the religious front in his own milieu. But that was turmoil within religion

[7] Montaigne, 641. The English is supplied from Florio's translation, itself a classic in its own right.
[8] Ibid. 364.

itself. The French Enlightenment, on the other hand, took shape as a vast confrontation between secularity and religion, with the very being of religion at stake. The great enemy of Enlightenment was the Catholic Church, and the great enemy of the Catholic Church was Enlightenment. For a single example, the jolting attacks on the Christian religion delivered by Diderot's 'Addition aux Pensées philosophiques', which were appended in 1762 to his *Pensées philosophiques* of 1746, constituted a programmatic fulfilment of Voltaire's oft-expressed desire to 'écraser l'infame'.[9] (Voltaire of course contributed numerous writings of his own to that agenda, as, for instance, his *Epître à Uranie*, or his *Sermon des cinquantes*, or his *Examen important de milord Bolingbroke*, or his *Dieu et les hommes*.)

Likewise, by taking the name of *Confessions* for his masterpiece, Rousseau co-opted and turned—or not to put too fine a point on it, perverted—a central function of the Catholic Church. Confession was a commonplace to a society conditioned to its purgative virtues through hundreds of years; but confession was always private, and Rousseau, in a momentous change, made it public. A recent study of Diderot makes the point that the *Encyclopédie* was a gigantic blabbing of the technological secrets of the power élite to the untutored masses;[10] by the same token, one may see Rousseau's self-examination as a blabbing to the secular world of the secrets reserved for the priesthood. By making public what had always been private, he not only mocked confession's role in an entire scheme of human personality, but at one stroke ensured a universal and avid audience for himself—an effect that still lingers in the title of sensationalistic journals such as *True Confessions*.

Rousseau's own true confessions not only turned literary attention from objectivity to the self, but recast the nature of that self. Now the emergence of the idea of the self from tribal social roles has occupied both classical scholarship and anthropology in recent years, and Georg Simmel suggests that the modern idea of the individual did not take shape until the Renaissance.[11] To that one may offer a corrective; it did not take shape until Rousseau. The selves idealized by the Renaissance, doubtless magnetized by a reality of which we know nothing today—that is, the fabulous prestige of kingship—tended to be heroic. Heroic in evil, such as that Cesare Borgia who so fascinated Machiavelli, or 'that Atheist' Tamburlaine, 'daring God out of heauen'; or heroic like Antony, whose

---

[9] For the centrality of the phrase, see e.g. Besterman, 594.
[10] Elisabeth de Fontenay, *Diderot, ou, le matérialisme enchanté* (Paris: Grasset, 1981).
[11] *Simmel*, 217.

legs bestrid the ocean, whose reared arm crested the world; or like Bayard, a chevalier 'sans peur et sans reproche'. Even of Coriolanus, who in modern conceivings might seem merely stupid, it is specifically said that 'his nature is too noble for the world'.

To be sure, Montaigne's conception of self undermined the heroic persona, and one may recall a long passage where he recites a whole catalogue of his personal clumsinesses and deficiencies of physical skill:

Of addressing, dexteritie, and disposition, I never had any. . . . As for musicke, were it either in voice, which I have most harsh, and very unapt, or in instruments, I could never be taught any part of it. As for dancing, playing at tennis, or wrestling, I could never attaine to any indifferent sufficiencie, but none at all in swimming, in fencing, in vaulting, or in leaping. My hands are so stiffe and nummie, that I can hardly write for my selfe, so that what I have once scribled, I had rather frame it a new than take the paines to correct it; and I reade but little better. . . . I was never good carver at the table, I could never make readie nor arme a horse; nor handsomely array a hawke upon my fist, nor cast her off.[12]

Rousseau's unheroic conception of self, however, went much further than that. For Rousseau's self was not merely ordinary and bumbling; it was discreditable as well. Here, too, the tradition of Catholic confession that empowered his book's enormous effect dictated the nature of the new self. For what is uttered in the confessional is always something discreditable, something hidden and not to be told abroad in society. With Rousseau's turning of the private to the public, the most unsavoury secrets of personality were declared with the same hope of public attention as earlier attended claims to virtue. The Bible bids us not to hide our light under a bushel; but it tells us to send our beams forth for the greater glory of God, not to use the light to inspect the cellar or to examine the cesspool. With Rousseau's making public the confessional, the entire structure of the self was changed. For whereas that which had heretofore been confessed in secrecy, within the sacrament of the church, had by that very fact been no longer operative in the conception of the individual, Rousseau's making public such matters, instead of expelling them from the personality, engrafted all the discreditable material into a new, vastly augmented, but never again to be heroic, model of how an individual could be conceived.

For a single pregnant example, Rousseau at one point tells of a disgraceful episode in which he stole a pink and silver ribbon from an employer's household. When the ribbon was found in his possession, he accused a lovely and entirely innocent servant girl of stealing it and giving it to him. She was discharged, along with Rousseau himself. As Rousseau says, 'I took away with me lasting memories of a crime and the unbearable weight of a remorse which, even after forty years, still burdens my conscience.'[13] After detailing his part in the shameful episode, he says that his inability to own up to his crime is one of the chief reasons why he began to write the *Confessions*:

Not with the most intimate friend, not even with Mme de Warens, has this been possible. The most I could do was to confess that I had a terrible deed on my conscience, but I have never said in what it consisted. The burden, therefore, has rested till this day on my conscience, without any relief; and I can affirm that the desire to some extent to rid myself of it has greatly contributed to my resolution of writing these *Confessions*.[14]

The episode of the ribbon is obviously of central importance in the psychic provenance of Rousseau's need to confess. It is important in what it reveals; and it is important in what it hides. For Rousseau, in the depths of his own mind, felt he had done something even worse than this, that required even greater efforts at expiation by confession: horrible though this episode is, it pales beside another 'terrible deed on my conscience'. What was that deed? We learn of it at the very beginning of the *Confessions*: Rousseau's mother died as a result of giving birth to Rousseau. We learn also that his father, throughout his childhood, never let him forget it.

In the context of feeling that he had killed his own mother, not only the stealing of the ribbon and the false witness against the girl, but all the unprecedented disclosures of baseness and imperfect behaviour seem refractions of that primary and terrible awareness. Certainly never before in the history of culture had so many self-denigrations been so calmly presented by an author. Indeed, it is Rousseau's calmness, his wide-eyed naïvety, as it were, as he moves from situation to situation, now comically, now disastrously, now disgracefully, now paranoiacally, that most truly authenticates his genius. 'Every true genius,' says Schiller with brilliant insight, 'must be naïve, or it is not genius. Only its naïvety makes for its genius, and what it is intellectually and aesthetically it cannot disavow morally.'[15] 'The naïve', he also says, 'is *childlikeness where it is no longer expected*.'[16] The specification exactly fits Rousseau. 'Although in certain respects I have been a man since birth,' he observes, 'I was for a long time,

13 Rousseau, i. 84.   14 Ibid. 86.
15 *Schiller*, ii. 548.   16 Ibid. 544.

and still am, a child in many others.'[17] It is not Voltaire's *Candide*, but
Rousseau's Jean-Jacques, who presents the most accurate pattern of the
naïve in world literature.

   It would not be correct to say, however, that the self-denigration
embodied in Rousseau's *Confessions* had no antecedence whatever.
Actually, traces of it were adumbrated in the self posited by Montaigne, as,
for instance, when Montaigne says that 'When I religiously confesse my
selfe unto my selfe, I finde the best good I have hath some vicious taint'.[18]
Yet Montaigne never reveals vicious taints the way Rousseau does.
Indeed, Rousseau explicitly measured his revelation of self against that of
Montaigne, and proudly proclaimed a deeper presentation of inadequacy:

Although up to that point my life had not been particularly interesting so far as
incidents were concerned, I felt that with the frank treatment I was capable of
giving it it might become so. For I decided to make it a work unique and
unparalleled in its truthfulness, so that for once at least the world might behold a
man as he was within. I had always been amused at Montaigne's false
ingenuousness, and at his pretence of confessing his faults while taking good care
only to admit to likeable ones; whereas I, who believe, and have always believed,
that I am on the whole the best of men, felt that there is no human heart, however
pure, that does not conceal some odious vice. I knew that I was represented in the
world under features so unlike my own and at times so distorted, that
notwithstanding my faults, none of which I intended to pass over, I could not help
gaining by showing myself as I was.[19]

Accordingly, Rousseau early refers to 'the dark and dirty labyrinth of my
confessions. It is not what is criminal that is hardest for us to tell, but what
makes us feel ridiculous and ashamed.'[20]

   A single charged instance, noisome in every detail, and devastating to
the judgement, honesty, common sense, and good will of Rousseau
himself, can usefully be adduced at length. The passage is rarely brought
forward by commentators, for it is embarrassing to read or to hear read.
But it is precisely such a passage that reveals the extent to which Rousseau
expanded the conception of self. To ignore it is to remain unaware of just
how radical Rousseau's new departure was. Indeed, the passage is
matched by two others from later in the *Confessions*, the three together
almost setting their own genre. The initial episode is here rehearsed, not to
embarrass the reader, but to illustrate as dramatically as possible the
uniqueness of Rousseau's confessional turn; for never before in the prior

[17] Rousseau, i. 174.   [18] Montaigne, 656.
[19] Rousseau, i. 516–17.   [20] Ibid. 18.

history of culture—never—had the self been talked about in the way that Rousseau talked about it.

In the course of receiving instruction for an insincere entry into the Catholic Church, the youthful Rousseau tells of what he calls 'a very unpleasant little experience', where he plainly encourages homosexual advances by a vagabond and then explodes into hysterical frenzies of denunciation:

There is no soul so vile [says Rousseau], no heart so barbarous as to be insusceptible to some sort of affection, and one of the two cutthroats who called themselves Moors took a fancy to me. He was fond of coming up to me and gossiping with me in his queer jargon. He did me little services, sometimes giving me some of his food at table, and he frequently kissed me with an ardour that I found most displeasing. But, frightened though I naturally was by his dusky face . . . and by his passionate glances, which seemed to me more savage than affectionate, I put up with his kisses, saying to myself, 'The poor man has conceived a warm friendship for me; it would be wrong to repel him.' But he passed by degrees to more unseemly conduct, and sometimes made me such strange suggestions that I thought he was wrong in the head. One night he wanted to share my bed, but I objected on the plea that it was too narrow. He then pressed me to come into his. I still refused, however, for the poor devil was so dirty and smelt so strongly of the tobacco he chewed that he made me feel ill.[21]

One stares in disbelief at this shameless recountal. After accepting repeated kisses from the man, Rousseau declines to go to bed with him, not because of the prospect of sexual encounter, which amazingly is here simply denied, but because of fastidiousness about the smell of tobacco. But worse is to follow. More coy than one of Richardson's heroines, Rousseau the next day entices his unlikely suitor to an inevitable conclusion:

Next day, very early in the morning, we were alone together in the assembly-hall. He resumed his caresses, but with such violence that I was frightened. Finally, he tried to work up to the most revolting liberties, and by guiding my hand, to make me take the same liberties with him. I broke wildly away with a cry and leaped backwards, but without displaying any indignation or anger, for I had not the slightest idea what it was all about. But I showed my surprise and disgust to such effect that he then left me alone. But as he gave up the struggle I saw something whitish and sticky shoot towards the fireplace and fall on the ground.[22]

Having descended into this abyss of prurient bad faith, Rousseau

---

[21] Ibid. 66–7.
[22] Ibid. 67.

contentedly paddles around in it. In the aftermath of the encounter he indulges himself in denunciation:

I could think of nothing better than to go and inform everybody of what had just happened. Our old woman attendant told me to hold my tongue. . . . As I could see no reason for holding my tongue, I took no notice of her but went on talking. I talked so much in fact that next day one of the principals came very early and read me a sharp lecture. . . . In addition to this rebuke he explained to me a number of things I did not know, but which he did not suspect he was telling me for the first time. For he believed that I had known what the man wanted . . . but had merely been unwilling. He told me gravely that it was a forbidden and immoral act like fornication, but that the desire for it was not an affront to the person who was its object. . . . The whole matter seemed so simple to him that he had not even sought privacy for our conversation.[23]

Later the principal shot Rousseau 'a far from affectionate glance, and from that time on spared no pains to make my stay at the hospice unpleasant'.[24] For his part, after he was finally confirmed in the church, Rousseau left and in an orgy of denial redoubled his thoughts about women: 'My memories of that phoney African transformed the plainest of sluts into an object of adoration.'[25]

In terms of the new conception of self, the point of the episode is not so much to lead us to ask of Rousseau what the First Lord asked of Parolles, 'Is it possible he should know what he is, and be that he is?'—although that question exactly applies—but rather to dramatize the truth that the new and augmented conception of self had no boundaries. The heroic self was an objectified structure in a surrounding world; the new self of Rousseau, huge now, and quite without limits of decorum or defining objective structure, was a subjective reconstitution of reality itself. As Starobinski notes of Rousseau's last work, the *Reveries of a Solitary Walker*, which carried forward the world of the *Confessions*,

For whom did Rousseau write the *Rêveries?* For himself and no one else. What does he discuss in this ultimate work? His destiny. Having chosen himself as recipient of his work, the author also chooses himself as theme. He pursues no outside end and avoids mentioning a possible audience. Rousseau has convinced himself that the world has turned a deaf ear to him; his mind is made up. His plea is hopeless, hence his words will circulate only within his own mind. They will reflect their author, and only their author will absorb their import. It is as if the author's mind were split in two, into a discursive consciousness and a receptive consciousness, an addressee feeding on its own substance.[26]

[23] Rousseau, i. 67–8.   [24] Ibid. 68.
[25] Ibid. 69.   [26] Starobinski, 352.

Such subjective reconstitution of reality, permuting and refracting in varied ways, was to provide the very stuff of Romanticism.

The importance of reverie, for instance, which was established by the work just invoked, worked synergistically with the even more widespread Romantic criteria of dream and imagination. It is entirely symptomatic of the hegemony of the new totalizing self that Coleridge gives 'The Ancient Mariner' (at Wordsworth's suggestion) the subtitle 'A Poet's Reverie' and 'Kubla Khan' the subtitle 'A Vision in a Dream'.

But 'The Ancient Mariner' was also, as Coleridge told Mrs Barbauld, a poem of 'pure imagination'. Imagination, indeed, which decreases emphasis on the stability of the objective world and rebestows it on the activities of the conscious self, is a major, perhaps even *the* major, criterion of Romanticism. James Engell calls the doctrine of imagination 'the quintessence of Romanticism';[27] and it is hardly accidental that not only Coleridge, but Blake, not only Shelley, but Hazlitt, not only Wordsworth, but Poe and Emerson and Baudelaire, devoted intense theoretical formulation to its centrality. It was Rousseau's reconstitution of reality that made a place for that centrality.

Though in *Émile* Rousseau had theoretically disapproved of too much imagination as harmful to the development of a child, in the *Confessions* he allows imagination virtually to govern his world. For instance, he says there that

my restless imagination took a hand which saved me from myself and calmed my growing sensuality. What it did was to nourish itself on situations that had interested me in my reading, recalling them, varying them, combining them, and giving me so great a part in them, that I became one of the characters I imagined, and saw myself always in the pleasantest situations of my own choosing. So in the end, the fictions I succeeded in building up made me forget my real condition, which so dissatisfied me. My love for imaginary objects and my facility in lending myself to them ended by disillusioning me with everything around me, and determined that love of solitude which I have retained ever since that time.[28]

But such an enormous role for the imaginative function could only be maintained where subjectivity, which was at once its propagator and its theatre, had virtually displaced other criteria of reality. Indeed, Rousseau's growing preoccupation with the conspiracies he felt were being mounted against him, which are so melancholy a feature of the latter books of the *Confessions*, are not merely paranoiac manifestations but in a larger sense a witness to imagination run wild.

[27] Engell, 4.   [28] Rousseau, i. 41.

That a new importance and a new conception had been given to self and its domain by Rousseau was recognized very early. Hazlitt, for one, saw with his customary clarity the absolute and radical nature of Rousseau's egotism. 'The only quality which he possessed in an eminent degree,' wrote Hazlitt of Rousseau,

which alone raised him above ordinary men, and which gave to his writings and opinions an influence greater, perhaps, than has been exerted by any individual in modern times, was extreme sensibility, or an acute and even morbid feeling of all that related to his own impressions, to the objects and events of his life. He had the most intense consciousness of his own existence. No object that had once made an impression on him was ever after effaced. Every feeling in his mind became a passion. His craving after excitement was an appetite and a disease. His interest in his own thoughts and feelings was always wound up to the highest pitch; and hence the enthusiasm which he excited in others. He owed the power which he exercised over the opinions of all Europe, by which he created numberless disciples, and overturned established systems, to the tyranny which his feelings, in the first instance, exercised over himself. The dazzling blaze of his reputation was kindled by the same fire that fed upon his vitals.[29]

Hazlitt speaks with great precision here. Indeed, perhaps no commentary on Rousseau surpasses Hazlitt's for justness, force, and exactness of formulation. He understands that Rousseau's 'genius was the effect of his temperament. He created nothing, he demonstrated nothing, by a pure effort of the understanding. His fictitious characters are modifications of his own being, reflections and shadows of himself.'[30] He understands that Rousseau

did more towards the French Revolution than any other man. Voltaire, by his wit and penetration, had rendered superstition contemptible, and tyranny odious; but it was Rousseau who brought the feeling of irreconcilable enmity to rank and privileges, *above humanity*, home to the bosom of every man,—identified it with all the pride of intellect, and with the deepest yearnings of the human heart.[31]

Most of all, Hazlitt understands just how Rousseau's new creation of self managed to enlist and mould all the untold selves that had not previously raised themselves to self-reflection:

Before we can take an author entirely to our bosoms [writes Hazlitt], he must be another self; and he cannot be this, if he is 'not one, but all mankind's epitome.' It was this which gave such an effect to Rousseau's writings, that he stamped his own character and the image of his self-love on the public mind—*there* it is, and there it will remain in spite of every thing. Had he possessed more comprehension of

---

[29] *Hazlitt*, iv. 88–9.   [30] Ibid. 89.   [31] Ibid. 89 n.

thought or feeling, it would only have diverted him from his object. But it was the excess of his egotism and his utter blindness to every thing else, that found a corresponding sympathy in the conscious feelings of every human breast, and shattered to pieces the pride of rank and circumstance by the pride of internal worth or upstart pretension.[32]

Hazlitt then goes on to credit Rousseau's self-love as the most important element in the propagation of the egalitarian convictions that have gained such unquestioned ascendancy in our own era:

Rousseau was the first who held the torch (lighted at the never-dying fire in his own bosom) to the hidden chambers of the mind of man—like another Prometheus, breathed into his nostrils the breath of a new and intellectual life, enraging the Gods of the earth, and made him feel what is due to himself and his fellows.[33]

Hazlitt's understanding of Rousseau's genius is everywhere almost impeccably pertinent. 'The best of all his works is the *Confessions*,' he judges:

It relates entirely to himself; and no one was ever so much at home on this subject as he was. From the strong hold which they had taken of his mind, he makes us enter into his feelings as if they had been our own, and we seem to remember every incident and circumstance of his life as if it had happened to ourselves. We are never tired of this work, for it everywhere presents us with pictures which we can fancy to be counterparts of our own existence.[34]

Following this, the great critic, in one of his virtuoso rhetorical cascades, enumerates at length memorable passages and incidents from Rousseau's masterpiece, and concludes with a tribute to the book's effect on his own Romantic sensibility:

There are no passages in the *New Eloise* of equal force and beauty with the best descriptions in the *Confessions*, if we except the excursion on the water, Julia's last letter to St. Preux, and his letter to her, recalling the days of their first loves. We spent two whole years in reading these two works. . . . They were the happiest years of our life. We may well say of them, sweet is the dew of their memory, and pleasant the balm of their recollection! There are, indeed, impressions which neither time nor circumstances can efface.[35]

Not everyone was so enthusiastic. But Rousseau's Romantic impress can be discerned even when an accompanying admiration is explicitly disowned. Coleridge, who came to dislike everything French, at one point said that 'scarcely anyone has a larger share of my aversion than Voltaire;

[32] Ibid. xi. 278.   [33] Ibid.
[34] Ibid. iv. 90.   [35] Ibid. 91.

and even of the better-hearted Rousseau I was never more than a very
lukewarm admirer'.[36] He says that Rousseau 'died, luckily for himself,
before he had seen a tenth part of the miserable effects of his doctrines'.[37]
Strangely enough, however, in view of such declared lack of sympathy,
Coleridge repeatedly tried to institute comparisons between Rousseau and
the theologian he most admired, Martin Luther; even though

> Rousseau, on the contrary, in the inauspicious spirit of his age and birth-place, had
> slipped the cable of his faith, and steered by the compass of unaided reason,
> ignorant of the hidden currents that were bearing him out of his course, and too
> proud to consult the faithful charts prized and held sacred by his forefathers.[38]

Despite all this, when Coleridge attempts to conceive his beloved
Luther ('He was a Poet indeed, as great a Poet as ever lived in any age or
country; but his poetic images were so vivid, that they mastered the Poet's
own mind!'[39]) as existing outside his own age and time, it is, amazingly,
and of all people, Rousseau in whom he finds the spirit of Luther:

> Conceive him [Luther] a citizen of Geneva, and a contemporary of Voltaire;
> suppose the French language his mother-tongue, and the political and moral
> philosophy of English Free-thinkers re-modelled by *Parisian Fort Esprits*, to have
> been the objects of his study;—conceive this change of circumstances, and Luther
> will no longer dream of Fiends or of Antichrist—but will we have no dreams in
> their place? His melancholy will have changed its drapery; but will it find no new
> costume wherewith to cloath itself? His impetuous temperament, his deep-
> working mind, his busy and vivid imaginations—would they not have been a
> *trouble* to him in a world, where nothing was to be altered, where nothing was to
> obey his power, to cease to be that which had been, in order to realize his pre-
> conceptions of what it ought to be? . . . Henceforward then, we will conceive his
> reason employed in building up anew the edifice of *earthly* society, and his
> imagination as pledging itself for the possible realization of the structure. We will
> lose the great reformer, who was born in an age which needed him, in the
> Philosopher of Geneva, who was doomed to misapply his energies to materials the
> properties of which he misunderstood, and happy only that he did not live to
> witness the direful effects of his system.[40]

That is witness indeed to the pervasive effect of Rousseau upon the minds
that succeeded him.

A different kind of effect obtained elsewhere. An especially instructive
example of how Rousseau's formless but vast world of self provided the
conditions for a gigantic Romantic literary achievement is afforded by
Wordsworth. The matter is of special interest, because Wordsworth's

---

[36] *Philosophical Lectures*, 306.   [37] Ibid. 308.   [38] *Friend*, i. 133–4.
[39] Ibid. 140.   [40] Ibid. 142–3.

'egotistical sublime' was marked by none of the embarrassing self-revelation of Rousseau; Wordsworth's self-presentation to the world was always one of dignity and high morality, however much his indulgence in usury, or his affair with Annette Vallon, or other unsavoury secrets might seem to qualify the truth of that self-presentation. Still, dignity and high morality were essential to the purified transcendence of feeling that was at the very core of what Wordsworth was trying to present. 'A Traveller I am,' he says, 'And all my tale is of myself—even so— | So be it, if the pure in heart delight | To follow me'.[41] Only if the tale of his inner self were at the same time a witness to purity of spirit could Wordsworth allow himself to violate his instinctive reserve.

Yet the absolute difference in tone between Wordsworth and Rousseau cannot mask their essential similarity. To take a trivial but suggestive example, Wordsworth habitually composed his poetry while he was out walking; Rousseau for his part said, 'I have never been able to do anything with my pen in my hand, and my desk and my paper before me; it is on my walks, among the rocks and trees . . . that I compose in my head.'[42] Again, when Wordsworth returns to nature as he found it a few miles above Tintern Abbey, he is happy to be out of the 'din | Of towns and cities', to escape 'the fretful stir | Unprofitable, and the fever of the world', and all that realm of 'greetings where no kindness is'.[43] Likewise Rousseau says, 'Paris life among pretentious people was so little to my taste . . . I found so little gentleness, open-heartedness, or sincerity even in the company of my friends, that in my disgust for that turbulent life I began to long ardently to live in the country.'[44]

And for still a third example, both men were notoriously resentful of criticism. As Hazlitt observed, 'Wordsworth would not forgive a single censure mingled with however great a mass of eulogy'; he was 'satisfied with nothing short of indiscriminate eulogy'.[45] Likewise, Mme de Staël said about Rousseau that 'Sometimes he would leave you still loving you; but if you had said a single word that could displease him, he recalled it, examined it, exaggerated it, thought about it for a week, and ended up by quarreling with you'.[46]

---

[41] Wordsworth, *Prelude*, 100 (bk. iii (1805), lines 196–9).

[42] Rousseau, i. 114.

[43] Wordsworth, *Poems*, ii. 260, 262 ('Tintern Abbey', lines 25–6, 53–4).

[44] Rousseau, i. 389–90.

[45] *Robinson*, i. 213, 179.

[46] Wilson, 181. Yet see De Man's 'Madame de Staël and Jean-Jacques Rousseau', where it is argued that 'Rousseau's influence covers the whole of Madame de Staël's work and is to be met with in her works of fiction as well as in her critical and political texts' (De Man, *Writings*, 171).

As in so many instances, Hazlitt saw the situation clearly:

Rousseau, in all his writings, never once lost sight of himself. He was the same individual from first to last. The spring that moved his passions never went down, the pulse that agitated his heart never ceased to beat. It was this strong feeling of interest, accumulating in his mind, which overpowers and absorbs the feelings of his readers. He owed all his power to sentiment. The writer who most nearly resembles him is the author of the *Lyrical Ballads*. We see no other difference between them, than that the one wrote in prose and the other in poetry. . . . Both create an interest out of nothing, or rather out of their own feelings; both weave numberless recollections into one sentiment; both wind their own being round whatever object occurs to them. . . . Rousseau . . . interests you in certain objects by interesting you in himself: Mr. Wordsworth would persuade you that the most insignificant objects are interesting in themselves, because he is interested in them.[47]

The insight is the more remarkable because Hazlitt attained it without a knowledge of *The Prelude*.

Rousseau's effect on Wordsworth is neither so overt nor so welcome as it was on Hazlitt. Indeed, it is everywhere masked. Nevertheless, it is very great, surely even greater than the enthusiasm engendered in Hazlitt. One is surprised, actually, that the relationship of Wordsworth and Rousseau has not received more attention than it has. George McLean Harper, however, in his biography of Wordsworth—a work, incidentally, that deserves to be made available again—after noting that Wordsworth was not much of a reader ('few other great poets', he says, 'are so little indebted to books'),[48] goes on to say that

One author, however, he almost certainly read before the close of 1791, and, curiously enough, this was a writer who himself had been indifferent to books. Rousseau it is, far more than any other man of letters, either of antiquity or of modern times, whose works have left their trace in Wordsworth's poetry. This poor, half-educated dreamer, just because he was poor, half educated, and a dreamer, found his way to the centre of his age, the centre of its intellectual and emotional life.[49]

In addition to whatever specific influences that may be isolated, there is often a suggestive agreement in tone and emphasis between Rousseau and

---

[47] *Hazlitt*, iv. 92.
[48] Harper, i. 127.
[49] Ibid. 127–8. Interestingly, Duncan Wu's recent study of Wordsworth's reading identifies external evidence for Wordsworth's having read only the *Discourses on Equality*, the *Social Contract*, and *Émile* by 1799 (Wu, 119–20). But the external likelihood and internal evidence for his having also read the *Confessions* are overwhelming.

Wordsworth. For instance, Wordsworth's apocalyptic passage in Gondo Gorge is an apex, a supreme moment, of his poetry:

> The immeasurable height
> Of woods decaying, never to be decayed,
> The stationary blasts of waterfalls,
> And everywhere along the hollow rent
> Winds threatening winds, bewildered and forlorn,
> The torrents shooting from the clear blue sky,
> The rocks that muttered close upon our ears—
> Black drizzling crags that spake by the wayside
> As if a voice were in them—the sick sight
> And giddy prospect of the raving stream,
> The unfettered clouds and region of the heavens,
> Tumult and peace, the darkness and the light,
> Were all like workings of one mind, the features
> Of the same face, blossoms upon one tree,
> Characters of the great apocalypse,
> The type and symbols of eternity,
> Of first, and last, and midst, and without end.[50]

Very few passages in world poetry, and perhaps not any prose, can match those ultimate lines. Nevertheless, much the same sense of awe amid stupendous mountain steeps, even if without the sublime diction and cadence of Wordsworth, is to be found in *La Nouvelle Héloïse*. Indeed, Rousseau's own cadences elicit an exaltation not entirely dissimilar to Wordsworth's, even if less intense:

Tantôt d'immenses roches pendoient en ruines au dessus de ma tête. Tantôt de hautes et bruyantes cascades m'inondoient de leur épais brouillard. Tantôt un torrent éternel ouvroit à mes côtés un abîme dont les yeux n'osoient sonder la profondeur. Quelquefois je me perdois dans l'obscurité d'un bois touffu. Quelquefois en sortant d'un gouffre une agréable prairie réjouissoit tout à coup mes regards. Un mélange étonnant de la nature sauvage et de la nature cultivée, montroit par tout la main des hommes, où l'on eut cru qu'ils n'avoient jamais pénétré; à coté d'une caverne on trouvoit des maisons; on voyait des pampres secs où l'on n'eut cherché que des ronces, des vignes dans des terres éboulées, d'excellens fruits sur des rochers, et des champs dans des précipices.[51]

But more important than any such confluence, or any traces of Rousseau's influence, is a single large effect. What Rousseau managed to do was turn Wordsworth out of his own natural disposition, and by the

---

[50] Wordsworth, *Prelude*, 218 (bk. vi (1805), lines 556–72).
[51] Rousseau, ii. 77.

force of his alien presence direct him into the channel of feeling by which Wordsworth was able to create the greatest poem of the nineteenth century.

To understand the ramifications of the claim just made, we need to realize two things about *The Prelude*, which, to reiterate, hardly has any genuine competitor as the greatest poem of the nineteenth century. First, as many and various critics have realized, *The Prelude* is Wordsworth's version of *Paradise Lost*. Not only does it take its urgency from its preoccupation with the lost paradise of Wordsworth's early life, but it constantly resonates with specific verbal recollections of Milton's great poem. Secondly, it is also very much the same poem as *The Excursion*, the controlling difference being that the latter poem is objective and public in form and focus, while *The Prelude* is a subjective revelation of an individual existence.

A subjective revelation of an individual existence is the more remarkable in this instance because Wordsworth, by background and social instinct, preferred his life to be veiled by the age-old social decorums against which Rousseau rebelled. Certainly Milton had availed himself of those decorums, for as Hazlitt well says, 'It is rarely that a man even of lofty genius will be able to do more than carry on his own feelings and character . . . into fictitious and uncommon situations. Milton has by allusion embodied a great part of his political and personal history in the chief characters and incidents of Paradise Lost.'[52] Wordsworth makes use of the same decorums. For instance, the public presentation of his grief about the deaths of his two children in 1812 is recast into the form of the Solitary's despondency in the third book of *The Excursion*; the affair with Annette Vallon is displaced into the poem of 'Vaudracour and Julia'.

Wordsworth in general did not like to make his private life public. When Barron Field proposed to publish his admiring *Memoirs* of Wordsworth's life and poetry in 1840, Wordsworth wrote him that 'I must regret that I am decidedly against the publication of your Critical Memoir';[53] and to the publisher Moxon he wrote, 'I set my face entirely against the publication of Mr. Field's MSS.'[54] To Field he indicated that his attitude was based on a rejection of self-revelation as such: 'it is far better not to admit people so much behind the scenes, as it has been lately fashionable to do.'[55] Again, to Sharp in 1804 Wordsworth wrote nervously about the incipient *Prelude*: 'it seems a frightful deal to say about one's self, and of course will never be published (during my lifetime, I mean).'[56]

[52] *Hazlitt*, viii. 42.   [53] *Barron Field*, 17.   [54] Ibid. 16.
[55] Ibid. 17.   [56] *Early Years*, 470.

To Sir George Beaumont in 1805 he said that *The Prelude* should come to 'not much less than 9,000 lines', which he called 'an alarming length! and a thing unprecedented in Literary history that a man should talk so much about himself'.[57]

Though one is bemused by the psychological ramifications of Wordsworth's palpable denial of Rousseau's precedent, one must also realize that his reasons for choosing the subjective mode are the very ones discovered by Rousseau himself, and by Montaigne before him: inexhaustible subject-matter and total control. 'I began the work,' confesses Wordsworth,

because I was unprepared to treat any more arduous subject, and diffident of my own powers. Here at least I hoped that to a certain degree I should be sure of succeeding, as I had nothing to do but describe what I had felt and thought, therefore could not easily be bewildered.[58]

Why, one asks, when the two geniuses were in accord on such large matters, do they seem so absolutely different? Why is the texture of *The Prelude* so wholly unlike that of the *Confessions*? That the textures are indeed radically different may be illustrated by adducing again a comparison I previously made in my book *Shapes of Culture*:

Take as single example the odd fact that both Wordsworth and Rousseau present among their earliest significant recollections not one but two episodes of boyhood theft. In book I of Wordsworth's *Prelude* we learn of the theft of other people's snares, with a characteristic admonitory moral animism in the memory:

> Sometimes it befell
> In these night wanderings, that a strong desire
> O'erpowered my better reason, and the bird
> Which was the captive of another's toil
> Became my prey; and when the deed was done
> I heard among the solitary hills
> Low breathings coming after me, and sounds
> Of undistinguishable motion, steps
> Almost as silent as the turf they trod.

Alongside this we may place Rousseau's first, characteristically near-ridiculous, memory of theft in his own book I:

There was a journeyman at my master's by the name of Verrat, whose mother lived in the neighborhood and had a garden a considerable distance from her house, where she grew very fine asparagus. Now it occurred to M. Verrat, who had not much money, to steal some of her asparagus. . . . As he was not very

[57] Ibid. 586.   [58] Ibid.

nimble and did not want to take the risk himself, he picked on me for the exploit. . . . I have never been able to resist flattery, and gave in. Every morning I went and cut the finest asparagus. . . . Thus I learnt that stealing was not so terrible as I had thought; and I soon turned my new knowledge to such good account that nothing I coveted and that was in my reach was safe from me.

Wordsworth's second memory of theft, the boat-stealing episode, is even more pregnant with moral animism than the first:

> One summer evening . . . I found
> A little boat tied to a willow tree
>
> .   .   .   .
>
> Straight I unloosed her chain, and stepping in
> Pushed from the shore. It was an act of stealth
> And troubled pleasure. . . .
>
> .   .   .   .
>
> She was an elfin pinnace; lustily
> I dipped my oars into the silent lake,
> And, as I rose upon the stroke, my boat
> Went heaving through the water like a swan;
> When, from behind that craggy steep till then
> The horizon's bound, a huge peak, black and huge,
> As if with voluntary power instinct
> Upreared its head. I struck and struck again,
> And growing still in stature the grim shape
> Towered up between me and the stars, and still,
> For so it seemed, with purpose of its own
> And measured motion like a living thing,
> Strode after me. With trembling oars I turned,
> And through the silent water stole my way
> Back to the covert of the willow tree;
> There in her mooring-place I left my bark,—
> And through the meadows homeward went, in grave
> And serious mood; but after I had seen
> That spectacle, for many days, my brain
> Worked with a dim and undetermined sense
> Of unknown modes of being; o'er my thoughts
> There hung a darkness . . .

As Wordsworth's second episode continues the grave tone of the first, so Rousseau's continues his own near-burlesque chatter:

One memory of an apple-hunt that cost me dear still makes me shudder and laugh at the same time. These apples were at the bottom of a cupboard which was lit from the kitchen through a high lattice. One day when I was alone in the house I climbed up on the kneading trough to peer into this garden of the Hesperides at those precious fruits I could not touch. Then I went to fetch the spit. . . . I probed several times in vain, but at last felt with delight that I was bringing up an apple.

He is unable to get the apple out, however, so:

Next day, when the opportunity offered, I made a fresh attempt. . . . But unfortunately the dragon was not asleep; the larder door suddenly opened; my master came out. . . . Soon I had received so many beatings that I grew less sensitive to them; in the end they seemed to me a sort of retribution for my thefts, which authorized me to go on stealing. . . . I reckoned that to be beaten like a rogue justified my being one.[59]

Despite the similarities of the episodes, the tone of Rousseau and the texture of his statement are so vastly different from the tone and texture of Wordsworth, that the question presents itself with renewed insistence, why is there such radical difference in the face of such similarity? The complete answer is doubtless complex, but perhaps an insight of Schiller's might serve to resolve at least a significant part of the problem. In his *Letters on the Aesthetic Education of Man*, Schiller states that 'Every individual man, it may be said, carries in disposition and determination a pure ideal man within himself, with whose unalterable unity it is the great task of his existence, throughout all its vicissitudes, to harmonize'.[60] In terms of this distinction, one might say that Rousseau's great work was devoted to recording his existence as an individual man, and that Wordsworth's great work, on the contrary, was devoted to extricating the ideal man within himself. That is not to say that there was no idealism in Rousseau's self-presentation; on the contrary, he was intensely idealistic. For a single instance, he says

This behaviour in a father of whose goodness and affection I am convinced, has caused me to reflect on my own conduct, and my reflections have had no small share in preserving the integrity of my conduct. They have taught me one great maxim of morality, the only one perhaps which is of practical use: to avoid situations which place our duties in opposition to our interests, and show us where another man's loss spells profit to us. For I am sure that, in such situations, however sincere and virtuous the motives we start with, sooner or later and unconsciously we weaken, and become wicked and unjust in practice, though still remaining good and just in our hearts.

I have carried this maxim firmly imprinted on my heart and applied it, although somewhat late in the day, to all my conduct. It has been one of the principal causes, indeed, of my seeming so foolish and strange in public, particularly in the eyes of my acquaintances. I have been accused of trying to be original and acting unlike other people, though really I have hardly even thought whether I was acting like others or unlike them. My sincere wish has been to do what was right, and I have

---

[59] *Shapes of Culture*, 164–7.   [60] *Schiller*, ii. 450.

strenuously avoided all situations which might set my interests in opposition to some other man's, and cause me, even despite myself, to wish him ill.[61]

But though the reader of the *Confessions* may, as Rousseau wanted him to do, come to love Rousseau in his indomitable attempt at candour, he must do so through the only doorway Rousseau allows him to enter, the doorway that takes him along a pitted path strewn with the ugly debris of multifarious mistakes, acts of baseness, experiences of humiliation, near-criminal errors of judgement, and even certifiable madness. He may, as I do, and many others besides me have done, come finally to regard Rousseau as none the less a very great man. But that recognition of greatness in some way emerges from Rousseau's iron resolve to tell it all at whatever cost; in that sense he is, as Nietzsche said of Schopenhauer, a man and a knight with a gaze of bronze:

The great object of my undertaking, always present to my eyes [says Rousseau, at the end of the eighth book of the *Confessions*], and my indispensable duty to fulfil it in its entirety, will not allow me to be deterred by weak considerations which might deflect me from my goal. In my strange, indeed unique, situation I owe too much to truth to owe anything more to any person. If I am to be known I must be known in all situations, good and bad. My *Confessions* are necessarily linked with the tales of many others; and in everything bearing on myself I record the truth about myself and others with equal frankness, in the belief that I owe no more consideration to other people than I show toward myself, although I should like to show them much more. I want always to be fair and truthful, to say as much good as I can of others, and only to speak evil when it concerns myself and in so far as I am compelled to do so. . . . My *Confessions* are not intended to appear in my lifetime, or in the lifetime of the persons concerned. . . . But since my name is fated to live, I must endeavour to transmit with it the memory of that unfortunate man who bore it, as he actually was and not as his unjust enemies unremittingly endeavour to paint him.[62]

Wordsworth, on the contrary, is less interested in detailing the actual facts of his existence than in searching for those transcendent moments that reveal the ideal person within. By their very definition, those moments always seemed not palpably present but glimpsed only:

> Oh! mystery of man, from what a depth
> Proceed thy honours. I am lost, but see
> In simple childhood something of the base
> On which thy greatness stands; . . .

                    .   .   .   .   .   .

---

[61] Rousseau, i. 56.   [62] Ibid. 399–400.

> The days gone by
> Return upon me almost from the dawn
> Of life: the hiding-places of man's power
> Open; I would approach them, but they close.
> I see by glimpses now; when age comes on,
> May scarcely see at all; and I would give,
> While yet we may, as far as words can give,
> Substance and life to what I feel, enshrining,
> Such is my hope, the spirit of the Past
> For future restoration.[63]

The transcendent moments that reveal the ideal man are, as that passage indicates, most characteristically remembered from the past. Thus it is that the six-years child becomes

> Mighty Prophet! Seer blest!
> On whom those truths do rest,
> Which we are toiling all our lives to find,
> In darkness lost, the darkness of the grave.[64]

Everywhere Wordsworth bypasses present reality in the quest for his transcendent self. 'Of my own heart | Have I been speaking',[65] he says, and Rousseau could and did say much the same thing; but Wordsworth's quest is not directed towards the same aspect of personality as Rousseau's. Everywhere Wordsworth feels that the incidents of his trip through life were 'in the end | All gratulant, if rightly understood'.[66] Rousseau, on the other hand, says that 'I was fated gradually to become an example of human misery'.[67] He was in very truth, in Byron's phrase, 'wild Rousseau, | The apostle of affliction'.[68] 'How shall I seek the origin?' asks Wordsworth, 'where find | Faith in the marvellous things which then I felt?'[69] The question, ecstatically searching for the highest moments of the self's experience, is at the antipode of Rousseau's gloomy determination to transmit the memory of that unfortunate man who bore the name of Rousseau, 'perdu dans la mer immense de mes malheurs'.[70]

But both Rousseau and Wordsworth were none the less committed to a new conception of subjectivity, and that conception provided the

---

[63] Wordsworth, *Prelude*, 433, 435 (bk. xii (1850), lines 272–86).
[64] Wordsworth, *Poems*, iv. 282 ('Immortality Ode', lines 115–18).
[65] Wordsworth, *Prelude*, 100 (bk. iii (1805), lines 176–7).
[66] Ibid. 478 (bk. xiii (1805), lines 384–5).
[67] Rousseau, i. 205.
[68] *Childe Harold*, canto III, stanza lxxvii.
[69] Wordsworth, *Prelude*, 85 (bk. ii (1850), lines 346–7).
[70] Rousseau, i. 544.

ideational ground of Romanticism, as well as the foundation of subsequent formations extending through, and even strengthening themselves within, the culture and history of our own era.

Yet Rousseau was not merely the hugely important shaper of a new conception of self; he was also, in another effect hardly less cataclysmic, the shaper of the French Revolution. As Byron said:

> . . . he was inspired, and from him came,
> As from the Pythian's mystic cave of yore
> Those oracles which set the world in flame,
> Nor ceased to burn till kingdoms were no more[71]

The thread of Rousseau's genius—'with ethereal flame | Kindled he was, and blasted'[72]—shall now be followed till our touching fingers encounter another densely woven configuration, one that reveals itself as a Romantic texture of a different pattern and different elaboration than the one just descried.

---

[71] *Childe Harold*, canto III, stanza lxxxi.
[72] Ibid., stanza lxxviii.

3

The Master Theme

ROUSSEAU, as discerned in the previous touching, not only changed for ever the direction of literary effort and the definition of the self, but also—more than any other single figure—prepared the way for the French Revolution. As Simon Schama has emphasized, 'A whole year before the Revolution is usually thought to have started, public utterances . . . were already saturated with Rousseau's rhetoric of virtue.'[1] And the participants in that mighty drama, regardless of which side they were on, were themselves almost all drenched in Rousseauism. Marat was deeply influenced by Rousseau, but so was his assassin, Charlotte Corday. Marie Antoinette read Rousseau; her antipode Robespierre studied him with assiduous attention.

Indeed, Rousseau almost totally occupied the mind of Robespierre, who deliberately tried to empty it of the other trophies of culture placed there by his excellent early education. A pastiche of quotations, referring to periods from early to late in Robespierre's life, may serve to dramatize the truth of Rousseau's hegemony in his thoughts (the quotations are drawn from the authoritative biography by J. M. Thompson). 'Robespierre's "head was full of Rousseau"; and one day, not long before 1778, there was perhaps a visit to the attic in which Jean-Jacques was nearing his end' (p. 9). 'Robespierre had, indeed, experienced, during that passage through the cheering crowds, a revelation of Rousseauism manifest in the flesh. He had heard for the first time, like Louis, the voice of the people, and thought that it was the voice of God' (p. 54). 'He was doubtless familiar with the chapter in the *Contrat Sociale* in which his hero Jean-Jacques declared that Christianity, properly understood, was too unworldly to be a state religion, and in which he outlined the "civic religion" necessary for the healthy life of society' (p. 84). 'The *Journal de Paris*, congratulating Robespierre on this speech, recalled the fact that a monument had recently been set up in honour of Rousseau. The allusion was just. Robespierre's religion was, indeed, the Deism that Jean-Jacques had learnt at Geneva . . . and had put into the mouth of his *vicaire savoyard*' (p. 217). 'Robespierre had been genuinely moved by the

---

[1] Schama, 279.

national enthusiasm of 1789. No one had laid so deeply to heart "that great moral and political truth preached by Jean-Jacques, that men have a sincere affection for those who really love them; that only the people is good, just and generous; and that corruption and tyranny are the monopoly of those who disdain the common crowd"' (p. 231). 'But Robespierre, again following Rousseau, sees a way out of the *impasse*, by way of the natural goodness of the people' (p. 281). 'Robespierre's doctrine of the State, upon which everything else rests, is clearly based on Rousseau's' (p. 359). 'There is, underlying all this, an important assumption, another of Robespierre's debts to Rousseau—the General Will' (p. 363). 'At every turn of events he was there, ready, like a Greek chorus, with appropriate comments; ready, like a Jewish prophet, with denunciation and warning; ready also, like any demagogue, with flattery of the people, and promises of a political millennium. Through it all, he was as sincere, as solemn, and as self-questioning as his master, the model of Jacobinism, Jean-Jacques Rousseau' (pp. 591–2).

Everywhere little rivulets of Rousseauism had trickled through the sides of the weakening dam of the *ancien régime*. The *Social Contract* of 1762 had proclaimed at its outset the striking paradox that man is born free, and is everywhere in chains: 'L'homme est né libre, et par-tout il est dans les fers.'[2] Later in the same work, Rousseau said, suggestively, that 'the institution of government is not a contract, but a law, that the depositaries of the executive power are not the people's masters, but its officers; that it can establish them and depose them as it likes'.[3] He continued:

When therefore the people set up a hereditary government, whether it be monarchical and confined to one family, or aristocratic and confined to a class, what it enters into is not at all a formal undertaking; it is a provisional form that it gives to administration until the people choose to order it otherwise.

It is true that such changes are always dangerous, and that the established government should never be touched except when it comes to be incompatible with the public good, but this circumspection is a maxim of politics and not rule of right, and the state is no more bound to leave civil authority to its rulers, than military authority to its generals.[4]

Again, the suggestively titled *Discours sur l'origine et les fondements de l'inégalité parmi les hommes* had, in 1754, much prior to Marx's delineation of the German ideology, stated an intent to 'mark, in the progress of things, the moment where, Right succeeding Violence, Nature was

---

[2] Rousseau, iii. 351.   [3] Ibid. 434.   [4] Ibid. 434–5.

subjected to Law; to explain by what chain of wonders the strong could resolve to serve the weak, and the people to buy a repose in idea at the price of a real hapiness'.[5] In that same treatise it was urged that

The first man who, having enclosed a piece of ground, to whom it occurred to say *this is mine* and found people sufficiently simple to believe, was the true founder of civil society. How many crimes, wars, murders, how many miseries and horrors mankind would have been spared by him who, pulling up the stakes or filling the ditch, had cried out to his kind: Beware of listening to this impostor, you are lost if you forget that the fruits are everyone's and the earth no one's.[6]

But even the enormous influence of Rousseau's political treatises could scarcely contend with the epoch-making effect of the flaming passion of *La Nouvelle Héloïse* in 1761. There may have been no single locus more premonitory of Revolutionary attitudes than Milord Edouard's argument with Julie's aristocratic father that St Preux, though not a nobleman, was a worthy suitor for Julie's hand. Generous hearts all over Europe thrilled to this vivid brief on behalf of human equality:

In what, then, continued Milord Edouard, consists the honour of that nobility of which you are so proud? What does it do for the glory of your country or the happiness of humankind? Mortal enemy of laws and liberty, what has it produced in most of the countries where it is conspicuous, except the force of tyranny and the oppression of the people?[7]

It is a twenty-to-one bet, said Milord Edouard in his coruscating diatribe, that a gentleman is descended from a scoundrel.[8] He himself would be sorry, said the symbolic English lord, not to have any other proof of his merit than that given him by a man dead for five hundred years.[9]

It was that sort of conditioning attitude that eventuated in what Thomas Paine, thirty years later, in his brilliant defence of the Revolution, proudly described this way:

The French constitution says *there shall be no titles*; and of consequence all that class of equivocal generation which in some countries is called '*aristocracy*,' and in others '*nobility*,' is done away, and the *peer* is exalted into the man.

It is, properly, from the elevated mind of France that the folly of titles has been abolished. It has outgrown the baby-clothes of *count* and *duke*, and breeched itself in manhood. France has not levelled, it has exalted. It has put down the dwarf to set up the man. The insignificance of a senseless word like *duke*, *count*, or *earl*, has ceased to please. Even those who possessed them have disowned the gibberish and, as they outgrew the rickets, have despised the rattle. The genuine mind of man,

---

[5] Ibid. 132.   [6] Ibid. 164.   [7] Ibid. ii. 170.
[8] Ibid. 169.   [9] Ibid. 170.

thirsting for its native home, society, contemns the gewgaws that separate him from it. Titles are like circles drawn by the magician's wand to contract the sphere of man's felicity. He lives immured within the Bastile of a word, and surveys at a distance the envied life of man.[10]

These and other attitudes, enunciated everywhere in Rousseau, found answering assent everywhere in cultivated society. It is hardly possible, indeed, to separate Rousseau's effect as founder of Romanticism, and his effect as instigator of the French Revolution.[11] For the great upheaval is inseparably entwined with the immediately following emergence of Romanticism.

A rich summoning of the texture of such entwinement may be supplied by considering a leading Romantic's political and intellectual involvement in the central issues of the Revolutionary cataclysm. The texture of such involvement is particularly complex and rewarding to touch, for it is full of the most intricate weaving and cross-weaving of fact and presumed fact, of assertion and counter-assertion. M. H. Abrams once complained that 'when critics and historians turn to the general task of defining the distinctive qualities of "Romanticism," or of the English Romantic movement, they usually ignore its relations to the revolutionary climate of the time'.[12] The complex texture to be descried in this chapter, by engaging in depth the relation of a leading Romantic, Coleridge, to the revolutionary climate of the times, seeks to fill that lacuna (though it has already been partly filled, in the interim since Abrams wrote, by an upsurge of new attention). Moreover, it seeks to fill it with special richness, by descrying an especially problematic texture, and by seeking to resolve a long-standing argument.

For few topics that occupy the borderland between Romantic literary history and political history are more problematic than the one posed by the political attitudes of Coleridge. Did Coleridge's attitudes over the course of his adult life represent a coherent development from primary assumptions, or, on the contrary, did they represent an incoherent line of thought characterized by opportunism and outright apostasy? To address the question is not simply to re-enter the political milieu of the Romantic

[10] Paine, 89.
[11] Cf. e.g. Hazlitt's vivid description of Rousseau's development and effect: 'after the anxious doubts and misgivings of his mind as to his own destiny . . .—after the slow dawn of his faculties, and their final explosion, that like an eruption of another Vesuvius, dazzling all men with its light, and leaving the burning lava behind it, shook public opinion, and overturned a kingdom . . .—after having been read by all classes, criticised, condemned, admired in every corner of Europe' (*Hazlitt*, xii. 366).
[12] Abrams, 46.

era, but to shed renewed light on Coleridge's mental attitudes and idiosyncratic modes of thought.

Both of the opposing cases were urged in Coleridge's day and are still being put forward in our own. The historian E. P. Thompson has repeatedly charged that Coleridge lacked political integrity, and that he in fact virtually defines one form of discreditable apostasy. In an essay called 'Disenchantment or Default? A Lay Sermon', Thompson attempts to distinguish between apostasy and disenchantment:

There is nothing in disenchantment inimical to art. But when aspiration is actively denied, we are at the edge of apostasy, and apostasy is a moral failure, and an imaginative failure. In men of letters it often goes with a peculiar disposition towards self-bowdlerization, whether in Mr. Southey or in Mr. Auden. It is an imaginative failure because it involves forgetting—or manipulating improperly—the authenticity of experience: a mutilation of the writer's own previous existential being. . . . Hazlitt commented that there need be no objection to a man changing his opinions. But

he need not . . . pass an act of attainder on all his thoughts, hopes, wishes, from youth upwards, to offer them at the shrine of matured servility: he need not become one vile antithesis, a living and ignominious satire of himself.[13]

And then Thompson says: 'Coleridge fell into this phase soonest.'[14]

Thompson argues that a creative tension between 'Jacobin affirmation and recoil' was good for Romantic poetry, but that apostasy, the abject giving up of former opinion, was bad: that for Wordsworth the moment of creative tension was 'far more protracted than it was for Coleridge'. He thus sees Coleridge's apostasy as not only an index to moral bankruptcy, but as the prime agent in his loss of poetic power (though others have ascribed that loss to other factors).

If Thompson's distinction may seem to start more questions than it answers, it at least serves as an introduction to his distaste for Coleridge. Ten years later, in a review of David Erdman's edition of Coleridge's *Essays on His Times*, Thompson indulged that distaste with greater vehemence. Coleridge's political essays, he says, are 'the spurious rhetoric of a chameleon'. Coleridge himself underwent 'interior redecoration'. 'Coleridge,' says Thompson, 'was an apostate, with a voracious appetite for hatreds.' 'These articles then are, in the main, both irresponsible and unprincipled.' 'These books are most damaging to Coleridge's reputation as an exalted political thinker, and, moreover, it is altogether proper that this inflated reputation should be so damaged. The *ingredients* of

[13] Thompson, 152–3.   [14] Ibid. 153.

Coleridge's political thought—historical, philosophical—were exception-
ally rich, but the results were always half-baked.'[15]

In truth, Thompson simply cannot abide Coleridge. 'I find these essays
objectionable, not on account of their opinions—although most of them
are lamentable—but on account of the unction with which they are
delivered.' Again: 'As one lays the volumes down one is sickened by the
surfeit of pharisaism and cliché. Coleridge is always writing "from my
inmost soul," he offers himself as "a teacher of moral wisdom." But the
content might be better entitled "Coleridge's Compendium of Cliché".'
Still again:

> The more he tried to work up his impulses into finished thoughts, the more
> unprincipled he became. He is chiefly of interest, in his political writings, as an
> example of the intellectual complexity of apostasy. He was, of course, a political
> apostate, and critics have confused the matter only because they have removed it
> from a political to an aesthetic court of judgment.

In a zenith of irritation Thompson even declares that 'Coleridge was
wrong on almost everything'.[16]

Now not everyone is likeable to everyone else, and doubtless there could
never be any possibility of rapprochement between the styles and opinions
of Coleridge and Edward Thompson. But that Coleridge was a committed
Jacobin who then became an apostate Tory is, on the evidence,
demonstrably not the case. Thompson's own political orientation is very
unlike that of Coleridge, and we should heed Coleridge's statement that

> he who infamizes another man as an Apostate and Renegado, does, *ipso facto*,
> confess that he himself continues to retain the opinions and principles which the
> other had *reneged* and . . . *turned against*. Had no other fragments of the works of
> the heretic Faustus been preserved but those in which he calls St. Augustine,
> Apostate and Deserter, yet these would have been amply sufficient to make it
> *certain* that Faustus himself had remained a Manichaean.[17]

Nor does Thompson's quoting Hazlitt against not passing an act of
attainder on all one's previous attitudes serve as more than a merely
rhetorical point against Coleridge. After all, Coleridge himself said the
same thing, more subtly:

> Why do we so very often see men pass from one extreme to another. . . . Alas they
> sought not the Truth but praise, self-importance, & above all to see something

---

[15] Review, 261–5.
[16] Ibid. 262–3.
[17] Coleridge, 'Mr. Southey and Wat Tyler, IV: Apostacy and Renegadoism' (2 April
1817), in *Essays*, ii. 474.

doing.—Disappointed they hate and persecute their former opinion, which no man will do who by meditation had adopted it, & in the course of unfeigned meditation gradually enlarged the circle & so got out of it—for in the perception of its falsehood he will form a perception of certain Truths which had made the falsehood plausible, & never can he cease to venerate his own sincerity of Intention.[18]

The setting up of Hazlitt against Coleridge, indeed, is a more complex matter than would appear on the surface. First of all, Hazlitt had not really been mature enough to experience the before-and-after shock of the Revolution, which, as shall presently appear, is so necessary to an understanding of the changes in political sentiment endemic to the time. Secondly, Hazlitt took a special, indeed a unique pride in not changing his opinions once they had formed, and this temperamental feature cannot be separated from the validity of his position as such:

In matters of taste and feeling, one proof that my conclusions have not been quite shallow or hasty, is the circumstance of their having been lasting. I have the same favourite books, pictures, passages that I ever had: I may therefore presume that they will last me my life—nay, I may indulge a hope that my thoughts will survive me. This continuity of impression is the only thing on which I pride myself.[19]

That statement occurs in an essay called 'A Farewell to Essay-Writing'. In an essay called 'On Consistency of Opinion' he proudly says:

I am not to be brow-beat or wheedled out of any of my settled convictions. Opinion to opinion, I will face any man. Prejudice, fashion, the cant of the moment, go for nothing. . . . If 'to be wise were to be obstinate,' I might set up for as great a philosopher as the best of them: for some of my conclusions are as fixed and as incorrigible to proof as need be. I am attached to them in consequence of the pains, the anxiety, and the waste of time they have cost me.[20]

Hazlitt was particularly 'fixed and incorrigible' with regard to the French Revolution, which he calls 'the great cause, to which I had vowed myself'. As he said in a haunting statement that affirmed his pride in the constancy of his beliefs, 'my earliest hopes will be my last regrets':

What sometimes surprises me in looking back to the past, is . . . to find myself so little changed in the time. The same images and trains of thought stick by me: I have the same tastes, likings, sentiments, and wishes that I had then. One great ground of confidence and support has, indeed, been struck from under my feet; but I have made it up to myself by proportionable pertinacity of opinion. The

---

[18] *Notebooks*, ii. 2121.
[19] *Hazlitt*, xvii. 318.
[20] Ibid. 22.

success of the great cause, to which I had vowed myself, was to me more than all the world: I had a strength in its strength, a resource which I knew not of, till it failed me for the second time [i.e. Napoleon's defeat at Waterloo]. . . . It was not till I saw the axe laid to the root, that I found the full extent of what I had to . . . suffer. But my conviction of the right was only established by the triumph of the wrong; and my earliest hopes will be my last regrets. One source of this unbendingness, (which some may call obstinacy,) is that, though living much alone, I have never worshipped the Echo. I see plainly enough that black is not white, that the grass is green, that kings are not their subjects; and, in such self-evident cases, do not think it necessary to collate my opinions with the received prejudices.[21]

Coleridge was quite different. He was not, however, different in the tenacity with which he held to his positions; for as I have elsewhere emphasized, he maintained the same principles throughout his adult career.[22] He was different rather in the complex structure of his tenacity: for unlike Hazlitt, who prided himself on seeing that black was not white, Coleridge was always trying to encompass both black and white. He did not simply jettison premature opinions; rather, as he says above, he 'in the course of unfeigned meditation gradually enlarged the circle and so got out of it'. He was temperamentally on all sides of a question at once,[23] and he was forever attempting to reconcile and include, rather than to separate and reject:

My system, if I may venture to give it so fine a name, is the only attempt I know, ever made to reduce all knowledges into harmony. It opposes no other system, but shows what was true in each; and how that which was true in the particular, in each of them became error, *because* it was only half the truth. I have endeavoured to unite the insulated fragments of truth, and therewith to frame a perfect mirror. I show to each system that I fully understand and rightfully appreciate what that system means; but then I lift up that system to a higher point of view, from which I enable it to see its former position, where it was, indeed, but under another light and with different relations; so that the fragment of truth is not only acknowledged, but explained.[24]

Coleridge, in brief, characteristically agreed both with what the Jacobins were attempting to do, and with what their opponents urged against them. For instance, he says in a compelling note of 1810 that

---

[21] *Hazlitt*, xvii. 316.   [22] CPT, 163–4, 358–9.
[23] For a single revealing example, John Thelwall commented, on Coleridge's endorsement in the *Biographia Literaria* of 'the EXISTENCE of the Supreme Being', that Coleridge 'seems to have received some new light upon the signification of the syllable *ex*, since he talked to me at Keswick of his design of writing an elaborate demonstration of the truth of Christian revelation which should commence with a denial of the *ex*istence of god' (Pollin, 88).
[24] TT, 12 Sept. 1831.

Atrocious were the crimes of the French Revolution, and dreadful has been their punishment. Do not then let us forget or transfer the benefits which it has produced. The Revolution was not brought about, any more than it was begun, by the Terrorists—No! nor which has been so endlessly asserted, by the irreligious doctrines of their philosophers: whatever share the just and humane doctrines of philosophers whom Vanity & Experience of Popery had misled into Irreligion, may have had in the complex cause of revolutionary Preparation.—The Infidels were, in numbers at least, an inconsiderable Minority in the Constitutional Assembly. No! Let the Truth be told! Ignorant, inexperienced, and presumptuous they were, most inex. most ign. most presumptuous!—But sanguinary, and dispisers of God and the Moral Law they were not—. Had they been so, never could they have effected what they did effect!—They broke down the Monasteries, Nunneries; restored the Lands & Domains of the Church to the independent agriculture of the Country; destroyed the whole Babel of feudal Vexations; & established the equal Descent of Property by Gavelkind—Were these, think you, small Blessings?[25]

In attempting to incorporate all positions into his own, Coleridge might well seem, to one who encountered him only on special issues, not to honour the difference between black and white; but the present author has described this being on both sides of a given issue as the idiosyncrasy and defining merit of his mental activity. As was affirmed at the conclusion of a work that surveyed the entire course of Coleridge's philosophical and religious thought:

through all the transformations of his 'it is'/pantheist interests on the one hand, and of his 'I am'/moral interests on the other, he remained true to the ineradicable fact of their tragic opposition—longing for their reconciliation, but foundering, as do we all, before the mysteries of existence.

In this equipoise Coleridge's philosophical achievement is both of its time and out of its time. His thought shares with that of his German contemporaries an emphasis upon the central importance of Spinozistic pantheism. But it differs in its idiosyncratic refusal to decide, either by pantheism or solipsistic scepticism, that which cannot be decided.[26]

So, too, as this chapter shall argue, Coleridge's voyage down the political stream, steering a course between the opposed banks of radicalism and reaction, seeming now to come close to one side and now to the other, is entirely consistent with his mental procedure on all topics of thought. Hazlitt sardonically recalled of a walk with him, that

I observed that he continually crossed me on the way by shifting from one side of the foot-path to the other. This struck me as an odd movement; but I did not at

---

[25] *Notebooks*, iii. 3845.   [26] CPT, 254.

that time connect it with any instability of purpose or involuntary change of principle, as I have done since. He seemed unable to keep on in a strait line.[27]

But Hazlitt, despite his disgust at what he thought of as Coleridge's defection from the cause of liberty, really did understand that Coleridge's political progress was precisely an intellectual version of the idiosyncratic fact that 'he continually crossed me on the way by shifting from one side of the foot-path to the other'. Coleridge did keep moving on the path; the shifting, however peculiar to his mode of progression, was not an opportunistic abandonment of one faith and adhesion to another. Even Hazlitt is unable to say that Coleridge was in fact a Jacobin, or for that matter, a Tory either:

I can hardly consider Mr. Coleridge as a deserter from the cause he first espoused, unless one could tell me what cause he ever heartily espoused, or what party he ever belonged to, in downright earnest. He has not been inconsistent with himself at different times, but at all times. He is a sophist, a casuist, a rhetorician, what you please; and might have argued or declaimed to the end of his breath on one side of a question or another, but he never was a pragmatical fellow. He lives in a round of contradictions, and never came to a settled point.[28]

Despite Hazlitt's scorn, his characterization of Coleridge's mental procedure here is compatible in its structure with what I praise, in the passage quoted above, as the special 'equipoise' of Coleridge's intellectual achievement. Coleridge, as shall presently appear in more detail, was committed, by theory and conviction, to see political health as the necessary and exclusive product of radically opposed adherences. He speaks beautifully of

the contest between the two great moving Principles of social Humanity— religious adherence to the Past and the Ancient, the Desire & the admiration of Permanence, on the one hand; and the Passion for increase of Knowledge, for Truth as the offspring of Reason, in short, the mighty Instincts of *Progression* and *Free-agency*, on the other. In all subjects of deep and lasting Interest you will detect a struggle between two opposites, two polar Forces, both of which are alike necessary to our human Well-being, & necessary each to the continued existence of the other.[29]

Moreover, to cleave, as did Hazlitt, to an unvarying course through all the subsequent vicissitudes of the French Revolution, was, as he himself conceded, 'unbendingness' and 'obstinacy'; for such a course could only

---

[27] *Hazlitt*, xvii. 113.
[28] Ibid. 29.
[29] *Collected Letters*, v. 35.

be maintained by radically downplaying—conniving at, really—the institutionalized murder that for Coleridge and for others changed the entire moral ambience of that Revolution.

Paine, writing in 1791 and hewing closely to Rousseau, had presented the Revolution as a noble and exalted change in human affairs:

But what we now see in the world, from the revolutions of America and France, are a renovation of the natural order of things, a system of principles as universal as truth and the existence of man, and combining moral with political happiness and national prosperity.

'I. Men are born and always continue free and equal in respect to their rights. Civil distinctions, therefore, can be founded only on public utility.

'II. The end of all political associations is the preservation of the natural and imprescriptible rights of man, and these rights are liberty, property, security and resistance of oppression.

'III. The nation is essentially the source of all sovereignty; nor can any individual, or any body of men, be entitled to any authority which is not expressly derived from it.'

In these principles there is nothing to throw a nation into confusion by inflaming ambition. They are calculated to call forth wisdom and abilities, and to exercise them for the public good and not for the emolument or aggrandizement of particular descriptions of men or families. Monarchical sovereignty, the enemy of mankind and the source of misery, is abolished; and sovereignty itself is restored to its natural and original place, the nation. Were this the case throughout Europe, the cause of wars would be taken away.[30]

Notable in that benign account is the implication that the Revolution was against violence, and would in truth eradicate violence. Likewise, one of Paine's insistent points against 'Mr. Burke's thundering attack on the French revolution'[31] was that the Revolution was free from violence:

Notwithstanding Mr. Burke's horrid paintings, when the French revolution is compared with that of other countries the astonishment will be that it is marked with so few sacrifices; but this astonishment will cease when we reflect that it was *principles*, and not *persons*, that were the meditated objects of destruction.[32]

Again: 'Whom has the national assembly brought to the scaffold? None.'[33] Still again: 'Not less than three hundred thousand persons arranged themselves in the procession from Versailles to Paris, and not an act of molestation was committed during the whole march.'[34]

---

[30] Paine, 140–1.   [31] Ibid. 59.   [32] Ibid. 63.
[33] Ibid. 69.   [34] Ibid. 75.

To be sure, though all this preceded the September Massacres of the following year, even by 1790 there had been enough violence to horrify Burke; and Taine always insisted that violence had been the character of the Revolution from the very first. Be that as it may, violence certainly became its subsequent character; the 'source of misery' was emphatically revealed to be something other than 'monarchical sovereignty'.[35] As Simon Schama has said:

The scholarly view of a limited Terror . . . hardly survives a scrutiny of the most dreadful enormity of the year II [1793]: the wholesale destruction of an entire region of France. Nowhere as much as in the area of the Vendée—including the neighboring departments of Loire-Inférieure and Maine-et-Loire—did the Terror fulfill Saint-Just's dictum that the 'republic consists in the extermination of everything that opposes it.'[36]

Schama goes on to insist on the apocalyptic and inexcusable nature of the savagery:

whatever claims on political virtue the French Revolution may make on the historian's sympathy, none can be so strong as to justify, to any degree, the unconscionable slaughters of the winter of the year II. Still less does it seem right to shunt off the Vendée into a special category of works set aside from the rest of the history of the Revolution, as though it were some sort of aberration. The exterminations practiced there were, in fact, the logical outcome of an ideology that progressively dehumanized its adversaries and that had become incapable of seeing any middle ground between total triumph and utter eclipse.[37]

But Hazlitt would have none of it. Ready to change reality rather than to change his opinions—shamefully ready, in truth—he writes that

The cant about the horrors of the French Revolution is mere cant—every body knows it to be so: each party would have retaliated upon the other: it was a civil

---

[35] No one has ever been able to justify the enormities of the Terror; but Michelet, the most devoted of all defenders of the French Revolution, provides the only possible, if not entirely convincing, defence: the Terror was horrible, but the Inquisition (whose own enormities were two centuries in the past), which was the result of the feudal complicity of kings and priests, was even worse: 'Que la Terreur révolutionnaire se garde bien de se comparer à l'Inquisition. Qu'elle ne se vante jamais d'avoir, dans ses deux ou trois ans, rendu au vieux système ce qu'il nous fit six cents ans! . . . Combien l'Inquisition aurait droit de rire! . . . Qu'est-ce que c'est que les seize mille guillotinés de l'une devant ces millions d'hommes égorgés, pendus, rompus, ce pyramidal bûcher, ces masses de chairs brûlées, que l'autre a montées jusqu'au ciel? La seule Inquisition d'une des provinces d'Espagne établit, dans un monument authentique, qu'en seize années elle brûla vingt mille hommes. . . . Mais pourquoi parler de l'Espagne, plutôt que des Albigeois, plutôt que des Vaudois des Alpes, plutôt que des beggards de Flandre, que des protestants de France, plutôt que de l'épouvantable croisade des Hussites, et de tant de peuples que le pape livrait à l'épée?' (Michelet, i. 34–5).   [36] Schama, 787.   [37] Ibid. 792.

war, like that for a disputed succession: the general principle of the right or wrong of the change remained untouched. Neither would these horrors have taken place, except from Prussian manifestos, and treachery within: there were none in the American, and have been none in the Spanish Revolution.[38]

Yet the American Revolution, Hazlitt should have known, was not a true revolution at all; and Hazlitt could not know that the next true revolution, the Russian Revolution, would precisely repeat the horrors of the French Revolution. In sum, if Coleridge's seeming vacillation between progressive and conservative modes might be thought to entail a moral cost, so too did Hazlitt's steadfastness. Moreover, Coleridge, it must emphatically be repeated, was fully as steadfast as Hazlitt, though in a different structure of concern.

To be sure, Coleridge was more conservative in the second decade of the nineteenth century than he had been in the first half of the last decade of the eighteenth. His enthusiasm for the liberation of human hopes, proclaimed by the Revolution, was very early tempered by repulsion, engendered by the horrifying human violations that so endemically occurred in the course of that Revolution. His own view of social desirability was in place from the first; but it was apparently in about 1798 and 1799—possibly a year or so earlier—that, as a recent commentator urges, Coleridge came to an overt insistence on 'insulation' against the electric shocks of Revolutionary violence:

The Plot Discovered looks back to Coleridge's optimistic pantisocratic phase, as well as forwards to his later conservatism. The disillusionment with the British people seen at the close of the pamphlet presages Coleridge's abandonment of democratic values publicly represented in his poem 'Fears in Solitude' (1798) where he criticises those who expect constitutional change to lead to moral improvement:

> Some, belike
> Groaning with restless enmity, expect
> All change from change of constituted power;
> As if a government had been a robe,
> On which our vice and wretchedness were tagged
> Like fancy-points and fringes, with the robe
> Pulled off at pleasure.

In so doing Coleridge is using the Commonwealthsman tradition to move from his radical reading of the constitution to one where the rights of property were sacrosanct. This shift, more than any other revision, marks the end of his radical phase. He publically signalled this in his Essay for the *Morning Post* of 7 December

1799 'On the French Constitution.' The pantisocratic view of property is completely abandoned:

> For the present race of men Governments must be founded on property; that *Government is good in which property is secure and circulates; that Government the best, which, in the exactest ratio, makes each man's power proportionate to his property.*

In *The Plot Discovered* Coleridge had declared that government to be best 'where every man is represented, and the representatives act according to instructions'. By 1799 Coleridge is arguing that the basis of government should no longer be upon personal representation but upon property: the shift is crucial. No longer is the discharge of the 'electric fluid of truth' a political necessity. Coleridge in 1799 is more interested in ways of insulating society from the too immediate enlightenment.[39]

Along the way to this shift in emphasis, gradually attained by enlarging the circle of his meditations, Coleridge gave noble voice to the generous hopes raised by the apocalyptic changes set in motion. As Lewis Patton summarizes Coleridge's language of reform in *The Watchman* of 1796, we hear the tropes likely to be used at that time by any young man of mind and heart. Thus Coleridge in 1796

> charged the Church of England with teaching hatred in the name of the God of love (p. 11) and ridiculed the miracles of the New Testament (p. 52); he called the Two Acts breaches of the Constitution (p. 13); he declared that the possessions of the rich rightfully belonged to the poor (p. 64); he predicted that by providential means kings and potentates would shortly be overthrown, and a good thing, too (pp. 65–6); he quoted with approval a declaration in favour of the rights of man (p. 372) and that nations other than France and the United States, which had been 'too long the dupes of perfidious kings, nobles, and priests, will eventually recover their rights' (p. 373); he urged the enlargement of the right of suffrage in England (p. 209); he asserted that in the purer and more radical days of the French Revolution 'the victories of Frenchmen' were 'the victories of Human Nature' (p. 270); and he likened Pitt to Judas Iscariot and hoped that he would be struck by a thunderbolt (p. 167). But if these extracts, chosen as instances of candour, give an impression of rashness or bombast, as well they might, the impression is false. The tone of *The Watchman* was prevailingly temperate.[40]

Such opinions were close to certain emphases of Jacobinism, but they were not congruent, as shall presently appear, to the most idiosyncratic emphases. Coleridge had been a youthful sympathizer with the radicalism of William Frend, a fellow of Coleridge's own Jesus College, who was expelled from the college because of his publication in February, 1793, of a pamphlet called *Peace and Union* (Nicholas Roe has well described the whole matter in his chapter called ' "Mr. Frend's Company": Cambridge, Dissent, and Coleridge'[41]). But even here, in Coleridge's closest approach to unalloyed sympathy for the French Revolution, he was guided by the significant fact that Frend was a Unitarian Christian, and one, moreover, who was much upset by the 'dreadful outrages' of the September Massacres: 'Frend was genuinely horrified', summarizes Roe, 'by the "assassinations, murders, massacres, burning of houses, plundering of property, open violations of justice, which have marked the progress of the French revolution".'[42]

Although Roe does not make the distinction that the present chapter does between Jacobinism and Coleridge's democratic leanings, careful reading both of his discussion, and of all other evidence pertaining to Coleridge's attitudes, fails to document any actual commitment to Jacobinism on Coleridge's part. On the contrary, Coleridge at all times was bound by the rejection of violence and the espousal of humanitarian beliefs. Even Frend, despite his Unitarianism, approved of the execution of Louis XVI. Even Wordsworth approved of the execution of Louis XVI. Coleridge, on the contrary, as Roe says in discussing the vogue of Godwin's *Political Justice*, felt that 'love and friendship were the means to human regeneration, and in this respect Coleridge was fundamentally at odds with Godwin's disinterested rationalism in *Political Justice*'.[43]

The more carefully one examines the situation, indeed, the more strikingly does it appear that Coleridge, despite his fellow-feeling for the democratic ardours of reform, was never really saying quite the same thing that his youthful companions were saying. Logan Pearsall Smith once pointed out that in Donne's sermons, which use the language and reference of their time, 'Donne is often saying something else. . . . It sometimes seems as if he were using the time-honoured phrases of the accepted faith, its hope of heaven, and its terror of the grave, to express a vision of his own—a vision of life and death, of evil and horror and ecstasy—very different from that of other preachers.'[44] *Mutatis mutandis*, the same might be affirmed of Coleridge. What he was really talking about, amid all the excited verbiage of the time, was not Revolutionary Jacobinism, but 'love and friendship'.

[41] Roe, *Wordsworth*, 84–117.   [42] Ibid. 104.

[43] Ibid. 115. Cf. Coleridge to Southey on 21 Oct. 1794: 'In the book of Pantisocracy I hope to have comprised all that is good in Godwin—of whom and of whose book I will write more fully in my next letter. (I think not so highly of him as you do—and I have read him with the greatest attention—)' (*Collected Letters*, i. 115).

[44] Pearsall Smith, p. xxv.

Nowhere does Coleridge countenance violence or justify civil disorder. For instance, Roe notes that 'Frend's loss in the riots of 1791 doubtless gave impetus to his strictures on mob violence in *Peace and Union*, an attitude which Coleridge also shared in his political lectures'.[45] Again, Roe points out that the Pantisocracy projection—which harks back to the pure currents of Rousseau's *Discourse on Equality*, and not to its aftermath forty years later—was concerned not so much with politics (or the grinding effect of 'general will') as it was with personal friendship:

Pantisocracy was 'a scheme of emigration on the principles of an abolition of individual property' that would be established in America on the banks of the River Susquehannah (CL. i. 96–7). For Coleridge, however, its equalitarian principles were not wholly political or economic, but religious and emotional as well: Pantisocracy was to be a 'family of Love' or, as he put it in a letter to Southey on 18 September 1794, 'frendotatoi meta frendous. Most friendly where all are friends' (CL. i. 103). Coleridge's pun on Frend's name was, I think, a deliberate acknowledgement. His letters of summer 1794 alternate between excited anticipation of 'the pure System of Pantocracy' (CL. i. 84), and a parallel concern to explain its systematic perfection through the workings of personal friendship to 'universal benevolence'.[46]

Coleridge himself recalls his involvement in the Pantisocracy plan. He does so in terms that precisely agree with the contention above that his partial parallelism to Jacobin radicalism always entailed something fundamentally different from Jacobinism. In very truth, his 'little world described the path of its revolution in an orbit of its own'. As he says in *The Friend*, speaking of his attitudes in the immediate aftermath of the Revolution:

My feelings, however, and imagination did not remain unkindled in this general conflagration; and I confess I should be more inclined to be ashamed than proud of myself, if they had! I was a sharer in the general vortex, though my little world described the path of its revolution in an orbit of its own. What I dared not expect from constitutions of government and whole nations, I hoped from Religion and a small company of chosen individuals, and formed a plan, as harmless as it was extravagant, of trying the experiment of human perfectability on the banks of the *Susquehannah*, where our little society in its second generation was to have combined the innocence of the patriarchal age with the knowledge and genuine refinements of European culture.[47]

---

[45] Roe, *Wordsworth*, 96.
[46] Ibid. 113.
[47] *Friend*, i. 223–4.

That projection, however critical it was of conservative mores, was not Jacobinism.

Moreover, if even in his extreme youth Coleridge's views were at most somewhat parallel to, rather than identical with, that Revolutionary groundswell known as Jacobinism, they changed rapidly into an outright and uncompromising rejection of Jacobinism, and this rejection continued unwaveringly to the end of his life. As Coleridge moved further from the Revolutionary climate and into middle age, his dislike for Jacobinism as such steadily intensified. 'I fear, and detest the *passions* and malignant *restlessness* of Jacobinism,' he wrote a correspondent in 1818, 'as much as I despise the shallowness and empiricism of it's principles. A Jacobin Spirit can thrive in a mob only: and whatever Society, it thrives in, becomes ipso facto a mob.'[48] Again—but even in this emphatic statement still steering his course between the radical and conservative in French politics—he says: 'I detest Jacobinism, and as to the French, Jacobins or Royalists, even as I love what's virtuous, *hate* I them!'[49]

In line with this intensifying repudiation, Coleridge tried to obliterate traces of Jacobin sympathy that might be found in his youthful utterances. Thus, just as Southey in 1817 was enraged by the unauthorized publication of his *Wat Tyler* of 1794, Henry Crabb Robinson can note in 1816 that 'I read at Montagu's Coleridge's beautiful *Fire, Famine, and Slaughter*, written in his Jacobinical days, and now reprinted to his annoyance by Hunt in the *Examiner*'.[50] To make sure that he would not be further embarrassed by having raw earlier formulations thrown in his face, Coleridge significantly altered his poem *To a Young Ass*. Where in 1794 the concluding lines read:

> Yea! and more musically sweet to me
> Thy dissonant harsh bray of joy would be,
> Than Handel's softest airs that soothe to rest
> The tumult of a scoundrel Monarch's Breast

by 1834 both Handel and the scoundrel Monarch were gone, and the lines now read

> Yea! and more musically sweet to me
> Thy dissonant harsh bray of joy would be,
> Than warbled melodies that soothe to rest
> The aching of pale Fashion's vacant breast![51]

[48] *Collected Letters*, iv. 866.   [49] Ibid. 815.
[50] *Robinson*, i. 198.   [51] Coleridge, *Poems*, i. 76.

In the same context, when the *Biographia Literaria* appeared in 1817, it contained in its tenth chapter a denial that Coleridge had at any time been a convert to Jacobinism, and in its third chapter presented a eulogy of Southey.[52] Hazlitt, in his ferocious review of the *Biographia*, took note of both:

Mr. Southey has come voluntarily before the public; and all the world has a right to speak of his publications. It is those only that have either been depreciated or denounced. We are not aware, at least, of any attacks that have been made, publicly or privately, on his private life or morality. The charge is, that he wrote democratical nonsense in his youth; and that he has not only taken to write against democracy in his maturer age, but has abused and reviled those who adhere to his former opinions; and accepted of emoluments from the party which formerly calumniated him, for those good services. Now, what has Mr. Coleridge to oppose to this? Mr. Southey's private character! . . . Some people say, that Mr. Southey has deserted the cause of liberty: Mr. Coleridge tells us, that he has not separated from his wife. They say, that he has changed his opinions: Mr. Coleridge says, that he keeps his appointments; and has even invented a new word, *reliability*, to express his exemplariness in this particular. It is also objected, that the worthy Laureate was as extravagant in his early writings, as he is virulent in his present ones: Mr. Coleridge answers, that he is an early riser, and not a late sitter up.[53]

As for Coleridge's claim that people he had met in the 1790s 'will bear witness for me how opposite even then my principles were to those of

---

[52] *Biographia*, i. 184 and 59–67. One can, as this chapter will continue to attempt to show, accept absolutely Coleridge's claim that he was 'never at any period of my life a Convert to the System' of Jacobinism (184 n.), and that friends could 'bear witness for me, how opposite even then my principles were to those of jacobinism' (184). The key word is 'principles' (just as in the first statement the key Coleridgean word is 'System'), which for Coleridge did not change. In the play of his mind and conversation, however, it might be more accurate to say that he was in his early years both inclined towards Jacobinism and inclined against it. A sonnet on Burke in 1794 exactly expresses this characteristically antithethical approach. Burke, the arch-enemy of Jacobinism, is hailed by 'FREEDOM' as 'Great Son of Genius!', but then blamed that 'in an evil hour with alter'd voice | Thou bad'st Oppressions hireling crew rejoice.' On the other hand, it is then said that 'never, BURKE! thou drank'st Corruptions bowl'; and the poem concludes by hailing Burke as 'Spirit pure' and wishing 'That Error's mist had left thy purgèd eye: | So might I clasp thee with a Mother's joy!' (Coleridge, *Poems*, i. 80–1). If Jacobin sympathies here co-exist with reverence for Burke, in *The Fall of Robespierre*, written in collaboration with Southey in 1794, the same antithetical pattern appears. As a commentator points out, 'Its dedication, which is plainly un-Jacobin in tone, speaks of Robespierre's "great bad actions" and of the "vast stage of horrors" on which the two young poets have set the events of their play. . . . But the play is as anti-monarchical as it is anti-Jacobin' (George Watson, 'The Revolutionary Youth of Coleridge and Wordsworth', *Critical Quarterly*, 18 (1976), 53). For a rejoinder to Watson's article, see John Beer, 'The "Revolutionary Youth" of Wordsworth and Coleridge: Another View', *Critical Quarterly*, 19 (1977), 79–87, which argues for more consistency and less prevarication in Coleridge's views than Watson concedes them.   [53] *Hazlitt*, xvi. 120.

Jacobinism or even of democracy',[54] Hazlitt comments with a verbal shrug:

We shall not stop at present to dispute with Mr. Coleridge, how far the principles of the Watchman, and the *Conciones ad Populum*, were or were not akin to those of the Jacobins. His style, in general, admits of a convenient latitude of interpretation. But we think we are quite safe in asserting, that they were still more opposite to those of the Anti-Jacobins, and the party to which he admits he has gone over.[55]

That Hazlitt, however, whose hatred for Coleridge was matched only by the extreme acuteness of his critical perceptions, does not choose actually to examine or assail the *Conciones ad Populum* is significant. Hugely significant. For the work is Coleridge's earliest political statement, and it is there and in those terms, or ultimately nowhere and in no terms at all, that an accusation of early Jacobinism and later apostasy must be substantiated.[56] It is, to reiterate, the argument of this chapter that neither charge can in fact be substantiated.

Indeed, one will be forced to recognize what Hazlitt himself, beneath his rancour, had to have known, that 'The Conciones are violently anti-polemic, violently anti-pittite—but least of all things, Jacobinical'.[57] 'From the very outset,' asserts Coleridge in 1833, the year before his death:

I hoped in no advancement of humanity but from individual mind & morals working onward from Individual to Individual—in short, from the *Gospel*—. This

---

[54] Indeed, as early as November 1794, Coleridge complained to his brother that 'People have resolved that I am a Dηmocrat—and accordingly look at every thing I do through the Spectacles of Prejudication.' He goes on to say: 'Solemnly, my Brother! I tell you—I am *not* a Dηmocrat. I see evidently, that the present is *not* the *highest* state of Society, of which we are *capable*—And after a diligent, I *may* say, an intense study of Locke, Hartley and others who have written most wisely on the Nature of Man—I appear to myself to see the point of *possible* perfection at which the World may perhaps be destined to arrive—But how to lead Mankind from one point to the other is a process of such infinite Complexity, that in deep-felt humility I resign it to that Being—"Who shaketh the Earth out of her place and the pillars thereof tremble"—.' 'I have been asked what is the best conceivable mode of meliorating Society—My Answer has been uniformly this—"Slavery is an Abomination to every feeling of the Head and the Heart—Did Jesus teach the *Abolition* of it? No! He taught those principles, of which the necessary *effect* was—to abolish all Slavery". . . . You ask me, what the friend of universal Equality *should* do—I answer—Talk not of *Politics—Preach the Gospel!*' (*Collected Letters*, i. 125–6). For an indication of the playful ebullience of Coleridge with regard to politics at this time, see a letter of 22 July 1794, where in Wales 'Welch Politics could not however prevail over Welch Hospitality—they all shook hands with me, (except the Parson) and said, I was an open-speaking, honest-hearted Fellow, tho' I was a *bit* of a Democrat' (ibid. 91).

[55] *Hazlitt*, xvi. 129.

[56] *Conciones ad Populum, or Addresses to the People* (February 1795), in *Lectures 1795*, 21–74. [57] *Collected Letters*, iv. 798.

in my first work, the Conciones ad Populum, I declared, in my 23rd year: and to this I adhere in my present 63rd. Liberty without Law can exist *no where*: and in nations in a certain state of general information & morality, Law without Liberty is as little possible. But in the state in which France *is*, and which England is becoming, there seems to me an equal incapability of either Law or Liberty.[58]

The statement seems eminently accurate in the light of the aims of the Pantisocracy scheme just rehearsed. Furthermore it is but one of many evidences that Coleridge did not change by abrupt repudiations and summary *voltes-face*; change, for Coleridge, was always a matter of evolving emphases and additional considerations. He was as tenacious of his originary beliefs as any thinker has ever been; and no intellectual life can have been more continuous and integrated in its development than was his. His beautiful statement of this ideal might profitably be compared with Thompson's furious denunciations:

It is a maxim with me, to make Life as continuous as possible, by linking on the Present to the Past: and I believe that a large portion of the ingratitude, inconstancy, frivolity, and restless self-weariness so many examples of which obtrude themselves on every man of observation and reflective habits, is attributable to the *friable*, incohesive sort of existence that characterizes the mere man of the World, a fractional Life made up of successive moments, that neither blend nor modify each other—a life that is strictly symbolized in the thread of Sand thro' the orifice of the Hour-glass, in which the sequence of Grains only *counterfeits* a continuity, and appears a *line* only because the interspaces between the Points are too small to be sensible. Without Memory there can be no hope—the Present is a phantom known only by it's pining, if it do not breathe the vital air of the Future: and what is the Future, but the Image of the Past projected on the mist of the Unknown, and seen with a glory round it's head.[59]

But whether or not Coleridge might in his statement of 1833 be thought by some—mistakenly thought, in the judgement of this author—to be slightly exaggerating his early disbelief in social action, as opposed to individual conscience, in the advancement of humanity, this chapter will argue that the link between his early and late attitudes can most fruitfully be understood, not as an oscillation between left-wing and right-wing politics, but rather as a continuing concern for the human. As he wrote in 1818, long after the Revolution and his own youth were past, but in words that may serve as an emblem of his stance from first to last:

Marat had a conviction amounting in his own mind to a moral certainty that the death of 200,000 of his Countrymen was indispensible to the establishment of the

[58] *Collected Letters*, vi. 965.   [59] Ibid. v. 266.

Liberty and ultimate moral and physical Well-being of France, and therein of all Europe. We will even assume, that events should have confirmed the correctness of this belief. And yet Marat was and will remain either execrable as a remorseless Ruffian, or frightful as an Insane Fanatic. And why? The proposal was frightfully disproportionate to the sphere of a poor fallible Mortal. It was a decisive symptom of an inhuman Soul, that, when the lives of myriads of his fellow-men were in question, the recollection of his necessary fallibility, and the probability of mistake where so many myriads of men possessing the same intellectual faculties with himself entertained different convictions with the same sense of positiveness, did not outweigh any confidence arising from his own individual insight.[60]

Marat, however, and it must be stressed, was an anomaly only by his higher degree of fanaticism, not by any difference from other Jacobins in his theoretical acceptance of reformist violence.[61]

Coleridge saw from the first that violence was essential to Jacobinism, and it was this inherent commitment to violence that constituted the unbridgeable and uncrossable chasm between his own attitudes and the system of Jacobinism. Despite his sympathy and personal friendship with some of the leading English Jacobins, Coleridge was always different from them. They were not themselves, like their French counterparts, brought to the actual test of violence. None of them became a Marat, a Fouché, a Fouquier-Tinville, a Tallien, an Hébert. But those monsters were merely ordinary enthusiasts, like their English counterparts, before the blood began to flow. We may perhaps see some indication of what the British Jacobins, too, would have done had the circumstances in England become those in France. Let us not forget that the youthful Wordsworth justified the execution of Louis XVI![62] Again, consider the reaction of one of the British Jacobins, James Watt, Junior, the son of the inventor, who happened to be in Paris at the time of the September massacres in 1792. He was appalled—yet he asserted that the deaths were not only necessary, but absolutely necessary![63]

---

[60] *Inquiring Spirit*, 130.

[61] For general background on Jacobinism, see Gérard Walter, *Histoire des Jacobins* (Paris: Aimery Somogy, 1946). For an important source collection of documents see Alphonse Aulard, *La Société des Jacobins: Recueil de documents pour l'histoire du club des Jacobins de Paris* (Paris: Librairie Jouast, 1889–97), 6 vols. For discussion of the kinds of people who became Jacobins, see e.g. Michael L. Kennedy, *The Jacobin Clubs in the French Revolution: The First Years* (Princeton, NJ: Princeton University Press, 1982), 73–8.

[62] *Prose*, i. 32.

[63] As Watt said, 'I am filled with involuntary horror at the scenes which pass before me and wish they could have been avoided, but at the same time I allow the absolute necessity of them. In some instances the vengeance of the people has been savage & inhuman.' (Erdman, 228–9.)

It is important to note this example of a British Jacobin's attitude when actually in the midst of reformist bloodshed. To be sure, as Carl Cone notes, 'English Jacobinism was not monolithic.'[64] At least at its outset, Jacobinism 'was a state of mind, a cluster of indignant sensibilities, a faith in reason, a vision of the future. It was also individuals and groups among whom Thelwall admitted there were "many different opinions . . . as to the extent" of change that was needed.'[65] But underlying all Jacobinism, as shall increasingly appear in this chapter, there was a leaning towards violence and a readiness for bloodshed. That these effects were not evident in England was a consequence of the extraordinary gentleness of the confrontation there between radicalism and the established government. For instance, John Augustus Bonney, while confined in the Tower of London, and in Newgate, in 1794, was treated with notable kindness. When he was first apprehended, he was 'taken in a Coach to the Hummums Govt. Garden where Gurnell left me with Miller—could get no beds went to Webbs Hotel King Street where I went to bed the Officer sat in a Chair & kept me awake by snoring.'[66] Again, on 'Tuesday June 3', Bonney writes that 'Tooke sent me a basket of strawberries'.[67] On Friday, 6 June, 'Tooke sent Strawberries & Artichokes'; on Sunday 8 June, 'Wife Mary & Mrs T. came & staid near hours under the new regulation—Yeoman Porter reprimanded Hemmons for not being in the room tho' Mr. Kinghorne was here'; on Monday, 9 June, 'Barington relieved Hemmons—Strawberries from Tooke. Mrs. B & her 2 Daughters came.'[68]

Strawberries and artichokes in an English prison were a far cry from tumbrils and the guillotine in France. As Cobban points out:

One of the remarkable features of the British situation during the Revolutionary decade was the absence of serious social disorder in the presence of generally deteriorating economic conditions. . . . The English courts of law, with an Erskine to keep them up to the mark, never lost their judicial character. . . . One cannot read trials such as those of Hardy, or Horne Tooke, without being moved by the humane and gentlemanly way in which they were conducted by the judges, and the moderation even of the prosecuting lawyers. At the same time the Revolutionary Tribunal in Paris was exhibiting a very different conception of the judicial function. Horne Tooke's trial ended in mutual felicitations between Lord Chief Justice Eyre and the accused; even the prosecuting lawyers could scarce forbear to cheer, and the crowd outside carried the defendant in triumph to his lodgings.[69]

But once the social climate of England was exchanged for that of France, as Watt's attitude shows, British Jacobinism exhibited a ready

[64] Cone, 5. [65] Ibid. [66] Roe, *Politics*, 85.
[67] Ibid. 87. [68] Ibid. [69] Cobban, 21–2.

acceptance of violence. The vegetarian John Oswald, a British enthusiast who went to France at the outset of the Revolution and joined the Jacobin Club in Paris, was possessed, in the words of Thomas Paine, of 'a most notable appetite for blood'. He was the author of bizarre and sanguinary proposals, and his career has received important attention in David Erdman's *Commerce des Lumières*; 'Oswald, too,' summarizes Albert Goodwin delicately, 'was an exponent of the pike.'[70] Again, the London Corresponding Society's 'Joint Address to the French National Convention', on 27 September 1792, exultantly proclaimed, 'how well purchased will be, though at the expence of much blood, the glorious, the unprecedented privilege of saying, "Mankind is free! Tyrants and Tyranny are no more!"'[71]

Coleridge was viscerally opposed to all this. It must be reiterated, and cannot be too strongly emphasized, that he saw clearly that Jacobinism was inextricably bound up with a commitment to programmatic violence that necessarily desecrated the human. About this commitment there can be no convincing historical disagreement: it was not the Girondins, but the Jacobins, and their Hébertist offshoots (as a recent commentator notes, 'Above all, though, the Hébertistes were for unrelenting surveillance, denunciation, indictment, humiliation, and death'[72]), who planned and executed the Terror in all its phases. Crane Brinton points out that the Jacobin Clubs from the first, well before the actual advent of the Terror, were permeated by a tropism to violence, sometimes even in slight ways.[73]

More recently a historian, speaking of the massacre of 10 August 1792, has insisted that

the carnage of the tenth of August was not an incidental moment in the history of the Revolution. It was, in fact, its logical consummation. From 1789, perhaps even before that, it had been the willingness of politicians to exploit either the threat or the fact of violence that had given them the power to challenge constituted authority. Bloodshed was not the unfortunate by-product of revolution, it was the source of its energy.[74]

For Coleridge, as will become evident, the knowledge that bloodshed was the source of the Revolution's energy became the impassable chasm. He saw from the first that such bloodshed alarmingly existed; till it ceased, he could not become a Revolutionary. When it did not cease, he became an opponent of all that Jacobinism in its essence stood for.

[70] Goodwin, 242 n.
[71] Ibid. 503. The complete text of the Address, along with part of the French text as read to the National Convention, 7 November 1792, is given in Goodwin, 501–4.
[72] Schama, 806.   [73] Brinton, 111–15.   [74] Schama, 615.

In truth, the only real question is whether Jacobin violence arose from circumstances, which was the position of the historian Alphonse Aulard,[75] or was, on the contrary, an essential condition of the Jacobin way of viewing the world, which was the contention of Hippolyte Taine.[76] The implications of Taine's analysis, indeed, are that it would have been better if the Revolution had never occurred at all, and that, though not entirely Coleridge's view, is not far from it. William Doyle, a historian more anxiously committed to seeing both sides than Taine, nevertheless concludes, at the end of a long and discriminating chapter called 'The Revolution in Perspective', that 'the men of 1789'

failed to see, as their inspirers had not foreseen, . . . that reason and good intentions were not enough by themselves to transform the lot of their fellow men. Mistakes would be made when the accumulated experience of generations was pushed aside as so much routine, prejudice, fanaticism, and superstition. The generation forced to live through the upheavals of the next twenty-six years paid the price. Already by 1802 a million French citizens lay dead; a million more would perish under Napoleon, and untold more abroad. How many millions more still had their lives

---

[75] e.g. 'there was nothing systematic in the creation of the Revolutionary Government. Nearly all the facts hitherto related go to prove that this Government was not the application of any system or any preconceived idea, but that it formed itself empirically, from day to day, out of the elements imposed on it by the successive necessities of the national defences of a people at war with Europe; a people in arms for the defence of its existence, in a country which resembled a vast military camp. . . . The Revolution . . . strove to govern by law and liberty until August 10, 1792. Then, the resisting forces of the past having formed an alliance, having brought about a civil war and a war of invasion . . . the Revolution put away and suspended the principles of '89, and turned against its enemies . . . the weapons with which it found itself attacked. The Terror consisted in the suspension of the principles of '89' (Aulard, *Revolution*, ii. 278–9).

[76] Taine finds that a 'homicidal idea'—*idée homicide*—characterized Jacobinism from the first: 'In his narrow brain, perverted and turned topsy-turvy by the disproportionate notions put into it, only one idea suited to his gross instincts and aptitudes finds a place, and that is the desire to kill his enemies; and these are also the State's enemies. . . . He carries this savagery and bewilderment into politics, and hence the evil arising from his usurpation. . . . As representing the State, he undertakes wholesale massacres, of which he has the means ready at hand. For he has not yet had time enough to take apart the old administative implements; at all events the minor wheels, gendarmes, jailers, employees, bookkeepers, and accountants, are always in their place and under control. There can be no resistance on the part of those arrested; accustomed to the protection of the laws and to peaceable ways and times, they have never relied on defending themselves nor ever could imagine that any one could be so summarily slain. As to the mass, rendered incapable of any effort of its own by ancient centralization, it remains inert and passive and lets things go their own way. Hence, during many long, successive days, without being hurried or impeded, with official papers quite correct and accounts in perfect order, a massacre can be carried out with the same impunity and as methodically as cleaning the streets or clubbing stray dogs. Let us trace the progress of the homicidal idea in the mass of the party. It lies at the very foundation of the revolutionary creed' (Taine, iii. 265–6).

ruined? Inspiring and ennobling, the prospect of the French Revolution is also moving and appalling; in every sense a tragedy.[77]

Certainly the question in retrospect is not whether good may have stemmed from the Revolution, but whether the cost of that good was too high.[78]

How radical such a conclusion was in terms of Romantic experience can scarcely be overemphasized, for that the Revolution did occur was the overwhelming fact of the era, and that it should occur was the almost equally overwhelming hope of the finest and most ardent sensibilities among those who were young. 'The French Revolution', wrote Shelley to Byron, was 'the master theme of the epoch in which we live.'[79] Hazlitt treated it as the originating moment of Romanticism itself;[80] and certainly no figure in the literature of the early nineteenth century is exempt from the impress of the revolutionary cataclysm.

And yet it is also true that hardly any figure is entirely consistent in his orientation towards that cataclysm. We must not forget that the most eloquent opponent of the French Revolution, Burke, had formerly been the most eloquent defender of the American Revolution. Yet the earlier event gave the later upheaval its pattern of hope and justification. 'For France,' remarks a commentator, 'the Revolution began in America.'[81] Indeed Blake's *America*, it is generally agreed, is actually a poem about the French Revolution, and its statement that 'The King of England looking

[77] Doyle, 425.

[78] See René Sedillot, *Le Coût de la Révolution française* (Paris: Perrin, 1987). The cost was not alone in lives, as has so often been rehearsed (17,000 executed in the Terror, the masses slaughtered in the Vendée, 2,000,000 more dead in the Napoleonic wars that erupted from the Revolution), but in wealth, goods, and national treasure—irrecoverably so (the destruction of Cluny alone makes one wonder what benefit could justify it; it was in the Revolution that the word 'vandalism' was coined). And great though the cost was as just described, a recent historian suggests that it was probably still greater: 'It has been customary for scholars to be skeptical of the claims of pro-Vendéan historians' estimates of massive population loss, and Donald Greer's figure of forty thousand deaths for the whole period of the Terror in all departments has been accepted as plausible. It is not necessary, though, to accept Raymond Sécher's characterization of the massacres as "genocide" to see that a human catastrophe of colossal proportions occurred in the Vendée in the year II that demands a substantial upward revision of these fatalities. Jean-Clement Martin, whose book on the same subject is a model of reasoned research, gives a total loss for the Vendée, Loire-Inférieure and Maine-et-Loire of just under a quarter of a million. . . . Confronted with evidence of an apocalypse, it does historians no credit to look aside in the name of scholarly objectivity. . . . whatever claims on political virtue the French Revolution may make on the historian's sympathy, none can be so strong as to justify, to any degree, the unconscionable slaughters of the winter of the year II' (Schama, 791–2).

[79] Shelley, *Letters*, i. 504.

[80] *Hazlitt*, v. 161–3.

[81] Schama, 24.

westward trembles at the vision'[82] should in the reality of 1793 be
understood as that the King is looking eastward. But as Hazlitt insisted:

> Mr. Burke, the opponent of the American war—and Mr. Burke, the opponent of
> the French Revolution, are not the same person, but opposite persons—not
> opposite persons only, but deadly enemies. In the latter period, he abandoned not
> only all his practical conclusions, but all the principles on which they were
> founded. He proscribed all his former sentiments, denounced all his former
> friends, rejected and reviled all the maxims to which he had formerly appealed as
> incontestable. In the American war, he constantly spoke of the rights of the people
> as inherent, and inalienable: after the French Revolution, he began by treating
> them with the chicanery of a sophist, and ended by raving at them with the fury of a
> maniac. In the former case, he held out the duty of resistance to oppression, as the
> palladium, and only ultimate resource, of natural liberty: in the latter, he scouted,
> prejudiced, vilified and nicknamed, all resistance in the abstract, as a foul and
> unnatural union of rebellion and sacrilege.[83]

Notable in Hazlitt's rhetoric is the tendency to treat Burke's attitudes
not as representing a legitimate approach to different situations, but as
nothing less than a breakdown of character and personality: the two
Burkes are 'not the same person, but opposite persons—not opposite
persons only, but deadly enemies'. The charge may serve as an index to the
extreme depth of feeling, both for and against, generated by the French
Revolution and the political opinions connected with it. In France, former
friends sent one another to the guillotine (for a single instance,
Robespierre abandoned his boyhood friend and schoolmate, Camille
Desmoulins, to the tumbril[84]). When Friedrich Schlegel repudidated his
earlier Revolutionary sentiments, joined the Catholic Church, became an
aide to Metternich, and espoused reaction in a virtually feudal
commitment—so strongly, indeed, that even Metternich was appalled—
his brother Wilhelm would have nothing further to do with him, and the
estrangement persisted to the end of Friedrich's life.[85]

Chameleon-like change, in truth, characterized even those closest to the
revolution; for forces were there unleashed that tossed ordinary
consistencies around like confetti. Robespierre, though it now seems
difficult to credit, was, virtually at the same time that he became the
foremost expediter of institutionalized murder, an opponent of capital
punishment![86] On 31 May 1791, in fact, he delivered to the Assembly a

---

[82] *Blake*, 53.   [83] *Hazlitt*, xvi. 130.
[84] See e.g. Korngold, 292–9.   [85] Eichner, 110–11, 112–17.
[86] See e.g. Jordan, 54. For an impressive catalogue of Robespierre's many humane and
enlightened beliefs, see 51–4.

long and humane speech calling for the abolition of the death penalty.[87]
Again, the Girondin orator Vergniaud spoke with great eloquence against
the execution of Louis XVI, and for a time carried the day;[88] only shortly
afterward to reverse himself completely, mount the rostrum, and vote for
death![89] In England, the stalwart friend of Revolution, John Thelwall,
could look back on his own course of action and say unrepentantly, 'If it be
of any importance to my enemies to know that the opinions of the boy of
nineteen, were not the same as those of the man of thirty, let them make
what use they please of my apostasy.'[90] And for a final example, John
Horne Tooke, Thelwall's mentor, and the most respected of the English
Jacobins, after a few years accepted an income and became moderate and
even cautious in his opinions—for which Thelwall could never forgive
him:

I still, indeed, respect the politician, but I abhor the man. I venerate the sage, but I
abhor the treacherous friend. . . . If Horne Tooke values posthumous reputation
he has reason to wish my memoirs never should be resumed. It became not him to
assist in driving me from society—to attempt to draw a line between his politics
and mine; for though we differed in some points most assuredly, the principal
demarcation between us was, that I was open and sincere, he subtle and
hypocritical.[91]

Those who turned against the French Revolution were bitter against
the Revolution's betrayal of their hopes; those who for their part remained
loyal to Revolutionary commitment were bitter against the apostates. As
Henry Crabb Robinson said in 1816, 'Europe was rising morally and
intellectually when the French Revolution, after promising to advance the
world rapidly in its progress towards perfection, suddenly, by the woeful
turn it took, threw the age back in its expectations.'[92] But Hazlitt, as
Robinson also recalls on an occasion in 1815, 'became warm on politics and
declaimed against the friends of liberty for their apostasy. He attacked me,
but was at the same time civil.'[93] Hazlitt was not always civil. As Crabb
Robinson records of a later occasion in the same year:

debated with Hazlitt, in which I was . . . not successful, as far as the talent of the
disputants was involved, though Hazlitt was wrong as well as offensive in almost all

---

[87] See e.g. Matrat, 106.   [88] Lamartine, ii. 70–74.
[89] 'Au nom de Vergniaud, les conversations cessèrent, les regards se portèrent sur lui seul.
Il monta lentement les degrés de la tribune, se recueillit un moment, la paupière baissée sur
les yeux, comme un homme qui réfléchit pour la dernière fois avant d'agir; puis, d'une voix
sourde, et comme résistant dans son âme à la sensibilité qui criait en lui, il prononça: *La mort*'
(Lamartine, ii. 210).
[90] *Thelwall*, i. 47.   [91] Ibid. 352.
[92] *Robinson*, i. 183.   [93] Ibid. 161.

he said. . . . Hazlitt and myself once felt alike on politics, and now our hopes and
fears are directly opposed. Hazlitt retains all his hatred of kings and bad
governments, and believing them to be incorrigible, he from a principle of revenge,
rejoices that they are punished.[94]

Robinson's diary, indeed, provides the very feeling of the political
acrimony that pervaded daily encounters. To avail ourselves of a pastiche
of examples, in 1812 he notes of a conversation that 'On politics of the time
of the French Revolution [Wordsworth] also spoke and attempted, but
unsuccessfully, against Anthony Robinson's attacks, to defend Coleridge's
consistency'.[95] Again, in 1813: 'A chat with Godwin. He expressed himself
in the ordinary commonplace way against Coleridge's honesty, accusing
him of a vulgar hypocrisy of which I am sure he is not capable; though he
wants courage in company. And he also seemed ready to extend this
reproach to Wordsworth, but did not persist in it.'[96] On another occasion,
however, Godwin clearly did persist in it: 'Spent from ten till half-past
eleven in a call on Godwin. He was lately with Wordsworth, and after
spending a night at his house seems to have left him with very bitter and
hostile feelings. I believe political opinions alone kept them aloof.'[97] This
was in 1816. A year earlier Godwin had turned on Robinson himself: 'I
spent the evening by appointment with Godwin. The Taylors were there.
We talked politics and not very comfortably. Godwin and I all but
quarrelled. He was very rude, I very vehement, both a little angry, and
equally offensive to each other.'[98]

The Revolutionary loyalists were bitter about the apostates; the
apostates were bitter about the Revolution: but the apostates were serene
about their apostasy. As Robinson writes in 1812: 'On telling Burrell of my
former attachment to Godwin and the French writers, he observed that I
had taken exactly his course; he is now an anti-Jacobin like me, and I
should infer a Wordsworthian in politics.'[99]

Yet even the Revolutionary loyalists displayed variations in their
attitudes. Blake himself, though he never repudiated his radical
sentiments, changed very noticeably in his attitude towards the French
Revolution as such. *America* had presented an ecstatic view of political
freedom:

> Let the slave grinding at the mill, run out into the field:
> Let him look up into the heavens & laugh in the bright air:
> Let the inchained soul shut up in darkness and sighing
> Whose face has never seen a smile in thirty weary years:

[94] *Robinson*, i. 164.   [95] Ibid. 103.   [96] Ibid. 127.
[97] Ibid. 183.   [98] Ibid. 171.   [99] Ibid. 115.

Rise and look out, his chains are loose, his dungeon doors
    are open.
And let his wife and children return from the oppressors
    scourge;
They look behind at every step & believe it is a dream.
Singing. The Sun has left his blackness, & has found a
    fresher morning
And the fair Moon rejoices in the clear & cloudless night;
For Empire is no more, and now the Lion & Wolf shall
    cease.[100]

A decade or so later, however, this intoxication with explicitly realized political freedom had given way to something much more internalized. In his address 'To the Deists' that prefaces the third chapter of *Jerusalem*, Blake specifically says that though the 'Tyrant Pride & the Laws' of 'Babylon' shall 'shortly be destroyed', it will be 'with the Spiritual and not the Natural Sword'.[101] In line with this internalization, the Revolutionary principle Orc is entirely absent from *Jerusalem*, though this figure had dominated the earlier prophetic books, as in Enitharmon's call in *Europe a Prophecy*:

Arise O Orc and give our mountains joy of thy red light.

   .   .   .   .

But terrible Orc, when he held the morning in the east,
Shot from the heights of Enitharmon;
And in the vineyards of red France appear'd the light of his
    fury.[102]

Blake was not the only intellectual to mute and internalize his Revolutionary commitments. John Thelwall, though he started out with Tory sympathies, became a protégé of Horne Tooke and in the 1790s was perhaps the most resolute of all the English Jacobins. About 1800, however, he abandoned Revolutionary provocation for the teaching of elocution and the remedy of speech defects, veered back into politics about 1818, then back to elocution until his death in 1834.[103] William Cobbett,

[100] *America a Prophecy*, plate 6, lines 6–15, in *Blake*, 53.

[101] *Jerusalem*, plate 52, in *Blake*, 200.

[102] *Europe a Prophecy*, plates 14–15, in *Blake*, 66.

[103] Though Thelwall always remained true to his democratic principles, he did say later that 'I no longer consider a stubborn consistency to two or three political dogmas, however excellent in themelves, as sufficient to atone for all deficiencies of heart and morals' (*Thelwall*, i. 352). And he became uncomfortable about the name 'Jacobin'. By 1817 he would say that 'Nothing betrays the destitution of principle more completely than the sophistical use of really unmeaning, but yet popular cant nick names. Thus Jacobin (a term of no definable signification, but conjuring up in the minds of alarmist & zealous royalists every emotion that

the most influential political reformer of the early nineteenth-century—
'unquestionably the most powerful political writer of the present day', said
Hazlitt[104]—oscillated wildly in his commitments (Coleridge once spoke of
'the glaring contempt of all principle in Cobbett, as Writer and Man';[105]
Hazlitt charged him with 'outrageous inconsistency'[106]). For instance, he
reversed himself from vilification of Thomas Paine in the 1790s to
glorification twenty years later, and even reverentially brought Paine's
bones back with him from America, to the vast scorn of his enemies.[107]

But these changes were like the turn of leaves in a California autumn.
For flaming colour one must visit the apostates. Wordsworth, who was the
only one of the major English Romantic poets who actually saw the French
Revolution first hand, changed from enthusiastic support of libertarian
principles to an almost legendary reaction.[108] 'Most intensely did I rejoice
at the Counter Revolution,' wrote Robinson in 1816. 'I had also rejoiced
when a boy at the Revolution, and I am ashamed of neither sentiment'; but
in the same breath he says, 'I am sorry that Wordsworth cannot change
with the times. . . . Of the integrity of Wordsworth I have no doubt, as of
his genius I have an unbounded admiration; but I doubt the discretion and
wisdom of his latest political writings.'[109]

The year before, Robinson noted that one evening Godwin, constantly
bitter on this topic, was 'abusive on Wordsworth, Coleridge, Southey, and

---

belongs to the hatred of all crimes & enormities) is used by the consistent [Coleridge] in such
way as to be apparently applicable to all reformers & *incliners* to republicanism—in short to
all who are dissatisfied with the established systems of *legitimate* despotism' (Pollin, 93).
Coleridge, however, said much the same thing, earlier: 'What is a Jacobin? Perhaps the best
answer to this question would be, that it is a term of abuse, the convenient watchword of a
faction'—and he goes on to speak eloquently of various uses of the term (*Essays*, i. 365).

[104] *Hazlitt*, viii. 50.

[105] *Collected Letters*, iv. 903.

[106] *Hazlitt*, viii. 57.

[107] Even Hazlitt, though for the most part sympathetic to Cobbett, said that 'The only
time he ever grew romantic was in bringing over the relics of Mr. Thomas Paine with him
from America to go a progress with them through the disaffected districts. Scarce had he
landed in Liverpool when he left the bones of a great man to shift for themselves; and no
sooner did he arrive in London than he made a speech to disclaim all participation in the
political and theological sentiments of his late idol, and to place the whole stock of his
admiration and enthusiasm towards him to the account of his financial speculations, and of
his having predicted the fate of paper-money. . . . The fact is, he *ratted* from his own project.'
(*Hazlitt*, viii. 58.)

[108] For Wordsworth's early Revolutionary radicalism, see Roe, *Wordsworth*, chs. 2, 4, and
5. For his later Tory attitudes, see e.g. the sympathetic account by Michael Friedman, *The
Making of a Tory Humanist: William Wordsworth and the Idea of Community* (New York:
Columbia University Press, 1979).

[109] *Robinson*, i. 183–4.

Stoddart—for what he calls their political tergiversation'.[110] And yet such reversals were not restricted to a small group in England. For a single Continental instance, Schiller, who in his youth more influentially than almost any other figure idealized the doctrines of liberty, equality, and fraternity, in later years withdrew his support of the Revolution.[111]

Why was there so much 'political tergiversation'? Why did so many intellectuals change their opinions about the French Revolution and the complex of sentiments surrounding it? The answer is both large and simple. The Revolution was not one thing, but two things: it was one thing in prospect, another in actuality and retrospect. The difference in the two introduced all the variations in attitude that afflicted the best sensibilities of the time. 'Southey has changed', wrote Shelley in 1811: 'I shall see him soon, and I shall reproach him of his tergiversation—He to whom Bigotry Tyranny and Law was hateful has become the votary of these Idols, in a form the most disgusting.'[112]

In prospect, the Revolution partook almost of the idea of paradise, and it was no accident that millenarian doctrines flourished with particular intensity as it gathered to its climax.[113] The overthrow of the Bastille seemed almost the beginning of a new order of peace, wisdom, and brotherhood:

> For, lo! the dread Bastille,
> With all the chambers in its horrid towers,
> Fell to the ground:—by violence overthrown
> Of indignation; and with shouts that drowned
> The crash it made in falling! From the wreck
> A golden palace rose, or seemed to rise,
> The appointed seat of equitable law and mild
> Paternal sway.
>
>   .   .   .   .   .
>
>   Meanwhile, prophetic harps
> In every grove were ringing, 'War shall cease;
>
>   .   .   .   .   .
>
> Bring garlands, bring forth choicest flowers, to deck
> The tree of liberty.'[114]

This, it must be emphasized, was what young and ardent spirits all over Europe looked to the Revolution to be. It was not simply that

---

[110] Ibid. 177.
[111] Wiese, 70, 72, 335, 345–7, 456–9, 808.
[112] Shelley, *Letters*, i. 208.
[113] See e.g. Paley, 120–36.
[114] Wordsworth, *Poems*, v. 100–1 (*The Excursion*, bk. iii, lines 709–26).

> Bliss was it in that dawn to be alive,
> But to be young was very Heaven![115]

but that 'the whole Earth, | The beauty wore of promise—'. It almost argued lack of soul not to participate in the great upsurge of hope. The cause was

> Good, pure, which no one could stand up against
> Who was not lost, abandoned, selfish, proud,
> Mean, miserable, wilfully depraved,
> Hater perverse of equity and truth.[116]

Of special significance is the fact that the Revolution, as idealistic focus, did not suddenly burst upon the scene on 14 July, 1789. That was merely the date at which it opened to full bloom. But the plant had been growing for years. Michelet, indeed, cutomarily spoke of it as an event that had been centuries in the coming, the rough beast, as it were, slouching towards Bethlehem. Thus when Hegel enrolled at the Tübingen Stift in 1788, his private readings were not devoted to the reigning king of philosophy, Kant, but towards the revolutionary prime-mover, Rousseau. With this as preamble, Hegel's circle of students in the spring of 1791 went up into a meadow outside of Tübingen one Sunday morning, and imitating the great events in France, put up a liberty tree. Then, young pedants that they were, they wrote 'Vive la liberté' and 'Vive Jean-Jacques' in one another's albums.[117] And we all know the Revolutionary direction of *Le Nozze di Figaro* and the subversive play by Beaumarchais on which it was based.

But the tree of liberty had been growing long before. In 1762, for instance, Rousseau wrote in his *Émile* that

You trust in the present order of society without thinking that this order is subject to inevitable revolutions. . . . The nobles become commoners, the rich become poor, the monarch becomes subject. . . . We are approaching a state of crisis and the age of revolutions. . . . I hold it to be impossible that the great monarchies of Europe still have long to last.[118]

In the lower branches, the seventeenth-century levellers and diggers discussed in Christopher Hill's studies were already mature in Revolu-

---

[115] Wordsworth, *Prelude*, 397 (bk. xi (1850), lines 108–9).
[116] Ibid. 327 (bk. ix (1850), lines 284–7).
[117] Wiedmann, 20–1.
[118] Rousseau, iv. 468.

tionary ideology.[119] Still further down the trunk, a century earlier, the ever-subversive Rabelais had Pantagruel say of the portentous King Anarche: 'These accursed kings are nothing but dolts. They know nothing, and they're good for nothing except harming their poor subjects, and troubling the whole world with wars, for their wicked and detestable pleasure. I mean to put him to a trade, and make him a hawker of green sauce.'[120]

The very roots of that vast tree of liberty, indeed, twine round the Peasants Revolt of 1381, and the figures associated with that revolution, Wat Tyler, Jack Straw, and John Ball, no less than Danton, Marat, and Robespierre in the French Revolution, were moved to action by the great and ever-renewed question, why should human hierarchies be allowed to perpetuate the exploitation of the many for the benefit of the few? 'When Adam delved and Eve span, | Who was then a gentleman?'[121] John Ball's speech to the peasants, as recorded by Froissart, seems forever modern:

Good people, things cannot go right in England and never will, until goods are held in common and there are no more villeins and gentlefolk, but we are all one and the same. In what way are those whom we call lords greater masters than ourselves? How have they deserved it? Why do they hold us in bondage? If we all spring from a single father and mother, Adam and Eve, how can they claim or prove that they are lords more than us, except by making us produce and grow the wealth which they spend? They are clad in velvet and camlet lined with squirrel and ermine, while we go dressed in coarse cloth. They have the wines, the spices and the good bread: we have the rye, the husks and the straw, and we drink water. They have shelter and ease in their fine manors, and we have hardship and toil, the wind and the rain in the fields. And from us must come, from our labour, the things which keep them in luxury. We are called serfs. . . . If we go in good earnest and all together, very many people who are called serfs and are held in subjection will follow us to get their freedom.[122]

That was the aspiration of the Revolution seen in prospect. As Wordsworth asks, 'What temper at the prospect did not wake | To

---

[119] See Christopher Hill, *The World Turned Upside Down: Radical Ideas during the English Revolution* (New York: Viking Press, 1972) and *Milton and the English Revolution* (New York: Viking Press, 1978).

[120] Rabelais, 304.

[121] This 'momentous couplet' provided the text for John Ball's speeech delivered 13 June 1381. For a magnificently learned but concise discussion of the couplet and its evocation over many years, and in many languages, see Albert B. Friedman, '"When Adam Delved . . .": Contexts of an Historic Proverb', *Harvard Studies in English*, ed. L. Benson, No. 5 (1974), 213–30.

[122] Froissart, 212.

happiness unthought of? The inert | Were roused, and lively natures rapt away!'[123] The ardent Schiller, in his school days, was, as a scholar says,

fascinated by Rousseau's glowing pictures of 'nature,' and shared all his burning scorn for despotism and conventionality. Why had man been endowed with powers if all of them were not to be freely exercised? What reason could there be in the nature of things for the advantages heaped on one class and denied to another? And was it not the clear duty of humanity to destroy institutions and customs that had been handed down from degenerate ancestors, and to return to primitive simplicity and happiness?[124]

Schiller's youthful and sensational play of 1781, *The Robbers*, incorporated these burning ideals. 'It is past one o'clock in the morning,' wrote Coleridge to Southey in November 1794,

—I sate down at twelve o'clock to read the 'Robbers' of Schiller—I had read chill and trembling until I came to the part where Moor fires a pistol over the Robbers who are asleep—I could read no more—My God! Southey! Who is this Schiller? This Convulser of the Heart? . . . Upon my Soul, I write to you because I am frightened—I had better go to Bed. Why have we ever called Milton sublime?[125]

Others beside Coleridge fell under the spell of Schiller's play. 'The Robbers was the first play I ever read,' said Hazlitt, 'and the effect it produced upon me was the greatest. It stunned me like a blow.'[126] As Heine summed up, 'Schiller wrote for the great ideas of the Revolution; he destroyed the Bastille of the intellect; he aided in building the temple of freedom.'[127] The National Assembly of the Revolution even went so far as to make Schiller an honorary citizen of France; the diploma was signed by Danton and accompanied by a letter from Roland.

In general, as a recent historian notes, the onset of the Revolution was greeted by profound excitement and the most widespread acclaim:

The news was romantic and thrilling. All over Europe people thronged bookshops and reading rooms, clamouring for the latest information. 'I do not know where to turn,' wrote a German lady, 'for the papers contain such great and splendid news that I am hot from reading.' The leaders of German literary life were almost unanimous in welcoming the events in France. Philosophers like Kant and Herder, poets like Klopstock, Hölderlin, and Wieland were enraptured by what they heard. . . . Richer and more adventurous Germans took the road to Paris to observe the new liberty at first hand, and one at least became notorious there— Anacharsis Clootz, a wealthy Prussian nobleman who had left France in 1785

[123] Wordsworth, *Prelude*, 397 (bk. xi (1850), lines 122–4). [124] Sime, 21.
[125] *Collected Letters*, i. 122. [126] *Hazlitt*, vi. 362.
[127] *Heine*, iii. 393.

vowing never to return until the Bastille had fallen. He was in Sicily when it did, and hurried back to throw himself into the democratic politics he had hitherto only dreamed of. The impact was similar among the intellectuals of Italy, who rejoiced to see what had seemed the most well established of states shattered by popular uprising and then rededicating itself to national reform. . . . As far away as Stockholm the news from France was the talk of the salons and cafés. 'Tell me,' wrote the young Swedish poet Kellgren to his brother, 'was there ever anything more sublime in History, even in Rome or Greece? I wept like a child, like a man, at the story of this great victory.'[128]

But that was the Revolution in prospect. At length there supervened the Revolution in retrospect, and that was a different entity for everyone. The zealots, as Wordsworth said, were 'compelled to exclaim │ As Brutus did to Virtue, "Liberty, │ I worshipped thee, and find thee but a Shade!" '[129] Even Hazlitt, who never gave up his libertarian commitments, nevertheless records the change from paradisal dawn to disappointment. He speaks of

that bright dream of our youth; that glad dawn of the day-star of liberty; that spring-time of the world, in which the hopes and expectations of the human race seemed opening in the same gay career with our own; when France called her children to partake her equal blessings beneath her laughing skies; when the stranger was met in all her villages with dance and festive songs, in celebration of a new and golden era.

But then, as Hazlitt goes on to lament,

The dawn of that day was suddenly overcast; that season of hope is past; it is fled with the other dreams of our youth, which we cannot recal, but has left behind it traces, which are not to be effaced by Birth-day and Thanks-giving Odes, or the chaunting of *Te Deums* in all the churches of Christendom. To those hopes, eternal regrets are due.[130]

Hazlitt was nostalgic for the golden days of Revolutionary prospect and melancholy at the onset of reaction. Others, however, in Revolutionary retrospect felt betrayed, and responded with revulsion rather than nostalgia. Burke's great attack of 1790 preceded the events that made him a true prophet: the many thousands of state murders undertaken in the name of John Ball's ideal.[131] After the execution of Louis XVI, Schiller

---

[128] Doyle, 160.

[129] Wordsworth, *Poems*, v. 102 (*The Excursion*, bk. iii, lines 775–7).

[130] *Hazlitt*, iv. 119–20.

[131] For the subsequent Terror, see e.g. M. Mortimer-Ternaux, *Histoire de la Terreur 1792–1794* (Paris: Michel Lévy, 1862–81), 8 vols.; Wilfred B. Kerr, *The Reign of Terror*

wrote to his friend Körner: 'for fourteen days I have been unable to look at
a newspaper—these butchers disgust me so!'[132] He turned his back on the
Revolution forever. He did not, like Friedrich Schlegel, retreat to
reactionary feudalism and religious ultra-montanism. He always maintained his ideals of human freedom and brotherhood; but he separated
them henceforth from the French Revolution as a means of achieving such
advancement. As he says at the end of a poem that was occasioned by the
advent of the new century, 'Freedom exists only in the realm of
dream | And beauty blooms only in song.'[133]

So, too, with others. Wordsworth, who had earlier proudly become 'a
patriot; and my heart was all | Given to the people, and my love was
theirs', now felt 'That he, who would sow death, reaps death, or
worse, | And can reap nothing better.' Earlier he had said that 'in the
People was my trust', but now he confessed to a 'loss of confidence in social
man'. The recognition of 'Lamentable crimes', of 'dire work | Of
massacre,' began to erode his commitment to 'arguments of civil polity'.
'O Friend!', he exclaims to Coleridge, 'It was a lamentable time for
man.'[134] Thenceforth his social views began to move towards the ideal of a
slow and natural evolution of human betterment, and towards a hardening
abhorrence of any and all state intervention in this process. He even
threatened to leave the country if the Reform Bill of 1832 were enacted!

Thus the split between the Revolution in prospect and the Revolution
in retrospect introduced a profound instability into the opinions of those
who experienced both entities masquerading under a single name.
Southey in his youth wrote a Jacobin play called *Wat Tyler*, in which he
expressed the rejection of kingship that became the insignia of all
Revolutionary sentiment: 'King,' exclaims Tyler, 'is all this just? | The
hour of retribution is at hand, | And tyrants tremble—mark me, King of
England.'[135] This is quite worthy to occupy a place of honour besides
Blake's alleged remark to the soldier Scholfield: 'damn the King and
Country, his Subjects and all you Soldiers are sold for Slaves.'[136] It accords

1793–4 (Toronto: University of Toronto Press, 1927); R. R. Palmer, *Twelve Who Ruled: The
Year of the Terror in the French Revolution* (Princeton, NJ: Princeton University Press,
1941). See also Colin Lucas, *The Structure of the Terror: The Example of Javogues and the
Loire* (London: Oxford University Press, 1973) for a detailed study of extreme terrorist
activity in one of the provinces.

[132] Schiller, *Letters*, 281.

[133] *Schiller*, i. 823.

[134] Wordsworth, *Prelude* (1850), 319, 395, 361, 395, 379 (bk. ix, lines 123–4; bk. xi, lines
67–8; bk. x, lines 41–3; bk. xi, line 77; bk. x, lines 383–4).

[135] Southey, ii. 43.   [136] Blake, *Life*, 147–9.

too with Shelley's proclamation in the Preface to *Hellas*: 'This is the age of the war of the oppressed against the oppressors, and every one of those ringleaders of the privileged gangs of murderers and swindlers, called Sovereigns, look to each other for aid against the common enemy and suspend their mutual jealousies in the presence of a mightier fear.'[137] The compatibility of all these sentiments with Jacobin doctrine is evident, as we see by considering the 26th and last proposition of Robespierre's own *Declaration of the Rights of Man*: 'Kings, aristocrats, tyrants of every description, are slaves in revolt against the sovereign of the earth, which is the *human race*, and against the legislator of the universe, which is *Nature*.'[138]

Shelley, however, had never experienced the French Revolution in its two forms, nor in truth had the consistently libertarian Hazlitt. Shelley therefore sounded in 1820 much as Thelwall sounded in 1791, and Hazlitt could heap scorn on Southey's political tergiversation. 'Poor Bob Southey! How they laugh at him!'[139] This was in 1817, before Byron's immortal riposte, *The Vision of Judgment*, showed them how really to laugh at the hapless poet-laureate. Hazlitt had said that 'Mr. Southey's Muse is confessedly not a vestal; but then she is what is much better, a Magdalen.'[140] And Southey's *A Vision of Judgment*, written in 1821 as laureate's lament for the death of George III, the erstwhile tyrant of *Wat Tyler*, was maudlin work in all senses. Summing it up in 1825, in *The Spirit of the Age*, Hazlitt judged that Southey was 'anomalous, incalculable, eccentric, from youth to age (the *Wat Tyler* and the *Vision of Judgment* are the Alpha and Omega of his disjointed career)'.[141]

But though Southey elicited more scorn than any other of the figures who changed their minds about the Revolution, his career is none the less a pattern for the political vicissitudes of the time. *Wat Tyler* was published in 1817 without Southey's permission and to his great embarrassment. 'Mr. Southey', said Hazlitt, 'calls the person who published "Wat Tyler" "a skulking scoundrel," . . . and says that it was published, "for the avowed purpose of insulting him, and with the hope of injuring him if possible."' Hazlitt went on to say that 'Mr. Southey is not a man to hear reason at any time of his life. He thinks his change of opinion is owing to an

[137] *Shelley*, iii. 9.

[138] *Robespierre*, ii. 140.

[139] *Hazlitt*, vii. 179. Again, 'Many people laugh at him, some may blush for him, but nobody envies him' (p. 89).

[140] Ibid. 178.

[141] Ibid. xi. 82.

increase of knowledge, because he has in fact no idea of any progress in intellect but exchanging one error for another.'[142]

Yet we see Southey in quite a different and more complex light in a diary entry by Robinson on 2 May 1817:

I had a call from Robert Southey the laureate. I had a pleasant chat and a short walk with him. Southey spoke gaily of his *Wat Tyler*. He understood thirty-six thousand copies had been printed. He was not aware how popular he was when he came to town. He did not appear to feel any shame or regret at having written the piece at so early an age as twenty. He wrote the drama in three [months], anno 1794. We spoke of his *Letter to W. Smith* [where Southey had defended himself against the imputation of political apostasy], of which I thought and spoke favourably. I did not blame Southey, but commended him for asserting the right of all men, who are wiser at forty than at twenty years of age, to act on such superiority of wisdom. 'I only wish,' I added, 'that you had not appeared to have forgotten some political truths you had been early impressed with. . . .' Southey said: 'I spoke of the present time only. I am still a friend to reform.'[143]

So Southey, interestingly enough, regarded himself as constant in his opinions; it was the Revolution itself that had proved disjointed. Certainly Southey's life in all other respects was one of enormous consistency and of a constancy to personal commitments that verged on the heroic.

Coleridge, who had known Southey in both youth and later years, wrote two letters to the *Courier* in March, 1817, vindicating him from the charge of political apostasy (he actually wrote four, two of which were published; those two were scathingly criticized by Hazlitt).[144] The vindicating letters might well have served as vindications of their author as well. For like Southey, like Wordsworth, Coleridge too veered from sympathy with the ideals of the Revolution to sympathy with the ideals of the established order. Indeed, though Southey was the most ridiculed apostate in his own time, and though Wordsworth changed more radically than either,[145] Coleridge has in our own day become the symbol *par excellence* of political apostasy.

---

[142] *Hazlitt*, xi. 82.   [143] *Robinson*, i. 206.

[144] *Essays*, ii. 449–60; *Hazlitt*, vii. 176–86. Hazlitt says wickedly that 'Instead of applying for an injunction against *Wat Tyler*, Mr. Southey would do well to apply for an injunction against Mr. Coleridge, who has undertaken his defence in *The Courier*' (vii. 176).

[145] Though E. P. Thompson, engrossingly intent on Coleridge's alleged apostasy, fails to charge Wordsworth in the same way, Byron, in 1818, is less benign; he refers to Wordsworth's place 'at Lord Lonsdale's table, where this poetical charlatan and political parasite licks up the crumbs with a hardened alacrity; the converted Jacobin having long subsided into the clownish sycophant of the worst prejudices of the aristocracy.' (Note to the 'Dedication' of *Don Juan*.) Likewise, in the 'Preface' to *Don Juan*, Byron calls Southey 'this Pantosocratic apostle of Apostasy'.

Not everyone even in his day liked the apparent change. On the appearance of the *Biographia Literaria*, Thelwall annotated a copy with the comment that at Stowey in 1797 'I visited and found him a decided Leveller—abusing the democrats for moderation.' Again, Thelwall remembered in 1817 that Coleridge had in 1797 been 'a down right zealous leveller', actually 'a man of blood' from the 'violence and sanguinary tendency of some of these doctrines'.[146] (Incidentally, in view of E. P. Thompson's charge about Coleridge's 'voracious appetite for hatreds', it is interesting to compare Coleridge's own later statement about Thelwall, in a lecture reported in 1813. 'A friend of the Lecturer (Mr. Thelwall) at one time was called a traitor, but though he did not deserve that appellation, he was doubtless a mistaken man: it was a period when men of all ranks, tailors and mechanics of various descriptions, thought they had a *call* for preaching politics, as Saints had a *call* for preaching the Gospel.'[147] Although the report may sound somewhat patronizing, it hardly seems to exhibit a 'voracious appetite for hatreds'. Coleridge, as De Quincey observes, 'had no real unkindness in his heart towards any human being'.[148]

Indeed, in the interests of historical justice, it may be well to summon still other testimony in mitigation of Thompson's singular statement about Coleridge's 'voracious appetite for hatreds'. In 1810 Basil Montagu, through some indiscreet remarks, precipitated a lifelong rupture in the ardent friendship of Coleridge and Wordsworth; and Coleridge, as might be supposed, for quite a while after referred to Montagu in the bitterest terms. They eventually reconciled, however, and Montagu became a still closer friend; not only that, but in 1834, in his edition of Bacon, Montagu paid tribute to Coleridge in this way: 'Wise as the serpent, gall-less as the dove, pious and pure of heart, tender, affectionate, and forgiving, this, and more than this, I can say, after the trial of forty years, was my friend and instructor, Samuel Taylor Coleridge.'[149]

So much for Montagu's own experience of Coleridge's 'voracious appetite for hatreds'. And Montagu was not the only friend who referred to Coleridge in such terms. Hyman Hurwitz, Coleridge's mentor in rabbinical studies, in 1828 spoke of Coleridge in public as 'a gentleman whom I am both happy and proud to call my friend—and where is the man who knowing his vast learning, genuine piety, and goodness of heart, that would not be proud of his friendship!'[150] And Robinson in 1812 notes that

[146] Pollin, 82, 81.
[148] *De Quincey*, ii. 209.
[150] Ibid. vi. 775 n.
[147] *Lectures 1808–1819*, i. 586.
[149] *Collected Letters*, v. 493 n.

Wordsworth, even after his rupture with Coleridge, 'praised' Coleridge's 'goodness of heart'.)[151]

With respect, again, to Thelwall's possible inaccuracy in his recollections, one must insist that Coleridge was never 'a man of blood'. Thelwall says that letters from Coleridge '(which I believe I yet have)' will bear out the 'sanguinary tendency' of some of Coleridge's doctrines. Yet Richard Holmes quietly points out that 'We do have those letters, but they do not bear Thelwall out'.[152] Of course it might be argued that the letters we have were not the ones to which Thelwall referred. But it seems far more likely that Thelwall simply misconstrued what Coleridge thought. Coleridge may have said many things in the glow and effervescence of conversation, but in the whole course of his writings, both public and private, nothing bears out the contention that he was a man of blood. After all, in his first political writing, he said, with great power and point—and the present discourse shall continually advert to the statement—that 'A system of fundamental Reform will scarcely be effected by massacres mechanized into Revolution.'[153] Can that be a statement issuing from a Jacobin, 'a man of blood'? And Coleridge said, also in 1795,

The filial and paternal affections discipline the heart and prepare it for that blessed state of perfection in which all our Passions are to be absorbed in the Love of God. For if we love not our friends and Parents whom we have seen—how can we love our universal Friend and . . . Parent whom we have not seen? Jesus was a Son, and he cast the Eye of Tenderness and careful regard on his Mother Mary, even while agonizing on the Cross. Jesus was a Friend, and he wept at the Tomb of Lazarus. Jesus was the friend of the whole human Race . . . Jesus knew our Nature—and that expands like the circles of a Lake—the Love of our Friends, parents and neighbours lead[s] us to the love of our Country to the love of all Mankind.[154]

Can that be a statement issuing from 'a man of blood?' And Nicholas Roe points out that the youthful Coleridge, with respect to Godwin's views, 'would also have insisted that love and friendship were the means to human regeneration'.[155] Is that a position characteristic of 'a man of blood'?

We may infer that the doctrines imputed to Coleridge by Thelwall, which were extensions of those of Thelwall himself, had been ones Thelwall was delighted to hear Coleridge express. In March 1798, Thelwall had written to Dr Crompton and said that 'Mount him [Coleridge] upon his darling hobby horse, "the republic of God's own

---

[151] *Robinson*, i. 80.					[152] Holmes, *Coleridge*, 158 n.
[153] *Lectures 1795*, 48.					[154] Ibid. 162–3.
[155] Roe, *Wordsworth*, 115.

making," & away he goes like hey go mad, spattering & splashing thro'
thick and thin & scattering more *levelling* sedition, & constructive treason,
than poor *Gilly* [that is, Gilbert Wakefield] or myself ever dreamt of'.[156]
But against Thelwall's version of Coleridge, who mirrored Thelwall so
satisfactorily, we may place Coleridge's own statement in a letter to Josiah
Wade of August 1797. The statement confutes, explicitly and absolutely,
everything that Thelwall thought:

John Thelwall is a very warm hearted honest man—and disagreeing, as we do, on
almost every point of religion, of morals, of politics, and of philosophy; we like
each other uncommonly well. . . . *Energetic activity*, of *mind* and of *heart*, is his
Master-feature. He is prompt to *conceive*, and still prompter to *execute*—. But I
think, that he is deficient in that *patience* of mind, which can look *intensely* and
frequently at the *same subject*. He believes and disbelieves with impassioned
confidence—I wish to see him *doubting* and *doubting*. However, he is the man for
action—he is intrepid, eloquent, and—honest.—Perhaps the only *acting* Democrat, that *is* honest for the *Patriots* are ragged cattle—a most execrable herd—
arrogant because they are ignorant, and boastful of the strength of reason, because
they have never tried it enough to know its *weakness*.[157]

Along with the dismissal here of the '*Patriots*'—presumably the French
Jacobins and their hard-line English supporters—as 'a most execrable
herd', there is the pointed avowal of disagreement with Thelwall:
'disagreeing, as we do, on almost every point of religion, of morals, of
politics, and of philosophy; we like each other uncommonly well'.[158]

It might be instructive to consider the implication of the flat
disagreement of Coleridge's statement at the very time, which is certainly
friendly and admiring enough with respect to Thelwall, and Thelwall's
own memories.[159] The implication can only be that there was a difference
between what Coleridge thought, and what friends perceived him to think.
We know that Coleridge was universally considered the greatest talker of
that, or possibly any other age. 'If Mr. Coleridge,' said Hazlitt in 1825,
'had not been the most impressive talker of his age, he would probably
have been the finest writer; but he lays down his pen to make sure of an

---

[156] Quoted in Thompson, 162; also Hanson, 242.
[157] *Collected Letters*, i. 339.
[158] In 1818 Coleridge recalled that he told Thelwall what 'he was so unwilling to
believe—viz. that alike on the grounds of Taste, Morals, Politics, and Religion, he and I had
no one point of coincidence' (*Collected Letters*, iv. 880).
[159] Memories of course can play tricks after a certain amount of time has passed. For
instance, in 1817 Thelwall at one point, when Coleridge refers to Fichte as a disciple of Kant,
recalls some details about Fichte. But then he says, 'P. S. In the shadowy recollections of past
times I have jumbled names—It was Knitch not Fichte—to whom the facts in the above note
have reference' (Pollin, p. 92).

auditor, and mortgages the admiration of posterity for the stare of an idler.'[160] Other testimonials abound.

We know, too, that there was a difference between Coleridge's talk in later years and his talk as a youth, the later talk being more like the seamless and droning flow immortalized in Carlyle's description,[161] the earlier talk being something more dazzling and dynamic. By 1798, in the words of Leslie Stephen, 'Coleridge had not only given proofs of astonishing power, but had won what was even more valuable, the true sympathy and cordial affection of young men who were the distinct leaders of the next generation.'[162] We can only shake our heads in perplexity as to how Coleridge so unerringly collected future famous men as his friends; we can perhaps hope to understand, however, how he managed to win their 'true sympathy and cordial affection'. By being a hypocrite? That can hardly be the case; the intellectual calibre of his interlocutors of itself refutes such a conclusion. Rather it was by mirroring, in his matchless, his truly unique conversational flow, their own deepest aspirations. Thelwall himself reported that Coleridge was 'one of the most extraordinary Geniuses & finest scholars of the age'.[163] The scarcely less radical Hazlitt, for his part, said that Coleridge was 'the only person I ever knew who answered to the idea of a man of genius'.[164]

As to why Coleridge gave himself so wholly to the mirroring of his friends' deepest and dearest aspirations, we surely find the answer in his lifelong sense of having been abandoned in his childhood. As he explained to Sir George Beaumont in 1803, 'Who then remained to listen to me? to be kind to me? to be my friends? . . . These offices of Love the Democrats only performed to me; my own family, bigots from Ignorance, remained wilfully ignorant from Bigotry.' Forever seeking the approval of surrogate brothers, Coleridge expended heroic effort in mirroring their hopes. 'With an ebullient Fancy,' he remembers, 'a flowing Utterance, a light & dancing Heart, & a disposition to catch fire by the very rapidity of my own motion, & to speak vehemently from mere verbal associations . . . I aided the Jacobins, by witty sarcasms & subtle reasonings & declamations full of genuine feeling against all Rulers & against all established Forms.'[165]

E. P. Thompson finds these explanations of 1803 particularly indicative of Coleridge's chameleon-like lack of principle. Perhaps we ourselves should regard them rather as extraordinarily perceptive self-analysis. Certainly they were no change of opinions uttered specifically for the

---

[160] *Hazlitt*, xi. 30.   [161] *Carlyle*, xi. 55–8.
[162] *Stephen*, iii. 324.   [163] Quoted in Thompson, 159.
[164] *Hazlitt*, v. 167.   [165] *Collected Letters*, ii. 1000–1.

benefit of Sir George Beaumont. For instance, in 1801, two years before the explanation to Beaumont, Wordsworth wrote to John Taylor that

Mr Coleridge and I had a long conversation [probably at Keswick on March 25] upon what you with great propriety call jacobinical pathos; and I can assure you that he deeply regretted that he had ever written a single word of that character, or given, directly or indirectly, any encouragement whatever to such writings; which he condemned as arguing both want of genius and of knowledge: he pointed out as worthy of the severest reprehension, the conduct of those writers who seem to estimate their power of exciting sorrow for suffering humanity, by the quantity of hatred and revenge which they are able to pour into the hearts of their Readers. Pity, we agreed, is a sacred thing, that cannot, and will not be prophaned. Mr C is as deeply convinced as myself that the human heart can never be moved to any salutary purposes in this way; and that they who attempt to give it such movements are poisoners of its best feelings. They are bad poets, and misguided men.[166]

Wordsworth, who of course knew Coleridge far better than is possible for E. P. Thompson, apparently found nothing chameleon-like in these sentiments; indeed, on the very same day, 9 April, that this letter was written, another one, to Thomas Poole, said that Coleridge 'is a great man, and if God grant him life will do great things'.[167]

In any event, Coleridge mirrored Thelwall's aspirations, as he had those of Hazlitt, as he had those of Southey. His first letter to Southey, in July 1794, mirrors Southey's ardent political radicalism, although no earlier letter of Coleridge's mentions anything at all of such matters. But to Southey he writes at the close, 'Farewell, sturdy Republican!', and in the body of the letter he has said that 'The Cockatrice is a foul Dragon with a *crown* on its head'; he has referred to 'the unfeeling Remarks, which the lingering Remains of Aristocracy occasionally prompt'; and he has said— we may well suspect the event to be an imaginary one constructed for purposes of illustration—'It is *wrong*, Southey! for a little Girl with a half famished sickly Baby in her arms to put her head in at the window of an Inn—"Pray give me a bit of Bread and Meat"! from a Party dining on Lamb, Green Pease & Sallad.'[168] Scant wonder that Southey in 1809, after Coleridge in *The Friend* had defied his 'worst enemy to shew, in any of my few writings, the least bias of Irreligion, Immorality, or Jacobinism',[169] irritably commented: 'It is worse than folly, for if he was not a Jacobine, in the common acceptation of the name, I wonder who the Devil was. I am sure I was, am still, and ever more shall be. I am sure that he wrote a

[166] *Early Years*, 325–6.   [167] Ibid. 324.
[168] *Collected Letters*, i. 83–4.   [169] *Friend*, ii. 26.

flaming panegyric of Tom Paine, and that I delivered it in one of my lectures.'[170]

Southey's ardent 'Jacobinism' of the early 1790s may have seemed wholly mirrored in Coleridge's language and action (and how truly it was a mirroring can be seen in a situation where Coleridge's own anti-Jacobin opinion is joined to, and softened by, an acquiescence in Southey's pro-Jacobin opinion. Speaking in August 1794, of 'Poor Robespierre!', Southey notes that 'Coleridge says "he was a man whose great bad actions cast a dis [. . .] lustre over his name." He is now inclined to think with me that the [. . .] of a man so situated must not be judged by common laws, that Robespierre was the benefactor of mankind and that we should lament his death as the greatest misfortune Europe could have sustained"[171]). How successful Coleridge's tactic of mirroring was, in winning the esteem he coveted, may be judged from Southey's introducing him, a fortnight later, to a friend: 'Coleridge brings this. As a man of the first genius and abilities, and as my friend you will welcome him.'[172] To another friend, he wrote: 'Coleridge left me yesterday. It was like the losing a limb to part with him.'[173]

Still more dramatic examples of Coleridge's unique ability to mesmerize his friends by mirroring their most cherished opinions can be supplied from elsewhere. The enthusiastic 'Jacobin' Southey found Coleridge an enthusiastic Jacobin. The nature-loving Wordsworth, however, found him an enthusiast for nature, who had 'sought | The truth in solitude, and thou art one, | The most intense of Nature's worshippers; | In many things my brother, chiefly here | In this my deep devotion'.[174] The joking Lamb, still again, found him a jokester: '*Summer*, as my friend Coleridge waggishly writes, has set in with its usual severity.'[175]

And always there was the awe before Coleridge's conversational powers. On an occasion in 1823, when Lamb said he 'dined in Parnassus, with Wordsworth, Coleridge, Rogers, and Tom Moore—half the Poetry of England constellated and clustered in Gloster Place!', Coleridge was at the top of his form. 'Coleridge was in his finest vein of talk, had all the talk, and let 'em talk as evilly as they do of the envy of Poets, I am sure not one there but was content to be nothing but a listener. The Muses were dumb,

[170] Southey, *New Letters*, i. 511.
[171] Ibid. 72–3.
[172] Ibid. 74.
[173] Ibid. 71.
[174] Wordsworth, *Prelude*, 90 (bk. ii (1805), lines 475–9).
[175] Lamb, *Letters*, iii. 44.

while Apollo lectured on his and their fine Art.'[176] Significantly, to poets Coleridge talked about poetry—'his and their fine Art'.

But perhaps Coleridge's mirroring powers are shown in most instructive relief in his comments on Swedenborg. Coleridge mentions Swedenborg infrequently in his correspondence, although he knew Swedenborgian thought extremely well. Benjamin Kurtz, who has investigated the matter, shows that Coleridge had read at least eleven volumes of Swedenborg's works, which means that he knew the seer as well as or better than Blake himself did.[177] On certain occasions, however, despite his usual silence about Swedenborg, Coleridge talks about the Swedish thinker so volubly, knowledgeably, and enthusiastically as almost to seem a Swedenborgian. Remarkably, these occasions, except when they appear in private entries in his notebooks, are nearly always in letters to a single person, Charles Tulk.[178] Who was Charles Tulk? A wealthy Swedenborgian, whose father had been a Swedenborgian before him. The younger Tulk, with John Flaxman, formed the society for publishing Swedenborg's works and devoted much of his own later writing to elucidating the underlying rationalism of Swedenborg's doctrines. To Tulk, Coleridge seemed a Swedenborgian adept. But Coleridge did not talk of Swedenborg in his letters to Thelwall, or those to Southey, or those to Wordsworth.

So too with Coleridge's alleged Jacobinism. Republican enthusiasm mirrored the aspirations of those who testified to its reality. It did not, however, by that fact reflect the intricacy of what Coleridge really thought. That it was, moreover, very possible for those who heard Coleridge to be mistaken about what he stood for may be shown from a significant example. It is almost a truism that Coleridge's deepest and most constant thoughts were directed towards the Christian religion, from the Unitarianism of the 1790s to the Trinitarianism of his final position. As Walter Jackson Bate, to name only one of many scholarly investigators, concludes: 'If we wish to understand and assess Coleridge's career, we must do so at least partly in terms of what mattered most to him: the hope that his life, whatever its failings, might ultimately be religious in shape, intention, meaning.'[179] As Coleridge himself said, 'I can truly affirm of myself, that my studies have been profitable and availing to me only so far, as I have endeavoured to use all my other knowledge as a glass enabling me to receive more light in a wider field of vision from the word of God.'[180]

---

[176] Ibid. ii. 376–7.   [177] Kurtz, 201.
[178] *Collected Letters*, iv. 835, 837; v. 9–10, 17–19, 86–91, 136–8.
[179] Bate, 213.   [180] *Lay Sermons*, 70.

That is the simple and ineluctable truth of Coleridge's career. And yet Henry Crabb Robinson says of Coleridge in 1812:

He afterward entered into a long series of observations on the Trinity, from which I could learn only that he is very desirous to be orthodox. . . . Coleridge is very desirous to be both a refined and subtle philosopher and metaphysician, and at the same time to conform with the people in its religion. That this desire is consciously excited by any unworthy suggestions, or that he is grossly insincere in any of his assertions, I do not believe; but I believe there is in him much self-deception.[181]

How utterly wrong Robinson was can be seen not only from Coleridge's deportment at the time of his death, but from an intense and momentary comment such as this: 'I regard my very life, as less vital to me than my faith as a follower of the suffering Messiah!'[182]

It is fascinating to consider how antithetical Robinson's eyewitness but totally mistaken report is to Bate's considered conclusion. Those companions who thought Coleridge a Jacobin, I suggest, are the complement of a Henry Crabb Robinson who, despite his good intentions, thought Coleridge not serious about Christianity. We correct both misapprehensions in the same way, by considering the course and ramification of Coleridge's intellectual commitment over many years.

If we look at that course and commitment, we see Coleridge as actually quite different politically from both Southey and Wordsworth. Instead of passing from committed Jacobinism to committed reaction, Coleridge developed, very early, an original and profound theory of politics that was not only far more sophisticated than the attitudes of either Southey or Wordsworth, but was, so far as one can judge, consistent throughout his adult life. For Coleridge, so weak and vacillating in some personal situations, was, as was stressed above and must continually be repeated, almost unbelievably constant in his intellectual views.

If we turn towards the Coleridge of later years, we do not quite see a Tory, though conservative opinion took much comfort from his views. But De Quincey, continually perceptive with regard to the Lake Poets, insists on the unsatisfactoriness of classifying Coleridge as a Tory.

One character in which Mr. Coleridge most often came before the public was that of politician. In this age of fervent partisanship it will, therefore, naturally occur as a first question to inquire after his party and political connexions: was he Whig, Tory, or Radical? Or, under a new classification, were his propensities Conservative or Reforming? I answer that, in any exclusive or emphatic sense, he

---

[181] *Robinson*, i. 108.
[182] *Collected Letters*, v. 4.

was none of these; because, as a philosopher, he was, according to circumstances, and according to the object concerned, all of these by turns.[183]

Unlike E. P. Thompson, De Quincey finds no lack of sincerity in Coleridge's political views. 'In his politics, Mr. Coleridge was most sincere and most enthusiastic. No man hailed with profounder sympathy the French Revolution; and, though he saw cause to withdraw his regard from many of the democratic zealots in this country, and even from the revolutionary interest as it was subsequently conducted, he continued to worship the original revolutionary cause in a pure Miltonic spirit.'[184]

Indeed, Coleridge himself, in 1831, said that he was 'neither Whig nor Tory'.[185] The next year he wrote that 'I almost despair of the Conservative Party—too truly, I fear, & most ominously self-designated, TORIES—& of course, Half-truthmen!'[186] The significant, and characteristically Coleridgean, term, 'Half-truthmen', compresses within itself the eternal Coleridgean demand for the confluence of opposed adherences in healthy political attitudes. He considered himself neither Whig nor Tory, because his political views were, in his own estimation, based on consistent principle, and so, as De Quincey said, at different times coincided with both conservatism and reform. The appeal to principle was unvarying; thus, in 1815, he writes:

I have not altered my *principles*—yet now I must join in pleading for Reform.—I assumed as the Ideal of a Legislature—that in which all the great component interests of the State are adequately represented, so that no one should have the power of oppressing the others, the whole being in sympathy of action & reaction with the feelings and convictions of the People—I now see that this is not the case—& I see the historical cause too.—Neither Blackstone or De Lolme have truly given the Theory of our Constitution—which would have realized in practice but for two oversights.—But of this hereafter—.[187]

To the extent that Coleridge did make common cause with the Tories, De Quincey urges, it was because the Whigs themselves had deserted their principles. With regard to Coleridge's alleged 'want of principle in his supposed sacrifice of his early political connexions,' says De Quincey, the 'explanation is involved in the strange and scandalous conduct of the Parliamentary Whigs':

Coleridge passed over to the Tories only in that sense in which all patriots did so at that time . . . by refusing to accompany the Whigs in their almost perfidious

---

[183] *De Quincey*, ii. 215.   [184] Ibid. 169.
[185] *Collected Letters*, vi. 863.   [186] Ibid. 884.
[187] Ibid. iv. 554.

demeanour towards Napoleon Bonaparte. . . . [H]is adhesion to the Tories was
bounded by his approbation of their foreign policy; and even of *that* rarely in its
executive details, rarely even in its military plans . . . but solely in its animating
principle . . . that Napoleon Bonaparte ought to be resisted. . . . Thus far he went
along with the Tories: in all else he belonged quite as much to other parties—so far
as he belonged to any.[188]

Certainly Coleridge did not move towards the hardened reaction of
Wordsworth. 'With respect to Mr. Coleridge,' notes De Quincey, 'he was
certainly a friend to all enlightened reforms; he was a friend, for example,
to Reform in Parliament.'[189]

De Quincey saw with his customary acuteness the complexity and
idiosyncrasy of Coleridge's later sympathy with conservative policies.
That complexity made Coleridge as difficult to dismiss as to classify. John
Stuart Mill, as Michael St John Packe points out, thought the aged
Coleridge the most formidable opponent of his own liberal and
intellectually powerful views:

Coleridge, then at the height of his prophetic powers, wielded tremendous
influence. He was writing little. . . . But he talked . . . and young men, eager and
adventurous like Maurice and Sterling, sat listening to him by the hour. As the
story-teller ran along in his soft sweet voice, his hearers forgot him and forgot
themselves. For he told of the white marble palaces of heart's desire. . . . Mill,
unlike most others, was bewitched less by the presence than by the written word.
In April 1834 he wrote, 'Few persons have exercised more influence over my
thoughts and character than Coleridge has; not much by personal knowledge of
him, though I have seen and conversed with him several times, but by his works,
pieced together by what I have otherwise learned of his opinions.' Everything
about him was directly contrary to radical beliefs. While Radicals worked
industriously, building up their man-made tower to heaven, he . . . said that
heaven was already in the world, all but the seeing of it. Where they dealt in proofs,
he dispensed faith.

The very delicacy of his opposition to radicalism made it all the more dangerous.
The general run of intuitionist defended Church, State, and the Aristocracy
simply and for what they were—their country right or wrong. Not so Coleridge:
his distinction between the apparent shadow and the spiritual substance enabled
him to attack the existing framework of the institutions while exalting the
possibility of what they might be made. None was ahead of him in deploring
inhumanities and injustices, the slave ships, the child labour, the presumption of
the rich, the complacency of the clergy. He was ahead of all in describing the spirit
of the whole . . . of a gracious civility between the orders of society working

---

[188] *De Quincey*, ii. 223.
[189] Ibid. 217.

together harmoniously towards a proud and placid destiny. . . . The opposed movements of Christian Socialism and Oxford Mysticism alike derived from him. In the great battle of the century between authority and the individual, between tradition and science, he was the most significant of the patricians.[190]

St John Packe's description of Coleridge's conservatism as involving political progressivism accurately reflects the dialectical basis of Coleridge's politics. Those politics, like Marx's, are based on the Romantic doctrine of the progression of opposites; Marx's were borrowed from Hegel, Coleridge's arose from the same sources that Hegel himself used. At the very heart of Coleridge's theory was an insistence on the 'harmonious balance of the two great correspondent, at once supporting and counterpoising, interests of the state, its permanence, and its progression'.[191]

The formula is characteristic of Coleridge, in that it serves as illustration for his lifelong tendency not to reject but to incorporate adverse data. Thus in order to combat Enlightenment *raison*, he changes the *raison* of Diderot and Voltaire into 'understanding', and nominates his own version as 'reason'; both, however, remain necessary to the definition of mind. Likewise, in order to combat the psychology of Locke's tradition, he calls that tradition's theory of mental imaging 'fancy', and nominates his own version as 'imagination'; both, however, remain necessary to the functioning of mind. So, too, with his great political polarity. The interests of his earlier libertarian sympathies are preserved in the word 'progression', which is cast into polar opposition with his conservative interests, under the word 'permanence'.

But certainly permanence lay deeper in the psychology and instinct of Coleridge. For, leaving aside his political opinions, his intellectual attitudes were always profoundly conservative, which, indeed, is precisely the reason for his immense and lifelong reading of other and earlier thinkers:

What is it [asks Coleridge] that I employ my Metaphysics on? To perplex our clearest notions, & living moral Instincts? To extinguish the Light of Love & of Conscience, to put out the Life of Arbitrement—to make myself & others . . . *Worthless*, *Soul*-less, *God* less?—No! To expose the Folly & the Legerdemain of those, who have thus abused the blessed Organ of Language, to support all old & venerable Truths, to support, to kindle, to project, to make the Reason spread Light over our Feelings, to make our Feelings diffuse vital Warmth thro' our Reason—these are my Objects—& these my Subjects.[192]

[190] Packe, 83–4.   [191] *Church and State*, 29.   [192] *Notebooks*, i. 1623.

In his commitment to 'support all old & venerable Truths', we see one reason why Coleridge could never have been in any real sense a Jacobin, nor have remained one if he temporarily did espouse such radicalism. As he said, the 'dreariest feature of Jacobinism' was the 'contempt of the Institutions of our Ancestors and of past wisdom'.[193] Coleridge, on the contrary, and it cannot be emphasized enough, found such contempt abhorrent. As he says in November of 1803, he always rejoiced 'to find his opinions plumed & winged with the authority of venerable Forefathers'.[194]

It is interesting that this statement about 'the dreariest feature of Jacobinism' was summoned in a context that deplores 'the Jacobinism of Anti-Jacobins', for it clearly reveals Coleridge's temperamental lack of radicalism, either of the left or of the right.[195] He hewed to his own line, which steered between the two extremes.

That idiosyncratic line is defined by the second of the reasons why Coleridge could never have been in any real sense a Jacobin: his commitment to the Christian religion. Not only is the *Conciones ad Populum* of 1795 shot through with Coleridge's Christianity, a fact that even Thelwall accepted, but in that same year he produced writings now entitled *Six Lectures on Revealed Religion its Corruption and Political Views*. As Peter Mann, the editor of Coleridge's *Lectures 1795 on Politics and Religion* points out: 'The Lectures on Revealed Religion allow one to see how deeply rooted Coleridge's religious and moral feelings were in 1795 and how they would necessarily bring him into conflict, intellectually and morally, with the extreme radical movement and lead him to a point of view that was different from that of such "friends of liberty" as Paine, Thelwall and Holcroft.'[196]

The Jacobins, on the other hand, were virulent anti-Christians. Embarking on a specific programme of 'dechristianization', they replaced Christianity with a religion of reason.[197] As Lefebvre says:

The new religion endowed itself with symbols and a form of liturgy, honoured the 'holy mountain' [the Jacobin side of the Assembly was called 'the mountain'], and venerated its martyrs, Lepeletier, Marat, and Chalier. On 3 Brumaire, Year II

---

[193] *Notebooks*, ii. 2150.

[194] Ibid. i. 1695.

[195] Again, 'If we are not greatly deceived we could point out more than one or two celebrated Anti-Jacobins who are not slightly infected with some of the worst symptoms of the madness against which they are raving; and one or two acts of parliament which are justifiable only upon Jacobin principles' (*Essays*, i. 370).

[196] Editor's Introduction, *Lectures 1795*, p. lxxix.

[197] See e.g. Michel Vovelle, *Réligion et révolution, la déchristianisation de l'An II* (Paris: Hachette, 1976). See also Aulard, *Christianity*.

(October 24, 1793) . . . the Convention adopted the revolutionary calendar. It attempted to dechristianize daily life by substituting the date of September 22, 1792, the first day of the Republic, for the Christian era; by replacing references to religious ceremonies and the saints with names borrowed from tools . . . and above all, by eliminating Sunday in favour of the Tenth day [*décadi*].[198]

Indeed, a Festival of Liberty was planned for 20 Brumaire, Year II (10 November 1793), for which the Commune seized Notre Dame, now called the Temple of Reason, and built a mountain in the choir, with an actress impersonating Liberty![199] As Brinton remarks, 'The Jacobins unquestionably held their political philosophy as a matter of faith.' Again: 'Jacobinism is, then, first of all a faith. . . . "Liberty, Equality, Fraternity," as words, may be subject to definition and contain the seeds of infinite dispute; as symbols, they were to the Jacobins a common property above logic.'[200]

It is tempting to linger over the implications of Jacobin anti-Christianity, which led directly to the doctrinal atheism of Marx.[201] What has been said, however, suffices to show how profound the division was between Coleridge and the Jacobins, especially since the Christian religion came to be elaborated into the very theory of Coleridge's view of the social organism. In his *Constitution of the Church and State*, which was his last published prose work, and which, as John Colmer says, is 'a brief but brilliant synthesis of the political and theological thinking of a lifetime',[202] Coleridge takes up a theme he had described twenty years earlier, and adhered to tenaciously all that time. In 1811 he writes:

Church and state—civil and religious rights—to hold these essential powers of civilized society in due relation to each other, so as to prevent them from becoming its burthens instead of its supports; this is perhaps the most difficult problem in the whole science of politics. . . . From the first ages of Christianity to the present period, the two relations of a rational Being, to his present and to his future state, have been abstracted and framed into moral personages, Church and State: and to each has been assigned its own domain and its especial rights.[203]

When, in 1830, Coleridge published the *Constitution of the Church and State*, the reconciliation of the two domains was effected as a large instance

[198] Lefebvre, ii. 77.
[199] For Coleridge's awareness of all this, see his reference to 'the Jacobins' Goddess of Reason' (*Collected Letters*, iv. 758).
[200] Brinton, 218, 240.
[201] Cf. Aulard: 'The peril thus run by Christianity at the time of the Worship of Reason and the Worship of the Supreme Being is the most outstanding episode in the religious history of the French Revolution' (Aulard, *Christianity*, 14).
[202] *Church and State*, p. xxxiii.   [203] *Essays*, ii. 308.

of the principle of interacting opposites. The 'two antagonist powers or opposite interests of the state, under which all other state interests are comprised, are those of PERMANENCE and PROGRESSION.' In a footnote Coleridge distinguishes between opposites and contraries:

The feminine character is *opposed* to the masculine; but the effeminate is its *contrary*. Even so in the present instance, the interest of permanence is opposed to that of progressiveness; but so far from being contrary interests, they, like the magnetic forces, suppose and require each other. Even the most mobile of creatures, the serpent, makes a *rest* of its own body, and drawing up its voluminous train from behind on the fulcrum, propels itself onward. On the other hand, it is a proverb in all languages, that (relatively to man at least) what would stand still must retrograde.[204]

Coleridge never wanted society to stand still; but to balance its progression, principles of rest were necessary. One of these was property, which he, like Burke, specifically summoned against the Jacobin spirit.[205] As he writes in 1802, in his 30th year:

We were never at any period of our life converts to the system of French politics. As far back as our memory reaches, it was an axiom in politics with us, that in every country in which property prevailed, property must be the grand basis of the government; and that that government was the best, in which the power was the most exactly proportioned to the property.[206]

The Revolution itself had not initially been opposed to private property. As the *Déclaration des droits de l'homme et du citoyen*, drafted by Lafayette and decreed on 26 August 1789 (and translated in its entirety in Paine's *Rights of Man* of 1791), emphasized in its seventeenth and final article, 'The right to property being inviolable and sacred, no one may be deprived of it, except in cases of evident public necessity, legally ascertained, and on condition of a previous indemnity.'[207] Robespierre

[204] *Church and State*, 24.
[205] For a brief conspectus of the overwhelmingly dominant earlier tradition—present even in Locke, Montesquieu, and Blackstone—by which liberty was tied to the ownership of property, see Cone, 4–18.
[206] *Essays*, i. 372–3.
[207] Lafayette, because of his youthful participation in the American Revolution, was a figure of great prestige in the early days of the French version. For the immense role of America in the evolution of the Revolution, see e.g. Pierre Gaxotte: 'La révolte américaine précipita encore l'évolution. Les Treize colonies étaient depuis longtemps un des thèmes principaux de la littérature sentimentale et humanitaire. On voyait en elles un peuple neuf, tout proche de la nature, tolérant, pieux, patriarcal, sans autre passion que celle du bien, sans autre fanatisme que celui de la vertu. Les chapitres que Raynal leur consacre sont la partie brillante de son *Histoire des Indes*. . . . La déclaration des droits rédigée par Jefferson en un

himself, as Louis Madelin points out, 'had three dogmas: *the support of Virtue by Terror*; *the existence of the Supreme Being*; and *the absolute sanctity of Property*'.[208]

But the Jacobin theories of taxation and of the subordination of property to personal rights (and the rights of society as prefigured in *The Social Contract*)—and the burgeoning socialism of figures like Chaumette and Fouché—tended to erode the status of property, a status still more compromised by the time of the *Communist Manifesto*. 'The theory of the Communists', says that enchiridion, 'may be summed up in the single sentence: Abolition of private property.'[209]

Yet property as a principle of rest, along with the church, does not exist in monolithic stagnation in Coleridge's scheme; it too is brought into the conciliating flux of permanence and progression. 'We have thus divided the subjects of the state into two orders,' Coleridge says in 1830, 'the agricultural or possessors of land; and the merchant, manufacturer, the distributive, and the professional bodies, under the common name of citizens.' The first group, he says, 'either by their interests or by the very effect of their situation, circumstances, and the nature of their employment', are 'vitally connected with the permanency of the state, its institutions, rights, customs, manners, privileges—and as such, opposed to the inhabitants of ports, towns, and cities, who are in like manner and from like causes more especially connected with its progression'.[210]

The one thing there was no room for in Coleridge's view of politics was reformist violence. And this, though connected with his commitment to Christianity, is the third and most unbridgeable of the reasons why he was never a Jacobin, and could never have been a Jacobin. Though, as Lefebvre observes, 'nothing contributed as much to spreading the Terror

---

style de code moral tourna la tête aux beaux esprits. Quelques-uns se firent quakers; d'autres—et des plus nobles—s'engagèrent à la suite de La Fayette dans les armées républicaines.' American influence crested with the arrival of Benjamin Franklin in Paris: 'Il est le grand prêtre des philosophes, le Messie des mécontents, le patron des faiseurs de systèmes. Ses portefeuilles sont plein de lettres qui montrent quelle place il tient dans l'esprit publie et quelle influence il a sur lui. On lui écrit de partout. On implore ses conseils. . . . Un cardinal—c'est Rohan, celui du Collier—organise des fêtes en son honneur. Un médecin—c'est Marat—lui soumet des expériences de physique. Un avocat—c'est Brissot—l'interroge sur le nouveau monde où il pense aller prendre une leçon de Révolution. Un autre lui dédie son premier plaidoyer, c'est Robespierre. Quand Franklin quitte la France, la légende des Etats-Unis est indestructible. . . . Les Etats-Unis avaient donné à la doctrine révolutionnaire ce que lui manquait encore: l'exemple.' (Gaxotte, 74–6).

[208] Madelin, 382.   [209] *Marxist Reader*, 38.   [210] *Church and State*, 26–7.

as dechristianization',[211] in the remainder of this chapter the Christian/
anti-Christian opposition of Coleridge and the Jacobins shall be muted in
favour of an emphasis on another contrast, that between Coleridge's
humanitarianism and the Jacobin commitment to reformist violence.
Thus, in his earliest political statement, the remarkable *Conciones ad
Populum* of 1795, Coleridge is clearly and unarguably not a Jacobin; for he
says, with epigrammatic terseness: 'A system of fundamental Reform will
scarcely be effected by massacres mechanized into Revolution.'[212]

Even Jacobin apologists have to take note of the truth of the oneness of
Jacobinism and massacre. Isser Woloch, for instance, in *Jacobin Legacy*,
says that Jacobinism had 'much to do with what Americans call grass-roots
democracy, and a commitment to equality in the sense of mitigating social
distinctions'—but in the same sentence he must also grant that Jacobinism
is also synonymous 'with the strange mantle of terrorism and fanaticism
that the sociétaires wore in the Year II'.[213] Lefebvre, whose history of the
Revolution is written as a partisan both of Robespierre and the Jacobins,
and though he does his best to mute the Terror, nevertheless must note
things like this: 'Proposals involving violence were more and more
frequently heard, even at the Assembly, where Merlin de Thionville
demanded that wives and children of émigrés be seized as hostages, while
Debry advocated a "tyrannicide corps" to exterminate kings. Marat had
many times insisted that the only way to save the Revolution was to
slaughter the aristocrats en masse.'[214] Or this: 'So, after Germinal the
sessions of the Convention became dreary, the committees worked in
silence, and the clubs disappeared, except for the Jacobins, where most of
the regulars were functionaries of the Terror.'[215]

That Coleridge was from the outset acutely aware of the Jacobin
commitment to violence is evident. In the Introductory Address to
Conciones ad Populum—the year is 1795 and Coleridge's age is not yet 23—
he says:

The Annals of the French Revolution have recorded in Letters of Blood, that the
Knowledge of the Few cannot counteract the Ignorance of the Many; that the
Light of Philosophy, when it is confined to a small Minority, points out the
Possessors as the Victims, rather than the Illuminators, of the Multitude. The
Patriots of France either hastened into the dangerous and gigantic Error of making
certain Evil the means of contingent Good, or were sacrificed by the Mob, with
whose prejudices and ferocity their unbending Virtue forbade them to
assimilate.[216]

[211] Lefebvre, ii. 119.   [212] *Lectures 1795*, 48.   [213] Woloch, 12.
[214] Lefebvre, i. 242.   [215] Ibid. ii. 92.   [216] *Lectures 1795*, 34.

The rejection of reformist violence, the arguing for humanity, the avoidance of the 'gigantic Error of making certain Evil the means of contingent Good', these, indeed, are the very hallmarks of Coleridge's political writings of 1795:

We should be cautious how we indulge the feelings even of virtuous indignation. Indignation is the handsome brother of Anger and Hatred. The Temple of Despotism, like that of Tescalipoca, the Mexican Deity, is built of human skulls, and cemented with human blood;—let us beware that we be not transported into revenge while we are levelling the loathsome Pile; lest when we erect the edifice of Freedom we but vary the stile of Architecture, not change the materials.[217]

The passage is a fair glimpse of Coleridge's line of thought in the process of steering itself between the extremes of Jacobinism and Toryism. The temple of despotism—that is, kingship and its supports— must be levelled; but the edifice of Freedom must be careful not to duplicate it in a different style. This steering of a path at once libertarian and humanitarian between the extremes of Jacobinism and reaction, so evident in 1795, is the very stuff of Coleridge's vision clear through to 1830. As he wrote in January 1800, at the age of 27:

We detest equally Jacobinism and usurpation in the French, and the principles of despotism preached by their opponents—we look with equal horror on those who murder a lawful Constitution, and those who, under pretence of medicine, administer poison to it. We deem it among the most fatal errors in some friends of freedom in England, that they have thought it necessary to a consistent opposition to Ministers, that they should *slur over* the follies or wickedness of France. We think otherwise. TRUTH is *our* policy. We despise the absurdities and dread the fanaticism of France; believing, however, at the same time [and here Coleridge presages the position of Aulard], that but for the war against France they would have died in their infancy.[218]

Such steering between extremes is the pilot's course throughout this exhortation of early 1800, which concludes by rejecting both Jacobinism and monarchical reaction, and doing so in terms of the interplay of permanence and progression. Coleridge said (and proved a true prophet):

Supposing for a moment, that Royalty could be restored—what reason have we for affirming its permanency? Will not the principles of Jacobinism remain? Can the faction of the Royalists boast more talent, more activity, more energy, than the Republicans? Will it not disturb the present state of property infinitely more than the usurpation of Buonaparte? And by the very act of disturbing property, will it not necessarily bring Jacobinism once more into play? And will not Royalty

[217] Ibid. 48.   [218] *Essays*, i. 78.

therefore, if restored, perish, like a bubble, by the very agitation that produced it?[219]

Coleridge understood not only the violence integral to and inseparable from Jacobinism, but also the nobler ideals that lay behind the Jacobin aspiration. In truth, it would be difficult to find a fairer or more perspicacious description of the Jacobin view of the world than the one he supplies in 1802:

A Jacobin, in *our* sense of the term, is one who believes, and is disposed to act on the belief, that all, or the greater part of, the happiness or misery . . . of mankind, depends on forms of government; who admits no form of government as either good or rightful, which does not flow directly and formally from the persons governed; who—considering life, health, moral and intellectual improvement, and liberty both of person and conscience, as blessings which governments are bound as far as possible to increase and secure to every inhabitant, whether he has or has not any fixed property, and moreover as blessings of infinitely greater value to each individual, than the preservation of property can be to any individual—does consequently and consistently hold, that every inhabitant, who has attained the age of reason, has a natural and inalienable right to an *equal* share of power in the choice of governors. In other words, the Jacobin affirms that no legislature can be rightful or good, which did not proceed from universal suffrage. In the power, and under the controul, of a legislature so chosen, he places all and every thing, with the exception of the natural rights of man, and the means appointed for the preservation and exercise of these rights, by a direct vote of the nation itself—that is to say, by a CONSTITUTION. Finally the Jacobin deems it both justifiable and expedient to effect these requisite changes in faulty governments, by absolute revolutions, and considers no violences as properly rebellious or criminal, which are the *means* of giving to a nation the power of declaring and enforcing its sovereignty.[220]

All this is not only accurate and comprehensive, but subtly articulated and exquisitely just.

Indeed the Jacobins, in Coleridge's masterly description here, sound more like bourgeois liberals in the Jeffersonian mould than architects of terror. Marx and Engels, in fact, distinguished Communism from the Jacobin revolution by claiming that their own revolution was to be a proletarian revolution that looked totally to the future, whereas the French Revolution had been a bourgeois venture that recapitulated the past. 'The social revolution of the nineteenth century', said Marx in *The Eighteenth Brumaire of Louis Bonaparte*, 'cannot draw its poetry from the past, but

---

[219] *Essays*, i. 79.   [220] Ibid. 368–9.

only from the future. It cannot make a beginning until it has stripped off all superstition of the past.'[221]

But Marx was not so much different from the Jacobin spirit as he affected to believe. After all, Shelley, the 'most Jacobinical of poets', as Richard Holmes calls him,[222] said that 'The system of society as it exists at present must be overthrown from the foundations with all its superstructure of maxims & of forms.'[223] Marx, however, not caring to see himself as pre-empted by Jacobin theorists and attitudes, disregarded this central truth of the Jacobin spirit and insisted on the bourgeois character of the French Revolution. He pointed out that it looked back to Roman Republican values as the English Revolution had looked back to Old Testament values. (Coleridge, incidentally, published three articles in 1802 on the comparison of Revolutionary France and ancient Rome.) Marx says:

Camille Desmoulins, Danton, Robespierre, Saint-Just, Napoleon, the heroes, as well as the parties and masses of the old French Revolution, performed the task of their time in Roman costume and with Roman phrases, the task of releasing and establishing modern *bourgeois* society. The first mentioned knocked the feudal basis to pieces and cut off the feudal heads which had grown from it. The other [Napoleon] created inside France the conditions under which free competition could first be developed . . . and outside the French borders he everywhere swept the feudal form away, so far as it was necessary to furnish bourgeois society in France with a suitable up-to-date environment on the European continent.[224]

Despite these arguments, Marx, with his acceptance of the cutting off of feudal heads, reveals himself as far closer to Jacobinism than Coleridge ever was. Violence, indeed, is cherished in Marxist theory as in Jacobin actuality. Writing on Engels's utopian phrase, 'the withering away of the state', Lenin, in *The State and Revolution*, sharply reminds true believers that this refers only to the proletarian state; violence, on the contrary, must and should be used by the proletariat to abolish the bourgeois state. 'In the same work of Engels, from which every one remembers his argument on the "withering away" of the State,' says Lenin, 'there is also a disquisition on the significance of a violent revolution. The historical analysis of its role becomes, with Engels, a veritable panegyric on violent revolution.' Lenin then quotes Engels as saying that 'force' is, 'in the words of Marx', the 'midwife of every old society that is pregnant with the new; that it is the instrument with whose aid social movement forces its way through and

---

[221] *Marxist Reader*, 119.   [222] *Coleridge* (Oxford, 1982), 69.
[223] Shelley, *Letters*, ii. 191.   [224] *Marxist Reader*, 117.

shatters the dead, fossilized political forms'.[225] And the conclusion of the *Communist Manifesto* proudly proclaims that 'The Communists disdain to conceal their views and aims. They openly declare that their ends can be attained only by the forcible overthrow of all existing social conditions.'[226]

It is the obsession with reformist violence that provides the final link in the chain joining Jacobinism to Communism. Though the Jacobin clubs were disestablished following Robespierre's fall on ninth Thermidor of the year II (27 July 1794), the Jacobin spirit did not die. A later strain of Jacobinism, Babouvism, transformed itself into outright communism.[227] Babeuf himself (the Chartist Bronterre O'Brien compared him to Jesus)[228] was not guillotined until 1797.[229] Coleridge, in listing the radical tenets of Babouvism in an issue of *The Watchman* for 27 April 1796, is confronting an enumeration perhaps even more unequivocal than that contained in the *Communist Manifesto*. Certainly he understood the tendency of the Jacobin spirit: for from the Democrats of the original Jacobin clubs, to the Terrorist functionaries of 1793 to 1794, to the Babouvian communism of 1796 and 1797, to the Communist Manifesto of 1848, to the Russian radicals described by Dostoevsky in *The Possessed*, to the latter-day Jacobins called Bolsheviks, and all the way to Lenin's arrival at the Finland Station, there is one united progression of a single spirit, the spirit of Jacobinism.[230]

---

[225] *Marxist Reader*, 581.   [226] Ibid. 59.

[227] For Babeuf's centrality in the line leading from Jacobin principles to Russian communism, cf. R. B. Rose: 'As the first revolutionary communist of modern times Gracchus Babeuf has been for many years a figure of considerable veneration for Marxists. In 1845 Marx and Engels paid their own tribute in *The Holy Family* to the rôle of Babeuf and the Conspiracy of Equals of 1796 in passing on the idea of communism from the utopians of the Enlightenment, through the mediation of Buonarotti, to the nineteenth century: in the *Communist Manifesto* Babeuf was recognized as the spokesman of the proletariat in the French Revolution. In 1919, on the morrow of the Bolshevik Revolution, Leon Trotsky proclaimed Babeuf the first of a long line of revolutionary heroes and martyrs whose struggle had prepared the way for the Communist International and the world proletarian revolution' (Rose, 1). Interestingly, Rose notes that 'the great French Revolution scholar Albert Mathiez always obstinately refused to distinguish between the Jacobin tradition and the Babouvist tradition' (p. 330).

[228] Buonarotti, 57 n.

[229] For Babeuf's career, see e.g. Gérard Walter, *Babeuf 1760–1797 et la conjuration des égaux* (Paris: Payot, 1937).

[230] Furet notes that 'the Leninist historian' of the twentieth century 'prefers Jacobins to Constituants, to say nothing of Thermidorians. With the men of 1793, the Leninist historian finds himself in familiar surroundings, since the Soviet experience also illustrated the necessity for dictatorship and terror' (Furet, 96). Feher points out that twentieth-century Marxists were all steeped in the Jacobinism of the French Revolution: 'After the victorious first generation of Russian Jacobins had laid the foundation of their work, the master narrative has gradually become absorbed into *their* story of foundation. Lenin's, Trotsky's

That spirit is inseparable from reformist violence. The Communist apotheosis of violence merely raised to theory what the Jacobins had discovered as praxis. Its institutionalization has borne the richest kind of historical fruit. As aftermath of Marxist and Leninist commandments, Pol Pot and the Khmer Rouge actually and in grotesque fact caused to be erected new temples of skulls to replace those Aztec temples of skulls metaphorically invoked by Coleridge. Stalin, using reformist violence to achieve the Communist goal of collectivizing Russian farmland, achieved also the death of staggering numbers of human beings—fourteen million of them, according to Robert Conquest's melancholy history of that late-Jacobin episode.[231] The non-violent reforms of American capitalism, on the other hand, which were undertaken in the presidencies of Theodore Roosevelt, Taft, and Franklin Roosevelt, were the sorts of action that were stigmatized by Marx, in *The Poverty of Philosophy*, as effects of 'the humanitarian school', or even worse, of 'the philanthropic school';[232] they were reforms, certainly, that were entirely in the spirit of Coleridge's reconciling and humane political vision.

---

and Luxemburg's generation still knew by heart what had happened in Paris in those distant days' (Feher, 153). For those who witnessed the 'Jacobin mania' of our own recent decade of the 1960s, Feher's description of the character of the Jacobin will seem especially just: 'The new French revolutionary . . . wanted only to live in social turbulence, promoting revolutions preferably from a position of power, but if things changed for the worse, then also to do so under persecution. These men shared three features in common. Firstly, they preferred process to consolidation. The term "permanent revolution" was coined later, but the way of life pertaining to it had already been invented by the Jacobin militant. . . . The second feature was the strong ideological motivation of the modern revolutionary . . . [T]he real life of human beings should cede to the imperatives of doctrine. Thirdly, the modern revolutionary was a professional: revolution was his *métier*. He lived from the revolution, mostly poorly but sometimes in a dandyish, well-provided manner' (p. 125). What Feher calls 'the strong ideological motivation', Taine stigmatizes as the 'theorizing mania' that scrambled the brains of the ordinary people who made up the Jacobins (Taine, iii. 41). In this same line, Brinton says that 'Of the very general truth that the Jacobins were thoroughly steeped in the writings of the eighteenth century philosophers there can be no doubt' (Brinton, 210).

[231] 'When we conclude that no fewer than fourteen million odd peasants lost their lives as a result of the events recounted in this book we may well be understating' (Conquest, 305). Conquest emphasizes that the massacre was not a result of inadvertency or mismanagement, but was precisely a furtherance of Marxist doctrine as envisioned by Stalin: 'In a more general sense, the responsibility for the massacre of the "class enemy" and the crushing of "bourgeois nationalism," may be held to lie with the Marxist conceptions in the form given them by the Communist Party as accepted by Stalin' (p. 328). 'The main lesson seems to be that the Communist ideology provided the motivation for an unprecedented massacre of men, women, and children. And that this ideology, perhaps all set-piece theory, turned out to be a primitive and schematic approach to matters far too complex for it' (p. 344).

[232] *Marxist Reader*, 264–5.

That political vision is, early and late, wholly at odds with the infatuation with force and violence that was the truest legacy of Jacobinism. 'To *reconcile*', said Coleridge in one of his most characteristic statements, 'is truly the work of the Inspired! This is the true *Atonement*.'[233] But the Jacobins were not interested in reconciling. As Saint-Just said, 'What constitutes the Republic is the destruction of everything opposed to it. A man is guilty against the Republic when he takes pity on prisoners: he is guilty because he has no desire for virtue: he is guilty because he is opposed to the Terror.'[234] And in the Marxist analysis, the Terror of 1793–4 was not an aberration but an accreditation, a necessary and desirable cleansing action.[235]

In Coleridge, on the other hand, one finds everywhere an express humanitarianism that stands in total opposition to this essential of the Jacobin spirit. For instance, in the very midst of the 23-year-old Coleridge's passionate democratic plea in *Conciones ad Populum*, we read of

the awful Truth, that in the course of this calamitous Contest more than a Million of men have perished—a MILLION of men, of each one of whom the mangled corpse terrifies the dreams of her that loved him, and makes some mother, some sister, some widow start from slumber with a shriek.[236]

To the Coleridge of 1795 the slave trade was not a matter of charts and statistics and moral guidelines:

I address myself first of all to those who independent of political distinction profess themselves Christian. As you hope you live with Christ hereafter you are commanded to do unto others as ye would that others should do unto you! Would you choose that Slave Merchants should incite an intoxicated Chieftain to make War on your Tribe to murder your Wife and Children before your face and drag them with yourself to the Market—Would you choose to be sold, to have the hot iron hiss upon your breast, to be thrown down into the hold of a ship ironed with so many fellow victims so closely crammed together that the heat and stench arising from your diseased bodies should rot the very planks of the Ship?[237]

[233] *Notebooks*, ii. 2208.
[234] Madelin, 394.
[235] Thus Marx in 1847: 'The terror in France could thus by its mighty hammer-blows only serve to spirit away, as it were, the ruins of feudalism from French soil. The timidly considerate bourgeoisie would not have accomplished this task in decades' (Furet, 173). Furet himself comments: 'The "hammer" of the Terror still finds its justification, just like 1789, in the necessity of realizing the bourgeois revolution . . . and of extirpating the last "feudal ruins" from French soil' (p. 55).
[236] *Lectures 1795*, 59.
[237] Ibid. 247–8.

That was the true substance of Coleridge's political libertarianism. Programmatic Jacobinism and its desecration of the human were alien to him. He avoided, as the Jacobins did not, 'the dangerous and gigantic Error of making certain Evil the means of contingent Good'.

If we wonder whether it was certain evil or contingent good that loomed larger in the French Revolution, we should in our musing heed the message of Taine's impassioned history, *The Origins of Modern France*.[238]

[238] Taine's fury against the Revolution predictably led to counterattacks by those historians who celebrated it as a great advance in human history. Aulard wrote an entire book in an attempt to discredit Taine: 'Ainsi toute la Terreur s'explique (je ne dis pas: se justifie) par les circonstances de guerre civile et étrangère où se trouvait alors la France. Taine ne parle pas de ces circonstances ou n'y fait que d'insignifiantes allusions. Les moyens de violence que les Montagnards employèrent pour assurer la défense nationale contre les insurgés vendéens, contre les Autrichiens, les Anglais, les Espagnoles, Taine ne les attribue qu'à un fanatisme philosophique' (A. Aulard, *Taine; historien de la révolution française* (Paris: Librairie Armand Colin, 1907), 326). He attempts, at great length but with indifferent success, to impeach Taine's learning ('J'ai moins voulu critiquer les théories philosophico-historiques de Taine que son érudition, dont l'appareil, d'aspect si imposant, a donné crédit à ses théories et lui a valu, en France et à l'étranger, une grande réputation d'historien' (p. 323); and he concludes that Taine's 'livre, tout compte fait, et en ses résultats généraux, me semble presque inutile à l'histoire. Il n'est vraiment utile qu'à la biographie intellectuelle de Taine lui-même ou à celle de quelques contemporains, ses disciples' (p. 330).

The majority of academic historians today (quite a few of whom are declared Marxists) are content with Aulard's position, and reject Taine as intolerably biased. As far as the present author can judge, however, Taine is less biased than Michelet was as the extoller of Revolution, and no more biased than Aulard himself, or Lefebvre, or other academic apologists for the great upheaval. As a single random case in point, Cobb can quaintly accuse Taine of progressing 'to pure insult' in his description of the personnel of the provincial armies, while Cobb himself is continually palliating their crimes (Cobb, 5). After all, Brinton at one point finds it fitting to speak of 'the madness of true Jacobinism' (Brinton, 240). 'They were in the main ordinary, quite prosperous middle-class people. And yet they behaved like fanatics. The Reign of Terror was marked by cruelties and absurdities which the greatest of misanthropes will hardly maintain are characteristic of ordinary human beings' (p. 232).

For those who, unlike Taine and Coleridge, did and do think that the Revolution justified its cost, the classic line of argument is that eloquently pleaded by Shelley: 'The oppressors of mankind had enjoyed . . . a long and undisturbed reign in France, and to the pining famine, the shelterless destitution of the inhabitants of that country had been added and heaped up insult harder to endure than misery. For the feudal system (the immediate causes and conditions of its institution having become obliterated) had degenerated into an instrument not only of oppression but of contumely, and both were unsparingly inflicted. Blind in the possession of strength, drunken as with the intoxication of ancestral greatness, the rulers perceived not that increase of knowledge in their subjects which made its exercise insecure. They called soldiers to hew down the people when their power was already past. The tyrants were, as usual, the aggressors. Then the oppressed, having been rendered brutal, ignorant, servile and bloody by long slavery, having had the intellectual thirst, excited in them by the progress of civilization, satiated from fountains of literature poisoned by the spirit and the form of monarchy, arose and took a dreadful revenge on their oppressors. Their desire to wreak revenge, to this extent, in itself a mistake, a crime, a calamity, arose from the same source as their other miseries and errors, and affords an additional proof of the necessity of that long-delayed change which it accompanied and disgraced' (*Shelley*, vii. 13).

To Taine, the real truth of that revolution was the triumph of violence and the desecration of the human: 'from the peasant, the laborer, and the bourgeois, pacified and tamed by an old civilization, we see suddenly spring forth the barbarian, and still worse, the primitive animal, the grinning, bloody, wanton baboon, who chuckles while he slays, and gambols over the ruin he has accomplished'.[239] To Taine, the Revolution was an orgy of violence from the start, and he records its enormities in passionate detail. 'To every impartial man', he quotes Malouet as saying, 'the Terror dates from the 14th of July [1789].'[240]

But Taine sees it as being brought to its edge of perfection by what he calls the 'homicidal idea' of the Jacobins. For the Jacobins themselves he has only revulsion and scorn:

From one end of the territory to the other, the machine, with its hundred thousand arms, works efficaciously in the hands of those who have seized the lever at the central point. Resolution, audacity, rude energy, are all that are needed to make the lever act, and none of these is wanting in the Jacobin.

First, he has faith, and faith at all times 'moves mountains.' Take any ordinary party recruit, an attorney, a second-rate lawyer, a shopkeeper, an artisan, and conceive, if you can, the extraordinary effect of this doctrine on a mind so poorly prepared for it, so narrow, so out of proportion with the gigantic conception which has mastered it. Formed for routine and the limited views of one in his position, he is suddenly carried away by a complete system of philosophy, a theory of nature and of man, a theory of society and of religion, a theory of universal history, conclusions about the past, the present, and the future of humanity, axioms of absolute right, a system of perfect and final truth, the whole concentrated in a few rigid formulas as, for example: 'Religion is superstition, monarchy is usurpation, priests are impostors, aristocrats are vampires, and kings are so many tyrants and monsters.' These ideas flood a mind of this stamp like a vast torrent precipitating itself into a narrow gorge; they upset it, and, no longer under self-direction, they sweep it away. . . . A plain bourgeois, a common laborer, is not transformed with impunity into an apostle or liberator of the human species.[241]

Taine speaks with equal contempt of the Jacobin clubs. 'In many of the large cities, in Paris, Lyons, Aix, and Bordeaux, there are two clubs in partnership, one, more or less respectable and parliamentary . . . and the other, practical and active. . . . The latter is a branch of the former, and, in urgent cases, supplies it with rioters. "We are placed amongst the people," says one of these subaltern clubs, "we read to them the decrees, and through lectures and counsel, we warn them against the publications and

---

[239] Taine, ii. 70.   [240] Ibid. 65.   [241] Ibid. iii. 66–7.

intrigues of the aristocrats. We ferret out and track plotters and their machinations. We welcome and advise all complainants." '[242]

But Taine's profoundest revulsion is for the leaders of the Jacobins. 'Three men among the Jacobins,' he says,

Marat, Danton, and Robespierre, merited distinction and possessed authority: owing to a malformation, or distortion, of head and heart, they fulfilled the requisite conditions. Of the three, Marat is the most monstrous; he borders on the lunatic, of which he displays the chief characteristics—furious exaltation, constant over-excitement, feverish restlessness, an inexhaustible propensity for scribbling.[243] . . . From first to last, he was in the right line of the Revolution, lucid on account of his blindness, thanks to his crazy logic, thanks to the concordance of his personal malady with the public malady, to the precocity of his complete madness alongside the incomplete or tardy madness of the rest, he alone steadfast, remorseless, triumphant, perched aloft at the first round of the sharp pinnacle which his rivals dared not climb or only stumbled up.[244]

Robespierre, to both Taine and Coleridge, was different from Marat. He was, says Taine, a '*cuistre*',[245], that is to say,

the hollow, inflated mind that, filled with words and imagining that these are ideas, revels in its own declamation and dupes itself that it may dictate to others. Such is his title, character and the part he plays. In this artificial and declamatory tragedy of the Revolution he takes the leading part; the maniac and the barbarian slowly retire into the background on the appearance of the *cuistre*. . . . If we would comprehend him we must look at him as he stands in the midst of his surroundings. At the last stage of an intellectual vegetation passing away, he remains on the last branch of the eighteenth century, the most abortive and driest offshoot of the classical spirit. He has retained nothing of a worn-out system of philosophy but its lifeless dregs amd well-conned formulas, the formulas of Rousseau, Mably, and Raynal, concerning 'the people, nature, reason, liberty, tyrants, factions, virtue, morality,' a ready-made vocabulary, expressions too ample, the meaning of which,

---

[242] Ibid. 48–9.   [243] Ibid. iv. 159.   [244] Ibid. 174.
[245] Gaxotte argues interestingly that Robespierre's special kind of mediocrity was especially fitted to be empowered by the structure of the Jacobin Club. 'Robespierre est l'homme de club par excellence. Tout ce qui le dessert dans la vie réelle lui devient au club un gage de succès. Il a l'esprit peu fécond, peu d'idées, peu d'invention? Il est au niveau de son auditoire, il ne l'effraie pas, il n'excite pas sa jalousie. Sa personnalité est apparemment faible, indistincte? Il se fond dans la personnalité collective, il se plie sans effort à la discipline démocratique. Sa situation sociale est presque nulle? Le club est fondé sur l'égalité de tous ses membres et il supporte mal les supériorités extérieures de rang et d'argent. Ses affaires l'occupent peu? Il n'en sera que plus assidu aux séances. Il a peu vécu, son expérience des hommes et des choses est bornée? Le club est une société artificielle construite au rebours de la société véritable. Il a l'intelligence formaliste, sans grande prise sur le réel? Au club l'action ne compte pas, mais la parole.' 'Cet homme médiocre a le sens, ou, si l'on veut, le génie de la Révolution et de son mécanisme.' (Gaxotte, 389–90, 391).

ill-defined by the masters, evaporates in the hands of the disciple. . . . It might be said that he never saw anything with his own eyes, that he neither could nor would see, that false conceptions have intervened and fixed themselves between him and the object; he combines these in logical sequences, and simulates the absent thought by an affected jargon, and this is all. . . . For hours, we grope after him in the vague shadows of political speculation, in the cold and perplexing mist of didactic generalities, trying in vain to make something out of his colourless tirades, and we grasp nothing. We then, astonished, ask what all this talk amounts to, and why he talks at all; the answer is, that he has said nothing, that he talks only for the sake of talking, the same as a sectary preaching to his congregation, neither the preacher nor the audience ever wearying, the one of turning the dogmatic crank, and the other of listening. So much the better if the hopper is empty; the emptier it is the easier and faster the crank turns. And better still, if the empty term he selects is used in a contrary sense; the grand words justice, humanity, mean to him piles of human heads, the same as a text from the gospels means to a grand inquisitor the burning of heretics.[246]

With Taine's reference to Robespierre's 'piles of human heads' we return to Coleridge's warning in 1795 about not building again the Aztec temple of skulls in the name of freedom. Indeed, Taine's burning volumes, motivated not by political prepossession but by humanitarian concern, are especially relevant to Coleridge's attitudes. As Taine says in the preface to his third volume:

I have again to regret the dissatisfaction which I foresee this work will cause to many of my countrymen. My excuse is, that almost all of them, more fortunate than myself, have political principles that serve them in forming their judgements of the past. I had none; if, indeed, I had any motive in undertaking this work, it was to seek for political principles. Thus far I have attained to scarcely more than one; and this is so simple that it will seem puerile, and I hardly dare enunciate it. . . . It consists wholly in this observation: that human society, especially a modern society, is a vast and complicated thing.[247]

Taine's implication, that human knowledge is not sufficient to balance hypothetical improvement against real massacre is identical with Coleridge's counsel to avoid 'the dangerous and gigantic Error of making certain Evil the means of contingent Good'.

And just as the French savant's portrait of Robespierre brings to burning focus his rejection of the crimes of Jacobin activity, so does the 23-year-old Coleridge's portrait of that same arch-Jacobin Robespierre serve as similar but even more finely calibrated focus, and serve to establish once and for all that Coleridge was never, and never in any true sense could have been, a Jacobin. Adumbrating Acton's famous dictum about power

---

[246] Taine, iv. 190–2.   [247] Ibid., vol. iii, pp. i–ii.

corrupting, Coleridge produces a dazzling evocation of Robespierre's meaning for history:

Robespierre, who displaced [Brissot], possessed a glowing ardor that still remembered the *end*, and a cool ferocity that never either overlooked, or scrupled, the *means*. What that *end* was, is not known: that it was a wicked one, has by no means been proved. I rather think, that the distant prospect, to which he was travelling, appeared to him grand and beautiful; but that he fixed his eye on it with such intense eagerness as to neglect the foulness of the road. If however his first intentions were pure, his subsequent enormities yield us a melancholy proof, that it is not the character of the possessor which directs the power, but the power which shapes and depraves the character of the possessor. In Robespierre, its influence was assisted by the properties of his disposition. . . . [E]nthusiasm in Robespierre was blended with gloom, and suspiciousness, and inordinante vanity. His dark imagination was still brooding over supposed plots against freedom—to prevent tyranny he became a Tyrant[248]—and having realized the evils which he suspected, a wild and dreadful Tyrant.—Those loud-tongued adulators, the mob, over-powered the lone-whispered denunciations of conscience—he despotized in all the pomp of Patriotism, and masqueraded on the bloody stage of Revolution, a Caligula with the cap of Liberty on his head.[249]

This, then, is enough. Not even Taine's portrait of Robespierre can quite match the point, the compression, the Roman parallelism so beloved by the Jacobins, of 'a Caligula with the cap of Liberty on his head'.[250] For Coleridge's beautiful prose not only validates his idiosyncratically humane political stance against any charge of Jacobinism, but in its depth, and cadence, perhaps gives us as well a fleeting glimpse of the conversational power that bemused so many among his most brilliant contemporaries.

[248] Cf. Madelin: 'The one and constant thought of that mediocre brain and narrow soul was to protect himself against "his enemies." These he discovered in every quarter; to destroy them he kept the guillotine permanently employed'. 'It was unsafe to look sad, or even thoughtful. Barras tells a story of one deputy who fancied Robespierre was looking at him when he was in a dreamy mood, and exclaimed in alarm: *"He'll be supposing I was thinking about something!"* ' (Madelin, 402–3).

[249] *Lectures 1795*, 35.

[250] It detracts in no way from the exquisite fittingness of Coleridge's metaphor to note that just as Robespierre was not actually the Emperor Caligula, so too in fact he was too much of a dandy to wear the red cap of liberty. 'He did not seem at all pleased,' notes a commentator, 'that the general had arrived wearing a red cap. He never wore one himself, but only had a tricolour cockade in his buttonhole. How could he put such a covering over his powdered hair that was so carefully combed? . . . . Even so, the cap had great success with the Parisians and members of the club, the majority of whom wore it. . . . At the end of the session one of those present tried to put one on Robespierre's head. No doubt he was an admirer and he did not want his idol to appear to disadvantage alongside Dumouriez. Robespierre immediately snatched it off and threw it to the ground. From anyone else but him the gesture would have seemed a sacrilege. Even so, no one protested. In fact, for a while fewer red caps were seen at the club' (Matrat, 144–5).

4

Beckoning from the Abode

THE two preceding textures of Romanticism have touched the two most important English founders, Wordsworth and Coleridge. The present touching will descry a texture from the so-called second generation. It was Shelley's admiration of Rousseau that originally heralded this volume's shift to the texture of origins; and it seems fitting, therefore, Rousseau and his effect having provided such important patternings up to now, that Shelley, Rousseau's celebrator and disciple, provide the texture to be descried in another part of the fabric called Romanticism. The present patterning, however, will have relatively little to do with previous studies (there are at least three treatments in recent years, one in English and two in French, on the relation of Shelley and Rousseau) that seek to assess the intellectual field of force existing between the two figures.[1]

It has been difficult to disentangle our contemporary response to Shelley from the damaging animadversions of Leavis and T. S. Eliot, and before that, of Arnold and even Hazlitt. The present tactile endeavour will attempt to further that disentanglement while not distorting what Shelley was—to concede against him what must be conceded, but at the same time to direct attention to his extraordinary intelligence and his supreme achievements: the poems, *Adonais* and 'Mont Blanc', and the essay, *A Defence of Poetry*.

Shelley's admirable intelligence is what has tended to get lost in the protracted moral debate about his actions, and the critical debate about the abstractness of his poetic voice. If one reads a biography, say that of Richard Holmes, one constantly sees a Shelley who quite properly appears eccentric, immature, and even foolish. But such a view seems, in significant degree, to be an effect of external description; if one approaches Shelley from within, through his letters, an entirely different picture emerges. Though he was beleaguered and confused, in his letters we hear a voice of moderation, courtesy, modesty, and perspicacity. We hear, above all, a voice pervasively characterized by coruscating intelligence.

That intelligence, one must repeat, should be our prime awareness about Shelley. Mary Shelley speaks with great justness and accuracy when

[1] See esp. Edward Duffy, *Rousseau in England: The Context for Shelley's Critique of the Enlightenment* (Berkeley: University of California Press, 1979).

she observes, 'And still less is his vast superiority in intellectual attainments sufficiently understood—his sagacity, his clear understanding, his learning, his prodigious memory; all these, as displayed in conversation, were known to few while he lived, and are now silent in the tomb'.[2] There are other testimonies available. Newman Ivey White, for instance, noted that

Nothing impressed Trelawny more deeply than Shelley's mental powers. 'Sometimes he would run through a great work on science, condense the author's laboured exposition, and by substituting simple words for the jargon of the schools, make the most abstruse work transparent.' 'He kept your brain in constant action.' His mental activity was infectious; it converted Williams from a sportsman to a scholar and writer; it elevated the tone of Byron's conversation whenever Shelley was present; it imposed upon Byron an unwonted docility toward Shelley's critical judgment.[3]

It is Shelley's extraordinary intelligence that places him, in the English Romantic pantheon, closest of all to Coleridge; and, indeed, the two figures exhibit important similarities: first of all, in clear-sighted and at times breathtaking intelligence; secondly, in a constant preoccupation with the classical languages (somewhat to my surprise, Hugh Lloyd-Jones, Regius Professor of Greek at Oxford, observed to me that he considered Coleridge's Greek to be even better than that of Shelley—which would make it very good indeed); and thirdly, in an absolute rightness in critical judgement. Coleridge is often, and correctly, considered the best of all English critics; certainly his judgement is amazingly correct and sympathetic. A tiny but exquisite example is supplied by his lines on Donne, which descry the contour of that poet with dazzling accuracy:

> With Donne, whose muse on dromedary trots,
> Wreathe iron pokers into true-love knots;
> Rhyme's sturdy cripple, fancy's maze and clue,
> Wit's forge and fire-blast, meaning's press and screw.[4]

That such compressed and happy description could only emerge from profound and just knowledge of Donne—even though that poet was little known in the Romantic era—should be apparent on the surface. If it is not, one only needs to consult other superbly just Coleridgean comments: 'If you would teach a scholar in the highest form how to *read*, take Donne, and of Donne [the third] satire.'[5] Again: 'After all, there is but one Donne! and now tell me yet, wherein, in *his own kind*, he differs from the similar power

[2] *Shelley*, iii. 220.   [3] White, ii. 358–9.
[4] Coleridge, *Poems*, i. 433.   [5] Brinkley, 521.

in Shakespeare?'[6] Or consider Coleridge's judgements of individual poems: of 'The Canonization', he remarked, 'One of my favorite poems'; of 'A Valediction forbidding Mourning', 'An admirable poem which none but Donne could have written'; of 'The Extasie', 'I should never find fault with metaphysical poems, were they all like this, or but half as excellent.'[7]

If Coleridge was here unerring in one of the most difficult of judgements, that of an unread poet for whom there existed no contemporary consensus of opinion; Shelley was unerring in a still more difficult judgement, that of a fellow poet whose reputation is still fluid. Alongside Coleridge's lines on Donne, we may place Shelley's exquisitely right lines in his sonnet on Wordsworth:

> Poet of Nature, thou hast wept to know
> That things depart which never may return[8]

In those two lines Shelley grasps the two profoundest truths about Wordsworth—the first a truth, as indicated elsewhere in this book, that important critics today have lost sight of—and the second, that 'the deepest current of feeling' in Wordsworth's entire nature, as a contemporary scholar has asserted, was 'the continuous presence of his own past'.[9] That the sonnet then goes on to grieve for Wordsworth's abandonment of his early Republican commitments and their replacement by Tory sentiment ('Deserting these, thou leavest me to grieve, | Thus having been, that thou shouldst cease to be') makes its sure identification of the inner essence of Wordsworth even more remarkable. But as Mary Shelley noted, for the youthful Shelley, 'The love and knowledge of nature developed by Wordsworth', was part of 'his favourite reading'.[10] Again, she says that 'No man ever admired Wordsworth's poetry more;—he read it perpetually, and taught others to appreciate its beauties'.[11] To be sure, this latter assertion is made somewhat to ameliorate Shelley's less than respectful portrait of Wordsworth as Peter Bell the Third:

He changes colours like a cameleon, and his coat like a snake. He is a Proteus of a Peter. He was at first sublime, pathetic, impressive, profound; then dull; then prosy and dull; and now dull—O, so very dull! it is an ultra-legitimate dulness.[12]

Yet this, especially considering its burlesque occasion, is a far from unjustified view of the later Wordsworth (Coleridge in 1822, as reported by Crabb Robinson, reproached 'Wordsworth with a disregard to the

---

[6] Brinkley, 522.   [7] Ibid. 523–4.
[8] *Shelley*, i. 206.   [9] Salvesen, 45.
[10] *Shelley*, i. 167.   [11] Ibid. iii. 307.
[12] Ibid. 255.

mechanism of his verse, and in general insinuates a decline of his faculties'[13]), especially the politically unsatisfactory later Wordsworth; and it does not impeach the poetic greatness of the essential Wordsworth. Again, Shelley's understanding of the merits of both Keats and Byron is also superb; especially when contrasted to Byron's blindness to the quality of Keats, and really of Wordsworth as well. Still again, nothing can surpass the generosity and accuracy of Shelley's judgement of cantos iii–v of *Don Juan*, expressed when he received them in 1821: 'It is a poem totally of its own species, & my wonder and delight at the grace of the composition no less than the free & grand vigour of the conception of it perpetually increase.'[14]

Coleridge and Shelley were also alike in the comprehensiveness and depth of their learning. Coleridge's learning was stupendous; the simple fact is that no scholar has ever even come close to sounding its depths. But Shelley's learning was of comparable depth, even if not of such massive scope—for Shelley lived only twenty-nine years, a fact which is always difficult to keep before one's eyes. Mary found 'a record of the books that Shelley read during several years', and it is awesome:

During the years of 1814 and 1815 the list is extensive. It includes in Greek: Homer, Hesiod, Theocritus—the histories of Thucydides and Herodotus, and Diogenes Laertius. In Latin: Petronius, Suetonius, some of the works of Cicero, a large proportion of those of Seneca and Livy. In English: Milton's Poems, Wordsworth's *Excursion*, Southey's *Madoc* and *Thalaba*, Locke on the Human Understanding, Bacon's *Novum Organum*. In Italian, Ariosto, Tasso, and Alfieri. In French, The *Rêveries d'un Solitaire* of Rousseau. To these may be added several modern books of travels.[15]

Of Shelley's reading in 1817, and of projects relating to his reading, his wife supplies an account as follows:

He projected translating the Hymns of Homer; his version of several of the shorter ones remain, as well as that to Mercury. . . . His readings this year were chiefly Greek. Besides the Hymns of Homer, and the Iliad, he read the Dramas of Aeschylus and Sophocles, the *Symposium* of Plato, and Arrian's *Historia Indica*. In Latin, Apuleius alone is named. In English, the Bible was his constant study; he read a great portion of it aloud in the evening. Among these evening readings, I find also mentioned the *Fairy Queen*, and other modern works, the production of his contemporaries, Coleridge, Wordsworth, Moore, and Byron.[16]

---

[13] *Miscellaneous Criticism*, 397.
[14] Shelley, *Letters*, ii. 357.   [15] *Shelley*, iii. 120.
[16] Ibid. 171. For a comprehensive listing of the virtual entirety of Shelley's reading, see 'Appendix VIII, Shelley's Reading', in Shelley, *Letters*, ii. 467–88.

Though they were alike in such important respects, Shelley and Coleridge were absolutely opposed in their relationships to Christianity. Coleridge devoted the chief effort of his life to the defence of 'Christianity, the one true Philosophy'. He speaks, characteristically, of 'the surpassing worth and transcendent reasonableness of the Christian Scheme';[17] and he insists that 'The two great moments of the Christian Religion are, Original Sin and Redemption'.[18] Shelley, on the other hand and in absolute antithesis, considered Christianity a superstition intertwined with all the exploitative social forms he despised:

Analogy seems to favour the opinion, that as, like other systems, Christianity has arisen and augmented, so like them it will decay and perish; that, as violence, darkness, and deceit, not reasoning and persuasion, have procured its admission among mankind, so when . . . time, that infallible controverter of false opinions, has involved its pretended evidences in the darkness of antiquity, it will become obsolete; that Milton's poem alone will give permanency to the remembrance of its absurdities; and that men will laugh as heartily at grace, faith, redemption, and original sin, as they now do at the metamorphoses of Jupiter, the miracles of Romish saints, the efficacy of witchcraft, and the appearance of departed spirits.[19]

Nevertheless, though this difference would appear to constitute an unbridgeable gulf between the two men; each of them—remarkably— seems to lean out longingly across that gulf towards the other. To Peacock in 1816 Shelley asked for news of 'the political state of England', and of 'its literature, of which when I speak Coleridge is in my thoughts'.[20] In 1820, in his 'Letter to Maria Gisborne', he speaks memorably of

> Coleridge—he who sits obscure
> In the exceeding lustre and the pure
> Intense irradiation of a mind,
> Which, with its own internal lightning blind,
> Flags wearily through darkness and despair—
> A cloud-encircled meteor of the air,
> A hooded eagle among blinking owls.[21]

Such deep respect is also present in the portrait of Coleridge provided in 'Peter Bell the Third':

> A man there came, fair as a maid,
> And Peter noted what he said,
> Standing behind his masters's chair.

---

[17] *Aids to Reflection*, 300.   [18] Ibid. 301.   [19] *Shelley*, i. 153.
[20] Shelley, *Letters*, i. 490.   [21] *Shelley*, iv. 8.

He was a mighty poet—and
    A subtle-souled psychologist;
All things he seemed to understand,
Of old or new—of sea or land—
    But his own mind—which was a mist.

This was a man who might have turned
    Hell into Heaven—and so in gladness
A Heaven unto himself have earned;
But he in shadows undiscerned
    Trusted,—and damned himself to madness.[22]

To be sure, Shelley's respect is here compromised by his rejection of Coleridge's Christianity, which makes Coleridge's mind 'a mist', which constitutes a trust in 'shadows undiscerned' that leave all his potentiality unfulfilled. Still, the praise is very great, and the curious description 'fair as a maid' comes much closer to describing Shelley himself than it does the sage of Highgate.

Shelley was at liberty to provide that description, because he never saw Coleridge. Mary Shelley says that

The poem beginning, 'Oh, there are spirits in the air,' was addressed in idea to Coleridge, whom he never knew; and at whose character he could only guess imperfectly, through his writings, and accounts he had heard of him from some who knew him well.[23]

Significantly, Shelley believed that Coleridge's political apostasy from the Jacobin principles of his youth—or rather, as discussed in the preceding chapter, his supposed political apostasy—could not represent the true Coleridge:

He regarded [Coleridge's] change of opinions as rather an act of will than conviction, and believed that in his inner heart he would be haunted by what Shelley considered the better and holier aspirations of his youth.[24]

If Shelley projected his own figure and conviction into the image of Coleridge, Coleridge, too, projected his own values into Shelley. He was immensely confident that he and Shelley would have become friends. 'I think as highly of Shelley's Genius—yea, and of his *Heart*—as you can do', wrote Coleridge to a correspondent some years after Shelley's death:

Soon after he left Oxford, he went to the Lakes, poor fellow! and with some wish, I have understood, to see me; but I was absent, and Southey received him instead. Now, the very reverse of what would have been the case in ninety-nine instances

---

[22] Ibid. iii. 273–4.   [23] Ibid. 120.   [24] Ibid.

out of a hundred, I *might* have been of use to him, and Southey could not; for I should have sympathized with his poetico-metaphysical Reveries, (and the very word metaphysics is an abomination to Southey).[25]

Coleridge's attribution of 'poetico-metaphysical Reveries' to Shelley is to the point. Shelley's inclination, Mary Shelley observed, led him 'almost alike to poetry and metaphysical discussions', and she speaks of the 'abstract and etherialised inspiration of Shelley'.[26] 'The metaphysical strain that characterises much of what he has written', she also says, 'was, indeed, the portion of his works to which, apart from those whose scope was to awaken mankind to aspirations for what he considered the true and good, he was himself particularly attached.'[27]

Even the seemingly unbridgeable gulf between Coleridge's Christianity and Shelley's atheism (or pantheism), did not deter Coleridge. Shelley, early in 1812, had told Southey of his beliefs:

I have lately had some conversation with Southey which has elicited my true opinions of God—he says I ought not to call myself an Atheist, since in reality I believe that the Universe is God.—I tell him I believe that God is another signification for the Universe.[28]

Hearing this, Southey had promptly declared Shelley a pantheist: 'Southey says I am not an Atheist but a Pantheist.'[29]

To be a pantheist rather than an atheist was, for Coleridge, who had spent almost his entire adult life thinking about the implications of these matters, not to change anything. 'Pantheism', he said, 'is equivalent to Atheism . . . there is no other Atheism actually existing, or speculatively conceivable, but Pantheism.'[30] Again, he spoke of 'Pantheism as the only possible *speculative* Atheism.'[31] Nevertheless, neither pantheism nor atheism disqualified Shelley in Coleridge's eyes:

His Atheism would not have scared *me*—for *me*, it would have been a semi-transparent Larva, soon to be *sloughed*, and, through which, I should have seen the true *Image*; the final metamorphosis. Besides, I have ever thought *that* sort of Atheism the next best religion to Christianity.[32]

Coleridge's respect for atheism, in truth, was a constant in his thought. 'Not one man in a thousand', he said:

has either strength of mind or goodness of heart to be an atheist. I repeat it. Not one

---

[25] *Collected Letters*, vi. 849–50.   [26] *Shelley*, i. 409.
[27] Ibid., p. xiii.   [28] Shelley, *Letters*, i. 215.
[29] Ibid. 219.   [30] Quoted in CPT, 190.
[31] *Collected Letters*, vi. 962.   [32] Ibid. 850.

man in ten thousand has goodness of heart or strength of mind to be an atheist. And were I not a Christian . . . I should be an atheist with Spinoza. . . . This, it is true, is negative atheism; and this is, next to Christianity, the purest spirit of humanity![33]

Southey had in a letter complacently assumed the role of philosophical mentor to Shelley ('He is come to the fittest physician in the world. At present he has got to the Pantheistic stage of philosophy, and, in the course of a week, I expect he will be a Berkeleyan, for I have put him on a course of Berkeley.'[34]). Coleridge, however, scoffed at Southey's fitness for understanding someone like Shelley:

As far as Robert Southey was concerned with him, I am quite certain that his harshness arose entirely from the frightful reports that had been made to him respecting Shelley's moral character and conduct—reports essentially false, but, for a man of Southey's strict regularity and habitual self-government, rendered plausible by Shelley's own wild words and horror of hypocrisy.[35]

Be that as it may, there can be little doubt that Coleridge would have engaged Shelley far more deeply than did Southey. No one ever called Southey a hooded eagle among blinking owls (even at the time of his early admiration, Shelley acutely noted that Southey was 'far from being a man of great reasoning powers');[36] and the much more brilliant Shelley would almost certainly have been overcome by Coleridge's corresponding brilliance, depth, and seductive sympathy.

Actually, the two minds were in accord on many issues. For instance, the myth of Prometheus, which so captivated Shelley, entranced Coleridge also. Coleridge speaks of 'the noblest Subject that perhaps a Poet ever worked on—the Prometheus', and he says that he has written 'a small volume almost to him [his son Hartley], containing all the materials & comments on the full import of this most pregnant and sublime Mythos and Philosopheme'.[37] Again, Shelley's plan, noted above, to translate the Homeric Hymns (which he actually did), is co-ordinate with a plan on Coleridge's part to translate and edit the Homeric Hymns (which of course he did not). Still again, Coleridge urged the heterodox opinion that Plato and Bacon were in agreement: he called Plato 'the Athenian Verulam' and Bacon 'the British Plato',[38] and he claimed that Bacon and Plato had 'radically one and the same system':[39]

[33] Allsop, 61.
[34] Quoted in Shelley, *Letters*, i. 219 n.
[35] *Collected Letters*, vi. 850.
[36] Shelley, *Letters*, i. 212.
[37] *Collected Letters*, v. 142–3.
[38] *Friend*, i. 488.
[39] Ibid. 487.

Thus the difference, or rather distinction between Plato and Lord Bacon is simply this: that philosophy being necessarily bi-polar, Plato treats principally of the truth, as it manifests itself at the *ideal* pole, as the science of intellect (i.e. de mundo intelligibili); while Bacon confines himself, for the most part, to the same truth, as it is manifested at the other, or material pole, as the science of nature (i.e. de mundo sensibili).[40]

For his part, Shelley too insisted on the conjunction of Bacon and Plato. 'Plato was essentially a poet—the truth and splendour of his imagery, and the melody of his language, is the most intense that it is possible to conceive'; but this role was also shared by Bacon: 'Lord Bacon was a poet. His language has a sweet and majestic rhythm, which satisfies the sense, no less than the almost superhuman wisdom of his philosophy satisfies the intellect.'[41] Again, 'Plato exhibits the rare union of close and subtle logic, with the Pythian enthusiasm of poetry. . . . His language is that of an immortal spirit, rather than a man. Lord Bacon is, perhaps, the only writer, who, in these particulars, can be compared to him.'[42] The twin comparisons not only attest the brilliance and critical discernment of their authors, but, across the gulf that separated Coleridge's Christian commitment from Shelley's contempt for 'that superstition which has disguised itself under the name of the religion of Jesus',[43] attest to their strong intellectual similarity.

Shelley's brilliant intelligence, as distinct from indications of poetic maturity, is nowhere more vividly present than in *Queen Mab*, the very poem in which he takes up most challengingly the roles of Christianity and atheism. One must be careful to discriminate an apprehension of the enormous intelligence behind *Queen Mab* from any claim that it is actually a great poem. But it is a poem of truly extraordinary intelligence, not less in its accompanying notes—'long philosophical, & Anti Christian'[44]—than in its verse lines. It is, to reiterate, not a great poem; Shelley was far too young at that time to produce a great extended poem. But it is very much better than Shelley's seeming later revulsion would have it:

Queen Mab [he writes in June 1821], a poem written by me when very young, in the most furious style, with long notes against Jesus Christ, & God the Father and the King & the Bishops & marriage & the Devil knows what, is just published by one of the low booksellers in the Strand, against my wish & consent.[45]

A few days later he writes Leigh Hunt's *Examiner* in the same vein. Hunt

[40] *Friend*, i. 492.
[41] *Shelley*, vii. 114–15.
[42] Ibid. 161.
[43] Ibid. 7.
[44] Shelley, *Letters*, i. 361.
[45] Ibid. ii. 300–1.

would have been so sympathetic to the original impetus of *Queen Mab*, that one's suspicion that the passage just quoted might have been designed to forestall action in the struggle over custody of Shelley's children, here seems reinforced. The passage may well have been deliberately planted with Hunt for future possible use as evidence of Shelley's abjuration of youthful errors. That, at any rate, is what Kelvin Everest has suggested to the present author, who finds the suggestion plausible:

A poem, entitled 'Queen Mab', was written by me at the age of eighteen [actually, it was written when he was 20], I dare say in a sufficiently intemperate spirit—but even then it was not intended for publication, and a few copies only were struck off, to be distributed among my personal friends. I have not seen this production for several years; I doubt not but that it is perfectly worthless in point of literary composition; and that in all that concerns moral and political speculation, as well as in the subtler discriminations of metaphysical and religious doctrine, it is still more crude and immature.[46]

All this seems to make prescient Coleridge's talk above of 'a Larva, soon to be *sloughed*, and, through which, I should have seen the true *Image*; the final metamorphosis'. Still, one regrets that Shelley, for whatever reason, should have deserted *Queen Mab*. Far better his proud statement in 1817:

It was composed in early youth, & is full of those errors which belong to youth, as far as arrangement of imagery & language & a connected plan, is concerned.—But it was a sincere overflowing of the heart & mind, & that at a period when they are most uncorrupted & pure. It is the Author's boast & it constitutes no small portion of his happiness that, after six years [four years] of added experience & reflection, the doctrines of equality & liberty & disinterestedness, & entire unbelief in religion of any sort, to which this Poem is devoted, have gained rather than lost that beauty & that grandeur which first determined him to devote his life to the investigation & inculcation of them—[47]

Yet *Queen Mab* is Shelley's first substantial work; and it is a truly remarkable work in its perspicacity, ardour, and high seriousness. The verse does not resonate with a unique urgency of imagery or diction, but, in the idiosyncratically Shelleyan manner, it is throughout workmanlike:

> How beautiful this night! the balmiest sigh,
> Which vernal zephyrs breathe in evening's ear,
> Were discord to the speaking quietude
> That wraps this moveless scene. Heaven's ebon vault,
> Studded with stars unutterably bright,
> Through which the moon's unclouded grandeur rolls,

---

[46] Ibid. 304.   [47] Ibid. i. 566–7.

> Seems like a canopy which love had spread
> To curtain her sleeping world. Yon gentle hills,
> Robed in a garment of untrodden snow;
> Yon darksome rocks, whence icicles depend,
> So stainless that their white and glittering spires
> Tinge not the moon's pure beam; yon castled steep,
> Whose banner hangeth o'er the time-worn tower
> So idly, that rapt fancy deemeth it
> A metaphor of peace;—all form a scene
> Where musing solitude might love to lift
> Her soul above this sphere of earthliness;
> Where silence undisturbed might watch alone,
> So cold, so bright, so still.[48]

Those lines are not contemptible; and the poem as a whole is an impressive performance. To say that it is an astonishingly precocious achievement is to say too little. It is a permanent addition to the literature of futurity.

Indeed, in the clearness of his vision of the future, Shelley has few equals. He saw more clearly than even Marx, whose chief prophecies—as opposed to his profound understandings about the nature of culture—have not been borne out by subsequent events. The workers, for instance, have never become 'immiserated'; and yet immiseration was an essential stage of the Marxist prediction of the future. But the vision of Shelley was not committed to the illusion that he could actually predict the specific details of the future, even though the future seems to be decidedly his. The causes he advocated as an outcast from society—the rights of women, the rights of animals, the equality of all people ('*Man* is equal; & I am convinced that equality will be the attendant on a more advanced & ameliorated state of society'[49]), the necessity of exchanging hierarchical society and class gradations for universal democracy—now flow in the full tide of society's aspiration.

Freud once said that John Stuart Mill, of all figures in the nineteenth century, was the least bound by the conventions of thinking in his time. To that nomination one would want to counter with the name of Shelley. For in the enormous convulsion of thought necessary to shake himself loose from the pieties of the early nineteenth century—'old Custom, legal Crime, | And bloody Faith, the foulest birth of time'[50]—Shelley not only summoned the intellectual strength for such a break, but set himself with great acumen on the path of the future. The passionate vision in *Prometheus Unbound*, which is the culmination of the effort begun in *Queen*

---

[48] *Shelley*, i. 90.   [49] Shelley, *Letters*, i. 28.   [50] *Shelley*, i. 206.

Mab, resonates with a vibrancy even greater now than when it appeared in 1820:

> And behold, thrones were kingless, and men walked
> One with the other even as spirits do,
> None fawned, none trampled;
>
> . . . . . .
>
> None frowned, none trembled, none with eager fear
> Gazed on another's eye of cold command,
> Until the subject of a tyrant's will
> Became, worse fate, an abject of his own
>
> . . . . . .
>
> None, with firm sneer, trod out in his own heart
> The sparks of love and hope
>
> . . . . . .
>
> None talked that common, false, cold, hollow talk
> Which makes the heart deny the *yes* it breathes,
> Yet question that unmeant hypocrisy
> With such a self-mistrust as has no name.
> And women, too, frank, beautiful, and kind
> As the free heaven which rains fresh light and dew
> On the wide earth, past; gentle radiant forms,
> From custom's evil taint exempt and pure;
> Speaking the wisdom once they could not think,
> Looking emotions once they feared to feel,
> And changed to all which once they dared not be
>
> . . . . . .
>
> The loathsome mask has fallen, the Man remains,—
> Sceptreless, free, uncircumscribed,—but man:
> Equal, unclassed, tribeless and nationless,
> Exempt from awe, worship, degree, the King
> Over himself; just, gentle, wise,—but man[51]

And yet *Queen Mab* seems almost a still more impressive achievement, taken in all its contexts, including Shelley's own later dismissal of its quality, than does *Prometheus Unbound* (despite the fact that it cannot claim the later poem's virtuosity of language). To say this may seem to imply the dislodging of *Prometheus Unbound* from its position as the apex of Shelley's achievement. If that be so, then so be it. Notwithstanding Shelley's own opinion that *Prometheus Unbound* was 'a poem in my best style, whatever that may amount to',[52] it is not this work, but *Adonais*, that should be seen as Shelley's greatest poem.

---

[51] *Shelley*, ii. 240–2.   [52] Shelley, *Letters*, ii. 127.

To say this is not to assert a simple preference. To say this is rather to attempt a readjustment of perspective on Shelley and the nature of his achievement. 'It is the most perfect of my productions', said Shelley of the *Prometheus*.[53] Yet of *Adonais* he said: 'It is a highly wrought *piece of art*, perhaps better in point of composition than any thing I have written.'[54] The praises for each poem seem to put them upon the same level. And yet there is a slight difference in these virtually equivalent encomia. The praise for *Adonais* seems to claim a more objective poem: 'a highly wrought *piece of art*'. The praise for *Prometheus*, on the other hand seems to imply a more idiosyncratically Shelleyan production: 'a poem in my best style'.

The diverging patterns are significant for an understanding of Shelley. Following them, an attempt can be made to descry, not just here, but throughout Shelley's work and the events of his life, two continuous but divergent threads of tone and emphasis. These strands take their origin in a connection to a single source: a massive wish for death. They constitute differing reactions to that wish—which, like Demogorgon, was 'a mighty darkness | Filling the seat of power, and rays of gloom | Dart round, as light from the meridian sun, | Ungazed upon and shapeless'.[55] In differing ways, the two concatenations weave themselves into patterns that almost seem to imply two Shelleys. The one, in accordance with the observation just made, may be thought of as the externally directed Shelley, and the second as the internally directed Shelley. Though the two often intertwine, they are none the less distinguishable.

It is the externally directed Shelley that produces his greatest work, that trio of masterpieces constituted by *Adonais*, 'Mont Blanc', and the *Defence of Poetry*, as well as a lesser poem like 'Ozymandias'. It is the internally directed Shelley that produces idiosyncratically Shelleyan—and in some estimations, great—work such as *Prometheus Unbound* and *Epipsychidion* and *Alastor*. Whenever the intertwining of externally-directed reference becomes sufficiently attenuated, there is likely to emerge what may almost be termed the hysterical Shelley—the Shelley who 'shrieked, and clasped my hands in extacy!';[56] the Shelley who says, 'I pant, I sink, I tremble, I expire!';[57] the Shelley who writes, 'I faint, I perish with my love!'[58] The hysterical poet is the direct counterpart of the man who, to an extent not sufficiently noted by commentators, felt overwhelmed by life: 'My heart faints within me,' writes Shelley in 1811, 'I am wretched, miserable.'[59]

[53] Shelley, *Letters*, ii. 127.
[55] *Shelley*, ii. 218.
[57] Ibid. 373.
[59] Shelley, *Letters*, i. 177.
[54] Ibid. 294.
[56] Ibid. 61.
[58] Ibid. iv. 119.

The internally directed Shelley subordinated the writing of poetry to pressing psychological needs; and it is this that makes many of the poems that ensued seem overlong, laden with too many words, tiringly abstract. The relentless flow of verbiage reminds one of the reports of Coleridge's conversational monologues; and one suspects that the source in each case might be the same: the anxiety that gripped the author when conversation or poetry-writing ceased. One tends to agree with Leavis on the issue of Shelley's overwrought and abstract verbosity:

Even when he is in his own way unmistakably a distinguished poet, as in *Prometheus Unbound*, it is impossible to go on reading him at any length with pleasure; the elusive imagery, the high-pitched emotions, the tone and movement, the ardours, ecstasies and despairs, are too much the same all through.[60]

Leavis charged Shelley with a 'weak grasp upon the actual';[61] and the indictment is substantially true with regard to much of Shelley's verse— though radically untrue with regard to his greatest poetry, which Leavis does not really address. The charge is in substance the same as the one made early on by Hazlitt, that Shelley 'gives us, for representations of things, rhapsodies of words'.[62] Hazlitt went on to judge severely that Shelley 'does not lend the colours of imagination and the ornaments of style to the objects of nature, but paints gaudy, flimsy, allegorical pictures on gauze, on the cobwebs of his own brain, "Gorgons and Hydras, and Chimeras dire" '.[63]

But as a matter of fact, Shelley himself might almost have concurred in the charge of a 'weak grasp upon the actual', for actuality did not rank highly in his scale of values; and much, though not all, of his internally directed verse was devoted to the alleviation of an inner stress that was the direct result of actuality. 'You know,' he writes to Peacock, 'I always seek in what I see the manifestation of something beyond the present & tangible object.'[64] Speaking of *Epipsychidion*, he said, 'As to real flesh & blood, you know that I do not deal in those articles,—you might as well go to a ginshop for a leg of mutton, as expect any thing human or earthly from me.'[65]

Indeed, the whole point of the composition of Shelley's internally directed verse was, as it were, to loosen the grasp of actuality. 'Any thing that prevents me from thinking does me good. Reading does not occupy me enough: the only relief I find springs from the composition of poetry, which necessitates contemplations that lift me above the stormy mist of

[60] Leavis, 211.
[61] Ibid. 206.
[62] *Hazlitt*, xii. 246.
[63] Ibid.
[64] Shelley, *Letters*, ii. 47.
[65] Ibid. 363.

sensations which are my habitual place of abode.'[66] The writing of internally directed poetry, in fact, served the same medicinal function as the relentless study of Greek: 'I have employed Greek in large doses, & I consider it the only sure remedy for diseases of the mind.'[67]

If the composition of poetry gave Shelley relief from 'the stormy mist of sensations' in which he found himself living, by that very fact it tended to loosen the chains of actuality, to take him from the real into the ideal. 'He loved to idealise reality,' observed Mary Shelley cannily, 'and this is a taste shared by few.'[68] Why such a commitment to idealization? The answer must be reiterated: actuality was what Shelley found intolerable. He speaks of 'the filthy world of which it is it's Hell to be a part'.[69] He speaks of 'this hellish society of men'.[70] 'My firm persuasion', he says, 'is that the mass of mankind as things are arranged at present, are cruel deceitful & selfish, & always on the watch to surprize those few who are not—& therefore I have taken suspicion to me as a cloak, & scorn as an impenetrable shield.'[71]

It was this grim view of actuality, expressed in those statements late in his life, but traceable from his childhood, that led to Shelley's wish for death. Where do we find that wish expressed? For one place, in the very first line of his very first significant poem, *Queen Mab*: 'How wonderful is Death'.[72] Even earlier, in 1811, he had said, 'Night comes,—Death comes—Cold, calm death, almost I would it were tomorrow.'[73] Still earlier, he says that 'Death closes all!—Wherefore should we linger, unhappiness disappointment enthusiasm & subsequent apathy follow our steps, wd. it not be a general good to all human beings that I should make haste away.'[74] Again, 'Is suicide wrong? I slept with a loaded pistol & some poison last night but did not die.'[75] Yet again, 'how beautiful does death appear, what a release from the crimes & miseries of mortality! To be condemned to feed on the garbage of grinding misery that hungry hyena mortal life!'[76]

Why did Shelley so fervently embrace the prospect of death? Why did he so desperately seek to flee reality? The answer is that he felt crushed and desolated by the anger of others, starting with the anger of his father, and proceeding to the anger of his schoolmates at Eton, then to the anger of the authorities at Oxford who expelled him, and in due course the anger of society at large. It is hardly possible to exaggerate the devastating effect of

[66] Shelley, *Letters*, ii. 296.   [67] Ibid. 360.   [68] *Shelley*, vol. i, p. xiii.
[69] Shelley, *Letters*, ii. 320.   [70] Ibid. 319.   [71] Ibid. 382.
[72] *Shelley*, i. 67.   [73] Shelley, *Letters*, i. 172.   [74] Ibid. 104.
[75] Ibid. 36.   [76] Ibid. 173.

this avalanche of anger, though commentators have tended to be misled by Shelley's defiance into thinking he was not so deeply hurt as he was. As a youth in 1810, he reacts with bravado: 'They attack me for my detestable principles I am reckoned an outcast, yet defy them & laugh at their inefficient efforts.'[77] In the same letter, he again reacts with youthful bravado: 'There lowers a terrific tempest, but I stand as it were on a Pharos, & smile exultingly at the vain beating of the billows below—'.[78]

He stopped smiling, however, as time went on. By 1816 he could write to Godwin: 'my blood boils in my veins, and my gall rises against all that bears the human form, when I think of what I, their benefactor and ardent lover, have endured of enmity and contempt from you and from all mankind.'[79] By the time of *Adonais*, Shelley felt himself 'neglected and apart' and likened himself to 'A herd-abandoned deer, struck by the hunter's dart'.[80] By that time, forced to live a nomadic outcast's life in Italy (he speaks of 'the dreary solitude of the understanding & the imagination in which we past the first years of our expatriation, yoked to all sorts of miseries & discomforts'[81]) he felt himself a 'phantom among men; companionless'.[82]

This had all been going on since his childhood. Some sort of psychological cataclysm occurred in Shelley's early life, the complete lineaments of which cannot be discerned. Clearly, however, it was connected with his relationship to his father (and, in psychoanalytical perspective, the very paucity of reference or documentation about the relationship to the mother suggests that all was not well there either). Whatever the intertwined dynamics of parental relationships, however, Shelley felt himself locked out of the warmth and nurture associated with home. He speaks memorably and poignantly, in *Alastor*, when he says of the poet that 'When early youth had past, he left | His cold fireside and alienated home'.[83] Indeed, that whole poem is a testament to the psychological ruin of Shelley's life. I have elsewhere said of *Alastor* (significantly subtitled *The Spirit of Solitude*) that

Shelley's awesomely despairing poem is surely one of literature's most painful testaments to wretchedness, a wretchedness so frantic, so alienated, and so alone

[77] Ibid. 27.
[78] Ibid. 28.
[79] Ibid. 459.
[80] *Shelley*, ii. 398 (Stanza xxxiii).
[81] Shelley, *Letters*, ii. 373.
[82] *Shelley*, ii. 398 (Stanza xxxi). Cf. a letter of 1819: 'I am regarded by all who know or hear of me, except I think on the whole five individuals as a rare prodigy of crime & pollution.' (Shelley, *Letters*, ii. 94.)   [83] *Shelley*, i. 179 (lines 75–6).

that it burdens the heart. The melancholy is compounded by Mrs Shelley's testimony that 'None of Shelley's poems is more characteristic than this'.[84]

Though details about Shelley's cold fireside and alienated home are in short supply, a certain amount of information is available about his relationship to his father. Timothy Shelley was doubtless a decent enough man, but he lacked the resources of sympathy and sensibility to understand his brilliant son. Indeed, Shelley's peculiar combination of enormous intelligence and disturbed immaturity was a particularly volatile compound in any relationship with authority. Shelley told Godwin that

I am the Son of a man of fortune in Sussex.—The habits of thinking of my Father and myself never coincided. Passive obedience was inculcated and enforced in my childhood: I was required to love because it was my *duty* to love—it is scarcely necessary to remark that coercion obviated its own intention.[85]

It is not known just what traumas might have been subsumed under the phrase 'inculcated and enforced'. Certain it is that Shelley, weak and never able to defend himself physically ('frail' is his lifelong adjective of self-description), developed an inflexible psychological opposition to rendering obedience to anyone—an attitude reinforced by his admired Godwin having maintained, in *Political Justice*, that 'one man can in no case be bound to yield obedience to any other man or set of men upon earth'.[86] Where there is love, obedience is gladly given; where there is no sense of love ('My father has ever regarded me as a blot and defilement of his honor'),[87] an attitude of defiance can be engendered, no matter how dearly the subject may pay for that defiance. Shelley's later philosophical celebrations of love seem to be reaction formations to the lack of the sense of being loved in early life.

In any event, obedience became a kind of adverse shibboleth for Shelley. In his very first surviving letter, the 12-year-old boy concludes with the defiant statement, 'I am not | Your obedient servant, | P. B. Shelley.'[88] In a letter to his father in 1811, he says, '*Obedience* is in my opinion a word which should have no existence—you regard it as necessary.'[89] To Elizabeth Hitchener later that same year, he says that '*Obedience* (were society as I could wish it) is a word that ought to be without meaning.'[90] And to her father, in 1812—and he might as well have been speaking to his own father—he writes sharply:

[84] Gravil, 19. [85] Shelley, *Letters*, i. 227.
[86] Godwin, i. 169. [87] Shelley, *Letters*, i. 228.
[88] Ibid. 1. [89] Ibid. 146.
[90] Ibid. 200.

I had some difficulty in stifling an indignant surprise on reading the sentence of your letter in which *you* refuse my invitation to your daughter. How are you entitled to do this? who made you her governor? did you receive this refusal from her to communicate to me? No you have not.—How are *you* then constituted to answer a question which can only be addressed to *her*? believe me such an assumption is as impotent as it is immoral, you may cause your daughter much anxiety many troubles, you may stretch her on a bed of sickness, you may destroy her body, but you are defied to shake her mind. . . . Neither the laws of Nature, nor of England have made children private property.—[91]

This remarkable statement seems to incorporate the whole structure of Shelley's reaction to his own childhood situation. Significantly for his experience of that situation, he poignantly concedes the 'much anxiety' and 'much trouble' created by disapproval from the father.

Indeed, the statement serves also as a compelling gloss for the larger structure of *Prometheus Unbound*. That poem was, at least on one level, a psychodrama of Shelley's family situation in childhood, one in which the conceptions of obedience and its enforcement were paramount. Its anxious cloud of feminine presences seems a shadowy refraction of Shelley's relations with his four sisters and his mother; Jupiter enforces the oppressive values of Timothy Shelley; and Demogorgon, shadowy and even more powerful than Jupiter, seems to embody the psychic meaning, in Shelley's unconscious mind, of the grandfather, Sir Bysshe Shelley.

Shelley was not close to his grandfather, but Sir Bysshe Shelley was none the less very important for the formation of his grandson's attitudes. Standing, in the hierarchy of power, above even Timothy Shelley, Sir Bysshe had been a democrat, opposed to tyrants and bigots, and by his several marriages had seemed an icon of free sexuality. It seems likely that Shelley's obsession with the necessity of opposing 'tyrants' was at least to some extent an attempt to adopt the putative values of his grandfather; and his belief that the grandfather was 'a complete Atheist'[92] by the same token must have had some role in the provenance of his own proudly flaunted atheism. Unable to identify with his own father, Shelley seems unmistakably to have attempted to identify himself with the shadowy figure of Sir Bysshe.

In this context, a letter he writes to his grandfather, the day after a defiant letter to Timothy Shelley, seems to convey a longing to find psychological succour there:

Excuse me, if never having addressed you before, I appeal in time of misfortune to your benevolence. I have forfeited I think unjustly my father's esteem, for having

[91] Ibid. 298.   [92] Ibid. 239.

consulted my own taste in marriage. If there is a question important to happiness it is this; certainly *he* whom the question most nearly concerns has the best right to decide upon its merits. Obedience in this case is misplaced. . . . I am accustomed to speak my opinion unreservedly; this has occasioned me some misfortunes, but I do not therefore cease to speak as I think. Language is given us to express ideas—he who fetters it is a BIGOT and a TYRANT, from these have my misfortunes arisen.—

I expect from your liberality and justice no unfavourable construction of what fools in power would denominate *insolence*.

This is not the spirit in which I write. I write in the spirit of truth and candor. If you will send me some money to help me and my wife (and I know you are not ungenerous) I will add to my respect for a grandfather my love for a preserver.[93]

The proud—and poignant—appeal was not successful; and Shelley's sense of a cold fireside and alienated home was thereby reinforced (we hear the hurt small boy in Shelley's later statement that 'I hear from my Uncle that Sir B Shelley is not likely to live long. . . . He is a bad man. I never had respect for him, I always regarded him as a curse on society.—I shall not grieve at his death. I will not wear mourning. I will not attend his funeral'[94]). But the appeal to Sir Bysshe, with the hopeful references to words that the grandfather might approve—words like TYRANT and BIGOT—show how much Shelley wanted to be able to feel himself his grandfather's epigone.

Indeed, Demogorgon, whose shadowy power defeats Jupiter, represents not merely Sir Bysshe, but also Shelley's hoped-for identification with Sir Bysshe; for Demogorgon reveals himself as Jupiter's own son. 'Awful shape, what art thou', asks Jupiter, only to hear the reply: 'I am thy child, as thou wert Saturn's child; | Mightier than thee: and we must dwell together | Henceforth in darkness.'[95] It is sad that Jupiter's answer, 'Detested prodigy!', seems precisely to incorporate Timothy Shelley's sentiments about his own child.

Shelley was the entailed heir of the estate; in fact, without the entail, his father would doubtless have disinherited him. In Shelley's psyche, accordingly, the entail seems to have assumed not only an economic but a psychological value; the psychological value, in truth, seems to have been the more important of the two. Few people can have been more generous or less avaricious than Shelley; nevertheless, the entail loomed large in his sense of self. He frequently mentions it either specifically or by implication[96] (the first thing he tells Godwin in the quotation above, for

[93] Shelley, *Letters*, i. 147.
[94] Ibid. 239.
[95] *Shelley*, ii. 228 (III. i. 51–6).
[96] For a single detailed example, see *Letters*, i. 457–8.

instance, is that he is the 'Son of a man of fortune'). His sense of the entail, which in his own mind indissolubly connected him with Sir Bysshe Shelley, seems, as it were, to have put the iron in his backbone. No matter how much his father detested him, he could not be disinherited; this knowledge was one by which, weak and physically abused though he was—first at home and then by his classmates at Eton—he was enabled to stand up in defiance, rather than cower in the terror he undoubtedly felt.

His always being defiant, however, cost him dearly. If he had bent before the blast, like the willow, his inner structures might have survived. Standing always on the Pharos, however, the outer man was, as it were, held upright by the entail, while the inner supports of his sensitive nature crumbled under the incessant pounding. 'I am, and I desire to be, nothing', he poignantly says, in 1821, in the context of his great admiration for Byron.[97] But this sense of inner annihilation had long been with Shelley, no matter what his flaming words of defiance. 'And what am I?', he writes to Hogg a decade earlier, 'nothing! a speck in an Universe'.[98] He refers to himself as 'the weakest, most slavish of beings that exists on the earth's face'.[99] Speaking in 1814 of the time before his marriage to Harriet, he says that 'I loathed the very light of day, & looked upon my own being with deep & unutterable abhorrence'.[100]

It is not enough to say that Shelley was unhappy. He was desperate, hanging by a thread. 'Alas! this is not what I thought life was', he exclaims in a fragment of 1820. 'I am half mad. I am wretchedly miserable', he blurts out in 1811.[101] In simple truth, Shelley fell upon the thorns of life—'I fall upon the thorns of life! I bleed!'[102] In face of the lifelong onslaught of anger and contempt from others, he felt himself unutterably frail and vulnerable. He repeatedly uses words that convey his sense of weakness and insubstantiality. The descriptions in *Adonais* poignantly convey that sense: 'Midst others of less note, came one frail Form'.[103] The sense of Shelley's weakness and inner desolation is almost overwhelming: 'A Love in desolation masked;—a Power | Girt round with weakness';[104] 'the ever-beating heart | Shook the weak hand that grasped it';[105] he speaks of 'his branded and ensanguined brow, | Which was like Cain's or Christ's.—Oh! that it should be so!';[106] and most piercingly of all, he writes:

---

[97] Shelley, *Letters*, ii. 344.   [98] Ibid. i. 171.   [99] Ibid. 184.
[100] Ibid. 389.   [101] Ibid. 172.
[102] *Shelley*, ii. 296 ('Ode to the West Wind', line 54).
[103] Ibid. 398 (*Adonais*, line 271).   [104] Ibid. (lines 281–2).
[105] Ibid. (lines 294–5).   [106] Ibid. 399 (lines 305–6).

> and now he fled astray
> With feeble steps o'er the world's wilderness
> And his own thoughts, along that rugged way,
> Pursued, like raging hounds, their father and their prey.[107]

His fleeing with feeble steps o'er the world's wilderness was almost literally an eviction caused by the anger and contempt of others:

You are perhaps aware that one of the chief motives which strongly urges me either to desert my native country, dear to me from many considerations, or resort to its most distant and solitary regions, is the perpetual experience of neglect or enmity from almost every one but those who are supported by my resources. I shall cling, perhaps, during the infancy of my children to all the prepossessions attached to the country of my birth, hiding myself and Mary from that contempt which we so unjustly endure. I think, therefore, at present only of settling in Cumberland or Scotland.[108]

The wrenching violence wrought upon Shelley's inner structures during his earliest years at home was perpetuated and augmented in his adolescent years at Eton. Lacking the kind of childhood confidence that would have allowed him to be accepted by the other boys, he incurred their anger and enmity, and further isolated himself from supportive social involvements. An especially affecting testament to his situation there is conveyed by his lines in dedication of *Laon and Cythna* to Mary:

> I do remember well the hour which burst
> My spirit's sleep: a fresh May-dawn it was,
> When I walked forth upon the glittering grass,
> And wept, I knew not why: until there rose
> From the near school-room voices, that, alas!
> Were but one echo from a world of woes—
> The harsh and grating strife of tyrants and of foes.[109]

Not only did the tyrants and foes ostracize Shelley, but it seems more likely than not, given his combination of personal attractiveness and physical weakness, and given the conditions of life at Eton at that time, that he was subjected to unwanted sexual intimacy (Coleridge, in 1826, writes of 'the moral corruption that was likely to be imparted by any boy fresh from Eton'[110]). Shelley's spirit could never be tamed; but he could offer scarcely any physical resistance.

---

[107] *Shelley,* ii. 398 (*Adonais,* lines 276–9).
[108] Shelley, *Letters,* i. 453.
[109] *Shelley,* i. 251 (lines 21–7).
[110] *Collected Letters,* vi. 645.

In any event, and most poignantly, he reacted against the society of tyrants and foes by an intensified idealism:

> And then I clasped my hands and looked around,—
> —But none was near to mock my streaming eyes,
> Which poured their warm drops on the sunny ground—
> So without shame, I spake:—'I will be wise,
> And just, and free, and mild, if in me lies
> Such power, for I grow weary to behold
> The selfish and the strong still tyrannise
> Without reproach or check.' I then countrouled
> My tears, my heart grew calm, and I was meek and bold.[111]

But this intensified idealism, which makes Shelley such an appealing figure among the heroes of culture ('Ah, did you once see Shelley plain?'), came at the appalling cost of ever-intensified aloneness:

> And from that hour did I with earnest thought
> Heap knowledge from forbidden mines of lore,
> Yet nothing that my tyrants knew or taught
> I cared to learn, but from that secret store
> Wrought linkèd armour for my soul, before
> It might walk forth to war among mankind;
> Thus power and hope were strengthened more and more
> Within me, till there came upon my mind
> A sense of loneliness, a thirst with which I pined.[112]

Just as the first line of Shelley's first significant poem hailed the surcease of death, so did the statement of his very last poem continue his unremitting sense of the misery attendant upon 'that hungry hyena mortal life'. 'The poem entitled the *Triumph of Life*', judged Hazlitt with elegant brevity, 'is in fact a new and terrific *Dance of Death*.'[113] But most of all, the wish for death suffuses and exalts Shelley's greatest and most magnificent poem, *Adonais*.

It is astonishing that so few commentators have seen this mighty truth about that supreme poem. No greater elegy—not *Lycidas* itself—has ever been written. And yet commentators cannot allow themselves to hear what it is saying, and what makes it so inconceivably powerful. 'Before its close,' says the otherwise admirable scholar Dowden, 'the poem rises into an impassioned hymn of immortality.'[114]

---

[111] *Shelley*, i. 252 (lines 28–36).
[112] Ibid. (lines 37–45).
[113] *Hazlitt*, xvi. 273.   [114] Quoted in *Shelley*, ii. 431.

162 *Beckoning from the Abode*

Immortality? That is precisely what *Adonais* does not offer. *Lycidas* offers immortality: 'Weep no more', commands Milton in an exultant and triumphant restoration of hope:

> Weep no more, woeful Shepherds weep no more,
> For *Lycidas* your sorrow is not dead,
> Sunk though he be beneath the wat'ry floor,
> So sinks the day-star in the Ocean bed,
> And yet anon repairs his drooping head,
> And tricks his beams, and with new spangled Ore,
> Flames in the forehead of the morning sky:
> So *Lycidas*, sunk low, but mounted high,
> Through the dear might of him that walk'd the waves,
> Where other groves, and other streams along,
> With *Nectar* pure his oozy Locks he laves,
> And hears the unexpressive nuptial Song,
> In the blest Kingdoms meek of joy and love.
> There entertain him all the Saints above
> In solemn troops, and sweet Societies
> That sing, and singing in their glory move,
> And wipe the tears for ever from his eyes.[115]

What a passage! Matchless in cadence, matchless in diction, matchless in its presentation of the apex of Christian hope, it seems to leave no possibilities for any rival. Particularly not for a rival such as Shelley, for whom Christian hope could not be summoned; who had, indeed, once closed a letter with an expression of devotion not until the advent of heaven but 'till annihilation'.[116] So how, in Shelley's lament, could the elegiac note of hope be sounded? The grief in Shelley's poem is especially plangent, but it is so precisely because of the irrevocability of Adonais's death:

> Alas! that all we loved of him should be,
> But for our grief, as if it had not been.
> And grief itself be mortal! Woe is me!
> Whence are we, and why are we?
>
> .   .   .   .   .
>
> *He* will awake no more, oh, never more![117]

As Shelley understands this frame of things, the stars could be termed immortal, but not ephemeral human life:

---

[115] *Lycidas*, lines 165–81.
[116] Shelley, *Letters*, i. 219.
[117] *Shelley*, ii. 395 (*Adonais*, stanza xxi, lines 181–4; stanza xxii, line 190).

> The sun comes forth, and many reptiles spawn;
> He sets, and each ephemeral insect then
> Is gathered into death without a dawn,
> And the immortal stars awake again;
> So is it in the world of living men[118]

In the face of this encompassing oblivion, how, to repeat, can the elegiac note of hope be sounded? By what means does Shelley's great poem ascend from despair to its gathering exultancy? The answer is twofold: one part psychological, the other rhetorical. Rhetorically, Shelley, in a truly dazzling turn, argues the progressive statement into a position where Adonais's death becomes an escape from life; and, as an escape, can be seen as preferable to life itself, and therefore co-ordinate with the value placed on immortality. That, it is evident, is apotheosis of the death wish indeed. The motive power for the progression is supplied by revulsion from the reviewers who have killed Adonais; they are still alive, therefore life is not desirable. It further follows that if life is not desirable, death, which is not infested by reviewers, must be eminently desirable:

> Our Adonais has drunk poison—oh!
> What deaf and viperous murderer could crown
> Life's early cup with such a draught of woe?[119]
>
> .   .   .   .   .   .
>
> Live thou, whose infamy is not thy fame!
> Live! fear no heavier chastisement from me,
> Thou noteless blot on a remembered name!
> But be thyself, and know thyself to be![120]
>
> .   .   .   .   .   .
>
> Nor let us weep that our delight is fled
> Far from these carrion kites that scream below;
> He wakes or sleeps with the enduring dead;
> Thou canst not soar where he is sitting now.—[121]

Its weeping abrogated, the poem, now in a huge crescendo of joy and affirmation, receives another influx of power. To the triumphant rhetorical progression just noted is now added an enormous emotional deepening, a sanctus-like organ tone supplied by Shelley's joining his own psychological situation to, or rather, merging it with, that of Keats. All the misery of

---

[118] Ibid. 397 (stanza xxix, lines 253–7).
[119] Ibid. 399 (stanza xxxvi, lines 316–18).
[120] Ibid. 399–400 (stanza xxxvii, lines 325–8).
[121] Ibid. 400 (stanza xxxviii, lines 334–7).

Shelley's own life is swept up into his longing for death, here, in sustained oxymoronic paradox, become the realm of sole value:

> Peace, peace! he is not dead, he doth not sleep—
> He hath awakened from the dream of life—
> 'Tis we, who lost in stormy visions, keep
> With phantoms an unprofitable strife,
> And in mad trance strike with our spirit's knife
> Invulnerable nothings—*We* decay
> Like corpses in a charnel; fear and grief
> Convulse us and consume us day by day,
> And cold hopes swarm like worms within our living clay.[122]

The poem had earlier prefigured this deepening, by which the *He* of Adonais changes to a *We* that includes Shelley, by Urania's plea ('her distress | Roused Death: Death rose and smiled'):[123]

> . . . my Adonais! I would give
> All that I am to be as thou now art
> But I am chained to Time, and cannot thence depart![124]

Still more had the deepening and merging been prefigured by the entrance of Shelley himself—to an extent that constitutes a radical departure in the tradition of the classical elegy—into the world of the poem. He comes as a figure markedly under a stress no less severe than the stress imputed to Keats. He is 'neglected and apart; | A herd-abandoned deer, struck by the hunter's dart'.[125] The 'one frail Form' who makes his entrance is precisely a figure under sore assault from life:

> and now he fled astray
> With feeble steps o'er the world's wilderness,
> And his own thoughts, along that rugged way,
> Pursued, like raging hounds, their father and their prey.[126]

Such a figure, by the very lineaments of his despair, makes it uncertain whether the funerary celebration be not as appropriate for him as for Adonais himself; certainly the need of such a figure for succour is very great.

But now the poem, Shelley's own longing pouring into it in exultant

---

[122] *Shelley*, ii. 400 (stanza xxxix, lines 343–51).
[123] Ibid. 396 (stanza xxv, lines 224–5).
[124] Ibid. (stanza xxvi, lines 232–4).
[125] Ibid. 398 (stanza xxxiii, lines 296–7).
[126] Ibid. (stanza xxxi, lines 271, 276–9).

release, begins triumphant and repeated paeans to the situation of Adonais, dead, yet by that very fact superior to life:

> He has outsoared the shadow of our night;
> Envy and calumny and hate and pain,
> And that unrest which men miscall delight,
> Can touch him not and torture not again;[127]
>
> .   .   .   .
>
> He lives, he wakes—'tis Death is dead, not he;
> Mourn not for Adonais.—Thou young Dawn,
> Turn all thy dew to splendour, for from thee
> The spirit thou lamentest is not gone[128]

To be sure, Keats lives only as a dispersal of his elements into nature, a pantheistic conclusion that brings solace only in the poem's transfigured language. Yet that language is here of a weight, its progression of a sureness and cadence, unequalled anywhere in all of Shelley's writing. Part of the weight, the sustained *gravitas*, of the poem is achieved by the gorgeous use of the decorative and objectifying conventions of classical elegy. Shelley's profound knowledge of Greek and Latin poetry supplies him a command that renders his verse here deliberate, grave, ornate and full; and the wonderful orotundity of the Spenserian stanzas imparts to it a stately and solemn movement—both *gravitas* and movement being here far removed from the frantic verbiage of the hysterical Shelley. The great pantheistic affirmation in this poem is a marvel of cadence and linguistic certainty:

> He is made one with Nature: there is heard
> His voice in all her music, from the moan
> Of thunder, to the song of night's sweet bird;
> He is a presence to be felt and known
> In darkness and in light, from herb and stone,[129]
>
> .   .   .   .
>
> He is a portion of the loveliness
> Which once he made more lovely: he doth bear
> His part, while the one Spirit's plastic stress
> Sweeps through the dull dense world, compelling there
> All new successions to the forms they wear;
> Torturing th' unwilling dross that checks its flight
> To it's own likeness, as each mass may bear;
> And bursting in it's beauty and its might
> From trees and beasts and men into the Heaven's light.[130]

---

[127] Ibid. 400 (stanza xl, lines 352–5).   [128] Ibid. 401 (stanza xli, lines 361–4).
[129] Ibid. (stanza xlii, lines 370–4).   [130] Ibid. (stanza xliii, lines 379–87).

Shelley's own wish for death now flooding passionately into the poem, in a total merging with his objective memorializing of Adonais's death, the language and its cadence become ever more musical and inevitable:

> And he is gathered to the kings of thought
> Who waged contention with their time's decay,
> And of the past are all that cannot pass away.[131]

And so the great poem rolls onward, to culminate in the majestic evocation, not of God, but of the impersonal and pantheistic One of Plotinus; and in the same overwhelming stanza to give full, direct, and unequivocal voice to Shelley's own wish for death:

> The One remains, the many change and pass;
> Heaven's light forever shines, Earth's shadows fly;
> Life, like a dome of many-coloured glass,
> Stains the white radiance of Eternity,
> Until Death tramples it to fragments.—Die,
> If thou wouldst be with that which thou dost seek![132]

No exhortation could be more unequivocal. Die! The command cannot be directed to Adonais, though it eagerly looks to his example. Die! The counsel may seem to be addressed to any for whom life is insufficient; yet the one person to whom it most surely is addressed is Shelley himself. 'Die, | If thou would be with that which thou dost seek!' No more startling, no more direct, advice is to be encountered in the annals of poetry.

It is advice that Shelley receives not with terror but with consent and gladness:

> Why linger, why turn back, why shrink, my Heart?
> Thy hopes are gone before: from all things here
> They have departed; thou shouldst now depart![133]

The lines, sighing and longing, bring to perfect focus the question of the tormented youth of 1811: 'Wherefore should we linger . . . would it not be a general good to all human beings that I should make haste away.'[134] The decision to die brings to full view the merging of Shelley and Adonais that had suggested itself from early in the poem; and the lines that convey their coming union are as soft as the breeze they invoke:

[131] *Shelley*, ii. 403 (stanza xlviii, lines 430–3).
[132] Ibid. 404 (stanza lii, lines 460–5).
[133] Ibid. (stanza liii, lines 469–71).
[134] Shelley, *Letters*, i. 104.

> The soft sky smiles,—the low wind whispers near:
> 'Tis Adonais calls! oh, hasten thither,
> No more let life divide what Death can join together.[135]

After these lines, what more is there to say? They constitute the pure and final triumph of Shelley's wish for death. His 'spirit's bark is driven' towards the place of Adonais:

> I am borne darkly, fearfully, afar;
> While burning through the inmost veil of Heaven,
> The soul of Adonais, like a star,
> Beacons from the abode where the Eternal are.[136]

The cumulative passion and intensity of Shelley's ultimate statement place the penultimate verb of his mighty poem under erasure. The noun 'beacon' is changed into the verb 'beacons'. Yet this changed function is itself also changed, in its import if not its hieroglyph, into the substitutive word 'beckons'. For the soul of Adonais, representing the death for which Shelley had so unremittingly longed, here beckons—' 'Tis Adonais calls!'—no less constantly, and even more enticingly, than it beacons; and throughout Shelley's great poem it has drawn everything towards its final rest.

Shelley knew what he had here achieved. Through the veil of his exquisite modesty, which was so beautiful a trait of his character, one must look carefully to find confirmation that he knew. But he did. He sent *Adonais* to Byron, with words of excessive self-deprecation: 'As to the Poem I send you, I fear it is worth little. Heaven knows what makes me persevere (after the severe reproof of public neglect) in writing verses; and Heaven alone, whose will I execute so awkwardly, is responsible for my presumption.'[137] Byron did not respond warmly to the poem, and we are perhaps justified in hearing disappointment in Shelley's comment: 'Before this you will have seen "Adonais". Lord Byron, I suppose from modesty on account of his being mentioned in it, did not say a word of "Adonais," though he was loud in his praise of "Prometheus." '[138] Earlier, on 8 June 1821, Shelley had found himself able to speak with less self-abnegation; to Claire Clairmont he wrote: 'I have lately been composing a poem on Keats; it is better than any thing that I have yet written, & worthy both of him & of me.'[139] To Claire he can continue to offer his unfettered opinion: 'My elegy on [Keats] is finished: I have dipped my pen in consuming fire

---

[135] *Shelley*, ii. 404 (stanza liii, lines 475–7).
[136] Ibid. 405 (stanza lv, lines 488, 492–5).
[137] Shelley, *Letters*, ii. 309.   [138] Ibid. 345.   [139] Ibid. 296.

to chastise his destroyers; otherwise the tone of the poem is solemn & exalted.'[140]

He wrote with more diffidence to Peacock on 10 August: 'I have sent you by the Gisbornes a copy of the *Elegy on Keats*. The subject, I know, will not please you; but the composition of the poetry, and the taste in which it is written, I do not think bad.'[141] Shyly, but obviously pleased, he writes to Horace Smith on 14 September: 'I am glad you like "Adonais", and, particularly, that you do not think it metaphysical, which I was afraid it was. I was resolved to pay some tribute of sympathy to the unhonoured dead, but I wrote, as usual, with a total ignorance of the effect that I should produce.'[142] To his publisher, Charles Ollier, on 25 September, he seems to have felt the need to be more assertive: 'The *Adonais*, in spite of its mysticism, is the least imperfect of my compositions, and, as the image of my regret and honour for poor Keats, I wish it to be so.'[143] To Hogg, on 22 October, he ventured to repeat his self-praise: 'Have you seen a poem I wrote on the death of Keats, a young writer of bad taste, but wonderful powers & promise. It is called Adonais—when you pass Ollier's you may tell him I desired you to call for one. It is perhaps the least imperfect of my pieces.'[144]

But to Ollier on 11 November, Shelley spoke of *Adonais* in a way that obliquely shows him to have been fully aware of its greatness: 'I am especially curious to hear the fate of Adonais.—I confess I should be surprised if *that* Poem were born to an immortality of oblivion'[145] (it is intriguing to note that Shelley's curious phrase 'immortality of oblivion' takes up in its linked nouns, though they are applied in a different direction, the unique concerns of *Adonais*'s argument).

In this same line, Shelley indicates that if he had had any hope of pleasing the poetic public, it rested in *Adonais*. Of Hunt he enquires, on 25 January 1822, 'what effect was produced by Adonais'?, and he continues: 'My faculties are shaken to atoms & torpid. I can write nothing, & if Adonais had no success & excited no interest what incentive can I have to write?'[146] To Peacock he indicated something of the same balance of despair and hope: 'You will have seen my Adonais & perhaps my Hellas, & I think, whatever you may judge of the subject, the composition of the first poem will not wholly displease you—I wish I had something better to do than furnish this jingling food for the hunger of oblivion, called *verse*: but I have not.'[147] But to John Gisborne, who was representing him in London,

[140] Shelley, *Letters*, ii. 302.   [141] Ibid. 330.   [142] Ibid. 349.
[143] Ibid. 354–5.   [144] Ibid. 362.   [145] Ibid. 365.
[146] Ibid. 382.   [147] Ibid. 374.

he spoke of his disillusionment with Ollier as a publisher, and said sharply: 'You know I don't think much about Reviews nor of the fame they give nor of that they take away—It is absurd in any review to criticize Adonais, & still more to pretend that the verses are bad.'[148] Shelley, in sum, knew how immense had been his achievement.

If *Adonais* managed to take Shelley's inner desolation and restructure it into an external and public situation, and thereby to become a poem of exalted rank in the history of poetry; much of Shelley's poetry—that which has been identified by the phrase internally directed—made scarcely any attempt to direct itself either towards external fact or the world's interest. A significant representative of this kind of effort is *The Witch of Atlas*, composed at about the same time as *Adonais* and also, as Mary Shelley says, 'under the Pisan hills'. During an expedition to the summit of Monte San Pelegrino, Shelley, as Mary records, 'conceived the idea and wrote, in the three days immediately succeeding to his return, the "Witch of Atlas." This poem is peculiarly characteristic of his tastes— wildly fanciful, full of brilliant imagery, and discarding human interest . . . , to revel in the fantastic ideas that his imagination suggested.'[149] It would be difficult to offer a more cogent description of Shelley's internally directed efforts, either with respect to their abandonment of what Leavis terms 'actuality,' or of their lack of function for anyone but Shelley himself. As Shelley said to Ollier, 'I send you the "Witch of Atlas", a fanciful poem, which, if its merit be measured by the labour which it cost, is worth nothing.'[150]

Shelley was not far wrong in his suggestion that the poem might be 'worth nothing'. It is an interesting example, however, both of his tireless ability to produce lengthy verse statement of craftsmanlike quality, and at the same time virtually to forfeit poetic urgency or interest for any external reader. The length of the poem is obsessive, while at the same time its content presents itself as nugatory. To be sure, much here suggests the Fairy and the Spirit of *Queen Mab*, but that poem, however ethereal and abstract in its imaginations, was anchored in a serious and at times brilliant ideational content. *The Witch of Atlas*, on the contrary, is a poem, to use Coleridge's distinction, of pure fancy, without any leaven at all of imagination.

Interestingly enough, even here, in this gossamer realm, Shelley longingly plays with variations on his ever-present wish for death. He

[148] Ibid. 388.
[149] *Shelley*, iv. 78.
[150] Shelley, *Letters*, ii. 257.

describes a 'Strange panacea' given by the Witch to those who were beautiful, which placed them in 'some controul, | Mightier than life'; and this is followed by an evocation of a sort of suspended animation that replaces the ordinary decay of death:

> the grave
> Of such, when death oppressed the weary soul,
> Was as a green and overarching bower
> Lit by the gems of many a starry flower.
>
> For on the night that they were buried, she
>   Restored the embalmers' ruining, and shook
> The light out of the funeral lamp, to be
>   A mimic day within that deathy nook;
> And she unwound the woven imagery
>   Of second childhood's swaddling bands, and took
> The coffin, its last cradle, from its niche,
> And threw it with contempt into a ditch.
>
> And there the body lay, age after age,
>   Mute, breathing, beating, warm, and undecaying,
> Like one asleep in a green hermitage,
>   With gentle smiles about its eyelids playing,
> And living in its dreams beyond the rage
>   Of death or life; while they were still arraying
> In liveries ever new the rapid, blind,
> And fleeting generations of mankind.[151]

The Witch of Atlas is a poem that simply abandons reality, and frolics in that abandonment with a high degree of poetic technique:

> This lady never slept, but lay in trance
>   All night within the fountain—as in sleep.
> Its emerald crags glowed in her beauty's glance;
>   Through the green splendour of the water deep
> She saw the constellations reel and dance
>   Like fire-flies—and withal did ever keep
> The tenour of her contemplations calm,
> With open eyes, closed feet, and folded palm.[152]

One might feel justified in hearing the breath of *The Ancient Mariner* sighing behind those lines, but unlike that poem, *The Witch of Atlas* does not move towards high meaning or significant moral consideration. The next stanza contentedly treads water, as it were, in its world of pure fancy:

[151] *Shelley*, iv. 35–6 (*The Witch of Atlas*, stanzas lxix to lxxi).
[152] Ibid. 24 (stanza xxviii).

> And when the whirlwinds and the clouds descended
>   From the white pinnacles of that cold hill,
> She passed at dewfall to a space extended,
>   Where in a lawn of flowering asphodel
> Amid a wood of pines and cedars blended,
>   There yawned an inextinguishable well
> Of crimson fire, full even to the brim,
> And overflowing all the margin trim:—[153]

Two stanzas later, the poem discovers a boat, that most typical of
Shelleyan images, the recurring symbol both of the frailness of his life and
of its movement towards death:

> She had a Boat which some say Vulcan wrought
>   For Venus, as the chariot of her star;
> But it was found too feeble to be fraught
>   With all the ardours in that sphere which are,
> And so she sold it, and Apollo bought
>   And gave it to this daughter: from a car
> Changed to the fairest and the lightest boat
> Which ever upon mortal stream did float.[154]

But this boat, unlike 'my spirit's bark' that carries Shelley to ultimate
meaning in *Adonais*—and unlike the 'little boat' that bears *Alastor*'s poet
to his death—undertakes no significant voyage at all. Indeed, three stanzas
later, the boat, instead of sailing, is still eddying in the verbiage of fancy:

> This boat she moored upon her fount, and lit
>   A living spirit within all its frame,
> Breathing the soul of swiftness into it.
>   Couched on the fountain like a panther tame,
> One of the twain at Evan's feet that sit—
>   Or as on Vesta's sceptre a swift flame,
> Or on blind Homer's heart a wingèd thought,—
> In joyous expectation lay the boat.[155]

All this highly competent verse pours forth for more than six hundred
lines, as if once Shelley had abandoned reality, he nourished no intention
of returning to that realm. When the boat finally gets under way, it does
not head for actuality:

> The water flashed like sunlight by the prow
>   Of a noon-wandering meteor flung to Heaven;

---

[153] Ibid. (stanza xxiv).   [154] Ibid. 25 (stanza xxxi).
[155] Ibid. 25–6 (stanza xxxiv).

> The still air seemed as if its waves did flow
>   In tempest down the mountains; loosely driven
> The lady's radiant hair streamed to and fro:
>   Beneath, the billows having vainly striven
> Indignant and impetuous, roared to feel
> The swift and steady motion of the keel.[156]

Indeed, even after the poem's more than six hundred fanciful lines, Shelley disembarks from its verbiage with visible reluctance. The last stanza declares simultaneously the work's unabashed indulgence in fancy and Shelley's determination to immerse himself in more of the same:

> These were the pranks she played among the cities
>   Of mortal men; and what she did to sprites
> And Gods, entangling them in her sweet ditties,
>   To do her will, and show their subtle sleights,
> I will declare another time; for it is
>   A tale more fit for the weird winter nights—
> Than for these garish summer days, when we
> Scarcely believe much more than we can see.[157]

Shelley recognized that he had here entered a fantasy designed only for himself. That he had wholly indulged 'The self-impelling steam-wheels of the mind'—to use the line from the 'Letter to Maria Gisborne'—is the burden of his playful dedication of the poem to his wife, which tries to equate his verses with the example of Wordsworth's 'Peter Bell', and bears the epigraph, 'To Mary | (On her objecting to the following poem, upon the score | of its containing no human interest)'.

It is important to understand that *The Witch of Atlas* is in no sense an anomaly in Shelley's poetical activity; it is, rather, the paradigm for a continuing discharge of his poetic effort. More of Shelley's verse is internally directed than externally directed, and *The Witch of Atlas* is a pure and representative example of the former mode. The purpose of that mode is always more directed towards inner therapy than towards what others might find of urgency. But whenever Shelley turns from his pure inner need to correlatives of outer fact or social entwinement, his poetry immediately mounts in general poetic significance. Think of 'The Masque of Anarchy', which trenchantly reacts to the Peterloo Massacre; think of 'Julian and Maddalo', which wonderfully renders aspects of his intellectual interchange with Byron; think of the 'Letter to Maria

---

[156] *Shelley*, iv. 29 (*The Witch of Atlas*, stanza xlvi).
[157] Ibid. 37 (stanza lxxviii).

Gisborne', which incorporates so well the sense of Shelley at ease among those dear to him.

Poetic production as a retreat from actuality, along with the intense study of Greek towards the same goal, are constants in Shelley's life. To the late quotations adduced above in support of that truth, one might add evidence that Shelley fixed himself in these twin modes very early. 'Classical reading, and poetical writing', he recalls at the age of 19, 'employed me during my residence at Oxford.'[158] Such activities helped maintain the veil that Shelley wanted to cast over an intolerable reality. In one of his better sonnets he urgently exhorts those who will listen not to lift that veil, for, as it were, the 'hyena mortal life' lurks beneath:

> Lift not the painted veil which those who live
> Call Life: though unreal shapes be pictured there,
> And it but mimic all we would believe
> With colours idly spread,—behind, lurk Fear
> And Hope, twin Destinies; who ever weave
> Their shadows, o'er the chasm, sightless and drear.
> I knew one who had lifted it—he sought,
> For his lost heart was tender, things to love,
> But found them not, alas! nor was there aught
> The world contains, the which he could approve
> Through the unheeding many he did move,
> A splendour among shadows, a bright blot
> Upon this gloomy scene, a Spirit that strove
> For truth, and like the Preacher found it not.[159]

The desolation emanating from this poem is even more strongly revealed in an early draft of lines 11–14:

> Like an unheeded shadow did he move
> Among the careless crowd that marked him not.
> I should be happier had I never known
> This mournful man—he was himself alone.[160]

In the context of strategies by which to withdraw and insulate himself against actuality, it seems that Shelley's unusually full commitment to poetic translation—translation from many languages, but especially from Greek and Latin, which has been powerfully explored in Timothy Webb's *The Violet in the Crucible: Shelley and Translation*—reveals itself as being

[158] Shelley, *Letters*, i. 228.
[159] *Shelley*, iii. 216–17,
[160] Ibid. 217.

the same kind of therapeutic activity as does the internally directed poetry. There was a great deal of such translational activity (in prose as well as poetry), which seems the more problematic in the matrix of Shelley's disbelief in the actual efficacy of translation. In the *Defence of Poetry*, he speaks memorably of 'the vanity of translation; it were as wise to cast a violet into a crucible that you might discover the formal principle of its colour and odour, as seek to transfuse from one language into another the creations of a poet. The plant must spring again from its seed, or it will bear no flower—and this is the burthen of the curse of Babel.'[161] Again, Shelley wrote to Leigh Hunt and said that instead of translating Tasso's *Aminta*, Hunt should create poetry of his own:

I am sorry to hear that you have employed yourself in translating the 'Aminta' though I doubt not it will be a just and beautiful translation. You ought to write Amintas. You ought to exercise your fancy in the perpetual creation of new forms of gentleness and beauty. You are formed to be a living fountain and not a canal however clear.[162]

But Shelley, however justly he might counsel Hunt to be 'a living fountain and not a canal however clear', did not heed this advice himself; his need to deaden himself to actuality overrode other considerations.

Sometimes, it should be noted, Shelley's internally directed concern mingles with external considerations to produce a special kind of texture. It does so with enormous results, as just noted, in *Adonais*. But a less strong though still considerable poem, rather more on the internally directed side, is *Lines Written Among the Euganean Hills*. Here, though the extended flow of words, which characterizes Shelley's seeming wish to hide as long as possible within the business of writing lines, is present, there is also present bitter recognition of the stress of actuality. The stress of actuality, in fact, is invoked, along with Shelley's ever-present wish for death and his symbolic movement on a boat, to form the very opening of the poem:

> Many a green isle needs must be
> In the deep wide sea of misery,
> Or the mariner, worn and wan,
> Never thus could voyage on
> Day and night, and night and day,
> Drifting on his dreary way,
> With the solid darkness black
> Closing round his vessel's track;

[161] *Shelley*, vii. 114.   [162] Shelley, *Letters*, ii. 152.

> Whilst above the sunless sky,
> Big with clouds, hangs heavily,
> And behind the tempest fleet
> Hurries on with lightning feet,
> Riving sail, and cord, and plank,
> Till the ship has almost drank
> Death from the o'er brimming deep;
> And sinks down, down, like that sleep
> When the dreamer seems to be
> Weltering through eternity;
> And the dim low lines before
> Of a dark and distant shore
> Still recedes, as ever still
> Longing with divided will,
> But no power to seek or shun,
> He is ever drifted on
> O'er the unreposing wave
> To the haven of the grave.[163]

The stress of actuality is present throughout the poem. At line 66, Shelley says:

> Ah, many flowering islands lie
> In the waters of wide Agony[164]

Though the focus of the poem is 'Many-domed Padua', its *basso ostinato*, as it were, is the pain of life. Shelley speaks desolatingly of 'remembered agonies' as enveloping the destination of 'The frail bark of this lone being'.[165] He goes on to note that

> Other flowering isles must be
> In the sea of life and agony:
> Other spirits float and flee
> O'er that gulf: even now, perhaps,
> On some rock the wild wave wraps,
> With folding wings they waiting sit
> For my bark, to pilot it
> To some calm and blooming cove[166]

—and then he projects a longing but wholly fanciful vision of momentary escape from the travails of life. The calm and blooming cove is one

---

[163] *Shelley*, ii. 49 (*Lines Written Among the Euganean Hills*, lines 1–26).
[164] Ibid. 51.
[165] Ibid. 58 (lines 330–1).
[166] Ibid. 58 (lines 335–42).

> Where for me, and those I love
> Many a windless bower be built,
> Far from passion, pain, and guilt,
> In a dell 'mid lawny hills,
> Which the wild sea-murmur fills,
> And soft sunshine, and the sound
> Of old forests echoing round,
> And the light and smell divine
> Of all flowers that breathe and shine:
> We may live so happy there,
> That the spirits of the air,
> Envying us, may even entice
> To our healing paradise
> The polluting multitude[167]

The same vision of a healing paradise is presented in the even more internally directed world of *Epipsychidion*. There, in his symbolic boat, Shelley sails towards a paradise described, with backward glances at *The Ancient Mariner*, at lavish length:

>   Emily,
> A ship is floating in the harbour now,
> A wind is hovering o'er the mountain's brow;
> There is a path on the sea's azure floor,
> No keel has ever ploughed that path before;
> The halcyons brood around the foamless isles;
> The treacherous Ocean has forsworn its wiles;
> The merry mariners are bold and free:
> Say, my heart's sister, wilt thou sail with me?
> Our bark is as an albatross, whose nest
> Is a far Eden of the purple East;
>
>   .   .   .   .   .
>
> It is an isle under Ionian skies,
> Beautiful as a wreck of Paradise,
>
>   .   .   .   .   .
>
> There are thick woods where sylvan forms abide;
> And many a fountain, rivulet, and pond,
> As clear as elemental diamond,
> Or serene morning air; and far beyond,
> The mossy tracks made by the goats and deer
> (Which the rough shepherd treads but once a year,)
> Pierce into glades, caverns, and bowers, and halls

---

[167] *Shelley*, ii. 58–9 (*Lines Written Among the Euganean Hills*, lines 343–56).

Built round with ivy, which the waterfalls
Illumining, with sound that never fails,
Accompany the noonday nightingales;
And all the place is peopled with sweet airs;
The light clear element which the isle wears
Is heavy with the scent of lemon-flowers,
Which floats like mist laden with unseen showers,
And falls upon the eye-lids like faint sleep;
And from the moss violets and jonquils peep[168]

But the hopefully projected fantasies of ameliorated existence, either here, or in the Euganean Hills poem, or elsewhere, are merely momentary veils cast over the true haven—'the haven of the grave'. The projected fantasies derive all their power from the desolation of Shelley's real situation. 'My greatest content,' he writes to Mary in the late summer of 1821, 'would be utterly to desert all human society. I would retire with you & our child to a solitary island in the sea, would build a boat, & shut upon my retreat the floodgates of the world.'[169]

Seeking to assuage the loneliness of his childhood and adolescence, Shelley reached out to marriage. It is important to understand that it was not adult sexual love—his physical attractiveness notwithstanding—that Shelley seems primarily to have sought in marriage, but solace for his isolation. Indeed, it seems likely that Shelley, the victim of a defective pattern of love in his childhood, did not fully experience adult love, sexually satisfying to women though he was. The women he loved, he loved primarily as sisters. His own sisters, all younger than he was, and therefore not threatening, were probably almost the sole source of kindness and solace in his early life (and this writer, at least, thinks it very likely that he had sexual relations with one or more of them). When he grew older, he sought to enlist Harriet and Mary as additions to the band of sisters.

That, in truth, is the essence of his attitude towards Harriet, and is, one suspects, the source of his appalling insensitivity toward her suffering as a wife. No one can rehearse the amazing course of Shelley's abandonment of his wife, and her subsequent suicide, without profound shock. But at the same time no one, it seems true to assert, has ever believed that Shelley actually intended to hurt Harriet. How, then, could this kind and sensitive man act like such an unfeeling blackguard? The answer must be that in Shelley's confused psyche there existed no true knowledge of what

---

[168] Ibid. 368–9 (*Epipsychidion*, lines 407–17, 422–3, 435–50).
[169] Shelley, *Letters*, ii. 339.

marriage was; Harriet was merely another sister, and though abandoned as a wife when he eloped with Mary, was never, in Shelley's own bizarre awareness of the situation, abandoned in her primary role as sister.

Indeed, Shelley never at any time was a Romeo towards Harriet's Juliet. He refers in October 1811 to 'Harriet, my new sister'.[170] At about the same time he writes to Elizabeth Hitchener and discloses the sister-entwined, entirely unromantic genesis of his marriage:

Some time ago when my Sister [Mary] was at Mrs. Fennings school, she contracted an intimacy with Harriet—at that period I attentively watched over my sister, designing if possible to add her to the list of the good the disinterested, the free.—I desired therefore to investigate Harriets character, for which purpose, I called on her, requested to correspond with her. . . . The frequency of her letters became greater during my stay in Wales, I answered them; they became interesting. They contained complaints of the irrational conduct of her relations, and the misery of living where she could *love* no one. Suicide was with her a favorite theme . . . her letters became more & more gloomy; at length one assumed a tone of such despair, as induced me to quit Wales precipately.—I arrived in London, I was shocked at observing the alteration of her looks, little did I divine it's cause; she had become violently attached to *me*, & feared that I should not return her attachment. . . . It was impossible to avoid being much affected, I promised to unite my fate with her's. . . . I came to London, I proposed marriage for the reasons which I have given you, & she complied.[171]

When his passion for Mary erupted on to this scene, Shelley argued, with a kind of twistedly valid logic, that Harriet's position, sisterly from its very inception, had not changed: 'It is no reproach to me that you have never filled my heart with an all-sufficing passion':[172]

Can your feelings for me differ, in their nature from those which I cherish towards you? Are you my lover whilst I am only your friend, the brother of your heart? . . . I wish that you could see Mary. . . . I murmur not if you feel incapable of compassion & love for the object & the sharer of my passion.[173]

Still urging the logic of sisterhood, Shelley invited Harriet to come join him and Mary in Switzerland:

I write to urge you to come to Switzerland, where you will at least find one firm & constant friend, to whom your interests will be always dear, by whom your feelings will never wilfully be injured. From none can you expect this but me.[174]

[170] Shelley, *Letters*, i. 152.   [171] Ibid. 162–3.
[172] Ibid. 390   [173] Ibid.
[174] Ibid. 391–2.

After raging at Harriet for her lack of understanding, Shelley magnani-
mously insisted on his own brotherly loyalty:

Do not imagine that my feelings towards you are ever bitter or unfriendly. . . . No
cold or distant feelings originated in me. I was desirous to be your friend in the
most emphatic meaning of the word. . . .
   Do not mistake me: I am & will be your friend in every sense of the word but that
most delicate & exalted one.—I solemnly protest to you that not the slightest
unkindness or enmity towards you has ever entered my heart.[175]

If Shelley's emotional perspective on Harriet was so distorted as to
constitute a kind of madness, the same pattern ruled in his bizarre
intellectual courtship of Elizabeth Hitchener. That plain and lonely
spinster was simply overwhelmed by the passion of Shelley's brotherly
approach:

I love you more than any relation I posess; you are the sister of my soul, its dearest
sister, & I think the component parts of that soul must undergo *complete*
dissolution before its sympathies can perish.[176]

And he concludes the letter: 'Sister of my soul adieu. With I hope *eternal*
love your | Percy Shelley—'[177]
   Such a relentless emotional assault could have only one outcome.
Elizabeth Hitchener fell in love with Shelley. And Shelley, bizarrely
uncomprehending, calmly led the relationship to catastrophe. He insisted
that Hitchener come live with him and Harriet, grandly insisting that
Harriet would not, could not, be jealous. His ardour fairly leaps off the
page:

O that you were with me!—My true and dear friend why should we be separated;
when may we unite. What might we not do if together, if two hearts panting for the
happiness and liberty of mankind were joined by union and proximity as they are
by friendship and sympathy what might we not expect? . . . How Harriet and her
sister long to see you, and how *I* long to see you *never* to part with you again. . . .
[Y]ou shall live with us.—at least some time hence; this time shall be indefinite
now. Harriet is above the littleness of jealousy of which you at first suspected her.[178]

   When Hitchener did join Shelley and Harriet, the results were as
disastrous as might have been expected. Shelley, despite the passion of his
language, was not in the least attracted to her; Harriet, like any young wife,
was jealous in the extreme. It must have been a miserable time, especially

[175] Ibid. 404–5.   [176] Ibid. 150.
[177] Ibid. 152.   [178] Ibid. 234.

for the unwitting visitor. Rather ungenerously, Shelley supplanted his
earlier caressings with the sobriquet 'Brown Demon':

The Brown Demon, as we call our late tormentor and schoolmistress, must receive
her stipend. I pay it with a heavy heart and an unwilling hand; but it must be so.
She was deprived by our misjudging haste of a situation, where she was going on
smoothly: and now she says, that her reputation is gone, her health ruined, her
peace of mind destroyed by my barbarity. . . . This is not all fact; but certainly she
is embarrassed and poor, and we being in some degree the cause, we ought to
obviate it. She is an artful, superficial, ugly, hermaphroditical beast of a woman,
and my astonishment at my fatuity, inconsistency, and bad taste was never so
great, as after living four months with her as an inmate.[179]

As the bewildered 'sister' Hitchener was hurt by Shelley's sexual
preference for Harriet, so the bewildered 'sister' Harriet was hurt by his
sexual preference for Mary. And had he lived longer, Mary would have
been bitterly hurt—she doubtless was hurt—by Shelley's subsequent
enthusiasm for Emilia (or Teresa) Viviani, or by his falling in love, near the
time of his death, with Jane Williams. The plurality of these relationships
doubtless reflects on some level the fact that he had not one sister but four
sisters.

Even Shelley's most fervid poem on love, *Epipsychidion*, in its very first
line hails Emilia Viviani as a sister figure:

> Sweet Spirit! Sister of that orphan one[180]

and promptly proceeds to invoke the category of sisterhood as the ideal
place for his new love:

> Emily,
> I love thee; though the world by no thin name
> Will hide that love, from its unvalued shame.
> Would we two had been twins of the same mother!
> Or, that the name my heart lent to another
> Could be a sister's bond for her and thee[181]

Perfervid apostrophe continues to nominate his new love as sister:

> Spouse! Sister! Angel! Pilot of the Fate
> Whose course has been so starless! O too late
> Beloved! O too soon adored, by me![182]

---

[179] Shelley, *Letters*, i. 336.
[180] *Shelley*, ii. 357 (*Epipsychidion*, line 1).
[181] Ibid. 358 (lines 42–7).
[182] Ibid. 360 (lines 130–2).

The status of sister slides easily into the status of wife in Shelley's lines:

> The day is come, and thou wilt fly with me,
> To whatsoe'er of dull mortality
> Is mine, remain a vestal sister still;
> To the intense, the deep, the imperishable,
> Not mine but me, henceforth be thou united
> Even as a bride, delighting and delighted.[183]

As he mounts his vision of flight to his Elysian isle, Shelley continues to think of Emilia as a sister, even though he says

> Our breath shall intermix, our bosoms bound,
> And our veins beat together; and our lips
> With other eloquence than words, eclipse
> The soul that burns between them . . .
>
> .   .   .   .   .
>
> We shall become the same, we shall be one
> Spirit within two frames[184]

Despite this intensity, Emilia is specifically categorized as sister:

> Emily,
> A ship is floating in the harbour now,
>
> .   .   .   .   .
>
> Say, my heart's sister, wilt thou sail with me?[185]

If Shelley's relationships with women were confused, and largely subsumed under the unrealistic categories established by his relationships with his sisters, his relationships with men were scarcely more comprehending. In particular, Shelley's failure to see the tendency of his relationship with Byron seems—one cannot speak with certain knowledge, but the likelihood is compelling—to have provided a kind of final shock that led directly to his death. That death fittingly occurred in 'the little boat' or 'spirit's bark' called, in gigantic Byronic relevance, *Don Juan*.

It is not possible to know whether Shelley deliberately committed suicide. It may be that he was torn, 'Longing with divided will, | But no power to seek or shun', as his boat drifted 'To the haven of the grave'.[186] Certain it is, however, that his sailing from Livorno to Lerici, on 8 July 1822, in a boat which had been modified to carry extra sail and floated, in

---

[183] Ibid. 368 (lines 388–93).
[184] Ibid. 373 (lines 565–8; 573–4).
[185] Ibid. 368 (lines 407–8; 415).
[186] *Shelley*, ii. 49 (*Lines Written Among the Euganean Hills*, lines 22–3, 26).

her quest for more speed, an extra three inches higher in the water, seems dangerous—especially for a Shelley who had never learned to swim ('if you can't swim, | Beware of Providence', Maddalo had forewarned[187]). To set off in deteriorating weather under full sail seems even more than dangerous. To refuse to shorten sail after the storm broke, or to return to port as local craft had done, seems like an added and absolute folly that in common parlance would readily be called suicidal.

Whether there was deliberate intent cannot be known. About three weeks before he died, Shelley wrote to Trelawny requesting poison:

His letter to Trelawny, whom he had only just waved off, was very strange. Most of it consisted of a long request for a lethal dose of 'the Prussic Acid, or essential oil of bitter almonds'. He explained that he had no intention of suicide at present, 'but I confess it would be a comfort to hold in my possession that golden key to the chamber of perpetual rest'.[188]

Various witnesses, including his wife, testify to Shelley's good spirits before the catastrophe; but the decision for suicide often lightens spirits. In any event, Shelley did not like to alarm people; as Mary says, 'Constant and poignant physical suffering exhausted him; and though he preserved the appearance of cheerfulness . . . yet many hours were passed when his thoughts, shadowed by illness, became gloomy, and then he escaped to solitude, and in verses, which he hid for fear of wounding me, poured forth morbid but too natural bursts of discontent and sadness.'[189] Shelley himself, less than three weeks before he died—his opinion of Mary now far more tempered than in his ecstatic statements at the time of their elopement—wrote that 'I only feel the want of those who can feel, and understand me. Whether from proximity and the continuity of domestic intercourse, Mary does not. The necessity of concealing from her thoughts that would pain her, necessitates this, perhaps.'[190]

Shelley's reluctance to alarm those around him is especially emphasized in the statements of the Maniac in 'Julian and Maddalo' ('We can hardly doubt', says his biographer, 'that this Madman is Shelley'[191]). 'Of the Maniac I can give no information,' says Julian/Shelley, and then adds shyly: 'He was evidently a very cultivated and amiable person when in his right senses.'[192] Indeed, the lengthy self-description of the Maniac—the year is 1818—is a prime witness not only to Shelley's mask of good spirits, but to his desperate inner unhappiness as well:

[187] *Shelley*, iii. 182 ('Julian and Maddalo', lines 117–18).
[188] Holmes, 725.   [189] *Shelley*, iii. 219–20.   [190] Shelley, *Letters*, ii. 435.
[191] White, ii. 46.   [192] *Shelley*, iii. 178.

'Month after month,' he cried, 'to bear this load
And as a jade urged by the whip and goad
To drag life on—which like a heavy chain
Lengthens behind with many a link of pain!—
And not to speak my grief—O, not to dare
To give a human voice to my despair,
But live and move, and wretched thing! smile on
As if I never went aside to groan,
And wear this mask of falsehood even to those
Who are most dear—[193]

The torment voiced by the Maniac corresponds with poignant exactness to the inner desolation of Shelley:

'What Power delights to torture us? I know
That to myself I do not wholly owe
What now I suffer, tho' in part I may.
Alas! none strewed sweet flowers upon the way
Where wandering heedlessly, I met pale Pain,
My shadow, which will leave me not again—
If I have erred, there was no joy in error,
But pain and insult and unrest and terror[194]

Newman Ivey White notes that 'the Madman thinks of suicide, as Shelley almost certainly did at the time, and as he later told Trelawny he did two months later at Naples'.[195]

In any event, Shelley's death seems both premature in the light of his 29 years, and highly apposite—almost foredoomed—in its form and its sense of inevitability. The frail bark is a constant symbol in his poetry; in his life, too, as Mary Shelley notes, 'Shelley's favourite taste was boating; when living near the Thames, or by the lake of Geneva, much of his life was spent on the water. On the shore of every lake, or stream, or sea, near which he dwelt, he had a boat moored.'[196] Indeed, in 1816, Shelley had come close to drowning in a boat that was almost swamped on Lake Geneva:

I felt in this near prospect of death a mixture of sensations, among which terror entered, though but subordinately. My feelings would have been less painful had I been alone; but I knew that my companion [Byron] would have attempted to save me, and I was overcome with humiliation, when I thought that his life might have been risked to preserve mine.[197]

[193] Ibid. 187 (lines 300–9).　　[194] Ibid. 188 (lines 320–7).
[195] White, ii. 44.　　[196] *Shelley*, iv. 122.
[197] Shelley, *Letters*, i. 483.

For the last boat voyage, Shelley's wife recorded her premonition: 'On the 1st of July they left us. If ever shadow of future ill darkened the present hour, such was over my mind when they went. During the whole of our stay at Lerici, an intense presentiment of coming evil brooded over my mind, and covered this beautiful place, and genial summer, with the shadow of coming misery.'[198]

The misery that came was, almost inevitably, death by water, and death by water was a peculiarly recurring fear among Shelley's friends. As Trelawny notes:

the old fellow pointed with his stick to a hat, books, and loose papers lying about, and then to a deep pool of dark glimmering water, saying 'Eccolo!' I thought he meant than Shelley was in or under the water. The careless, not to say impatient, way in which the Poet bore his burden of life, caused a vague dread amongst his family and friends that he might lose or cast it away at any moment.[199]

Whether Shelley deliberately cast away his life, or whether he was merely extraordinarily careless about preserving it, his demise occurred shortly after a rupture with Byron. It is this rupture, one suspects, that became, as it were, the last straw in Shelley's psychological burdening. The inner distress caused by Timothy Shelley, by the Eton classmates, by the Oxford authorities, by the censorious public, and by the guilt over Harriet (he had confessed to Byron in 1817 that 'My late wife is dead. The circumstances which attended this event are of a nature of such awful and appalling horror, that I dare hardly avert to them in thought.'[200]), here was augmented in a way so painful and destructive that it seems no surprise that death followed soon after.

Scholars have in the main attributed the rupture with Byron to Shelley's advocacy of Claire Clairmont in a dispute over the custody of Allegra. In a letter to Claire in February 1822, Shelley says that 'It is of vital importance both to me and to yourself, to Allegra even, that I should put a period to my intimacy with L[ord] B[yron], and that without *éclat*. No sentiments of honour or justice restrain him (as I strongly suspect) from the basest insinuations . . .'[201] By 30 May 1822 he had said to Claire that between him and Byron 'there is a great gulph fixed, which by the nature of things must daily become wider'.[202]

But though Shelley's championship of Claire certainly must be considered a factor in the rupture, careful reading of the matter in its

---

[198] *Shelley*, iv. 211.   [199] Trelawny, 113.
[200] Shelley, *Letters*, i. 529.   [201] Ibid. ii. 391–2.
[202] Ibid. 429.

verbal contexts seems to suggest the presence of an additional factor, one that, at least to this author, is more convincing—especially in terms of the intensity of Shelley's language. To retrace the episode makes it seem that Byron, always unabashedly bisexual, misinterpreted Shelley's almost adoring closeness and proposed a sexual liaison. Repulsed, he coldly rejected Shelley. Shelley, for his part, was stunned and panic-stricken. It may seem almost ironic that Shelley, who liked to flaunt free-love ('I attach little value to the monopoly of exclusive cohabitation.'[203]), and indeed, in *Laon and Cythna*, defended incest, should be so totally destroyed by a sexual proposition from Byron; but homosexual panic is one of the most unreasoning fears that humans know, and if Shelley had had previous unfortunate homosexual experience, his terror might well have been augmented.

Be that as it may, no other explanation really seems to fit the facts. It seems clear that Shelley was an unusually attractive man; he was also, one must remember, still a very young one ('in appearance extraordinarily young', noted Edward Williams, 'of manners mild and amiable, but withal full of life and fun'[204]). Byron had come to live in Pisa at Shelley's warm insistence. Before that, Shelley had visited him in Ravenna, and wrote Mary approvingly:

He lives in considerable splendour, but within his income which is now about 4000 a year—1000 of which he devotes to purposes of charity. He has had mischievous passions, but these he seems to have subdued; and he is becoming what he should be, a virtuous man.[205]

Shelley had said in the same letter that

He has read to me one of the unpublished cantos of Don Juan, which is astonishingly fine.—It sets him not above but far above all the poets of the day: every word has the stamp of immortality.—I despair of rivalling Lord Byron, as well I may: and there is no other with whom it is worth contending.[206]

It was with the greatest delight, therefore, that Shelley announced in August 1821 that 'Lord Byron is immediately coming to Pisa—He will set off the moment I can get him a House. Who would have imagined it!'[207] By October he is asking, 'When may we expect you? . . . Your house is ready

---

[203] Ibid. i. 175. Cf. *Epipsychidion*: 'I never was attached to that great sect, | Whose doctrine is, that each one should select | Out of the crowd a mistress or a friend, | And all the rest, though fair and wise, commend | To cold oblivion, though it is in the code | Of modern morals' (*Shelley*, ii. 361 (lines 149–54).

[204] White, ii. 283.   [205] Shelley, *Letters*, ii. 322.

[206] Ibid. 323.   [207] Ibid. 338.

& all the furniture arranged. . . . The Countess tells me that you think of
leaving Allegra for the present at the convent. Do as you think best—but I
can pledge myself to find a situation for her here such as you would
approve, in case you change your mind.'[208] In that same letter he expresses,
if possible, an even more rapturous judgement of *Don Juan*: 'This poem
carries with it at once the stamp of originality and a defiance of imitation.
Nothing has ever been written like it in English—nor if I may venture to
prophesy, will there be; without carrying upon it the mark of a secondary
and borrowed light.'[209]

By January 1822 Shelley was writing with great pleasure to Peacock that

> Lord Byron is established now, [& gives a weekly dinner *deleted*] & we are constant
> companions: no small relief this after the dreary solitude of the understanding &
> the imagination in which we past the first years of our expatriation, yoked to all
> sorts of miseries & discomforts.—Of course you have seen his last volume, & if you
> before thought him a great Poet what is your opinion now that you have read
> *Cain*?[210]

But being 'constant companions' may have meant something different to
Byron than it did to Shelley. Indeed, in some aspects Shelley's intellectual
courtship of Byron bizarrely reprises his courtship of Elizabeth Hitchener.
In each case Shelley's purely intellectual enthusiasm was accompanied by
such an outpouring of affect as to mislead its recipient. This would not
have been the first time that Shelley, quite without intending it, had
aroused a deep attraction in others. 'She had become violently attached to
me,' said Shelley in palpable surprise, when speaking of his first meetings
with Harriet.[211]

Shelley's admiration of Byron was given without stint. 'What think you
of Lord Byrons last Volume? In my opinion it contains finer poetry than
has appeared in England since the publication of Paradise Regained.—
Cain is apocalyptic—it is a revelation not before communicated to man.'[212]
That last statement was written to John Gisborne in London on 26
January. But by 15 February a change has occurred; there is a different
tone in the air. Shelley writes a correct but formal letter to Byron about
money for Leigh Hunt; and in a letter of 17 February he tells Hunt that
'Lord Byron begs me to inclose the ci-jointe letter. He has furnished with
tolerable willingness the sum requested, accepting my guarantee for the
payment with a tacit agreement that he is not to call on me for it before my
father's death.'[213] In the same letter, Shelley cryptically refers to

---

[208] Shelley, *Letters*, ii. 358.   [209] Ibid. 357.
[210] Ibid. 373.   [211] Ibid. i. 162.
[212] Ibid. ii. 388.   [213] Ibid. 389.

difficulties with Byron: 'Many circumstances have occurred between myself & Lord B, which make the intercourse painful to me, & this last discussion about money particularly so.'[214]

What, one asks, were the circumstances that made 'the intercourse painful to me'? The plural of 'many circumstances' of course might allow for more than one assessment. Doubtless, at least one aspect of the matter is conveyed by Shelley's expression of distaste for Byron's dinner parties: 'Lord Byron unites us at a weekly dinner where my nerves are generally shaken to pieces by sitting up, contemplating the rest making themselves vats of claret &c. till 3 o'Clock in the morning.'[215] On 18 June 1822 a letter to John Gisborne states that 'I detest all society—almost all, at least—and Lord Byron is the nucleus of all that is hateful and tiresome in it.'[216] So the distaste for Byron's parties, like the advocacy of Claire, must be accounted a factor in the rupture. But the disliked parties do not necessarily preclude an intertwinement with the sexual factor. One might speculate that at three o'clock in the morning, after Byron had drunk heavily—and Shelley evidently far less heavily and probably not at all—the conditions for inappropriate suggestions would seem to be ideal. In any case, neither drunken dinner parties, nor disagreements about Allegra, quite seem to account for the intensity of words like 'repugnance' ('a repugnance to a continuance of intimacy with Lord Byron so close as that which now exists').[217]

Shelley was perhaps not aware of Byron's homosexual tropisms; but he prided himself on somewhat reclaiming Byron from the debauchery of his Venetian days: 'I then talk, & he listens to reason and I earnestly hope that he is too well aware of the terrible & degrading consequences of his former mode of life.'[218] That, as with Harriet and Elizabeth Hitchener, might have been another example of Shelley's lack of comprehension as to his own role in relations with others.

In any case, disagreements about Allegra or about money, or disgust with drunken parties, hardly seem to justify the total reversal that follows. On 2 March Shelley refers again to 'circumstances', and to this author's ear, at least, only the homosexual hypothesis can adequately account for the tone:

Particular circumstances,—or rather I should say, particular dispositions in Lord B's character render the close & exclusive intimacy with him in which I find myself, intolerable to me; thus much my best friend I will confess & *confide* to you.[219]

---

[214] Ibid. 390. [215] Ibid. 379. [216] Ibid. 434.
[217] Ibid. 393. [218] Ibid. 336. [219] Ibid. 393.

One notes that there is no reference to a stated issue like too much drink, but to 'particular dispositions in Lord B's character', which relate explicitly to a 'close & exclusive intimacy'. Shelley, his enormous earlier adulation notwithstanding, now finds close and exclusive intimacy 'intolerable'. Moreover, what these 'particular dispositions' are apparently cannot be named, but only hinted—and that only partly: 'thus much my best friend I will confess & *confide* to you.' Can this plausibly refer to anything other than Byron's homosexuality?

The same interpretation seems to be sustained by Shelley's statement to Claire on 20 March 1822—though Mary's accompanying letter has referred at length to Byron's exasperation over Shelley's urging of Allegra's removal from the convent. Shelley says: 'I shall certainly take our house *far* from Lord Byron's, although it may be impossible suddenly to put an end to his detested intimacy.'[220] The phrase 'detested intimacy' seems to convey a weight somewhat different from Mary's reference to Byron's 'hypocrisy & cruelty'. It is almost as though Mary is talking of public matters on which she and Shelley agree, but that Shelley himself is invoking something secret and private.

Whatever the truth of this supposition, the great warmth between Shelley and Byron was no more:

Certain it is, that Lord Byron has made me bitterly feel the inferiority which the world has presumed to place between us and which subsists nowhere in reality but in our own talents, which are not our own but Nature's—or in our rank, which is not our own but Fortune's.[221]

This was on 10 April. Less than three months later, Shelley was dead.

Indeed, the significance of the name of Shelley's death boat, *Don Juan*, seems more a witness to Shelley's panic-stricken withdrawal (Shelley actually uses the phrase, 'equivocation of sex', in the context of his disgust at the name), than homage to Byron—the name, indeed, may even have constituted a deliberate taunt by Byron. Of a situation in mid-May a biographer writes:

Apart from insufficient reefing, their only problem was how to remove the huge black lettering *Don Juan* which had been painted on the forward mainsail. Mary said it looked like a coal barge, and Shelley said acidly to Trelawny that he 'supposed the name to have been given her during the equivocation of sex which her godfather suffered in the Harem.' It was suspected that Byron had arranged this desecration through Trelawny, and Shelley was indignant out of all proportion to the crime. Hours were spent trying to remove the paint at Lerici with

[220] Shelley, *Letters*, ii. 399.   [221] Ibid. 405.

'turpentine, spirits of wine, and buccata'. It would not come off, but Shelley absolutely refused to sail under the title of Byron's greatest work, and finally had the section of the sail cut out altogether, and a new patch put in by a local sailmaker, disguised by a line of reefs.[222]

In the opinion of the present author, Shelley's frantic intensity of scrubbing, and its almost obsessive extension as a necessity of cutting out, more compellingly and plausibly implies homosexual panic than does any other possibility. The attempted substitution of the markedly asexual and idealistic name *Ariel*, as the new name of the little sailing ship, seems further to emphasize the repudiation of the repugnant sexuality associated with Byron.

Because of the confusion and disappointment that beset Shelley's human relationships, much of his work was affected. A poem such as *Epipsychidion*, which hails in extravagant terms one of those unreal relationships, palpably falls into the internally directed mode of Shelley's productivity, with all which that implies of idiosyncrasy and too-muchness. 'Mont Blanc', on the other hand, which is definitively directed towards the external, achieves greatness. It is second in Shelley's canon only to *Adonais*, and not by a very large margin. It is in the same class of excellence as 'Tintern Abbey' and the 'Immortality Ode', though slightly below those tremendous poems in absolute rank. It is a very great poem.

The poem is, of course, a wonderful exemplification of the Romantic preoccupation with the sublime. More specifically in terms of Shelley's own practice, it is a poem about a relationship, a relationship not between Shelley and a woman, or another human, but between Shelley and an immovable object of great power and weight: Mont Blanc. It is this, the palpable weight of Mont Blanc as an object, that, much like the classical conventions of *Adonais*, counteracts the Shelleyan tendency to volatility, and supplies the *gravitas* that places the poem in the highest rank of achievement.

The mountain, as subject, ballasts the poem against the frenzied ethereality of much of Shelley's verse; as object of relationship it paradoxically activates, by its absolute non-humanness, all the emotions of awe, reverence, and obedience, that a youth naturally feels towards his father, but that Timothy Shelley was never able to summon in his son. In the human paternal relationship, Shelley's natural instincts of awe and devotion were always channelled into confusion and rebellion; in the contemplation of the mighty mountain they pour forth in clarity and focus.

[222] Holmes, 716.

The impersonality of the mountain is central to the poem's achievement. Mont Blanc's non-human substitution for the paternal authority, which no human had ever supplied to Shelley, exactly parallels the efficacy of the impersonal Plotinian One that, instead of the Christian God, reigns in *Adonais*. Certain it is that Shelley's lifelong war against the Christian God contained within it something of his despairing war against his own father. Jupiter bore the hallmark of Timothy Shelley; the Plotinian One, non-human, could be revered without the confusing intermixture of such human contamination (as Coleridge noted, 'the superessential ONE of Plotinus' was an entity 'to whom neither Intelligence, or Self-consciousness, or Life, or even *Being* dare be attributed'[223]).

Yet, from its ontological status as the non-human, the mountain continually mounts forays into the world of the human:

> The wilderness has a mysterious tongue
> Which teaches awful doubt, or faith so mild,
> So solemn, so serene, that man may be,
> But for such faith, with nature reconciled;
> Thou hast a voice, great Mountain, to repeal
> Large codes of fraud and woe; not understood
> By all, but which the wise, and great, and good
> Interpret, or make felt, or deeply feel.[224]

The natural realm of the non-human, in fact, is conceived as in explicit dialogical relationship with the human world of the poet:

> My own, my human mind, which passively
> Now renders and receives fast influencings,
> Holding an unremitting interchange
> With the clear universe of things around[225]

This dialogical relationship, however, is not presented as one of equality, but one of overwhelming inequality. The poet, as throughout Shelley, is weakness personified; the mountain is absolute power: 'Mont Blanc yet gleams on high;—the power is there.'[226] The subtext of the relationship seems to be that Shelley will accept virtual annihilation before the awesome power of the mountain, for he has always been powerless; but the arrogance of the world of Timothy Shelley, which thinks itself

---

[223] *Aids to Reflection*, 162.
[224] *Shelley*, i. 231 ('Mont Blanc', lines 76–83).
[225] Ibid. 230 (lines 37–40).
[226] Ibid. 232 (line 127).

powerful, will also be overwhelmed—will be revealed as without power or substance:

> The race
> Of man flies far in dread; his work and dwelling
> Vanish, like smoke before the tempest's stream,
> And their place is not known. Below, vast caves
> Shine in the rushing torrents' restless gleam,
> Which from those secret chasms in tumult welling
> Meet in the vale, and one majestic River,
> The breath and blood of distant lands, for ever
> Rolls its loud waters to the ocean waves,
> Breathes its swift vapours to the circling air.[227]

The image of immense power and energy (certainly informed by the tumult and flow of 'Kubla Khan'), which is so overwhelming to 'The race | Of man', is nevertheless itself overwhelmed by the still grandeur of Mont Blanc, with the word 'yet' assuming a special pregnancy in the line that follows that passage: 'Mont Blanc yet gleams on high;—the power is there.'

Indeed, three words, 'everlasting', 'infinite', and 'power', all of them in absolute opposition to the weakness of the poet, virtually govern the tone and cadence of the poem. The radical inequality of human poet and outer reality is the burden of the immensely powerful beginning:

> The everlasting universe of things
> Flows through the mind, and rolls its rapid waves[228]

The opening stanza ends with an image of kinetic power ('a vast river | Over its rocks ceaselessly bursts and raves'[229]) that, after being awesomely developed, will be superseded by the still greater image of Mont Blanc itself. Such kinesis is especially focused as power; the river is the Arve, and the 'awful scene' is one

> Where Power in likeness of the Arve comes down
> From the ice gulphs that gird his secret throne,
> Bursting thro' these dark mountains like the flame
> Of lightning thro' the tempest[230]

After the opening lines establish the power of the natural elements, the weakness of the poet, and the unremitting interchange between them, at line sixty the poem shifts into a higher gear, as it were—in a way that

[227] Ibid. (lines 117–26).   [228] Ibid. 229 (lines 1–2).
[229] Ibid. (lines 10–11).   [230] Ibid. (lines 15–19).

perhaps Handel alone was able to do in music—and in still more awesome majesty invokes the summit of the mountain itself. There are thus three layers of power: at the bottom the poet, frail and awe-stricken; in the middle, the gigantic kinesis of the Arve and the realm of foothill; and at the top, suddenly reversing itself from kinesis to absolute stillness, the mighty mountain itself:

> Far, far above, piercing the infinite sky,
> Mont Blanc appears,—still, snowy, and serene—[231]

What a statement! The poet's task is to confirm the sublimity of the Arve's kinesis, and at the same time to cap it. What can cap the rolling grandeur of 'The everlasting universe of things'? What can rise higher even than power? Shelley's magnificent lines give the answer. The word 'infinite' here caps 'power'; all the kinesis of the preceding lines is frozen into the verb 'pierces'. Mont Blanc's peak pierces the infinite sky, and reveals itself—as nowhere else in Shelley's tumultuous and frantic existence, and the tumultuous and frantic poetry that mirrored it—as 'still, snowy, and serene'. The mountain is not revealed; rather it itself, as the ultimate, 'appears', enters the scene.

Shelley has just said that at the contemplation of ultimate grandeur 'the very spirit fails'. It fails, too, the critic wants to say, at the contemplation of Shelley's wondrous statement. And perhaps the most remarkable single element in that statement is the repetition of 'far'. The second 'far' functions exponentially; it dramatically elevates the mental gaze, raising stillness and serenity to the condition of the infinite.

The turbulence of power is capped by the serenity of the infinite. Two great runs repeat that enormous reversal. The first is the vision of serenity far, far above, with images of power in subjection below:

> Far, far above, piercing the infinite sky,
> Mont Blanc appears,—still, snowy, and serene—
> Its subject mountains their unearthly forms
> Pile around it, ice and rock; broad vales between
> Of frozen floods, unfathomable deeps,
> Blue as the overhanging heaven, that spread
> And wind among the accumulated steeps;
> A desart peopled by the storms alone
>   . . . how hideously
> Its shapes are heaped around! rude, bare, and high,
> Ghastly, and scarred, and riven.[232]

---

[231] *Shelley*, i. 230 ('Mont Blanc', lines 60–1).   [232] Ibid. 230–1 (lines 60–71).

The second run reverses the process; the kinesis of earth gives way to the invocation of serenity. In this reversal, however, power itself is divested from the kinetic and relocated in the realm of the serene:

> The fields, the lakes, the forests, and the streams,
> Ocean, and all the living things that dwell
> Within the daedal earth; lightning, and rain,
> Earthquake, and fiery flood, and hurricane,
>
> . . . .
>
> The works and ways of man, their death and birth,
> And that of him and all that his may be;
> All things that move and breathe with toil and sound
> Are born and die; revolve, subside, and swell.
> Power dwells apart in its tranquillity,
> Remote, serene, and inaccessible[233]

Power henceforth merges with the summit of Mont Blanc; in doing so it abandons the kinesis of the world below. The 'race | Of man flies far in dread; his work and dwelling | Vanish', to be replaced by the awesome diapason of 'Below, vast caves | Shine in the rushing torrents' restless gleam'. But caves no less than man are dwarfed by the serene power of Mont Blanc: 'Mont Blanc yet gleams on high;—the power is there.'[234] At this juncture Shelley's own sense of insignificance is brought into the poem, more functionally than in any other of his statements. For, in a beautiful turn, Shelley's human mind, weak though it is, becomes necessary as that alone which can know and revere the power of the mountain. The infinite is once again invoked, but then, in an argument that somewhat parallels, but does not derive from, Kant's conceivings about the sublime, is finally revealed as needing the mind of man for its realization:

> The secret Strength of things
> Which governs thought, and to the infinite dome
> Of heaven is as a law, inhabits thee!
> And what were thou, and earth, and stars, and sea,
> If to the human mind's imaginings
> Silence and solitude were vacancy?[235]

It is startling to realize that this mighty dialectic of power and weakness, of stillness and kinesis, of higher and lower, of outer and inner, was

[233] Ibid. 231 (lines 84–97).
[234] Ibid. 232 (lines 117–19, 120–1, 127).
[235] Ibid. 233 (lines 139–44).

composed when Shelley was only 23. But it is a dialectic that emerges from the very roots of Shelley's awareness of the world, and in that sense seems not so much precocious as essential. Its depth and urgency for Shelley's own perspectives are witnessed by his prose statements about Mont Blanc, which contain virtually the same intensity that informs the poem itself. Of special interest in these statements is their witness that Mont Blanc, by the very fact of its being an impersonal object, allowed the release of personal awe in Shelley. That awe, normally elicited by the father, had been muted by Shelley's tragic relationship with his own father; but here the impersonal object takes on lineaments of the human: 'One would think that Mont Blanc was a living being & that the frozen blood forever circulated slowly thro' his stony veins.'[236]

With the human thus merging with the non-human, the subject merging with the object, Shelley's contemplation of the Arve and the mountain itself, now totally emptying his feelings into the external, is fraught with the full weight of his capacity for awe and reverence:

For an hour, we proceed along the valley of the Arve—a valley surrounded on all side by immense mountains whose jagged precipices were intermixed on high with dazzling snow: Their base was still covered with the eternal forest which perpetually grew darker & profounder as it approached the regions of snow.— After having visited a waterfall which was very fine we turned to the left & still following the valley, or now rather the vast ravine which is the couch and the creation of the terrible Arve, approached Chamounix. We ascended winding between mountains whose immensity staggers the imagination.[237]

As he approaches the mountain—here, intriguingly, it does not 'appear', but is hidden in clouds—Shelley's rapture becomes ever deeper:

Mont Blanc was before us but was covered with cloud, & its base furrowed with dreadful gaps was seen alone. Pinnacles of snow, intolerably bright, part of the chain connected with Mont Blanc shone thro the clouds at intervals on high. I never knew I never imagined what mountains were before. The immensity of these aerial summits excited, when they suddenly burst upon the sight, a sentiment of extatic wonder.[238]

As Shelley's poetry in 'Mont Blanc' is given depth, power, and weight by the characteristics of the mountain itself, which forms so mighty an objective correlative for his own awe and intensity, so in *A Defence of Poetry* does another external focus allow the full deployment of Shelley's

---

[236] Shelley, *Letters*, i. 500.
[237] Ibid. 496.
[238] Ibid. 497.

remarkable intelligence. This chapter began with an insistence on that intelligence, and it is fitting that it end with a renewed recognition of its quality. For nowhere is the exercise of high intelligence more in evidence than in the *Defence*. Only someone who had thought long and hard about the nature of poetry, and seen very deeply and clearly into what it is, could have composed that flaming essay.

The flame and flare of the piece, however, have always somewhat compromised an understanding of its enormous intelligence. By many a reader it is considered a rich piece of prose but little more. Students, particularly, have to be virtually forced to attend to the precise nature of the statement, a task made more difficult by their own relative paucity of understanding as to the nature of poetry.

But it is the burning quality of the essay that most surely indicates its depth. The understanding of poetry that it presents is not, as a surface encounter might suggest, the casual screed of a young man in his twenties, but the passionate utterance—passionate because it erupts from so deep within Shelley's habitual studies and thoughts, indeed, from within the very dedication of his life—of a totally committed poetic craftsman fortified by profound and intense study of the works of other practitioners of his art. A vast cultural knowledge, and a vast cultural awareness, underlie the statements of *A Defence of Poetry*.

Here there is none of the confusion that attended Shelley's relationships with women, none of the confusion and pain that vitiate so much of his internally directed verse. Shelley talks of an objective topic of great intellectual importance, not just for himself but for others, and one on which he is supremely qualified to speak. The passion and immediacy of his commitment lend to many of the statements a kind of coruscatingly aphoristic quality, as though a mighty fountain were flinging shining droplets into the sunlight. But the internal logic of the *Defence* is tight and coherent: the droplets are all created by the power of the single fountain.

There is a marvellous impatience in the essay. It is as though its thoughts must take shape in the most compressed and pregnant form in order to make way for other thoughts of the same urgency; truth follows truth in tumultuous pouring forth:

Poetry is indeed something divine. It is at once the centre and circumference of knowledge; it is that which comprehends all science, and that to which all science must be referred. It is at the same time the root and blossom of all other systems of thought; it is that from which all spring, and that which adorns all; and that which, if blighted, denies the fruit and the seed, and witholds from the barren world the nourishment and the succession of the scions of the tree of life. It is the perfect and consummate surface and bloom of things; it is as the odour and the colour of the rose to the texture of the elements which compose it, as the form and the splendour of unfaded beauty to the secrets of anatomy and corruption. What were Virtue, Love, Patriotism, Friendship— . . . what were our consolations on this side of the grave, and what were our aspirations beyond it, if Poetry did not ascend to bring light and fire from those eternal regions where the owl-winged faculty of calculation dare not ever soar?'[239]

Seamlessly following these impassioned statements, aphoristically but nevertheless consequentially, Shelley then urges that 'Poetry is not like reasoning, a power to be exerted according to the determination of the will'; that when 'composition begins, inspiration is already on the decline, and the most glorious poetry that has ever been communicated to the world is probably a feeble shadow of the original conception of the Poet'.[240]

It is very important to understand that this cascade of rich language is also a cascade of true and profound thoughts. Take, as single example, the statement above that poetry is 'the perfect and consummate surface and bloom of things'. The statement embodies an absolute realization of the unique nature of poetry in the spectrum of man's discourse. In a disquisition on poetry entitled 'Poetry and the Poem: The Structure of Poetic Content', it is argued that one of the most important features of poetry, called there *'essentia'*, involves a tension between the sense of nowness and evanescence:

Essentia, in its disposition of awareness between 'now' and 'then,' is accordingly fleeting and intangible—is in the nature of an *evanescence*. Indeed, the most immediate awareness of 'now' is that which not only vanishes into 'then,' but is in itself fragile.[241]

After illustrations from Rilke and Poe, the discussion then summons Coleridge:

The linkage between intensified nowness and evanescence is further underscored in Coleridge's statement that 'poetry is the blossom and the fragrancy' of human thoughts and emotions.[242]

It is evident that Shelley's words, 'the perfect and consummate surface and bloom of things', would illustrate the contention as precisely as Coleridge's 'blossom and the fragrancy'.

A single further example might be useful. One of Shelley's chief insistences is that poetry 'strips the veil of familiarity from the world'.[243]

---

[239] McElderry, 30.   [240] Ibid.   [241] McFarland, *Romanticism*, 277.
[242] Ibid. 278   [243] McElderry, 32.

The insistence is reiterated in various forms. How, specifically, it relates to a deep understanding of poetic function may perhaps be grasped by comparing it with one of the chief tenets of Russian Formalism in our own century. In 1917, Viktor Shklovsky coined the term 'defamiliarization' to indicate one of the indispensable means by which poetic language is 'foregrounded':

Habitualization devours works, clothes, furniture, one's wife, and the fear of war. . . . And art exists that one may recover the sensation of life; it exists to make one feel things, to make the stone *stony*. . . . The technique of art is to make objects 'unfamiliar', to make forms difficult.[244]

As Shelley says, in explicit congruence to this theoretical point, not only does poetry strip 'the veil of familiarity from the world', but it 'creates anew the universe, after it has been annihilated in our minds by the recurrence of impressions blunted by reiteration'.[245]

One of the reasons for the mistaken tendency to think of Shelley's tract as merely a beautiful effusion of language, rather than a deep-probing contemplation of the true nature of poetry, is that the intellectual quality of its stimulus—Peacock's 'The Four Ages of Poetry'—is generally underestimated. Underneath its caustic irony, Peacock's small treatise contains a hard and challenging, and immensely deflating, counter-conception of what poetry is. It will not do to dismiss Peacock's arguments as only half-serious, or Philistine, or clownish. On the contrary, Peacock says things that the claque of poetry-lovers does not want to hear, and will not allow to be heard; but that many, outside the arena of poetry, may often have thought. Peacock is the voice, as it were, of all those voiceless people, from merchants to engineers, who find themelves uncharmed by poetry and resistant to its self-adulating chorus.

His arguments are not attractive, but they can be formidable. For instance, it is not enough to hear merely cynical Philistinism in his account of the origin of poetry; his statement is a powerful example of proto-Marxist understanding, whereby cultural superstructures are always reared upon a materialist base:

The successful warrior becomes a chief; the successful chief becomes a king: his next want is an organ to disseminate the fame of his achievements and the extent of his possessions; and this organ he finds in a bard, who is always ready to celebrate the strength of his arm, being first duly inspired by that of his liquor. This is the origin of poetry, which, like all other trades, takes its rise in the demand for the commodity, and flourishes to the extent of the market.

[244] Lemon, 12, 21.   [245] McElderry, 32.

Poetry is thus in its origin panegyrical. The first rude songs of all nations appear to be a sort of brief historical notices, in a strain of tumid hyperbole, of the exploits and possessions of a few pre-eminent individuals.[246]

Peacock's chief argument rings changes on the thesis that poetry does not participate in the progress of science and utilitarian improvement, and it is thus little more than an obsolete vestige of the childhood of man: 'Poetry was the mental rattle that awakened the attention of intellect in the infancy of civil society.'[247] He observes that 'in whatever degree poetry is cultivated, it must necessarily be to the neglect of some branch of useful study'.[248] He argues that society's movement towards the subordination of 'the ornamental to the useful' will more and more drive poetry from modern consideration.[249] He insists that

A poet in our times is a semi-barbarian in a civilized community. He lives in the days that are past. His ideas, thoughts, feelings, associations, are all with barbarous manners, obsolete customs, and exploded superstitions. . . . The highest inspirations of poetry are resolvable into three ingredients: the rant of unregulated passion, the whining of exaggerated feeling, and the cant of factitious sentiment: and can therefore serve only to ripen a splendid lunatic like Alexander, a puling driveller like Werter, or a morbid dreamer like Wordsworth. It can never make a philosopher, nor a statesman, nor in any class of life an useful or rational man. It cannot claim the slightest share in any one of the comforts and utilities of life of which we have witnessed so many and so rapid advances.[250]

It was this insistence of Peacock on the practical that made so fitting Shelley's own insistence on poets as 'the unacknowledged legislators of the world'.[251] Shelley specifically took note in his *Defence* that 'poets have been challenged to resign the civic crown to reasoners and mechanists'.[252]

His answer, spurred by 'a sacred rage', almost exploded into existence.[253] Peacock's article had 'excited my polemical faculties' and done so 'violently'.[254] 'It is very clever, but, I think, very false,' he says of Peacock's essay.[255] At all events, Shelley's answer, which grew longer than he had at first intended, and was even at that to have been longer still, was written with the intent 'to silence cavil'.[256]

And silence cavil it did. It is a masterpiece of style and thought, as easily bearing comparison with Sidney's *Defence* as *Adonais* does with Milton's

[246] McElderry, 159.   [247] Ibid. 171.
[248] Ibid.   [249] Ibid. 172.   [250] Ibid. 170.
[251] Ibid. 36. The phrase had earlier appeared in the *Philosophical View of Reform* (*Shelley*, vii. 20).
[252] Ibid. 26.   [253] Shelley, *Letters*, ii. 261.
[254] Ibid. 258.   [255] Ibid.   [256] Ibid. 275.

Lycidas. Its profound and beautiful formulations cascade forth in memorable profusion:

Poets, according to the circumstances of the age and nation in which they appeared, were called, in the earlier epochs of the world, legislators, or prophets: a poet essentially comprises and unites both these characters. For he not only beholds intensely the present as it is, and discovers those laws according to which present things ought to be ordered, but he beholds the future in the present, and his thoughts are the germs of the flower and the fruit of latest time.[257]

Their language is vitally metaphorical; that is, it marks the before unapprehended relations of things and perpetuates their apprehension.[258]

A poem is the image of life expressed in its eternal truth.[259]

Poetry is a mirror which makes beautiful that which is distorted.[260]

But Poetry acts in another and diviner manner. It awakens and enlarges the mind itself by rendering it the receptacle of a thousand unapprehended combinations of thought. Poetry lifts the veil from the hidden beauty of the world and makes familiar objects be as if they were not familiar.[261]

. . . that great poem, which all poets, like the co-operating thoughts of one great mind, have built up since the beginning of the world.[262]

Poetry thus makes immortal all that is best and most beautiful in the world; it arrests the vanishing apparitions which haunt the interlunations of life,[263]

Poetry redeems from decay the visitations of the divinity in Man.[264]

But there are more—many more—exquisite formulations of deeply cognized truths. Indeed, this brief work, taken merely by itself, serves to admit Shelley to the ranks of the select and serious few in the annals of culture. When taken with his two other masterpieces, *Adonais* and 'Mont Blanc', the *Defence of Poetry* secures for its author not only a position as one of the most important of all Romantic writers, but a permanent place among the true masters of world literature.

---

[257] McElderry, 7. [258] Ibid. 6. [259] Ibid. 10.
[260] Ibid. [261] Ibid. 12. [262] Ibid. 19.
[263] Ibid. 32. [264] Ibid.

5

The Instrument of Good

IN its attempt to descry diverse textures within the text called Romanticism, the discourse of this book, following its theoretical contract, has proceeded, first, from the touching of a modern texture ancillary to Romanticism—Alan Liu's approach to Wordsworth—which is located along the edge of the fabric, and from there moved to a texture located in the very centre of the tapestry: Rousseau's originating cultural formations with regard to self and its implications. Following complexly interwoven threads from Rousseau to Revolution, it has then engaged the texture of Revolutionary attitude as woven into the life and thought of a central figure of English Romanticism: Coleridge. Next, gathering threads radiating both from Rousseau and from Coleridge, it has moved across the fabric to touch another textural configuration, this woven into a pattern supplied by the second-generation Romantic, Shelley.

The present chapter, in its touching of the Romantic fabric, will in effect turn the tapestry over and begin tracing the weaving as encountered on the other side. From a predominate concern with patterns as configured by central figures such as Shelley and Coleridge and Rousseau—and important modern interpreters such as Liu—it will now move to the touching of a less personal, more ideational collocation of textures. In this chapter it will touch the extraordinarily rich texture woven by the Romantic preoccupation with imagination. It will trace its way into this texture by following a thread supplied by Shelley, combine it with a longer length previously descried in the touching of Rousseau, and follow them both in their intertwinement with the many strands eventuating in the focal pattern supplied by Coleridge.

Now Shelley's *Defence of Poetry*, as just argued, is replete with deeply cognized and beautifully expressed conceptions that seem almost to be cast up as encapsulated worlds of wisdom. One of special beauty and point, not heretofore brought forward, is Shelley's insistence that all morality depends on imagination:

A man, to be greatly good, must imagine intensely and comprehensively; he must put himself in the place of another and of many others; the pains and pleasures of his species must become his own. The great instrument of moral good is the imagination; and poetry administers to the effect by acting upon the cause. Poetry enlarges the circumference of the imagination by replenishing it with thoughts of ever new delight, which have the power of attracting and assimilating to their own nature all other thoughts, and which form new intervals and interstices whose void for ever craves fresh food. Poetry strengthens that faculty which is the organ of the moral nature of man, in the same manner as exercise strengthens a limb.[1]

The formulation is profound. It is also noteworthy for displacing morality from a position as a primary factor or foundation of human awareness, to a secondary, or derived, position. After all, the great philosopher Kant, working near the headwaters of the vast Romantic current, had in 1788, in his *Kritik der praktischen Vernunft*, said that two things filled the spirit with 'Bewunderung und Ehrfurcht'—'wonderment and awe'—and they were 'der bestirnte Himmel über mir und das moralische Gesetz in mir'—'the starry heavens above and the moral law within'.[2] Morality, for Kant, existed absolutely, and was not grounded in this world. As a commentator, Norman Kemp Smith, emphasizes:

The moral consciousness is the key to the meaning of the entire universe as well as of human life. Its values are the sole ultimate values . . .[3]

. . . the consciousness of the moral law is thus noumenally grounded; it has a validity with which nothing in the phenomenal world can possibly compare. It is the one form in which noumenal reality directly discloses itself to the human mind.[4]

Another commentator, Lewis White Beck, emphasizes that

Morality stands independent in Kant's philosophy. The contributions made to it by theology are at most supplements. In establishing the principle of morality, even the 'highest good'—faith in which implies practical-metaphysical propositions—can be completely disregarded.[5]

Kant elaborated his view of the bedrock nature of morality in many places; it was propounded in the first critique of 1781, exhaustively discussed again in the second critique of 1788, exhaustively discussed in the interim in the treatise called *Grundlegung der Metaphysik der Sitten*, in 1785. In his last great work, the *Kritik der Urteilskraft* of 1790, he even subordinated the aesthetic to the moral: he compares the moral feeling to the aesthetic feeling, and he considers the beautiful as a 'symbol' of the moral.[6] The sum total of his lucubrations on the subject of the moral makes him one of the very greatest figures in the entire history of ethical thought.

---

[1] McElderry, 12–13.   [2] *Kant*, v. 161.   [3] Smith, 571.
[4] Ibid. 573.   [5] Beck, 45–6.   [6] *Kant*, v. 353.

Interestingly enough for the arguments of this book, Kant's enormous contribution to the theory of morality was intertwined both with Rousseau and with the French Revolution. As Beck says:

Rousseau prepared men's minds for the Revolution, but it was Kant's deepening of Rousseau's criticism of law imposed from above that gave philosophical dignity to *liberté, égalité, fraternité*. Indeed, George Herbert Mead, in his *Movements of Thought in the Nineteenth Century*, gave to Kant the title usually reserved for Rousseau, 'the philosopher of the Revolution.'[7]

To glimpse how Kant himself stated his obligation to Rousseau in this respect, and to see how important the obligation is, one may turn from Beck back to the commentary of Kemp Smith, who says that one of Kant's 'abiding convictions' was

that in matters which concern all men without distinction nature is not guilty of any partial distribution of her gifts, and that in regard to the essential ends of human nature the highest philosophy cannot advance beyond what is revealed to the common understanding. . . . Kant has himself placed on record his sense of the great debt which in this connection he . . . owed to the teaching of Rousseau:

'I am by disposition an enquirer. I feel the consuming thirst for knowledge, the eager unrest to advance ever further, and the delights of discovery. There was a time when I believed that this is what confers real dignity upon human life, and I despised the common people who know nothing. Rousseau has set me right. This imagined advantage vanishes. I learn to honor men, and should regard myself as of much less use than the common labourer, if I did not believe that my philosophy will restore to all men the common rights of humanity.'

The sublimity of the starry heavens and the imperative of the moral law are ever present influences on the life of man; and they require for their apprehension no previous initiation through science and philosophy. The naked eye reveals the former; of the latter all men are immediately aware. In their universal appeal they are of the very substance of human existence.[8]

Yet in this major concatenation, linking together Rousseau, Revolution, and the greatest philosopher of the age, Shelley seems to have no connection. His secondary derivation of the moral, as depending on imagination, appears to be an isolated insistence.

It does not follow, however, that Shelley's view lacks either pertinence or cultural resonance. It is, indeed, tantamount to Freud's view of the cruelty of savages to their foes; although he does not use the word imagination, Freud in effect makes the same argument as Shelley. The savage can cognize his own weal or woe, but he seems unable to make the imaginative substitution by which he sees himself in his foe's predicament, or inserts their feelings into his own situation.

Indeed, Shelley's grounding of morality upon imagination, though not participating in the emphasis that links together Rousseau and Kant, connects itself with Rousseau in another way. For in *Émile* Rousseau presents, fully and eloquently, precisely the same view that Shelley propounds:

To become sensitive and pitying, the child must know that there are beings like him who suffer what he has suffered, who feel the pains he has felt, and that there are others whom he ought to conceive of as able to feel them too. In fact, how do we let ourselves be moved by pity if not by transporting ourselves outside of ourselves and identifying with the suffering animal, by leaving, as it were, our own being to take on its being? . . . Thus, no one becomes sensitive until his imagination is animated and begins to transport him out of himself.[9]

If the ultimate insistence on morality, as found in Kant's philosophy, is here somewhat vitiated by Rousseau's making it a form of imaginative activity, the raising of imagination to such an immensely important place constitutes direct documentation for Engell's formula, adduced in Chapter 2 above, that imagination is 'the quintessence of Romanticism'.[10]

It is this line of conceiving, defined by Rousseau and Shelley, that leads directly into the apotheosis of imagination in Poe and Poe's epigone, Baudelaire. As morality, for Kant, was 'the one form in which noumenal reality discloses itself to the human mind', in Poe and Baudelaire the one form of noumenal reality is transferred to the imagination. In his *Notes nouvelles sur Edgar Poe*, Baudelaire says that

for Poe, the imagination is the queen of the faculties; but by the word he understands something much greater than is understood by the common reader. Imagination is not fancy; it is not, moreover, sensibility, although it would be difficult to conceive an imaginative man who would not have sensibility.

No, imagination is not fancy, it is 'une faculté quasi divine'—'a faculty almost divine'—which

perceives at once, dispensing with the methods of philosophy, the intimate relationships and secrets of things, their correspondences and analogies. The honors and functions he confers on the faculty give it a value such . . . that a learned man without imagination would appear as no more than a false savant, or at least as an incomplete savant.[11]

[9] Rousseau, iv. 505–6.
[10] See above, Ch. 2, n. 27.
[11] Baudelaire, ii. 328–9.

We are in this chapter touching a texture of extraordinary richness and complexity. Though Baudelaire's insistence accords with the high dignity conferred on imagination by Shelley and Rousseau, it also interweaves threads ultimately stemming from Coleridge—as the invocation of the distinction between imagination and fancy attests—and Swedenborg—as the reference to correspondences and analogies guarantees. In the interest of cognizing a full weaving of textural richness, however, this chapter, instead of attempting to survey the whole realm of imagination, will be restricted to a more circumscribed aim. It will limit itself to the touching of a single intriguing truth about the Romantic apotheosis of imagination: that apotheosis was not a raising of certain intellectual considerations from an already elevated place in human valuation, but was rather the dramatic reversal of a tradition of devaluation and suspicion with regard to imaginative functions. Imagination is a texture whose configuration rises notably above the common fabric of Romanticism, but thereby contains intaglioed depths of unusual steepness.

The absoluteness of the Romantic apotheosis can hardly be overestimated. Baudelaire carries over his reverential phrase about imagination, 'the queen of the faculties' ('la reine des facultés') into his aesthetic testament in the *Salon de 1859*. He gives one of that work's chapters the title 'La Reine des facultés', and in it he invokes in awed tones the power and mystery of this almost divine faculty: 'Mystérieuse faculté que cette reine des facultés! Elle touche à toutes les autres; elle les excite, elle les envoie au combat. . . . Elle est l'analyse, elle est la synthèse.' He continues:

It is the imagination that has taught man the moral sense of colour, of contour, of sound and smell. It has created, at the beginning of the world, analogy and metaphor. It decomposes the whole creation, and, with the materials amassed and disposed according to rules whose origin is to be found only in the depths of the soul, it creates a new world. . . . As it has created the world (one may say this, I believe, even in a religious sense), it is right that it should rule it.[12]

And he goes on, in the same accents of transcendence, to say that 'L'imagination est la reine du vrai, et le *possible* est une des provinces du vrai. Elle est positivement apparentée avec l'infini.'[13]

Baudelaire, joining Shelley and Rousseau, even explicitly nominates the imagination as the instrument of moral good:

Finally, imagination plays a powerful part even in the moral; for, permit me to go so far, what is virtue without imagination? You might as well say virtue without pity, virtue without heaven.[14]

---

[12] Baudelaire, ii. 620–1.   [13] Ibid. 621.   [14] Ibid.

In awarding the very highest value to the faculty of imagination, Baudelaire resumes the tradition most influentially enunciated by Coleridge.

Coleridge is undoubtedly the best-known formulator of the importance of imagination, and his apotheosizing emphasis, characteristically, is yoked in binary evocation with the less honorific conception of fancy. He first refers to the differentiation in 1802, though in an offhand context that suggests that its terms had been well in hand earlier:

In the Hebrew Poetry you find nothing of this poor Stuff—as poor in genuine Imagination, as it is mean in Intellect— | At best, it is but Fancy, or the aggregating Faculty of the mind—not *Imagination*, or the *modifying*, and *co-adunating* Faculty.[15]

The distinction appears repeatedly in Coleridge's thought. He refers, for random instance, to 'Bernini, in whom a great genius was bewildered and lost by excess of fancy over imagination, the aggregative over the unifying faculty'.[16] For another instance, also at random, Henry Crabb Robinson in 1810 recorded that Coleridge in conversation

made an elaborate and somewhat obscure distinction between fancy and imagination. The excess of fancy is delirium; of imagination, mania. Fancy is the arbitrary bringing together of things that lie remote, and forming them into a unity. The materials lie ready formed for the mind, and the fancy acts only by a sort of juxtaposition. In imagination, on the contrary, the mind from the excitement of some slight impression generates and produces a form of its own.[17]

But it is, of course, in the *Biographia Literaria* that Coleridge's most influential formulations occur. Broaching the matter in the fourth chapter, he says that repeated meditations had led him to suspect 'that fancy and imagination were two distinct and widely different faculties,'[18] and that 'Milton had a highly *imaginative*, Cowley a very *fanciful* mind'.[19] In chapter 13, however, in a notable augmentation, Coleridge's famous paragraphs distinguishing 'the imagination, or shaping and modifying power' from 'the fancy, or the aggregative and associative power'[20] begin with a direct apotheosis of the imaginative function:

The IMAGINATION then I consider either as primary, or secondary. The primary IMAGINATION I hold to be the living Power and prime Agent of all human

---

[15] *Collected Letters*, ii. 865–6.
[16] Ibid. iv. 569.
[17] *Miscellaneous Criticism*, 387–8.   [18] *Biographia*, i. 82.   [19] Ibid. 84.
[20] Ibid. 293. Cf. Coleridge elsewhere: 'Fancy, the aggregative, Imagination, the modifying & *fusive*' (*Notebooks*, iii. 3827).

Perception, and as a repetition in the finite mind of the eternal act of creation in the infinite I AM. The secondary I consider as an echo of the former, co-existing with the conscious will, yet still as identical with the primary in the *kind* of its agency, and differing only in *degree*, and in the *mode* of its operation. It dissolves, diffuses, dissipates, in order to re-create; or where this process is rendered impossible, yet still at all events it struggles to idealize and to unify. It is essentially *vital*, even as all objects (*as* objects) are essentially fixed and dead.

FANCY, on the contrary, has no other counters to play with, but fixities and definites. The Fancy is indeed no other than a mode of Memory emancipated from the order of time and space; and blended with, and modified by that empirical phenomenon of the will, which we express by the word CHOICE. But equally with the ordinary memory it must receive all its materials ready made from the law of association.[21]

That statement constitutes the absolute apex of Romantic assertions of imagination's transcendent importance. It is the only place where Coleridge posits the 'primary' imagination—it is always the 'secondary' imagination that is brought forward in other distinctions of imagination and fancy—and one large function of the positing of 'primary' imagination is to make unmistakable the apotheosis of the faculty. All active functions of imagination within the mind's control are subsumed under secondary imagination; the primary imagination's function is to provide the world and hold it in place: all reality exists only in the images supplied in the mind. Primary imagination, in other words, is virtually interchangeable with Berkeley's formula, *esse* is *percipi*.[22] It does not—*pace* Jonathan Wordsworth—have anything to do with the production of poetry or the conscious use of the mind.

Though Coleridge's formulation does not appear to have been known to Baudelaire, a refracted version, in a work of 1848 by Catherine Crowe, is quoted by Baudelaire as 'justificative paraphrase' for his own statement that 'Comme l'imagination a créé le monde, elle le gouverne'.[23] Baudelaire first quotes the English and then translates it:

'By imagination, I do not simply mean to convey the common notion implied by that much abused word, which is only *fancy*, but the *constructive* imagination, which is a much higher function, and which, in as much as man is made in the likeness of God, bears a distant relation to that sublime power by which the Creator projects, creates, and upholds his universe.'—'Par imagination, je ne veux pas seulement exprimer l'idée commune impliquée dans ce mot dont on fait si

[21] *Biographia*, i. 304–5.
[22] See *Originality*, 141–2, esp. n. 36.
[23] Baudelaire, ii. 623.

grand abus, laquelle est simplement *fantaisie*, mais bien l'imagination *créatrice*, qui est une fonction beaucoup plus élevée, et qui, en tant que l'homme est fait à la resemblance de Dieu, garde un rapport éloigné avec cette puissance sublime par laquelle le Créateur conçoit, crée et entretient son univers.'[24]

In the light of the unanimity and strength of these apotheosizing sentiments with regard to the Romantic view of imagination, a statement by Wallace Stevens in 1950 provides an unintentionally ironic footnote. Stevens was very much the reluctant heir of Coleridge's distinctions, as of Romanticism in general. But, under the influence of New Criticism's dismissal and abject misunderstanding of Romanticism and Romantic achievement, he says—with wild historical disconnectedness and inaccuracy—that

we must somehow cleanse the imagination of the romantic. We feel, without being particularly intelligent about it, that the imagination as metaphysics will survive logical positivism unscathed. At the same time, we feel, and with the sharpest possible intelligence, that it is not worthy to survive if it is to be identified with the romantic. The imagination is one of the great human powers. The romantic belittles it. The imagination is the liberty of the mind. The romantic is a failure to make use of that liberty. It is to the imagination what sentimentality is to feeling. It is a failure of the imagination precisely as sentimentality is a failure of feeling. The imagination is the only genius. It is intrepid and eager and the extreme of its achievement lies in abstraction. The achievement of the romantic, on the contrary, lies in minor wish-fulfillments and it is incapable of abstraction.[25]

That passage rather vividly reveals that Stevens's conceptualizing powers were, to put it kindly, hardly on the same level as his poetic abilities. Abysmally uninformed and ill-judged as his statement is, however, it does highlight the need for a careful touching of imagination, rather than a mere expression of opinion.

Imagination is ineluctably interwined with the cultural fabric of Romanticism. As the present author's *Originality and Imagination* argues, 'The historical rise of imagination's importance witnessed a transfer of mental energy from the weakening concept of soul to an alternative vehicle. Imagination, and its twin Romantic idea, originality, were then, and still are, transformations of the human intensity earlier conveyed by soul.'[26] The book goes on to take note of the special numinous aura that surrounded the term imagination by Romantic times:

'The word, Imagination,' says Wordsworth, 'has been overstrained, from impulses honorable to mankind, to meet the demands of the faculty which is perhaps the

[24] Ibid. 624.   [25] Stevens, 138–9.   [26] *Originality*, p. xii.

noblest of our nature.' This overstraining, as with originality, lifts itself from the *principium individuationis* to the highest principle of self, which is soul. Wordsworthian 'imagination,' as Geoffrey Hartman defines it, is 'consciousness of self raised to apocalyptic pitch.'

Because both terms, *originality* and *imagination*, historically accumulated value in inverse ratio to their clear and distinct definition, they tended not only to share a common aura but also to restore that numinous which by the eighteenth century was increasingly divested from *soul* as a term in its own right.[27]

Thus imagination, which by the Romantic era occupied a progressively larger and richer role in the estimation of mental faculties, was impelled in that upward ascent by human needs no longer satisfied by the concept of soul. The metonymy was possible, for since the time of Aristotle's *De Anima*, the imagining function was subsumed under the larger conception of soul. As long as that conception was current, imagination did not rise in importance. Descartes, for instance, who often discusses imagination, never augments its importance. He does not especially denigrate it; but he considers it merely a subsidiary function in the total realm of human mentation:

But what then am I? A thing which thinks. What is a thing which thinks? It is a thing which doubts, understands, conceives, affirms, denies, wills, refuses, which also imagines and feels.[28]

In this role, imagination is not an especially honored participant in the business of human thought:

For it is so evident of itself that it is I who doubts, who understands, and who desires, that there is no reason here to add anything to explain it. And I have certainly the power of imagining likewise; for although it may happen (as I formerly supposed) that none of the things which I may imagine are true, nevertheless this power of imagining does not cease to be really in use, and it forms part of my thought.[29]

More specifically, as Descartes says in section xx of his *Les Passions de l'âme*, under the rubric 'Of the imaginations and other thoughts which are formed by the soul':

When our soul applies itself to imagine something which does not exist, as when it represents to itself an enchanted palace or a chimera, and also when it applies itself to consider something which is only intelligible and not imaginable, e.g. to consider its own nature, the perceptions which it has of these things depend

---

[27] *Originality*, 88.
[28] *Descartes*, i. 153.
[29] Ibid.

principally on the act of will which causes it to perceive them. That is why we usually consider them as actions rather than passions.[30]

In the next section, Descartes speaks of 'the imaginations which have the body only as a cause', and here he takes note of 'the illusions of our dreams, and also the day-dreams which we often have when awake, and when our thought wanders aimlessly without applying itself to anything of its own accord'.[31] Both versions of imaginative activity bear on their face the stigma of disconnection from reality.

In his greatest work, the *Meditationes de prima philosophia*, Descartes analyses the difference between understanding (*intellectio*) and imagination (*imaginatio*), and there he speaks of

the faculty of imagination which I possess, and of which, experience tells me, I make use when I apply myself to the consideration of material things, is capable of persuading me of their existence; for when I attentively consider what imagination is, I find that it is nothing but a certain application of the faculty of knowledge to the body which is immediately present to it, and which therefore exists.

And to render this quite clear, I remark in the first place the difference that exists between the imagination and pure intellection. For example, when I imagine a triangle, I do not conceive it only as a figure comprehended by three lines, but I also apprehend these three lines as present by the power and inward vision of my mind, and this is what I call imagining.[32]

In that statement there resides both a downgrading of imagination ('nothing but a certain application of the faculty of knowledge to the body which is immediately present to it'), and a faint foreshadowing of the later Romantic escalation of the numinous aura of the imagination ('by the power and inward vision of my mind'). But Descartes, apart from this one adumbrative hint, keeps imagination firmly in a subservient role:

I remark besides that this power of imagination which is in one, inasmuch as it differs from the power of understanding, is in no wise a necessary element in my nature, or in the essence of my mind. . . . and although I examine all things with care, I nevertheless do not find that from this distinct idea of corporeal nature, which I have in my imagination, I can derive any argument from which there will necessarily be deduced the existence of body.[33]

It was imagination's connection with things that might not be true that dictated Descartes's relative lack of enthusiasm for the imaginative function ('A man might quite easily imagine that he rightly understood something which in reality he did not understand'[34]). Impelled as he was

---

[30] Ibid. 341.   [31] Ibid.   [32] Ibid. 185.
[33] Ibid. 186-7.   [34] Ibid. 438.

by the overwhelming and idiosyncratic need not to be 'deceived',
Descartes could hardly hail the mental faculty that led to the possibility of
misapprehending reality. The great French thinker, with his passion for
'clear and distinct ideas', virtually inaugurated the age of 'reason', and
reason and imagination could not easily be made to coincide.

His seventeenth-century compeers shared his distrust of this foe of
reason. 'Cette faculté trompeuse'[35]—'this fraudulent faculty'—is what
Pascal calls the imagination: 'The greatest philosopher in the world,
standing on the brink of a precipice, on an amply wide plank, and
convinced by his reason that he was perfectly safe, would be undone by his
imagination.'[36] Like Descartes a mathematician of the first rank, Pascal
casts his lot wholly with reason (and with faith), and not at all with
imagination.

Indeed, of imagination he says: 'It is man's dominant part, this mistress
of error and of falsehood, and all the greater for that she does not always
deceive; for she would be an infallible touchstone of truth, if she were a
touchstone of falsehood. But being most often false, she leaves no sure
mark of her quality, for she marks with the same character the true and the
false.'[37] Pascal's nomination of imagination as 'maîtresse de erreur et
fausseté' stands as the antipode of Baudelaire's reverential naming of
imagination as 'la reine du vrai'.

Indeed, Pascal's stigmatizing of imagination as the begetter of 'error'
was repeatedly reversed in high Romanticism. For instance, Shelley
lavishes extravagant praise on precisely imagination's ability to 'kill' error:

> Imagination! which from earth and sky,
> And from the depths of human phantasy,
> As from a thousand prisms and mirrors, fills
> The Universe with glorious beams, and kills
> Error, the worm, with many a sun-like arrow
> Of its reverberated lightning.[38]

Pascal does, however, accord imagination important powers. 'The
imagination disposes of everything,' he says, 'she creates beauty, justice,
and happiness, which are mankind's whole aim.'[39] But none of this counts
in the scale of truth, because imagination works against reason:

This haughty power, enemy of reason, which loves to control and dominate reason,
in order to show how in all things she is able to, has established in man a second
nature. She has her happy followers, her unhappy ones, her healthy ones, her sick

[35] Pascal, 505.   [36] Ibid. 504.   [37] Ibid.
[38] *Shelley*, ii. 361 (*Epipsychidion*, lines 164–9).   [39] Pascal, 505.

ones, her rich ones, her poor ones. She causes reason to believe, to doubt, to deny. She suspends the senses, and she makes them feel. She has her fools and her wise men. And nothing annoys us so much as to see her fill her partisans with a satisfaction more full and entire than reason does.[40]

A third great thinker of the seventeenth century, Spinoza, shares the distrust of imagination exhibited by Descartes and Pascal. In his *De intellectus emendatione*, Spinoza says that 'we have distinguished between a true idea and other perceptions, and shown that ideas fictitious, false, and the rest, originate in the imagination'.[41] He says, again, that 'we may also see how easily men may fall into grave errors through not distinguishing accurately between the imagination and the understanding'.[42] Like Descartes, Spinoza looked to understanding or reason, *intellectus*, as the guide of mankind, and rejected imagination as a false path.

Such a disposition of value had a long provenance. The most influential of all philosophers, Plato, had distrusted imagination. In the sixth (and seventh) book of *The Republic*, he had described a fourfold division of mental functioning, in which *eikasía* is the lowest. By *eikasía* Plato refers to the imaging faculty, imagination, and this is a faculty that cannot be trusted. Three faculties stand superior to it, the highest being *noesis* or the exercise of reason. As he says:

And now, answering to these four sections, assume these four affections occurring in the soul—intellection or reason for the highest, understanding for the second, belief for the third, and for the last, picture thinking, or conjecture—and arrange them in a proportion, considering that they participate in clearness and precision in the same degree as their objects partake of truth and reality.[43]

In his distinguished lectures on *The Republic*, R. L. Nettleship elucidates just why imagination ranked so low in Plato's scale. Nettleship emphasizes that 'the relation between each higher and lower stage is expressed by Plato as the relation between seeing an image or shadow and seeing the thing imaged or shadowed. This metaphor bears a great part in his theory of knowledge.'[44] Of the stages themselves he says,

The four stages of mental development are called (beginning with the lowest) εἰκασία, πίστις, διάνοια and νόησις (later called ἐιστήμη). The two former are stages of what has previously been described as δόξα; the two latter are stages of what has been called γνῶσις or επιστήμη and is later on called νόησις (a term which in this passage is limited to the higher of them).[45]

40 Ibid. 504. 41 *Spinoza*, ii. 32.
42 Ibid. 32–3. 43 Plato, *Republic*, 511 D–E.
44 Nettleship, 240. 45 Ibid. 241.

Commenting on this paragraph, Nettleship says that 'the most superficial view of the world, that which conveys least knowledge of it, is called by Plato ἐικασία'. He continues:

The word has a double meaning; it has its regular meaning of conjecture, and an etymological meaning of which Plato avails himself, the perception of images, that state of mind whose objects are of the nature of mere images (εἰκόνες). There is a connexion between the two meanings; when we talk of a conjecture we imply that it is an uncertain belief, and we imply also that it arises from a consideration of the appearance or surface of the thing in question. Plato has availed himself of both meanings of the word, so as to express a certain character or property of the object of mental apprehension and a certain state of mind in the subject; the mental state is one of very little certitude, its objects are of the nature of 'images', shadows and reflexions.[46]

We note at the outset that Plato's rejection of what we may call imagination is very much the same argument propounded in different ways by Descartes, Pascal, and Spinoza: imagination cannot be trusted to reveal truth. Nettleship goes on to expand on the centrality of the connection, in Plato, of images with shadows and reflections:

Why does he describe this lowest group of objects as shadows or reflexions? Shadows, images, and dreams, are the most obvious types of unreality, and the contrast between them and realities is very striking to early thinkers, as it is to a mind which is just beginning to think. In what respect does a shadow differ from the real thing? It resembles it merely in the outline, and that is often very vague and inexact; the rest of the real thing, its solidity, its constitution, even its colour, vanishes in the shadow. In what respect does a reflexion differ from the real thing? A reflexion reproduces more of the real object than a shadow does; its outline is very fairly defined and exact; the colour of the object is retained to a certain extent; but a reflexion is still only in two dimensions. Any state of mind of which the object stands to some other object as a shadow or reflexion does to the real thing, is ἐικασία.[47]

Nettleship does try to hold the door open, as it were, for the more honorific use of 'imagination' in Coleridge and later thinkers. But after holding it open, he immediately closes it, by noting that Plato would allow none of the honorific significance:

The literal translation of εἰκασία is 'imagination'. But it would be very misleading to translate the one word by the other; for, while εἰκασία expresses the superficial side of what we call imagination, it does not express the deeper side. Imagination in English has two senses. In one sense it really does answer to Plato's conception of

[46] Nettleship, 241.　　　　[47] Ibid. 242.

seeing images. When we say that something is a mere imagination, or that a man is the slave of his own imagination, we do mean to describe a very superficial view of things. But when we say that a poet is a man of great imagination we mean almost the exact opposite.[48]

Plato himself, however, would notoriously have none of the great imagination of the poet, and Nettleship is forced to concede that

Plato seems much more impressed by the possible misuse of imaginative work than by its possible use, though he himself is a standing example of what the union of thought and imagination can do.[49]

Be that as it may, Plato was opposed to the poetic use of imagination. No amount of refined observation can convert his distrust of imagination into an acceptance. True, his own work is supremely imaginative; true, that work amply attests that he himself loved poetry and knew it extremely well. But his theoretical opposition was too strong to be compromised by his personal tropisms. As Nettleship says:

If any one then were so far taken in by the perspective and colouring as to think the picture before him the actual thing, he would be in a state of εἰκασία. The moment a man knows that a shadow is only a shadow, or a picture only a picture, he is no longer in a state of εἰκασία in that particular respect. But, though the arts do not produce illusion of that simple kind, Plato attacks them in Book X, entirely on the ground that they are constantly used to produce and stimulate a multitude of illusory ideas of another kind. He takes painting as the most obvious instance of imitative art, but he applies the principles which he makes it illustrate to words. Poetry and rhetoric are the great sources of the kind of illusion he has in mind.[50]

Thus, from Plato through the great thinkers of the seventeenth century, there existed a powerful tradition of distrust and denigration of imagination. This tradition, though beginning to be vitiated in the eighteenth century, remained strongly visible up to the advent of Romanticism in the second half of that century.

It was always the conception of reason that depressed the stock of imagination; so long as the 'Age of Reason' persisted, imagination could not be highly valued. For a single instance, in 1728 Zachary Mayne said that

the Faculties of *Perceiving*, which *Brutes* have, as well as *Men*, namely *Sense* and the *Imagination*, are not *Intellectual*. . . . And consequently, it is *Reason* and *Understanding* alone, which constitutes the true and real Difference between

---

[48] Ibid. 245.   [49] Ibid. 246.   [50] Ibid. 243.

Mankind, and those Creatures of an inferiour Rank and Order, called *Brutes*, to denote their being destitute of Understanding.[51]

Such a sentiment was entirely co-ordinate with Descartes's opinion that imagination was 'in no wise a necessary element in my nature, or in the essence of my mind'.

By Romantic times, the weight of reason and understanding no longer depressed imagination. For merely one illustration to counterpoise against the statement of Mayne, Shelley insists that 'The imagination is a faculty not less imperial and essential to the happiness and dignity of the human being, than the reason'.[52]

The turning of the cultural tide, from distrust of imagination to apotheosis of imagination, can perhaps better be seen in Addison than anywhere else. In 1712, in a series of articles in the *Spectator*, Addison bore witness to, and furthered as well, the ascent of imagination in cultural valuation. Addison launches upon his topic by observing (with Aristotle, whom he does not name) that 'Our sight is the most perfect and most delightful of all our Senses. . . . It is this Sense,' he goes on, 'which furnishes the Imagination with its Ideas; so that by the Pleasures of the Imagination or Fancy (which I shall use promiscuously) I here mean such as arise from visible Objects.'[53] The connection of imagination with visible objects resumes the tradition from Plato onward, but Addison promptly indicates a complexity that will serve as the base of a happier contemplation of imagination's power:

There are few Words in the *English* Language which are employed in a more loose and uncircumscribed Sense than those of the *Fancy* and the *Imagination*. I therefore thought it necessary to fix and determine the Notion of these two Words, as I intend to make use of them in the Thread of my following Speculations, that the Reader may conceive rightly what is the Subject which I proceed upon. I must therefore desire him to remember, that by the Pleasures of the Imagination, I mean only such Pleasures as arise originally from Sight, and that I divide these Pleasures into two Kinds: My Design being first of all to discourse of those Primary Pleasures of the Imagination, which entirely proceed from such Objects as are before our Eyes, and in the next place to speak of those Secondary Pleasures of the Imagination which flow from the Ideas of visible Objects, when the Objects are not actually before the Eye, but are called up into our Memories, or formed into agreeable Visions of Things that are either Absent or Fictitious.[54]

[51] Mayne, 'To the Reader'.
[52] *Shelley*, vii. 107.
[53] Addison, iii. 276–7.
[54] Ibid. 277.

In this inaugurating division of his subject, Addison distinctly fore-shadows Coleridge's later threefold division of primary imagination, secondary imagination, and fancy. Addison's invoking of the 'Secondary Pleasures of the Imagination' could almost be a gloss for Coleridge's conception of a 'secondary' imagination; for Coleridge's secondary imagination, like Addison's, forms 'Visions of Things that are either Absent or Fictitious'.

In proleptic realization of the numinous ascent of Romantic imagina-tion, and entirely separating itself from the downtrodden imagination of the tradition stemming from Plato, Addison's imagination moves at once to an adjacence to soul:

Our Imagination loves to be filled with an Object, or to grasp at any thing that is too big for its Capacity. We are flung into a pleasing Astonishment at such unbounded Views, and feel a delightful Stillness and Amazement in the Soul at the Apprehension of them.[55]

Having thus lifted the place of imagination, Addison continues to urge a nearness between imagination and soul:

But there is nothing that makes its way more directly to the Soul than *Beauty*, which immediately diffuses a secret Satisfaction and Complacency through the Imagination, and gives a Finishing to any thing that is Great or Uncommon.[56]

Addison continues, using the alternative word 'fancy', to elevate the implications of his proximate terms:

The Supreme Author of our Being has so formed the Soul of Man, that nothing but himself can be its last, adequate, and proper Happiness. Because, therefore, a great Part of our Happiness must arise from the Contemplation of his Being, that he might give our Souls a just Relish of such a Contemplation, he has made them naturally delight in the Apprehension of what is Great or Unlimited. Our Admiration, which is a very pleasing Motion of the Mind, immediately rises at the Consideration of any Object that takes up a great deal of room in the Fancy.[57]

From such an elevation, it is natural to connect 'imagination' with 'the sublime': '*Homer* fills his Readers with Sublime *Ideas*, and, I believe, has raised the Imagination of all the good Poets that have come after him.'[58]

In *Originality and Imagination*, a tradition is pointed to, running from Ficino through Sidney to Coleridge, that sees the creativity of the poet as

[55] Ibid. 279.　　[56] Ibid. 280.
[57] Ibid. 282–3.　　[58] Ibid. 295–6.

imitating the creativity of God.[59] That same tradition surfaces in Addison. He does not, in the succeeding passage, specifically invoke the idea of the divine, but the implication is there, and the passage fits easily and proudly with the insistences of Ficino, Sidney, and Coleridge:

The Imagination can fancy to it self Things more Great, Strange, or Beautiful, than the Eye ever saw, and is still sensible of some Defect in what it has seen; on this account it is the part of a Poet to humour the Imagination in its own Notions, by mending and perfecting Nature where he describes a Reality, and by adding greater Beauties than are put together in Nature, where he describes a Fiction.

He is not obliged to attend her in the slow Advances which she makes from one Season to another, or to observe her Conduct in the successive Production of Plants and Flowers. He may draw into his Description all the Beauties of the Spring and Autumn, and make the whole Year contribute something to render it the more agreeable. His Rose-trees, Wood-bines, and Jessamines may flower together, and his Beds be covered at the same time with Lilies, Violets, and Amaranths. His Soil is not constrained to any particular Sett of Plants, but is proper either for Oaks or Mirtles, and adapts it self to the Products of every Climate. Oranges may grow wild in it; Myrrh may be met with in every Hedge, and if he thinks it proper to have a Grove of Spices, he can quickly command Sun enough to raise it.[60]

That magnificent passage, taking its wonderful invocations from the English love of gardening, dramatically illustrates the elevation of the deceiving imagination of Plato and Pascal to the Romantic status of Godlike creativity. Addison concludes with virtually a fanfare of trumpets:

Thus we see how many ways Poetry addresses it self to the Imagination, as it has not only the whole Circle of Nature for its Province, but makes new Worlds of its own, shews us Persons who are not to be found in Being, and represents even the Faculties of the Soul, with her several Virtues and Vices, in a sensible Shape and Character.[61]

Yet, though Addison richly heralds the Romantic apotheosis of imagination, it would nevertheless be several score years before that line of thought gained cultural ascendancy. Thinkers and theorists throughout the eighteenth century customarily addressed themselves to the definition and consideration of imagination, but by and large the imaginative power was not accorded enthusiastic recognition. Condillac speaks very much for the bulk of eighteenth century conceiving, when he says, in 1754, that 'I have called imagination this vivid memory, which makes that which is

[59] *Originality*, 121–3.   [60] Addison, 298–9.   [61] Ibid. 301–2.

absent seem present'.[62] He goes on to identify the most extended sense of the word imagination, which is to combine qualities of objects to make new objects not found in nature: 'Voilà la signification la plus étendue qu'on donne au mot *imagination*: c'est de le considérer comme le nom d'une faculté, qui combine les qualités des objets, pour en faire des ensembles, dont la nature n'offre point de modèles.'[63] These two statements, too, tepidly prefigure Coleridge's distinction between primary imagination, secondary imagination, and fancy.

Condillac was the most devoted follower of Locke in eighteenth-century France. The most devoted follower in eighteenth-century England, David Hartley, spoke of imagination even more limply. In his influential treatise of 1749, *Observations on Man, His Frame, His Duty, and His Expectations*, Hartley, after dutifully enumerating the pleasures of imagination, could find little more to say than to provide an unenthusiastic cautionary note: 'It is evident, that the Pleasures of Imagination were not intended for our primary Pursuit, because they are, in general, the first of our intellectual Pleasures, which are generated from the sensible ones by Association, come to their Height early in Life, and decline in old Age.'[64]

So much for the mainstream of eighteenth-century attitudes towards imagination. The texture of imagination descried in this chapter, it must be emphasized, raises its configured threads high above the plane of the fabric, but by that very fact sends them deep into shadowed and lowered weavings. But both the shadowed weavings of Plato, Descartes, Pascal, and Spinoza, and the elevated and highlighted designs of Coleridge and Baudelaire, are all parts of the same texture. To transfer the metaphor into less figured statement, both the depressed tradition of imagination, and the apotheosized tradition, mutually imply one another. More than that, they are actually interwoven. The depressed tradition, as shall be presently observed, maintained itself throughout the nineteenth century, while the apotheosized tradition, as pointed out above, was present *in parvo* in the denigrations of Pascal and Descartes.

This realization is especially important with regard to the apotheosizing activity of Addison just adduced. Though the two concluding quotations seem to raise his views almost to the same plane as Coleridge and Baudelaire, his papers, influential though they were, did not evict the depressed tradition. For a detailed instance, one may turn to the persisting attitudes of Dr Johnson, expressed later than Addison but earlier than Romanticism.

---

[62] Condillac, 146–7.   [63] Ibid. 147.   [64] Hartley, ii. 244.

Johnson was no friend to imagination. He distrusted it with the same intensity as did Plato and Pascal. For instance, he says at one point, in 1759, that

He that travels in theory has no inconveniences; he has shade and sunshine at his disposal, and wherever he alights finds tables of plenty and looks at gaiety. These ideas are indulged till the day of departure arrives, the chaise is called, and the progress of happiness begins.

A few miles teach him the fallacies of imagination. The road is dusty, the air is sultry, the horses are sluggish, and the postilion brutal. He longs for the time of dinner that he may eat and rest. The inn is crowded, his orders are neglected, and nothing remains but that he devour in haste what the cook has spoiled, and drive on in quest of better entertainment.[65]

As Johnson there reinvokes the old charge of imagination's tendency to deceive, in the previous year he had assailed imagination on the same grounds, but had added to them the almost equally old charge that it was also the enemy of reason:

Many have no happier moments than those that they pass in solitude, abandoned to their own imagination, which sometimes puts sceptres in their hands or mitres on their heads, shifts the scene of pleasure with endless variety, bids all the forms of beauty sparkle before them, and gluts them with every change of visionary luxury.

It is easy in these semi-slumbers to collect all the possibilities of happiness, to alter the course of the sun, to bring back the past, and anticipate the future, to unite all the beauties of all seasons, and all the blessings of all climates, to receive and bestow felicity, and forget that misery is the lot of man. All this is a voluntary dream, a temporary recession from the realities of life to airy fictions; and habitual subjection of reason to fancy.[66]

It is interesting to contrast that passage's denigrative emphasis on imagination in solitude, with Rousseau's approving statement on the same topic. The latter statement was quoted previously in Chapter 2 above, but it deserves re-perusal in this augmented context:

my restless imagination took a hand which saved me from myself and calmed my growing sensuality. What it did was to nourish itself on situations that had interested me in my reading, recalling them, varying them, combining them, and giving me so great a part in them, that I became one of the characters I imagined, and saw myself always in the pleasantest situations of my own choosing. So in the end, the fictions I succeeded in building up made me forget my real condition, which so dissatisfied me. My love for imaginary objects and my facility in lending myself to them ended by disillusioning me with everything around me, and determined that love of solitude which I have retained ever since that time.[67]

[65] *Idler*, ii. 181.   [66] Ibid. 101.   [67] Rousseau, i. 41.

The two passages, despite their similarity, dramatically illustrate the change in imagination's fortunes that marked the advent of Romanticism. The shift in sensibility is further dramatized by contrasting Rousseau's scarcely veiled implication of masturbation with the entirely veiled decorum with which Dr Johnson presents the same possibility: 'to receive and bestow felicity'.

Dr Johnson was almost unvarying in his opposition to imagination. In accordance with the depressed tradition surveyed earlier in this chapter, he repeatedly aligns himself with reason and against imagination. In the following passage that alignment provides the whole structure of discourse, with the subtext of imagination's incitement to sexual excess:

Such, therefore, is the importance of keeping reason a constant guard over imagination, that we have otherwise no security for our own virtue, but may corrupt our hearts in the most recluse solitude, with more pernicious and tyrannical appetites and wishes, than the commerce of the world will generally produce . . .

In this disease of the soul, it is of the utmost importance to apply remedies at the beginning . . .

The recollection of the past is only useful by way of provision for the future; and therefore, in reviewing all occurrences that fall under a religious consideration, it is proper that a man stop at the first thoughts, to remark how he was led thither, and why he continues the reflexion. If he is dwelling with delight upon a stratagem of successful fraud, a night of licentious riot, or an intrigue of guilty pleasure, let him summon off his imagination as from an unlawful pursuit . . .

In futurity chiefly are the snares lodged, by which the imagination is intangled.[68]

Other strictures are equally firm. Johnson, in 1751, says that 'Imagination, a licentious and vagrant faculty, unsusceptible of limitations, and impatient of restraint, has always endeavoured to baffle the logician, to perplex the confines of distinction, and burst the inclosures of regularity'.[69] In the same tone of distaste, he says that 'It is certain that any wild wish or vain imagination never takes such firm possession of the mind, as when it is found empty and unoccupied'.[70]

If the depressed tradition of imagination, which deplored its capacity for deceiving and its opposition to reason, maintained itself in full flower in the powerful cultural ambience of Dr Johnson, in another, and only marginally later, eighteenth-century cultural field of force, imagination dramatically displayed the characteristics that would eventuate in the Romantic apotheoses of Coleridge and Baudelaire. For Kant, in his philosophical analyses of the 1780s, raised imagination to something far

---

[68] *Rambler*, iii. 43–5.   [69] Ibid. iv. 300.   [70] Ibid. 86.

higher than 'a licentious and vagrant faculty'.[71] He did not, as seen above, go so far as Shelley and place imagination above his beloved 'moral law within'; but in every other way he too apotheosized imagination.

Indeed, he says, in 1781, that it is one of three fundamental sources of human knowledge:

There are three subjective sources of knowledge upon which rests the possibility of experience in general and of knowledge of its objects—*sense*, *imagination*, and *apperception*. Each of these can be viewed as empirical, namely, in its application to given appearances. But all of them are likewise *a priori* elements or foundations, which make this empirical employment itself possible.[72]

In line with that important role, Kant says that 'the reproductive synthesis of the imagination is to be counted among the transcendental acts of the mind',[73] and even more strongly, that 'we must assume a pure transcendental synthesis of imagination as conditioning the very possibility of all experience'.[74] No longer a 'faculté trompeuse' or 'maîtresse de erreur et fausseté', the imagination, for Kant, is a fundamental component of mind: 'Thus the principle of the necessary unity of pure (productive) synthesis of imagination, prior to apperception, is the ground of the possibility of all knowledge, especially of experience.'[75]

He laments that 'psychologists have hitherto failed to realize that imagination is a necessary ingredient of perception itself'.[76] As to the role of that necessary ingredient, he says:

Now, since every appearance contains a manifold, and since different perceptions therefore occur in the mind separately and singly, a combination of them, such as they cannot have in sense itself, is demanded. There must therefore exist in us an active faculty for the synthesis of this manifold. To this faculty I give the title, imagination. Its action, when immediately directed upon perceptions, I entitle apprehension. Since the imagination has to bring the manifold of intuition into the form of an image, it must previously have taken the impressions up into its activity, that is, have apprehended them.[77]

Kant, like all other philosophers, understands imagination to mean, strictly speaking, the faculty of presenting images to the mind:

---

[71] Kant's large interest in imagination was apparently mediated through the *Philosophische Versuche* of the psychologist Tetens, which appeared in 1777. As a commentator says: 'Disons donc provisoirement que tout prête à croire que le thème de l'imagination doit son origine à l'ouvrage de Tetens. Nous allons corroborer cette conclusion en montrant qu'avec une probabilité aussi forte la déduction subjective découle de la même source' (De Vleeschauwer, *Déduction*, i. 315).

[72] *Kant*, iv. 86.   [73] Ibid. 79.   [74] Ibid. 78.
[75] Ibid. 88.   [76] Ibid. 89 n.   [77] Ibid. 89.

'*Einbildungskraft* ist das Vermögen, einen Gegenstand auch *ohne dessen Gegenwart* in der Anschauung vorzustellen'—'*Imagination* is the faculty of representing in intuition an object that is *not itself present.*'[78] (Still more exactly, Spinoza had said that 'Imaginatio est idea, qua Mens rem aliquam ut praesentem contemplatur'—'Imagination is the idea by which the mind contemplates a thing as present'.[79]) In contemplating the nature of that faculty, however, Kant is led, like Coleridge after him, to dichotomized and discriminated divisions:

In so far as imagination is spontaneity, I sometimes also entitle it the *productive* imagination, to distinguish it from the *reproductive* imagination, whose synthesis is entirely subject to empirical laws, the laws, namely, of association, and which therefore contributes nothing to the explanation of the possibility of *a priori* knowledge.[80]

That passage occurred in the second edition of the *Kritik der reinen Vernunft* of 1787. It expanded a definition of the first edition of 1781, where Kant says that 'since the imagination is itself a faculty of *a priori* synthesis, we assign to it the title, productive imagination. In so far as it aims at nothing but necessary unity in the synthesis of what is manifold in experience, it may be entitled the transcendental function of imagination.'[81]

Kant still further discriminated imaginative function by developing a distinction between schema and image

The schema is in itself always a product of imagination. Since, however, the synthesis of imagination aims at no special intuition, but only at unity in the determination of sensibility, the schema has to be discriminated from the image.[82]

The schema is thus a mental synthesis in the imagination divorced from a specific image:

If five points be set alongside one another, thus, ... , I have an image of the number five. But if, on the other hand, I think only a number in general, whether it be five or a hundred, this thought is rather the representation of a method whereby a multiplicity, for instance a thousand, may be represented in an image in conformity with a certain concept, than the image itself. For with such a number as a thousand the image can hardly be surveyed and compared with the concept.[83]

Kant goes on to illustrate more finely this precise and elegant refinement of imaginative function. When we pass beyond the specific

---

[78] Ibid. iii. 119–20.   [79] *Spinoza*, ii. 301.
[80] *Kant*, iii. 120.   [81] Ibid. iv. 91.
[82] Ibid. 100.   [83] Ibid.

image we do not cease to think; the continuation rather takes place as a schematism:

It is schemata, not images of objects, which underlie our pure sensible concepts. No image could ever be adequate to the concept of a triangle in general. It would never attain that universality of the concept which renders it valid for all triangles, whether right-angled, obtuse-angled, or acute-angled; it would always be limited to a part only of this sphere. The schema of the triangle can exist nowhere but in thought. It is a rule of synthesis of the imagination, in respect to pure figures in space. Still less is an object of experience or its image ever adequate to the empirical concept; for this latter always stands in immediate relation to the schema of imagination, as a rule for the determination of our intuition, in accordance with some specific universal concept.[84]

The matter is clearly of greatest importance, if imagination is truly to be considered one of the fundamental faculties of knowledge. Of course, by Romantic times, imagination could be, and often was, apotheosized purely by rhetorical or emotional charging. Blake provides an instance that comes readily to mind. 'Man is All Imagination God is Man & exists in us & we in him.'[85] That is apotheosis indeed! But it is a statement presented as an intuition, not as a consequence of argument. Indeed, the intuitive apotheosis is always Blake's preference when speaking of imagination: 'One Power alone makes a Poet—Imagination The Divine Vision' (p. 665). 'Imagination The Real Man' (p. 664). 'Imagination is the Divine Vision not of The World nor of Man not from Man as he is a Natural Man but only as he is a Spiritual Man' (p. 666). 'To the Eyes of the Man of Imagination Nature is Imagination itself. . . . To Me This World is all One continued Vision of Fancy or Imagination' (p. 702). 'The Real Man The Imagination which Liveth for Ever' (p. 783). 'Nature has no Outline: but Imagination has. Nature has no Tune: but Imagination has! Nature has no Supernatural & dissolves: Imagination is Eternity' (p. 270). 'Adam is only The Natural Man & not the Soul or Imagination The Eternal Body of Man is The IMAGINATION' (p. 273). 'Vision or Imagination is a Representation of what Eternally Exists' (p. 554). 'The Nature of my Work is Visionary or Imaginative it is an Endeavour to Restore what the Ancients calld the Golden Age' (p. 555).

As with Blake, so with Emerson. 'Imagination', he says, is 'the cardinal human power.'[86] As with Emerson, so with Keats. In a situation where imagination was established as 'the quintessence of Romanticism', Keats, like Emerson, like Blake, did not have to argue its case, but could simply

---

[84] *Kant*, iv. 101.   [85] *Blake*, 664.   [86] *Emerson*, x. 243.

enter discourse at a supreme and sacred level of assumption: 'I am certain
of nothing but of the holiness of the Heart's affections and the truth of
Imagination.'[87] As *Originality and Imagination* comments on that passage:

> The 'Heart's affections' is virtually a synonym for one definition of soul, and
> 'holiness' drives toward the religious grounding of that conception. But 'Heart's
> affections' is placed in double harness with imagination's truth, and the two
> represent in effect a dividing, a new economy, as it were, of soul's powers.[88]

But Kant, committed to systematic reasoning ('*Philosophy* is the system
of all philosophical knowledge'[89]), needed particularization and discrimination. Hence the distinction of schema and image. Hence his elegant care
in defining what he meant. And yet Kant, too, at least foreshadows the
extreme elevation of imagination's texture in the Romantic era. The
foreshadowing is especially apparent when he calls the true nature of
schematic activity 'an art concealed in the depths of the human soul':

> The concept 'dog' signifies a rule according to which my imagination can delineate
> the figure of a four-footed animal in a general manner, without limitation to any
> single determinate figure such as experience, or any possible image that I can
> represent *in concreto*, actually presents. This schematism of our understanding, in
> its application to appearances and their mere form, is an art concealed in the depths
> of the human soul, whose real modes of activity nature is hardly ever to allow us to
> discover, and to have open to our gaze.[90]

Nevertheless, the distinction between image and schema is essential, in
Kant's analysis, to any satisfactory view of imaginative function:

> This much only we can assert: the *image* is a product of the empirical faculty of
> reproductive imagination; the *schema* of sensible concepts, such as figures in space,
> is a product and, as it were, a monogram, of pure *a priori* imagination, through
> which, and in accordance with which, images themselves first become possible.
> These images can be connected with the concept only by means of the schema to
> which they belong. In themselves they are never completely congruent with the
> concept. On the other hand, the schema of a *pure* concept of understanding can
> never be brought into any image whatsoever. It is simply the pure synthesis,
> determined by a rule of that unity, in accordance with concepts, to which the
> category gives expression. It is a transcendental product of imagination, a product
> which concerns the determination of inner sense in general according to conditions
> of its form (time), in respect of all representations, so far as these representations
> are to be connected *a priori* in one concept in conformity with the unity of
> apperception.[91]

[87] Keats, *Letters*, i. 184.   [88] *Originality*, 139.
[89] *Kant*, iii. 542.   [90] Ibid. iv. 101.
[91] Ibid.

But though both the schema—'a transcendental product of imagination'—and the image are necessary in any full functioning of the faculty of imagination, here far removed from the role of 'a licentious and vagrant faculty', both functions coalesce in Kant's radical elevation of imaginative activity. That elevation sounds a clarion call, as it were, heralding the advent of Romanticism: 'Wir haben also eine reine Einbildungskraft als ein Grundvermögen der menschlichen Seele, das aller Erkenntniss *a priori* zum Grunde liegt'—'We have thus a pure imagination, which lies at the base of all *a priori* knowledge, as one of the fundamental faculties of the human soul.'[92]

And yet we must never lose sight of the fact that the texture of Romantic imagination was truly interwoven, its threads genuinely intertwined. The apotheosis of imagination, as here with Kant, and with Addison before him, wove itself back into the 'Age of Reason'; with Johnson, however, and with Rousseau himself, its denigration was intertwined with patterns impinging almost upon the efflorescence of Romanticism. Rousseau, as noted in Chapter 2, in his *Confessions* put imagination at the forefront of the new conception of self he so strikingly promulgated. But it was also noted there that in *Émile* he addressed the imaginative faculty in a more negative manner.

In *Émile* Rousseau adhered to the depressed tradition that looked back to Pascal and Descartes—a striking fact in view of his role as groundbreaker for Romanticism. Though imagination is frequently invoked in *Émile*, its desirability is there at best equivocal. To the extent that the term implies heightened individuality—as *a fortiori* in Blake—in *Émile* it is approached with caution: 'Sophie is well born; she has a good nature; she has a very sensitive heart, and this extreme sensitivity sometimes makes her imagination so active that it is difficult to moderate.'[93] 'No matter what one does, the most dangerous of all the enemies that can attack a young man, and the only one that cannot be put out of the way, is himself. This enemy, however, is dangerous only through our own fault, for as I have said countless times, the senses are awakened only by the imagination alone. Their need is not properly a physical need.'[94] 'This child saw God everywhere, and what I would be afraid of, if this air of mystery were inopportunely affected, is that one might influence a young man's imagination too much, thereby troubling his brain and finally making a fanatic of him rather than a believer.'[95] 'Nature's instruction is late and slow; man's is almost always premature.

---

[92] *Kant*, iv. 91.
[94] Ibid. 662.

[93] Rousseau, iv. 746.
[95] Ibid. 557.

In the former case the senses wake the imagination; in the latter the imagination wakes the senses; it gives them a precocious activity which cannot fail to enervate and weaken individuals first and in the long run the species itself.'[96]

Even when Rousseau treats imagination as a desirable function, he is careful to insist on its restriction. 'Do not stifle his imagination; guide it lest it engender monsters.'[97] In the same vein, with the old counterbalance of reason and imagination, he says: 'Consider how I gain time for him doubly by delaying the progress of nature to the advantage of reason. But have I actually delayed this progress? No, I have only prevented imagination from accelerating it. I have counterbalanced the premature lessons the young man receives elsewhere with lessons of another kind.'[98] Imagination, in short, is almost always treated as a potentially dangerous faculty in need of restriction and control: 'The real world has its limits; the imaginary world is infinite. Unable to enlarge the one, let us restrict the other, for it is from the difference between the two alone that are born all the pains that make us truly unhappy.'[99]

In line with his reining in of imagination in the education of the child, Rousseau, in this work, reins in the concept of imagination itself, drawing it back to the fundamental definitions of Spinoza and Kant:

Before the age of reason the child receives not ideas but images; and the difference between the two is that images are only absolute depictions of sensible objects, while ideas are notions of objects determined by relations. An image can stand all alone in the mind that represents it, but every idea supposes other ideas. When one imagines, one does nothing but see; when one conceives, one is comparing.[100]

Though *Émile* was completed in 1762, and thereby might seem rather early to fall under the rubric of Romanticism, the same ambivalence that characterized Rousseau appears, at the very apex of Romanticism in America, in the writings of Emerson. In accordance with his high Romantic credentials, Emerson places imagination at the forefront of human powers:

All thinking is analogizing, and it is the use of life to learn metonymy. The endless passing of one element into new forms, the incesssant metamorphosis, explains the rank which the imagination holds in our catalogue of mental powers. The imagination is the reader of these forms.[101]

[96] Ibid. 495.	[97] Ibid. 651.
[98] Ibid. 638.	[99] Ibid. 305.
[100] Ibid. 344.	[101] *Emerson*, viii. 15.

Notable in that pregnant statement is the fact that Rousseau's distinction, just adduced, between 'images' and 'ideas', is here collapsed into a single function for the imagination. Where for Rousseau an image can stand alone, 'but every idea supposes other ideas', the 'comparing' that is essential to conceiving is precisely the 'analogizing' that for Emerson is the nature of thinking. Thus Rousseau's 'comparing', which holds fast to the Cartesian view of reason, in Emerson's emphasis becomes not a function of reason, but the domain of a new and immensely elevated conception of the imagination.

So Emerson celebrates imagination in terms as high as does Baudelaire; in terms, certainly, that constitute pure apotheosis: 'The act of imagination is ever attended by pure delight. It infuses a certain volatility and intoxication into all Nature. It has a flute which sets the atoms of our frame in a dance. . . . The very design of imagination is to domesticate us in another, in a celestial nature.'[102] With Emerson, in this same line, the reciprocity of soul and imagination becomes very explicit:

Nature is the true idealist. When she serves us best, when, on rare days, she speaks to the imagination, we feel that the huge heaven and earth are but a web drawn around us, that the light, skies and mountains are but the painted vicissitudes of the soul.[103]

As with Baudelaire, Coleridge's distinction of imagination and fancy surfaces again in Emerson, to provide even higher exaltation for the concept of imagination:

It is a problem of metaphysics to define the province of Fancy and Imagination. The words are often used, and the things confounded. Imagination respects the cause. It is the vision of an inspired soul reading arguments and affirmations in all Nature of that which it is driven to say. But as soon as this soul is released a little from its passion, and at leisure plays with the resemblances and types, for amusement, and not for its moral end, we call its action Fancy. . . . Imagination is central; fancy superficial. Fancy relates to surface, in which a great part of life lies. . . . Fancy amuses, imagination expands and exalts us.[104]

Despite these encomia for imagination, Emerson's enthusiasm for the faculty overlaid an older strand of distrust in imagination, whereby, as variously noted above, imagination is the enemy of reason, and therefore a misleader or potential misleader of man. Asking, 'what is the imagination?', Emerson supplies a diminishing answer: 'Only an arm or weapon of the interior energy, only the precursor of reason.'[105] As only the precursor

---

[102] *Emerson*, viii. 18, 20.				[103] Ibid. 26.
[104] Ibid. 28–9:					[105] Ibid. vii. 214.

of reason, imagination could not be entirely trusted; and Emerson went so far as to propose an essay on the evils of imagination:

I propose to write an Essay on the *Evils of imagination* which after such a panegyrick on this beautiful faculty as it easily shall admit may treat of those egregious errors that growing out of some favourite fancy have shot up into whole systems of philosophy or bodies of divinity, & have obstructed truth for thousands of years. The Essay should exemplify its statement by some of the most signal instances of this captivity in which the Imagination has held the Reason of Man.[106]

The essay, in short, would have been a signal exemplification of Pascal's seventeenth-century reproach that imagination was the 'mistress of error and falsehood'.

But just as that older tradition wove itself into the fabric of Emerson's conceivings about imagination, and thus into the Romantic texture of imagination, so too, in the very centre of adverse valuation of the imagination, did breezes of futurity waft back from high Romanticism. Despite Dr Johnson's uniformly dim and distrustful view of imagination, at one point he adumbrates, not strongly but unmistakably, the supreme apotheosis by which Shelley makes morality itself the handmaiden of imagination. 'All joy or sorrow for the happiness or calamities of others,' writes Johnson in 1750, 'is produced by an act of the imagination, that realises the event however fictitious, or approximates it however remote, by placing us, for a time, in the condition of him whose fortune we contemplate; so that we feel, while the deception lasts, whatever motions would be excited by the same good or evil happening to ourselves.'[107] Here, though tenaciously holding to the conception by which imagination is always entwined with 'deception', Johnson reaches towards, even though he does not fully grasp, the exalted understanding by which imagination is the sole and necessary instrument of good.

Such intertwinings of two ostensibly opposed conceptions of imagination occur both in the plantings and in the flowerings of Romanticism. They are all constitutive of this hugely important Romantic texture, and all bear witness to the complexity, and subtlety, with which the theorizing of the imaginative faculty emblazoned the extended fabric of the text called Romanticism.

[106] Emerson, *Journals*, 306.
[107] *Rambler*, iii. 318–19.

6

The Highest Faculty of Knowledge

IN the foregoing chapter an attempt was made to descry the vertical dimensionality of the texture of imagination, which figures so richly and intricately in the tapestry of Romanticism. It was repeatedly noted that when imagination was depressed and denigrated in its function, it was because of its opposition to reason. In the 'Age of Reason', accordingly, the pre-eminence of reason led historically to a persisting rejection of imagination. 'It is *Reason* and *Understanding* alone', said a commentator in 1728, 'which constitutes the true and real Difference between *Mankind*, and those Creatures of an inferiour Rank and Order, called *Brutes*, to denote their being destitute of Understanding.'[1] Imagination, which Descartes had rejected as not belonging to the essence of mind, was absent, nowhere to be seen, in this ranking.

But as sensibility shifted to those emphases that collocate in what is now termed Romanticism, such vast moving of the intellectual landscape cast up another mountain, one that vied with reason for supremacy of elevation. The new peak was constituted by the raising up of the previously depressed imagination. When Kant now insisted that imagination was 'one of the fundamental faculties of the human soul', reason could no longer claim an unchallenged ascendancy.[2] 'The imagination', said Shelley, in witness to the changed contours of intellectual landscape, 'is a faculty not less imperial and essential to the happiness and dignity of the human being, than the reason.'[3]

Indeed, imagination in its new dignity even encroached upon the high prerogatives of reason. Understanding itself, in Kant's view, depended on imagination: '*The unity of apperception in relation to the synthesis of imagination* is the *understanding*', he defined, 'and this same unity, with reference to the *transcendental synthesis* of the imagination, is the *pure understanding*.'[4] But reason itself was not vitiated by this astonishing elevation of imagination's claims. What saved it was that Kant had split apart the terms 'reason' and 'understanding'; and though the latter was now partially subsumed by imagination, the former remained inviolate,

---

[1] See above, Ch. 5, n. 51. [2] See above, Ch. 5, n. 92.
[3] See above, Ch. 5, n. 52. [4] *Kant*, iv. 88.

proudly maintaining its supremacy as what Kant called the 'highest faculty of knowledge' (*oberste Erkenntniẞkraft*).[5]

The splitting apart—or 'desynonymizing', to use one of Coleridge's favourite principles ('the whole process of human intellect is gradually to desynonymize terms')[6]—of 'imagination' and 'fancy' (one and the same term in Addison and his milieu) had allowed an unparalleled elevation to the imagination. Thus freed from encumbrance by functions that held it down—like a rocket jettisoning its fuel tanks after they have served their purpose—imagination soared high into regions of transcendence. So now by that same process of separation was reason made invulnerable to the new forces at large in the intellectual universe.

The desynonymizing of reason and understanding endorsed by Kant was adopted not just by his successor, Hegel, but by thinkers throughout the nineteenth century—Thomas Arnold, Julius Charles Hare, Thomas Carlyle, F. D. Maurice, are English epigones identified by the scholars Charles Richard Sanders and C. F. Harrold. But it was in Coleridge that the desynonymization was developed most fully and subtly, and there, with its Continental interweavings, it constitutes one of Romanticism's most finely patterned textures.

Indeed, as this volume chose to touch the texture of the French Revolution by following the threads of Coleridge's idiosyncratic interweavings into it, so, in parallel treatment, it will touch the texture of Romantic reason by following the threads of Coleridge's interweavings in that regard also. Such an approach allows the fullest and richest touching possible, one that presents for tactile awareness not only Coleridge but Kant and Kant's opponent Jacobi, as well as Diderot and Hume. Furthermore, Coleridge's opinions on reason, as will presently appear, offer a natural, rather than arbitrary, parallel to his attitudes towards the French Revolution.

It comes as something of a surprise to the merely casual student of Coleridge to realize that it is not imagination—so universally linked with the theories of Coleridge, and so enormously important in Romanticism—but reason, that is the most potent term in the arsenal of Coleridge's thought. But the truth must be emphasized: reason is much the most valued word in Coleridge's philosophical vocabulary, and the distinction between reason and understanding is the absolute fulcrum of his mentation.

Reason and understanding, to reiterate, are incomparably more decisive

[5] *Kant*, iii. 237.
[6] *Philosophical Lectures*, 173.

for the full spectrum of Coleridge's thought than are imagination and fancy. 'My philosophy (as metaphysics)', says Coleridge, 'is built upon the distinction between the Reason and the Understanding.' He continues:

He who, after fairly attending to my exposition of this point in the 'Friend,' . . . and in the Appendix to the *first* Lay-Sermon, can still find no meaning in this distinction . . . for him the perusal of my *philosophical* writings, at least, will be a mere waste of time.[7]

Though Coleridge here restricts the distinction's importance to his philosophical writings, rather than his poetical or critical writings, true Coleridgians understand the enormous weight of the statement. Indeed, another shibboleth for distinguishing true students of Coleridge from dabblers is whether an understanding is reached as to the immensely more urgent role, in his intellectual economy, of philosophy and theology, than of literature and poetry. As Walter Jackson Bate, for a single instance, has said:

Coleridge's career as a poet has no parallel among the major European poets since the Renaissance. . . . There is in fact nothing quite like it in the other arts.

To begin with, no other poet of comparable stature has devoted so little time and effort to his poetry. Second, and more important, none has considered it so incidental to his other interests, hopes, or anxieties. Failure to recognize these two facts alone, at the start, has led to misinterpretations of his career that are still accepted and passed on without examination. Most common among them is the stock premise that one of the major modern poets, after being delayed by domestic and personal troubles, hit his true stride in the 'Ancient Mariner,' 'Christabel,' and 'Kubla Khan,' and then, because of opium, and general weakness of will, was forced to fritter away the next thirty-five years in chasing philosophical and theological will-of-the-wisps, to which he would not have resorted unless his true talent had deserted him.[8]

As with the relative ranking of poetry and philosophy in Coleridge's conception of his life effort, so too with the relative ranking of philosophy and criticism. As J. R. de J. Jackson has said: 'The conclusion is inescapable. Much of Coleridge's admiration of literary works depends upon the extent to which they exemplify what he takes to be the most important issues of philosophy and theology.'[9] Coleridge himself at one point interrupts his critical discourse to observe that 'Illustration of principles [is] my main object; therefore [I am] not so digressive as might appear'.[10]

[7] *Collected Letters*, vi. 1049–50.   [8] Bate, 40–1.
[9] Jackson, 161.   [10] *Shakespearean Criticism*, i. 180.

Again, Jackson maintains that 'Perhaps the most telling proof of the real bias of Coleridge's mind . . . is that he appears in the end almost to reverse his priorities and to discuss literature largely as a means to understanding and expounding philosophical and theological problems'.[11] Still again,

There can be little doubt that philosophy was his central activity, and that the criticism along with other journalistic enterprises was a digression from it . . . it is clear that his criticism . . . is his astonishing substitute for hack-work; that while he undertook it earnestly in the hope of doing good, he regarded it as being of a lower order than the serious treatises to which he was devoting his life.[12]

When Coleridge says that his philosophy, therefore, was built on the distinction between reason and understanding, he is saying everything. His emphasis on the importance of that distinction never wavers. He says at one point that he has 'endeavoured to explain myself at large on that distinction between the Reason and the Understanding, which I deem of such vital Importance'.[13] He was here speaking of the *Statesman's Manual* in 1816. But the insistence was a constant in his thought. One of the aims of the *Aids to Reflection*, in 1825, was to 'substantiate and set forth at large the momentous distinction between REASON and Understanding', and this is preliminary to the intent to 'exhibit a full and consistent Scheme of the Christian Dispensation'.[14] Late in life, in his last work, he says:

It is now thirty years since the diversity of REASON and UNDERSTANDING, of an Idea and a Conception, and the practical importance of distinguishing the one from the other, were first made evident to me. And scarcely a month has passed during this long interval in which either books, or conversation, or the experience of life, have not supplied or suggested some fresh proof and instance of the mischiefs and mistakes, derived from that ignorance of this Truth, which I have elsewhere called the Queen-bee in the Hive of Error.[15]

In truth, it is hardly possible to overestimate the centrality of the distinction in Coleridge's thought: he refers at one point to the 'unspeakable importance of the Distinction between the Reason and the Human Understanding, as the only Ground of the Cogency of the Proof *a posteriori* of the existence of a God'.[16] He even goes so far as to say that 'all the labors of my life' will have 'answered but one end, if I shall have only succeeded in establishing the diversity of Reason and Understanding'.[17] The distinction, in short, and beyond the possibility of countervailing

[11] Jackson, 149.
[12] Ibid. 15.
[13] *Collected Letters*, iv. 670.
[14] *Aids to Reflection*, pp. viii–ix.
[15] *Church and State*, 58–9.
[16] *Inquiring Spirit*, 382.
[17] Snyder, 135.

argument, was the keystone in the arch of Coleridge's thought. It was the ultimate, the *ne plus ultra*, of all his mental activity.

But the distinction between reason and understanding, and the efficacy of that distinction, are not easy to grasp, and Carlyle converted that difficulty of comprehension into the cutting edge of his powerful and hilarious attack on the pertinence of Coleridge's thought:

The constant gist of his discourse [wrote Carlyle] was lamentation over the sunk condition of the world; which he recognised to be given up to Atheism and Materialism, full of mere sordid misbeliefs, mispursuits and misresults. All science had become mechanical; the science not of men, but of a kind of human beavers. . . . Men's souls were blinded, hebetated; and sunk under the influence of Atheism and Materialism, and Hume and Voltaire: the world for the present was as an extinct world, deserted of God. . . . The remedy, though Coleridge himself professed to see it as in sunbeams, could not, except by processes unspeakably difficult, be described to you at all. On the whole, those dead Churches, this dead English Church especially, must be brought to life again. . . . Atheistic philosophy was true on its side, and Hume and Voltaire could on their own ground speak irrefragably for themselves against any Church: but lift the Church and themselves into a higher sphere of argument, *they* died into inanition, the Church revived itself into pristine florid vigour. . . . But how, but how! By attending to the 'reason' of man, said Coleridge, and duly chaining-up the 'understanding' of man: The *Vernunft* (Reason) and *Verstand* (Understanding) of the Germans, it all turned upon these, if you could well understand them,—which you couldn't.[18]

Carlyle's words constitute a quite marvellous piece of prose, and the wicked 'it all turned upon these, if you could understand them,—which you couldn't' places the incomprehensibility of the distinction between reason and understanding at the very forefront of his rejection of Coleridge as philosopher and theologian.

But we should not allow our delight at Carlyle's devastating thrust to obscure important matters. Carlyle's wonderful tone of a man of hard sense reporting on some strange and exotic monster masks the fact that, until the final moment, the report on Coleridge is impeccably accurate in its representation of his standpoint. It is, moreover, not only accurate, but based on a deep knowledge of all the subjects, from Hume and Voltaire to the contemporary situation of the Anglican Church, that it takes up. Carlyle speaks of 'the *Vernunft* (Reason) and *Verstand* (Understanding) of the Germans' as though he were gingerly holding the words with tongs— as though, to vary the metaphor, it were a distinction reported by a traveller to distant Cathay; but we must not allow ourselves to forget that

[18] *Carlyle*, xi. 58–9.

Carlyle himself was steeped in the German language and German culture. In fact, no less a judge than Goethe himself exclaimed of Carlyle, 'how he has studied us Germans! He is almost more at home in our literature than we are ourselves.'[19]

In this context, Carlyle's dismissal of the distinction as incomprehensible takes on a different significance. He admits that reason and understanding constitute the linchpin, as it were, of Coleridge's position ('it all turned upon these'), at the same time that he dismisses the distinction as emanating from a culture with which a sane man could hardly concern himself. In other words, his dismissal of the distinction between reason and understanding, as a matter of no purport for the hard-headed Scotsman he seems to be, is totally at odds with his own profound immersion in German culture. It becomes clear that the dismissal is purely a tactic, and that it is a tactic that, seen in the context of Carlyle's Germanism, becomes exactly the opposite of what it is proclaimed to be. It now seems as though Carlyle's declaration of John Bull's lack of concern for a distant and foolish distinction is the only opportunity he has to discredit Coleridge; it almost seems that an actual examination of reason and understanding might bulwark Coleridge's cause. Carlyle declares incomprehensible what he well knows to be exactly the reverse.

But if deconstructive analysis tends to make equivocal Carlyle's equation of irrelevance and things German, such consideration may also reveal other parts of his statement as also of equivocal import. Carlyle says that Coleridge's distinction is the same as that of the Germans. It may be pointed out parenthetically that in referring to 'the Germans' rather than to Kant, Carlyle impressively demonstrates that sophistication in things Germanic indicated by Goethe's praise. For it was not merely Kant, but a plurality of Germans, who espoused the distinction between reason and understanding. In *Coleridge and the Pantheist Tradition*, that point was made with reference to the animadversions of James Stirling, the author of *The Secret of Hegel*, and one of Coleridge's most airily contemptuous dismissers:

Stirling denies the legitimacy of Coleridge's use of such polarities as 'subjective' and 'objective', 'transcendent' and 'transcendental', because they involve, he says, distinctions 'absolutely and exclusively Kant's'. 'Of *reason* and *understanding*', he continues, 'we may speak in precisely the same tone. This distinction, also, is Kant's, and Kant's alone.' But Stirling's claims are simply without historical validity. It is a point of historical fact that 'reason' and 'understanding' were not

[19] Goethe, xxiv. 293.

'Kant's and Kant's alone', but that, quite the contrary, the distinction formed the very core of the philosophical thought of Kant's opponent, Jacobi. So important, in fact, is the dichotomy for Jacobi's position, that the transcendentalist sophisticate Frederic Henry Hedge, who was the chief purveyor of German culture to nineteenth-century America, even says baldly that 'the distinction between reason and understanding, now so widely accepted' was one that 'Jacobi was the first to point out, or, at least, to make prominent'.[20]

To that quotation the observation may be appended that Hedge really did speak with authority: he became the most important professor of German at Harvard University in the entire nineteenth century.

Another observation that may be appended is that the important Kantian commentator, Herman de Vleeschauwer, has demonstrated, convincingly, that Kant's own distinction of reason and understanding was taken over by Kant from Tetens. Noting that Kant assiduously studied Tetens's *Philosophische Versuche* of 1777, De Vleeschauwer, after pointing out the influence of this work in Kant's theories of the concept and of apperception, says that 'It can hardly be doubted that Kant profited greatly from his study of the psychological essays of his predecessor in this field. The story is much the same with regard to the distinction between reason and understanding':[21]

Finally a third chapter [in Tetens] is devoted to the distinction between understanding and reasoning reason. The perfect analogy between this doctrine and that of Kant will be noted not only in the method of formulating the questions about reason which interest him and in the general solution which he reserves for them, but also in the dominating thesis that an identical spiritual function is at work in reason and in understanding which are distinguished one from the other by the matter with which they are called on to deal. Tetens suspects, just like Kant, that an internal conflict menaces reason itself, a point which Kant expounds in great detail in the chapter on the antinomies.

We can therefore conclude that the reading of Tetens must have made a very great impression on Kant, struggling with the same problem although from a very different general standpoint, when he noticed how the researches of Tetens corroborated the ruling thesis of his own transcendental epistemology. The impression was so great that he could not resist the pleasure of making not only his work but his readers benefit from it.[22]

Carlyle, in brief, shows his superior sophistication in referring to 'the Germans', rather than to Kant, at the same time that he is using the imprecision to affect lack of interest in the topic.

---

[20] CPT, p. xxxii.   [21] De Vleeschauwer, 87.   [22] Ibid.

But Carlyle seems to be doing something else as well. Though Germans in the plural are nominated, no single German is specified. And when Carlyle does specify, the names that are supplied are, surprisingly, not German at all. They are, on the contrary, two of the foremost luminaries of the Enlightenment: Voltaire and Hume. As Carlyle says, mockingly describing Coleridge's position,

Atheistic Philosophy was true on its side, and Hume and Voltaire could on their own ground speak irrefragably for themselves against any Church: but lift the Church and themselves into a higher sphere of argument, *they* died into inanition. . . . But how, but how! By attending to the 'reason' of man, said Coleridge, and duly chaining-up the 'understanding' of man: The *Vernunft* (Reason) and *Verstand* (Understanding) of the Germans, it all turned upon these, if you could well understand them,—which you couldn't.

Seen through the spectacles of deconstruction, Carlyle has given the game away. Starting with two apostles of the Enlightenment, Voltaire and Hume, he has sardonically proceeded to the supposedly not understand-able cul-de-sac indicated by his nomination of 'the Germans'. But actually, 'the Germans' always had less to do with 'reason' than did the thinkers of the Enlightenment; the Enlightenment's chief shibboleth was 'reason'—so much so that in intellectual history the period is more commonly known as 'the Age of Reason'. It is reason to which Hume and Voltaire appeal. Taken in this light, Coleridge's own appeal to 'the "reason" of man' becomes something much more direct and understand-able than Carlyle's attempt to channel it into the mists of Germanic incomprehensibility.

That, the French Enlightenment—the so-called 'Age of Reason'—is the true background of Coleridge's discrimination of reason and understanding, and the true background, as well, of the urgency of his emphasis on reason. The 'reason' which Coleridge made the linchpin of his philosophy was far more deeply involved with 'la raison' than with 'die Vernunft'. The continuing agenda of Coleridge's philosophical life was an attempt to defend Christianity against the rationalism of the French Enlightenment, and his use of German thought was merely instrumental in this larger commitment. 'During five and twenty, I might say thirty years,' he says, 'I have been resolutely opposing the whole system of modern illumination, in all the forms of Jacobinism, . . . Epicurean (in our country Pelagian) Christianity, Pelagian morals, Pelagian politics.'[23]

Coleridge's opposition to what he calls 'the whole system of modern

[23] *Collected Letters*, v. 453.

illumination' was precisely an opposition to the total relevance of the Enlightenment. In such massive opposition, he found himself confronting opponents as varied as the fields of concern in which he was trying to defend Christianity. In ultimate theological philosophy he was opposing pantheism, and the greatest of pantheistic thinkers, Spinoza. In the conception of life, he was opposing the evolutionary trends, starting with Maupertuis, that led to Darwin. In psychology, he was opposing Locke, the Enlightenment Lockean tradition of Condillac, and Hartley. In Christian morality he was opposing Paley; in Christian community, Unitarianism. Espousing the tradition of Plato and Pythagoras, he opposed materialism, and its concomitant, mechanism. He rejected 'the cheerlessness, vulgarity, and common-place character of the mechanical philosophy, and Paleyian Expedience'.[24]

It was against the whole cultural fabric of the late eighteenth century, as represented by the French 'Age of Reason', that Coleridge therefore aligned himself. He condemned 'the bran, straw and froth which the Idols of the age, Locke, Helvetius, Hume, Condillac, and their Disciples have succeeded in passing off for metaphysics'.[25] With anxious scorn he asked, 'What then must be the fate of a nation that substitutes Locke for Logic, and Paley for Morality, and one or the other for Polity and Theology?';[26] and his legendary *magnum opus* was to be 'my (Anti-Paleyo-grotian) Assertion of Religion as necessarily implying Revelation, and of Xtianity as the only Revelation of universal validity.'[27] In brief, he stood four-square against 'French philosophy and modern Materialism'.[28]

One can, indeed, hardly overestimate Coleridge's antipathy to French thought, which was even greater than his eventual disillusionment with French Revolutionary sentiment, though it was intertwined with that disillusionment. 'Prurient, bustling, and revolutionary,' he says, 'this French wisdom has never more than grazed the surfaces of knowledge.'[29] He accuses French thought as resulting in 'a heartless frivolity alternating with a sentimentality as heartless—an ignorant contempt of antiquity—a neglect of moral self-discipline—a deadening of the religious sense . . .—a scornful reprobation of all consolations and secret refreshings from above—and as the caput mortuum of human nature evaporated, a French nature of rapacity, levity, ferocity, and presumption'.[30]

Thus it was that the very word that was the emblem of the French

---

[24] *Collected Letters*, v. 464–5.
[25] Brinkley, 138.
[26] *Collected Letters*, v. 138.
[27] Ibid. 134.
[28] Ibid. 8.
[29] *Lay Sermons*, 76.
[30] Ibid. 76–7.

Enlightenment, 'reason', became the focal centre of Coleridge's counter-attack. Indeed, in what for Coleridge had to be an ultimate blasphemy, even if levelled against that Catholic Church he despised, in 1793 the Commune seized the cathedral of Notre Dame and renamed it the Temple of Reason. So the Enlightenment and its aftermath, in Coleridge's view, were guilty of 'usurping the name of reason', and thereby French thought 'openly joined the banners of Antichrist'.[31]

How pertinent such an opinion was to the demonstrable historical truth may be gauged from a single locus in Diderot, who was one of the triumvirate—'Voltaire, D'Alembert, Diderot'—singled out by Coleridge as leading the defection to Antichrist. In a ferocious attack on Christianity called 'Addition aux Pensées philosophiques', which was appended in 1762 to the *Pensées philosophiques* of 1746, Diderot employs 'la raison' virtually as a sledge-hammer to batter open a door to scornful mockery. By section XV Diderot is saying, 'if there are a hundred thousand damned for one saved, the Devil always has the advantage, without having abandoned his son to death.'[32] By section XXIV he asks, 'Why are the miracles of Jesus Christ true, and those of Esculapius, of Apollonius of Tyana and of Mahomet false?'[33] By section XXXI he is saying, 'The religion of Jesus Christ, annunciated by some ignorant people, made the first Christians. The same religion, preached by the learned and by doctors, makes today only unbelievers.'[34]

Diderot's scorn matches that of Hume ('the same Scotch philosopher', said Coleridge, 'who devoted his life to the undermining of the Christian religion'[35]). Hume, in perhaps his most famous act of undermining, had in 1748 appealed to 'reason' against Christianity:

upon the whole, we may conclude, that the *Christian Religion* not only was at first attended with miracles, but even at this day cannot be believed by any reasonable person without one. Mere reason is insufficient to convince us of its veracity: And whoever is moved by *Faith* to assent to it, is conscious of a continued miracle in his own person, which subverts all the principles of his understanding, and gives him a determination to believe what is most contrary to custom and experience.[36]

In that passage alone we may see the entire urgency of Coleridge's distinction of reason from understanding.

Where Hume, like Diderot, enlists reason against the Christian religion, Coleridge is, by that very fact, immensely concerned and profoundly committed to raising reason's siege of Christianity. He does so by

---

[31] Ibid. 75.   [32] Diderot, 60.   [33] Ibid. 61.
[34] Ibid. 63.   [35] *Lay Sermons*, 22.   [36] Hume, 131.

converting the 'reason' of Hume and Diderot into 'understanding', and marching to relieve the beleaguered garrison of Christianity under the generalship of a new understanding of reason. After all, both 'reason' and 'understanding', in the philosophical backgrounds of Diderot, Hume, and Kant, were rendered by the single Latin word *intellectus*; and Coleridge's distinction, or 'desynonymization', of the intellectual modes existing under that single word is entirely fitting in terms of the meaning of *intellectus*, and of his habitual intellectual procedure as well.

In Diderot's parallel attack on Christianity, the tone for the scornful thrusts noted above had been prepared by the first nine sections, which constantly invoke the efficacy of 'la raison', concluding, in section IX, with the statement, 'If my reason comes from on high, it is the voice of heaven that speaks to me by it; it is necessary that I listen to it.'[37] But 'la raison' has figured in all eight preceding sections. Thus, for instance, section I says that

Doubts in the matter of religion, far from being acts of impiety, should be regarded as good works, when they are raised by a man who humbly recognizes his ignorance, and when they are born from the fear of displeasing God by the abuse of reason.[38]

Again, section II says:

To admit some conformity between the reason of man and the eternal reason, which is God, and pretend that God demands the sacrifice of human reason, is to establish that he wills and does not will at the same time.[39]

Still again, section IV says:

If I renounce my reason I have no guide: it is necessary blindly to adopt a secondary principle, and to presuppose the issue that is in question.[40]

Yet once more, section VII says:

Pascal, Nicole, and others have said: 'That a God punishes by eternal torments the fault of a guilty father toward all his innocent children, is a proposition superior to and not contradictory of reason.' But what then is a proposition contrary to reason, if not this one that enunciates evident blasphemy?[41]

And in section VIII, Diderot says:

Lost in an immense forest during the night, I have only a little light to lead me. There comes a stranger who tells me: my friend, blow out the candle the better to find the way. Such a stranger is a theologian.[42]

[37] Diderot, 59.   [38] Ibid. 57.   [39] Ibid. 57–8.
[40] Ibid. 58.   [41] Ibid.   [42] Ibid. 59.

The import of all these invocations of 'la raison' is the same. 'Reason' or 'la raison', for the brilliant intellect of Diderot, as for all the formulators of Enlightenment argument against which Coleridge set himself, was precisely the faculty whose use discredited the validity claimed by the Christian religion. In this sense, as characteristically used—or 'usurped'—by the French thinkers, reason was in very truth the instrument of Antichrist.

Indeed, the upsurge of religiosity so closely associated with the rise of Romanticism found it necessary, as the very condition of its emergence, to reject the thought of the French Enlightenment. For a single significant example, the seminal German Romantic, Schleiermacher, who subsequently became the most influential theologian of the nineteenth century, in his epoch-making *Reden über die Religion* of 1799, specifically turned away from French thinking. As he said:

I turn myself away from the French, whose sight can scarcely be borne by one who reverences religion, because in every action, in every word almost, they tread its holiest laws under foot. The coarse indifference with which millions of their people, no less than the witty jests with which individual brilliant minds among them, regard the most sublime act of history . . . suffices to prove how little they are capable of a holy awe and a true devotion.[43]

Coleridge, in his attempt to wrest 'reason' from the hands of Antichrist, was at the same time attempting to place that baton firmly in the hands of Christianity. For 'reason' is the fullest translation of the Greek word *logos* that figured in the opening verse of the Gospel of St John, to which Coleridge attached so much importance that he intended to write a full commentary. Moreover, under the name 'Logosophia, or on the Logos human & Divine, in six Treatises'[44] *logos* was taken up into one of the names for the fabled *magnum opus* itself. *Logos*, it can hardly be too strongly stressed, was a central term and conception for Coleridge's systematic philosophico-theological endeavour; and *logos* meant not only 'word', as it usually is translated in the Bible, but 'reason' even more (even though, in the *Aids to Reflection*, in order to keep the slate clean for his own Johannine inscribings of 'reason', he equates *logos* with 'understanding': 'In Greek, Logos (Anglicé, Word), means likewise the Understanding').[45] As a recent writer has asked:

How can one understand the word *logos*, for example, from any one English

[43] *Schleiermacher*, I. i. 153.
[44] *Collected Letters*, iv. 591.
[45] *Aids to Reflection*, 25.

translation, when the definition of this famous term—in all its rich complexity and creative evolution—requires more than five full columns of small type in the massive unabridged Liddell–Scott–Jones *Greek–English Lexicon?* A thousand years of philosophic thought are embodied in a term that begins by meaning 'talk' in Homer, develops into 'Reason'—with a capital R, as the divine ruler of the universe—in the Stoics, and ends up in the Gospel of St. John—by a subtle borrowing from biblical sources—as the creative word of God, His instrument in the Creation.[46]

Coleridge's agenda for the reclamation of 'raison', on the one hand, and his agenda for the systematic exposition of *logos*, on the other, dovetailed neatly in the focal importance he attached to 'reason'.

There was still another aspect to Coleridge's attempt to snatch 'reason' back from 'la raison'. We need only think of the vicissitudes of Blake's Urizen to realize that 'reason' was a term in general eclipse in Romanticism, and that it had been largely supplanted, in public and popular prestige, by 'feeling'. The impetus for the shift was largely supplied by Rousseau, himself conditioned by the eighteenth-century English novel of sensibility. In the *Confessions*, and even more in *La Nouvelle Héloïse*, Rousseau dramatically indicates the new hegemony of feeling over reason. A small but sufficing example is his comment, in the former work, on Mme de Warens:

All her faults, I repeat, came from her lack of judgment, never from her passions. She was of gentle birth, her heart was pure, she loved decency; she was born for an elegant way of life, which she always loved but never followed, because instead of listening to her heart, which gave her good counsel, she listened to her reason, which gave her bad.[47]

For Romanticism in general, there was an acceleration in the desirability of listening to the 'heart'—an acceleration very much assisted by Jacobi—and a corresponding depression in the prestige of 'reason'. Coleridge, with his commitment to systematic philosophy, needed badly to elevate the prestige of reason once again.

So all these factors were present in his desire to redraw the map of reason and resurvey its domain. To wrest the function back from its usurpation by the French, however, remained the chief motivation for his labours. His task was urgent. To discharge it, he proceeded in the reconciling way that always characterized his intellectual activity: instead of jettisoning the alienated and degraded term, he split the conception of reason into 'reason and understanding', precisely as he split off the

[46] Stone, p. xi.   [47] Rousseau, i. 197.

conception of imagination into 'imagination and fancy'.[48] Thus French 'raison' became what Coleridge called 'understanding' and Coleridgian 'reason' resumed the thread of seventeenth-century theologizing to become the guarantor of Christianity. Coleridge's 'reason', conceived as the antipode of the Enlightenment's 'raison', was 'Λόγος', 'the supreme Reality, the only true *Being* in all things visible and invisible! the Pleroma, in whom alone God loveth the world!'[49] Though the distinction between *Vernunft* (reason) and *Verstand* (Understanding) was an essential of Kantian analysis (and later, of Hegel's), and perhaps almost as pertinently to Coleridge's own position, an essential of Jacobi's thought, it must be reiterated that there can be little doubt that the distinction was, for Coleridge, not nearly so much a simple exchange for Germanic currencies as it was a defensive tactic against 'la raison'.

In his campaign against 'la raison', however, he availed himself of the terms most exhaustively promulgated by Kant, who himself, in his monumental inspection and analysis of the human mind, was impelled by the Enlightenment's admiration for 'la raison'. Hence the title of his great work, *Kritik der reinen Vernunft* ('Critique of Pure Reason'). Kant, though enormously important for the formation of Romanticism, was in his own matrix, as Friedrich Paulsen has said, the last product of the *Aufklärung*. In assessing the functioning of the mind—and one must not forget that he was steeped in the tradition of Locke and of the faculty psychology of his eighteenth-century predecessors and contemporaries—Kant decided that ramified distinctions had to be made if the subject were not simply to remain on the surface. So he departed from a distinction supplied by what he called 'general logic', which is 'built up on a plan that coincides accurately with the division of the higher faculties of knowledge. These are, *understanding*, *judgement*, and *reason*.'[50] From this initial division an entire network of related distinctions emerged: inner and outer, subject and object, transcendental and transcendent, intuition and concept, concept and idea, analytic and dialectic—these binary conceptions and more, and most important of all, understanding (*Verstand*) and reason (*Vernunft*). Moreover, since Kant customarily translated the Latin *intellectus* as *Verstand*, the word *Vernunft* from the outset was partially freed from its 'ordinary language' implications.

Coleridge knew Kant's work in precise and thorough detail; indeed, it would be difficult to overestimate his saturation in it, not merely the three

[48] For Coleridge's characteristic dichotomizing of problems, see McFarland, *Romanticism*, 289–341, esp. pp. 340–1.
[49] *Collected Letters*, vi. 600.   [50] *Kant*, iv. 95.

great critiques, but even the least-known pre-critical writings, including Kant's Latin inaugural dissertation. In truth, one of the persisting difficulties in the evaluation of Coleridge's thought has been the fact that none of Coleridge's commentators has ever known the Kantian *œuvre* with anything approaching the thoroughness with which Coleridge knew it. He speaks only the simple truth when he says, in the *Biographia Literaria*, that

The writings of the illustrious sage of Königsberg, the founder of the Critical Philosophy, more than any other work, at once invigorated and disciplined my understanding. The originality, the depth, and the compression of the thoughts; the novelty and subtlety, yet solidity and importance, of the distinctions; the adamantine chain of the logic; and I will venture to add (paradox as it will appear to those who have taken their notions of IMMANUEL KANT, from Reviewers and Frenchmen) the *clearness* and *evidence*, of the 'CRITIQUE OF THE PURE REASON'; of the 'JUDGMENT'; of the 'METAPHISICAL ELEMENTS OF NATURAL PHILOSOPHY'; and of his 'RELIGION WITHIN THE BOUNDS OF PURE REASON,' took possession of me as with a giant's hand. After fifteen years' familiarity with them, I still read these and all his other productions with undiminished delight and increasing admiration.[51]

What Coleridge found most important in all this enormous investment of reading and understanding were logical instrumentalities, not a final position with which he agreed. Among these instrumentalities, the foremost was the one that Kant also emphasized: the all-pervading distinction between reason and understanding.

Understanding, for Kant, was 'a nonsensuous faculty of knowledge'. It came into play subsequent to the formation of the data of immediate awareness (intuition), but was itself under the sway of the faculty of principles, which was reason. As Kant says in his first *Kritik*:

As without sensibility we cannot have any intuition [*Anschauung*], it is clear that the understanding is not a faculty of intuition. Besides intuition, however, there is no other kind of knowledge except by concepts [*Begriffe*]. The knowledge, therefore, of every understanding, or at least of the human understanding, must be by means of concepts, not intuitive [*intuitiv*], but discursive [*discursiv*]. All intuitions, being sensuous, depend on affections, concepts on functions. By function I mean the unity of the act of arranging different representations under one common representation. Concepts are based therefore on the spontaneity of thought, sensuous intuitions on the receptivity of impressions. The only use the understanding can make of concepts is to form judgements by them.[52]

When Kant refers to 'every understanding, or at least . . . the human understanding', he virtually invites Coleridge to adopt a distinction by

---

[51] *Biographia*, i. 153.   [52] *Kant*, iii. 85.

which 'the human understanding' becomes a faculty subsidiary and inferior to reason (which Kant does not mention in the foregoing passage). Coleridge was resolutely opposed to the implications of the thought of Locke and Hume; the title of Locke's incredibly influential treatise of 1690 had been *An Essay Concerning Human Understanding*, and Hume's treatise of 1748 had been named *An Enquiry Concerning Human Understanding*. By Kant's distinction, Coleridge was, as it were, able to concede Locke and Hume their claim to 'understanding', while retaining for his own religious purposes the superior conception of 'reason'. It was a solution exactly in accord with his reconciling and including temperament. As Carlyle, in the paradigmatic passage above, cannily says, Coleridge was willing to concede that 'Hume and Voltaire could on their own ground speak irrefragably for themselves against any Church: but lift the Church and themselves into a higher sphere of argument: *they* died into inanition, the Church revived itself into pristine florid vigour.' For Coleridge, 'their own ground' could be conceded to be the human 'understanding'; his own 'higher sphere of argument' was provided by the human reason.

For in another aspect of the intellective function, Kant discerns an activity that he calls 'reason' as such, which has a double function of dealing in illusion (*Schein*) and of supplying meaning to the understanding:

All our knowledge begins with the senses, proceeds thence to the understanding, and ends with the reason, than which nothing higher can be met with in us for working up the material of intuition and bringing it under the highest unity of thought. And as it here becomes necessary to give a definition of that highest faculty of knowledge, I begin to feel considerable misgivings.[53]

Kant's misgiving about an actual definition of that highest faculty, it seems apparent, allowed Coleridge latitude in his own conceptions. But Kant had no difficulty in defining, if not the essence, at least the schematic function of 'reason'. 'In the first part of our transcendental logic,' he says, 'we defined the understanding as the *faculty of rules*, and we now distinguish reason from it, by calling it the *faculty of principles*.'[54] More specifically:

If the understanding is a faculty for producing unity among phenomena, according to rules, reason is the faculty for producing unity among the rules of the understanding, according to principles. Reason therefore never looks directly to experience, or to any objects, but to the understanding, in order to impart *a priori* through concepts to its manifold kinds of knowledge a unity that may be called the

[53] Ibid. 237.   [54] Ibid. 238.

unity of reason, and is very different from the unity that can be produced by the understanding.[55]

Reason, therefore, does not deal at all with objects or with nature, but generates ideas that relate solely to the rules of the understanding. There is an absolute break between reason and the outer world.[56] This break is what, as shall presently appear, was of the very greatest consequence in Coleridge's own use of the distinction.

The general relationship between reason and understanding is perhaps nowhere more concisely stated than in the following passage from Kant's *Grundlegung der Metaphysik der Sitten*, a treatise of 1785 that Coleridge knew in minutest detail:

Now man actually finds in himself a power that distinguishes him from all other things—and even from himself so far as he is affected by objects. This power is *reason*. As pure spontaneity reason is elevated even above *understanding* in the following respect. Understanding . . . cannot produce by its own activity any concepts other than those whose sole service is to *bring sensuous ideas under rules* and so to unite them in one consciousness; without this employment of sensibility it would think nothing at all. Reason, on the other hand—in what are called 'ideas'—shows a spontaneity so pure that it goes far beyond anything sensibility can offer: it manifests its highest function in distinguishing the sensible and intelligible worlds from one another and so marking out limits for understanding itself.[57]

To find a guarantee for the autonomy of the mind itself, free from the reign of objects, or, as the matter is elucidated in *Coleridge and the Pantheist Tradition*, the 'it is', was the most essential goal in Coleridge's intellectual agenda. 'Reason', which as Kant says, 'goes far beyond anything sensibility can offer', frees the sense of 'I am' from the tyranny of the external—a tyranny, in Coleridge's view, most devastatingly espoused by the thought of Locke and Newton. 'The pith of my system,' Coleridge once said, 'is to make the senses out of the mind—not the mind out of the senses, as Locke did.'[58]

The need to counter the philosophies of Locke and Newton, which asserted the hegemony of outer reality, was a constant and never-fading urgency of Coleridge's thought. The common view in Coleridge's young manhood was that Locke and Newton were irrefragable in their united effect. As Godwin said in 1793, 'Locke and others have established certain maxims respecting man, as Newton has done respecting matter, that are

[55] *Kant*, iii. 239.
[56] Cf. Coleridge: 'The reason & the proper objects of reason are wholly alien to sensation.'
[57] *Kant*, iv. 452.   [58] TT, 25 July 1832.

generally admitted for unquestionable.'[59] Against this Coleridge pitted his entire intellectual force. One of his plans for Wordsworth's *Recluse* was that it should refute 'the sandy Sophisms of Locke, and the Mechanic Dogmatists' by 'demonstrating that the Senses were living growths and developements of the Mind & Spirit in a much juster as well as higher sense, than the mind can be said to be formed by the Senses'.[60] Like Blake, who was forever trying to cast off Bacon, Locke, and Newton from Albion's covering, Coleridge aligned the position of Locke and that of Newton as the absolute focus of his opposition to the rule of objects over spirit:

Newton was a mere materialist—*Mind* in his system is always passive—a lazy Looker-on on an external World. If the mind be not *passive*, if it be indeed made in God's Image, & that too in the sublimest sense—the Image of the *Creator*—there is ground for suspicion, that any system built on the passiveness of the mind must be false, as a system.[61]

Mind was not only passive in Newton, but was passive in the reigning philosophies of Coleridge's own day against which he rebelled. 'In volition, if the doctrine of necessity be true,' had said Godwin in *Political Justice*, 'the mind is altogether passive.'[62] 'Man is in reality a passive, and not an active being.'[63]

The faculty of 'reason', as elucidated by Kant, totally freed mind from being a 'lazy looker-on' on an external world. Reason made the mind not passive but active, and guaranteed that man was not a passive but an active being. Understanding was restricted to 'sensuous ideas'; but reason was free. 'The pure concepts of understanding can *never* admit of *transcendental* use, but always only of *empirical* employment'[64] (hence Coleridge's concession, as reported by Carlyle, that the atheism of Hume and Voltaire was true 'on their own ground', but lifted into 'a higher sphere'—of the transcendental use of reason—their arguments 'died into inanition').

Kant is insistent upon the limitation of the objects of 'understanding' to the sensuous world of empirical experience:

When, therefore, we say that the senses represent objects *as they appear*, and the understanding objects *as they are*, the latter statement is to be taken, not in the transcendental, but in the merely empirical meaning of the terms, namely as meaning that the objects must be represented as objects of experience, that is, as appearances in thoroughgoing interconnection with one another, and not as they

[59] Godwin, i. 20.   [60] *Collected Letters*, iv. 574.
[61] Ibid. ii. 709.   [62] Godwin, i. 323.
[63] Ibid. 310.   [64] *Kant*, iii. 207.

may be apart from their relation to possible experience (and consequently to any senses), as objects of pure understanding. Such objects of pure understanding will always remain unknown to us; we can never even know whether such a transcendental or exceptional knowledge is possible under any conditions—at least not if it is to be the same kind of knowledge which stands under our ordinary categories. *Understanding* and *sensibility*, with us, can determine objects *only when they are employed in conjunction*. When we separate them, we have intuitions without concepts, or concepts without intuitions—in both cases, representations which we are not in a position to apply to any determinate object.[65]

Reason, on the other hand, in absolute contrast, 'contains within itself the source of certain concepts and principles which it does not borrow either from the senses or from the understanding'.[66]

Kant uncompromisingly insists on the absolute difference of the two faculties, despite their co-ordination:

Understanding may be regarded as a faculty which secures the unity of appearances by means of rules, and reason as being the faculty which secures the unity of the rules of understanding under principles. Accordingly, reason never applies itself directly to experience or to any object, but to understanding, in order to give to the manifold knowledge of the latter an *a priori* unity by means of concepts, a unity which may be called the unity of reason, and which is quite different in kind from any unity that can be accomplished by the understanding.[67]

The connection of reason with unity was especially suggestive for Coleridge, who was always seeking for rational ground for the belief in God. As Coleridge said, 'The Reason first manifests itself in man by the *tendency* to the comprehension of all as one. We can neither rest in an infinite that is not at the same time a whole, nor in a whole that is not infinite. Hence the natural Man is always in a state either of resistance or of captivity to the understanding and the fancy, which cannot represent totality without limit.'[68]

Kant's other point in the preceding passage, that 'reason never applies itself directly to experience or to any object,' could also be extrapolated for Coleridge's intent of establishing rational grounds for belief in God. Coleridge writes that 'This primal act of faith is enunciated in the word, GOD: a faith not derived from experience, but its ground and source, and without which the fleeting *chaos of facts* would no more form experience, than the dust of the grave can of itself make a living man.'[69]

Now Kant was perhaps ultimately as concerned with faith in God as was

[65] *Kant*, iv. 167–8. [66] Ibid. 191. [67] Ibid. iii. 239.
[68] *Lay Sermons*, 60. [69] Ibid. 18.

Coleridge. A major difference between them, however, was that Kant sought the grounding of that faith through his beloved 'moral law within', and not through reason as such ('It was the moral ideas that gave rise to the concept of the Divine Being which we now hold to be correct—and we so regard it not because speculative reason convinces us of its correctness, but because it completely harmonizes with the moral principles of reason'[70]). To be sure, near the end of the *Kritik der reinen Vernunft* Kant says, in a memorable statement, that

The ultimate aim toward which the speculation of reason in its transcendental employment is directed concerns three objects: the freedom of the will, the immortality of the soul, and the existence of God.[71]

Coleridge unequivocally concurred:

God created man in his own image ... gave us REASON ... gave us CONSCIENCE—that law of conscience, which ... unconditionally *commands* us attribute *reality*, and actual *existence*, to those ideas and to those only, without which the conscience itself would be baseless and contradictory, to the ideas of Soul, of Free-will, of Immortality, and of God![72]

And yet the two passages, despite their common alignment of freedom of the will, the immortality of the soul, and the existence of God, are not identical. Coleridge is patently more affirmative about the existence of God. It is as though Kant directs reason tantalizingly close to the realization of God, and then at the last moment snatches it away. As far as he will let reason go is for it to open an 'empty space' (*leerer Raum*),[73] which God might (or might not) fill. Speaking of the 'noumenon', he says:

But since we can apply to it none of the concepts of the understanding, the representation remains for us empty, and is of no service except to mark the limits of our sensible knowledge and to leave open a space which we can fill neither through possible experience nor through pure understanding.[74]

Kant, however, in his first *Kritik* did say, tantalizingly, that

The argument of our Critique, taken as a whole, must have sufficiently convinced the reader that although metaphysics cannot be the foundation of religion, it must always continue to be a bulwark of it, and that human reason, being by its very nature dialectical, can never dispense with such a science, which curbs it, and by a scientific and completely convincing self-knowledge, prevents the devastations of which a lawless speculative reason would otherwise quite inevitably be guilty in the field of morals as well as in that of religion.[75]

---

[70] *Kant*, iii. 530.   [71] Ibid. 518.   [72] *Friend*, i. 112.
[73] *Kant*, iv. 169.   [74] Ibid. 185.   [75] Ibid. iii. 548–9.

But what Kant seemed to proffer, he also seemed to take back.

So Kant did not wholly satisfy Coleridge's needs. The distinction between reason and understanding, which pointed so alluringly to God, did not actually arrive there. Despite Kant's seeming comfort to religion, the antinomic nature of the critical enterprise made it offer the same comfort to the opposed possibilities. Indeed, as a commentator acutely observed of the great German thinker, 'it is doubtless true that his vast influence comes from the very fact that he sympathetically agrees with the fundamental contentions of everybody.'[76]

How it was possible for Kant's analysis of reason to be on both sides of the issue at once can be understood if we recall that he insisted at the outset that reason had a double function: one was to prescribe rules to the understanding, but the other was to deal in illusion (*Schein*). It was this second tendency of reason that caused Kant to declare it unfit for the task of filling the empty space with God. In a section of the *Kritik* called 'Criticism of all Theology out of Speculative Principles of Reason', Kant declared rational theology a species of illusion (*Schein*): 'reason, in its purely speculative application, is utterly insufficient for this great undertaking, namely, to prove the existence of a Supreme Being [*eines obersten Wesens*].'[77] 'What I maintain then,' said Kant,

is that all attempts at a purely speculative use of reason, with reference to theology, are entirely useless and intrinsically null and void, while the principles of their natural use can never lead to any theology, so that unless we depend on moral laws, or are guided by them, there cannot be any theology of reason.[78]

Such a conclusion was entirely unacceptable to Coleridge. Having come so far with Kant, he could accompany him no longer. He did not entirely share Kant's consuming fascination with moral law (the English thinker once said that he was inclined 'to believe that morality is conventional'). He instead was interested in clearing the rational ground to a point where a philosophical approach could be made to the realm of Christian faith, a faith in which even someone as morally tattered as he could find safe haven. 'All we can or need say' said Coleridge, going palpably farther than Kant, 'is, that the existence of a necessary Being is so transcendently Rational, that it is Reason itself.'[79] He was firm in this position. 'Man alone was created in the image of God: a position groundless and inexplicable, if the reason in man do not differ from the understanding.'[80] 'Reason and Religion are their own evidence.'[81] 'Reason and Religion differ only as a

[76] Randall, 110.   [77] *Kant*, iii. 425.   [78] Ibid. 423.
[79] Brinkley, 128.   [80] *Lay Sermons*, 19.   [81] Ibid. 10.

two-fold application of the same power.'[82] Still again, he speaks of 'the Reason, of which spiritual Faith is even the Blossoming and the fructifying process'.[83] At one point, indeed, he says with unequivocal explicitness that he is attempting to make the reflecting Reader *apprehend*, 'and thus to feel and know, that CHRISTIAN FAITH IS THE PERFECTION OF HUMAN REASON'.[84] The defiant casting of the statement into small capitals, one can hardly doubt, serves as a throwing down of the gauntlet to the claims of Kant.

Coleridge therefore gravitated away from Kant, at least from this aspect of Kant, towards the conception of reason put forth by Kant's opponent, Friedrich Jacobi.[85] Jacobi, who had first alerted the philosophical world to the full meaning of Spinoza, who had first detected the Achilles heel in Kant's reasoning about the '*Ding-an-sich*'—'the thing-in-itself', who had availed himself of Hume's scepticism to denounce all our knowledge as fragmentary piecework (and had set against even that claim to knowledge what he called his 'unphilosophy'), who had argued that all systematic demonstration in philosophy led to fatalism, was one of the most tenacious, consistent, and penetrating of all opponents of Enlightenment 'raison'.

Where, for Kant, the understanding worked with materials supplied by the senses, while the reason had no separate source of material but could work only with what the understanding supplied to it; Jacobi radically urged a different formula. For him, 'reason', like understanding, had direct access to intuitive knowledge. In this instance, however, it was not intuitive knowledge of sense data, but intuitive knowledge of God. 'Just as there is a sensible intuition,' said Jacobi, 'an *intuition* through sense, so there is a rational intuition through *reason*.'[86]

Thinking along lines parallel to his much older contemporary, Rousseau, Jacobi enormously elevated the role of 'feeling':

I appeal to an imperative, unconquerable feeling as the first and immediate ground of all philosophy and religion; to a feeling which allows man to become inwardly aware and to perceive this: he has a sense for the supersensible. This sense I call *reason* [*Vernunft*], in distinction from the sense for the visible world.[87]

Impregnated by the new emphasis on feeling, 'reason' took on an added aura: 'Human reason is the symptom of the highest life that we know.'[88] Divested of the coldness that the word implied in Diderot, the new warmth of the term 'reason' in Jacobi made it a welcome presence as the

[82] Ibid. 59. [83] *Aids to Reflection*, 254 n. [84] Ibid. 58.
[85] For a brief conspectus of Jacobi's criticisms of Kant, see Wilhelm Weischedel, *Streit um die göttliche Dinge* (Darmstadt: Wissenschaftliche Buchgesellschaft, 1967).
[86] *Jacobi*, ii. 59. [87] Ibid., vol. iv-1, p. xxi. [88] Ibid. vi. 191.

highest faculty of knowledge: 'Cold is the understanding,' said Jacobi, in a pregnant and characteristic passage of his *Fliegende Blätter*, 'but reason is a flame that is at once warming and illuminating.'[89] Indeed, in *Woldemar*, a work that so accentuated moral feeling as to become, in the words of a famous review by Friedrich Schlegel, a 'moral debauch',[90] Jacobi said that 'reason' was 'the life of the spirit—the feeling of divinity and its power'.[91] 'We do not say of the reason in man,' said Jacobi,

> that it uses mankind; but of the man, that he uses his reason. Reason is the original art, that immediate instrument of the spirit uncovered in the sensuous; it is the uniting consciousness, incessantly striving towards unity. So arise her images of the common and universal, pure images; so she creates, orders, rules and commands, through the wonderful force of the word that goes forth from her, as she herself goes forth from the spirit. Unweariedly finding, joining, the word to the fact, the fact to the word, she brings forth, dissolving and binding, science and art; she grounds theoretical and practical systems.[92]

Reason, for Jacobi, was, on the one hand the Kantian reason pushed farther than Kant himself could countenance; on the other hand it was a restatement of the 'heart's reason' of Pascal. 'Le cœur a ses raisons,' said Pascal, 'que la raison ne connait point'—'the heart has its reasons, that the reason does not know.'[93] Immediately after this famous aphorism, Pascal says that 'the heart naturally loves the universal being and naturally loves itself'.[94] Elsewhere he says that 'we know the truth not only by the reason but by the heart',[95] a statement in which Jacobi's *Verstand* could easily substitute for reason, and Jacobi's *Vernunft* for heart. (It is intriguing to note that while Pascal rejected imagination because of his allegiance to reason and faith, he paradoxically put the whole weight of his intellect behind the apotheosis of 'heart'—'C'est le cœur qui sent Dieu', he says (p. 552).)

The influence of Pascal is equally apparent in Jacobi's emphatic avowal of 'feeling' as the foundation of philosophy. Jacobi was reputed to know French more perfectly than any German thinker since Leibniz, and among all French writers he loved Pascal most. Almost equal to his saturation in Pascal was a saturation in Rousseau (though he thought the revelations of the *Confessions* testified to madness: 'Traurig', was his comment). The combined influence of his French predecessor and of his older French contemporary, however, allowed the assignment of the greatest importance to 'heart' or feeling:

---

[89] *Jacobi*, vi. 140–1.   [90] *Kritische Schriften*, 281.   [91] *Jacobi*, v. 215.
[92] Ibid. 123.   [93] Pascal, 552.   [94] Ibid.   [95] Ibid. 512.

And so we admit without timidity, that our philosophy arises from feeling, objective and pure; that it recognizes feeling's authority as an ultimate, and grounds itself, as doctrine of the supersensible, upon this authority.

The faculty of feeling, we maintain, is the faculty in human beings elevated above all others. It is the one that alone specifically differentiates man from animal, in kind, not merely in degree, i.e., raises him above the animal *beyond comparison.* The faculty of feeling, we maintain, is one and the same with reason [*Vernunft*], or, as also can properly be said, that which we call reason and raises us above the mere understanding, which is applied to nature alone, arises solely and singly out of the faculty of feeling.[96]

As background to such an avowal, it is interesting to recall Henry Crabb Robinson's report of a conversation he had in Germany with the intellectual historian Friedrich Schlosser:

An interesting chat with Fritz Schlosser about the men of the last age—our youth. He said that F. Jacobi anxiously wished to be a Christian, and would hail him as a benefactor who should relieve him from his doubts. . . . He hated Kantianism because he thought it wanted life and feeling. He loved Spinoza's character, but thought himself wronged in being treated as his follower. He was fond of quoting Pascal and Hemsterhusius.[97]

One must not, however, in discussions of background, in any way underestimate the pervasive presence of Rousseau, and of the way his attitudes conditioned the whole question of feeling and its relation to reason. The chief witness of *La Nouvelle Héloïse*, in truth, is to the supremacy of feeling. Even in its most beleaguered moments, the heart is there accorded a dignity equal to the most sublime heights of reason: 'I dare count also on his heart,' writes Milord Edouard of St Preux:

it is made to struggle and conquer. A love like his is not so much weakness as a force ill employed. A flame ardent and unfortunate is capable of absorbing for a while, perhaps for always, a portion of his faculties; but it is itself a proof of their excellence, and of the account to which they can be turned in cultivating wisdom; for sublime reason only sustains itself by the same vigour of soul that makes great passions, and one only serves philosophy worthily with the same fire that one feels for love.[98]

By the time of high Romanticism, feeling had become an unchallenged component in intellectual formulations. To restrict argument to merely three instances, Hazlitt acutely says of Wordsworth, 'He only sympathises with those simple forms of feeling, which mingle at once with his own

---

[96] *Jacobi*, ii. 61.   [97] *Diary*, ed. Godler, iii. 49.   [98] Rousseau, ii. 193.

identity, or with the stream of general humanity.'[99] 'The general and the permanent, like the Platonic ideas, are his only realities. All accidental varieties and individual contrasts are lost in an endless continuity of feeling, like drops of water in the ocean-stream!'[100] To tax his superb criticism of Wordsworth for the final example as well, Hazlitt insists, again, that the core of Wordsworth's poetic genius is 'intensity of feeling'.[101]

The elevation of feeling to the ontological heights was accompanied by an undercurrent of hostility to reason. Early on in *La Nouvelle Héloïse*, Rousseau speaks of 'un Anglois généreux et brave, toujours passionné par sagesse, toujours raisonnant sans raison'—'an Englishman generous and brave, always passionate for the sake of wisdom, always reasoning without reason'.[102] He says that if one goes back into himself he will *feel* what is good, discern what is beautiful: 'Si tôt qu'un veut rentrer en soi-même, chacun sent ce qui est bien, chacun discerne ce qui est beau.'[103] St Preux tells Julie that it is not the cold language of books, but our heart that teaches us love: 'Qu'apprendions nous de l'amour dans ces livres? Ah, Julie notre cœur nous en dit plus qu'eux, et le langage imité des livres est bien froid pour quiconque est passionné lui-même!'[104]

All these emphases were in Jacobi's mind, and they all helped condition his elevation of feeling to a first principle of philosophy, and therewith his radical alteration of the Kantian distinction between reason and understanding. It would not be fair to say that he was dependent on Rousseau, or even on Pascal, but both must be seen as important figures in his way of thinking.

Coleridge was thoroughly acquainted with all of Jacobi's major writings, from the *Ueber die Lehre des Spinoza* of 1785 (second edition 1789), to the *David Hume über den Glauben, oder Idealismus und Realismus* of 1787; from the *Jacobi an Fichte* of 1799, to the *Von den göttlichen Dingen und ihrer Offenbarung* of 1811. He was well aware of this kind of argument from the last-named of those treatises:

One will be a naturalist or a theist according to whether one subordinates reason to understanding or understanding to reason. Or, what is the same thing, according to whether one accepts or denies, outside the existence of necessity in nature, another existence of freedom above nature.

---

[99] *Hazlitt*, iv. 113.   [100] Ibid.
[101] Ibid. xi. 89. Still again, and most interestingly, Hazlitt maintains that 'in general the strength and consistency of the imagination will be in proportion to the strength and depth of feeling' (Hazlitt, viii. 42).
[102] Rousseau, ii. 12.   [103] Ibid. 58.   [104] Ibid. 61.

Reason maintains the existence of freedom without denying the existence of necessity and its unlimited power in *the whole realm of nature outside reason*. The understanding, however, denies the existence of freedom as such, because it departs from the law of causality . . . as a supreme law and highest principle. The law of causality, however, resolves itself into the proposition: *Nothing is unconditioned; there is no all-highest, supreme and first being.*[105]

It is interesting to note that where Kant says that reason 'manifests its highest function in distinguishing the sensible and intelligible worlds from one another', Jacobi in effect says that the reason not only distinguishes the intelligible world but renders it to the human intellect. That is very close to Coleridge's own position. Coleridge also came to know and agree with Jacobi's insistence that 'the true God is a living God, who knows and wants, says to himself that I am THAT I am; not a mere I and absolute Not-I'.[106] He certainly agreed with Jacobi's statement that 'My philosophy asks: who is God; not, what is he?'[107]

Coleridge, in brief, found especially congenial Jacobi's insistence upon 'person' and 'faith' as components of reason, and he was sympathetic to Jacobi's rejection of pantheism. He did not, however, accept Jacobi's 'radikale Unwissenheit' (radical unknowingness), nor Jacobi's rejection of system. His own view of reason, accordingly, stands somewhere between Jacobi and Kant without exclusively adhering to either. For a single instance, where Jacobi says that 'reason affirms, what understanding denies',[108] Coleridge on the contrary says, halfway, so to speak, between Jacobi and Kant, that 'reason is the irradiative power of the understanding, and the representative of the infinite'.[109]

Indeed, rather than precisely replicating the distinctions of either Jacobi or Kant, Coleridge's distinction resumes the tradition of Descartes and foreshadows the noetic/noematic analyses of Husserl. Coleridge seems proleptically close to Husserl when he says:

First, in Reason there is and can be no *degree*. Deus introit aut non introit.—Secondly in Reason there are no *means* nor ends: Reason itself being one with the ultimate end, of which it is the manifestation. Thirdly, Reason has no concern with *things* (i.e. the impermanent flux of particulars) but with permanent Relations; & is to be defined, even in it's lowest or theoretical attribute, as the Power which enables man to draw *necessary* and *universal* conclusions from

[105] *Jacobi*, iii. 412–13.
[106] Ibid. 344. The formulation radically rejects the reigning philosophical language and thought of Fichte and Schelling.
[107] Ibid., vol. iv-1, p. xxiv.
[108] Ibid., p. xliv.   [109] MS. of Coleridge's *Opus Maximum*.

particular facts or forms—ex gr. from any 3 cornered thing that the 2 sides of a Triangle are & must be greater than the third.[110]

Though Husserl's philosophy is, of course, on one level an attempt to extend and shore up the philosophy of Kant, in his own emphasis, as his *Cartesian Meditations* show, it was a further thinking of Descartes and his insistence on the primacy of the self as compared to the claims of the material world. As Husserl says at the end of his 'Paris Lectures' prefixed to *Die Cartesianische Meditationen*:

the necessary way to an ultimately grounded, or what is the same thing, a philosophical, knowledge, is that of a universal self-knowledge, first monadic and then inter-monadic. The delphic phrase, *Gnothi seauton* has won a new meaning. Positivist *Wissenschaft* is *Wissenschaft* lost in the world. One must first lose the world through *epoché* in order to win it again in a universal self-reflection. *Noli foras ire*, says Augustine, *in te redi, in interiore homine habitat veritas.*[111]

Husserl's quotation from Augustine, which he makes programmatic for the entirety of the *Cartesian Meditations* and of phenomenology itself, may be translated as 'Do not seek to go forth, go back into yourself, truth dwells in the inner man.' Augustine's standpoint, which Husserl thus explicitly accepts as his own, may be compared to that of Coleridge, who says: 'That, which we find in ourselves, is . . . the substance and the life of *all* our knowledge.'[112] And he says, 'That which we find in ourselves, which is more than ourselves, and yet the ground of whatever is good or permanent therein, is the substance and life of all our knowledge.'

What Coleridge found in himself that was more than himself was reason:

Philosophy, properly so called, began with Pythagoras. He saw that the mind, in the common sense of the word, was itself a fact, that there was something in the mind not individual; this was the pure reason, *something in which we are*, not *which is in us*.

In this line, those things that Leibniz adduced against the 'human understanding' of Locke partake of reason. Leibniz noted, against the tradition of *tabula rasa* by which 'nothing is in the intellect which was not first in the senses', that there is a palpable exception: the intellect itself. 'Now the soul contains ideas of being, of substance, of unity, of sameness, of cause, of perception, of reasoning, and of numerous other notions that are not given by the senses.'[113]

[110] *Collected Letters*, v. 137–8.   [111] Husserl, 39.
[112] *Lay Sermons*, 78.   [113] *Leibniz*, v. 100–1.

Coleridge at one point says that 'Reason is the knowlege of the laws of the WHOLE considered as ONE: and as such it is contradistinguished from the Understanding, which concerns itself exclusively with the quantities, qualities, and relations of *particulars* in time and space.'[114] Indeed, he rarely relinquished an opportunity to 'contradistinguish' understanding and reason, always with the insistence on reason's superiority in kind as well as in degree:

By the UNDERSTANDING, I mean the faculty of thinking and forming *judgments* on the notices furnished by the sense, according to certain rules existing in itself, which rules constitute its distinct nature. By the pure REASON, I mean the power by which we become possessed of principle, (the eternal verities of Plato and Descartes) and of ideas, (N.B. not images) as the ideas of a point, a line, a circle, in Mathematics; and of Justice, Holiness, Free-Will, &c. in Morals.[115]

Another contradistinction casts the opposition in a different language, but still with reason pre-eminent:

The ground-work, therefore, of all true philosophy is the full apprehension of the difference between the contemplation of reason, namely, that intuition of things which arises when we possess ourselves, as one with the whole, which is substantial knowledge, and that which presents itself when transferring reality to the negations of reality, to the ever-varying framework of the uniform life, we think of ourselves as separated beings, and place nature in antithesis to the mind, as object to subject, thing to thought, death to life. This is abstract knowledge, or the science of the mere understanding.[116]

The wording in that particular opposition hints at pantheism and the thought of Schelling—recurring problems in Coleridge's philosophical position. But such wording does not often figure in the contradistinction of the two faculties. More often Coleridge revelled in the 'distinction between the *Reason*, as the source of principles, the true celestial influx and *porta Dei in hominem internum*, and the *Understanding*'[117]—with the phrase, *porta Dei in hominem internum*, meaning 'doorway of deity into the inner man'. Sounding much like Jacobi, he said, 'All we can or need say is, that the existence of a necessary Being is so transcendentally Rational, that it is Reason itself.'[118]

Coleridge's closeness to Jacobi is especially evident in *The Friend*. There he says, while writing on tolerance, 'And here I fully coincide with Frederic H. Jacobi, that the only true spirit of Tolerance consists in our conscientious toleration of each other's intolerance.'[119] He is referring here

---

[114] *Lay Sermons*, 59.   [115] *Friend*, i. 177 n.   [116] Ibid. 520–21.
[117] *Collected Letters*, v. 137.   [118] Brinkley, 128.   [119] *Friend*, i. 96.

to a passage in *Von den göttlichen Dingen*; and on his next page he produces a statement that is permeated with Jacobi's (and Pascal's) generic emphasis on heart: 'There is one heart for the whole mighty mass of Humanity, and every pulse in each particular vessel strives to beat in concert with it.'[120] But it is in Coleridge's discussions of reason and understanding, which constitute so important a part of his discourse in the *Friend*, that Jacobi appears insistently. For instance, Coleridge says:

If further confirmation be necessary, it may be supplied by the following reflections, the leading thought of which I remember to have read in the works of a continental Philosopher. It should seem easy to give the definite distinction of the Reason from the Understanding, because we constantly imply it when we speak of the difference between ourselves and the brute creation.[121]

Coleridge is here referring to Jacobi's *David Hume*; and he continues his discussion of the existence of understanding in animals with an overt naming of Jacobi:

But Reason is wholly denied, equally to the highest as to the lowest of the brutes; otherwise it must be wholly attributed to them, with it therefore Self-consciousness, and *personality*, or Moral Being.

I should have no objection to define Reason with Jacobi, and with his friend Hemsterhuis, as an organ bearing the same relation to spiritual objects, the Universal, the Eternal, and the Necessary, as the eye bears to material and contingent phaenomena. But then it must be added, that it is an organ identical with its appropriate objects. Thus God, the Soul, eternal Truth, &c. are the objects of Reason; but they are themselves *reason*. We name God the Supreme Reason; and Milton says, 'Whence the Soul *Reason* receives, and Reason is her being.'[122]

This important passage has been quoted at some length—and will be continued at still further length—because it illustrates so well the intertwinement of Coleridge's emphasis with that of Jacobi. Kant's steel-edged analysis of reason probably had the greater role in Coleridge's deep commitment to that function; but Kant's tantalizing way of proffering, and then withdrawing, reason as a basis for belief in God, was not what Coleridge needed. He needed, rather, a conception of reason that allowed him the basis for a rational belief in the 'Redeemer' he so desperately felt he had to have ('Christianity and REDEMPTION are equivalent terms'[123]).

[120] *Friend*, i. 97. It is also interesting to note the congruence of the statement to Wordsworth's 'we have all of us one human heart' (Wordsworth, *Poems*, iv. 239 ('The Old Cumberland Beggar', line 153)).

[121] *Friend*, i. 154.

[122] Ibid. 155–6.

[123] *Aids to Reflection*, 303.

That basis Jacobi's conception could supply, though Jacobi himself was in many ways a radical sceptic.

Indeed, it is important not to confuse Coleridge's fellow-feeling with Jacobi on the issues of reason and personality with a similarity in other respects. In particular, Coleridge's large commitment to external nature and to science found no counterpart in Jacobi, who was interested only in abstractions and moral feelings. 'The secret of the moral sense and moral feeling is the secret of lasting life', said Jacobi: 'Faith and experience are therefore the only way by which we can attain to knowledge of the truth.'[124] As Friedrich Schlegel finely said, 'The elastic point from which the philosophy of Jacobi departs is not an objective imperative, but an individual optative.'[125] Schlegel concedes that 'the polemical part of Jacobi's writings have great philosophical value: he has discovered the holes, the consequences, the disconnection not merely of this or that system, but also of the reigning intellectual mode of the century'.[126] Nevertheless Jacobi's 'positive faith-philosophy [*Glaubenslehre*] can throughout not claim philosophical validity'.[127] That was, said Schlegel, because Jacobi cavalierly dismissed all claims outside his own inner need:

By nature inclined to sink into himself and luxuriate in his own modes of conceiving, he could at first only through mistrust in his love [of the invisible], and doubt as to the reality of its object, be moved to tear himself out of himself, and be active towards the outside, where one must struggle for each step forward.[128]

So it was that Jacobi maintained, said Schlegel, that 'philosophizing in general is nothing other than what his own philosophy really is: the spirit of an individual life rendered in concepts and words.'[129]

As a result of this overriding focus on his own individual existence, Goethe's green and golden world is entirely absent in Jacobi. 'God', wrote Goethe once to his friend, 'has punished you with metaphysics . . . he has, on the other hand, blessed me with physics.'[130] Goethe's commitment to 'physics', not shared by Jacobi, was entirely shared by Coleridge.

Coleridge's discussion of reason and understanding in *The Friend*, just cited, continues, urgently intertwined with consideration of the mental functioning of animals:

Whatever is conscious *Self*-knowledge is Reason; and in this sense it may be safely defined the organ of the Super-sensuous; even as the Understanding wherever it

---

[124] *Jacobi*, vi. 138.
[126] Ibid. 274–5.
[128] Ibid. 273.
[130] *Goethe*, xviii. 924.

[125] *Kritische Schriften*, 272–3.
[127] Ibid. 275.
[129] Ibid. 274.

does not possess or use the Reason, as another and inward eye, may be defined the conception of the Sensuous, or the faculty by which we generalize and arrange the phaenomena of perception: that faculty, the functions of which contain the rules and constitute the possibility of outward Experience. In short, the Understanding supposes something that is *understood*. This may be merely its own acts or forms, that is, formal Logic; but *real* objects, the materials of *substantial* knowledge, must be furnished, we might safely say *revealed*, to it by Organs of Sense. The understanding of the higher Brutes has only organs of outward sense, and consequently material objects only; but man's understanding has likewise an organ of inward sense, and therefore the power of acquainting itself with invisible realities or spiritual objects. This organ is his Reason.[131]

Interestingly enough, Coleridge's intense need to discriminate reason from understanding, so that his hope in a Redeemer might receive a rational basis, leads him into more finely-fingered illustrations than are to be found in either Jacobi or Kant, let alone Diderot, for whom 'la raison' is monolithically simply a given.

The conditioning factor for Diderot's 'la raison' being simply a given, one should make sure to understand, is that the hegemony of the term in France was a direct result of the overwhelming influence of Descartes on European culture of the seventeenth century, and on French culture well into the eighteenth century. For it was Descartes who really inaugurated the Age of Reason. That amazingly subtle work of 1637, the *Discours de la méthode*, adopts an authorial persona of studied naïvety, despite the fact that Descartes was in actuality a wonderfully well-educated and supremely sophisticated thinker. Here, however, he seems as naïve and wide-eyed as Candide or Jean-Jacques; and all the naïvety is adopted to provide the black velvet background for effective display of a pristine and gleaming jewel, which is 'raison'. The black velvet is constituted by Descartes's repeated suspicions that he may be mistaken, that he knows nothing for certain, that (in the *Meditationes*) a powerful deceiver may be at work to mislead him. The jewel, radiant with intense light, is reason, exempt from, and exempting all else from, the blackness of the background. It is not the *cogito*, but reason, which is the ruler of the Cartesian intellectual cosmos. The formula *je pens, donc je suis* is merely a specific conclusion of reason.

The necessity for a supreme apotheosis of reason, indeed, is the cause of the denigration of imagination noted in the previous chapter. Descartes early on notes ominously that 'fables make one imagine many events possible which in reality are not so', and that even readers of history 'are

[131] *Friend*, i. 156.

liable to fall into the extravagance of the knights errant of Romances'.[132] He explicitly forms his four rules of method because

I did not wish to set about the final rejection of any single opinion which might have crept into my beliefs without having been introduced there by means of Reason, until I had first of all employed sufficient time in planning out the task which I had undertaken, and in seeking the true Method of arriving at a knowledge of all the things of which my mind was capable.[133]

In this task it seems to me, I succeeded pretty well, . . . trying to discover the error or uncertainty of the propositions which I examined, not by feeble conjectures, but by clear and assured reasonings.[134]

Accordingly, he admits to 'occupying my whole life in cultivating my Reason, and in advancing myself as much as possible in the knowledge of the truth in accordance with the method which I had prescribed myself'.[135]

For Descartes the light of reason shines ever more clearly in the gloom of deception and uncertainty: 'For, finally, whether we are awake or asleep, we should never allow ourselves to be persuaded excepting by the evidence of our Reason. And it must be remarked that I speak of our Reason and not of our imagination nor of our senses.'[136] 'Reason tells us that since our thoughts cannot possibly be all true, because we are not altogether perfect, that which they have of truth must infallibly be met with in our waking experience rather than in that of our dreams.'[137] In those statements, the rejection of what were to become important Romantic criteria, dreams and imagination, is especially prominent.

The apotheosis of reason in Descartes allows his epigone Diderot to invoke the faculty without discussion or justification. Coleridge, on the other hand, against a different background, continually seeks for compelling distinction in his own formulations:

Again, the Understanding and Experience may exist without Reason. But Reason cannot exist without Understanding; nor does it or can it manifest itself but in and through the understanding, which in our elder writers is often called *discourse*, or the discursive faculty, as by Hooker, Lord Bacon, and Hobbes: and an understanding enlightened by reason Shakespear gives as the contra-distinguishing character of man, under the name *discourse of reason*. In short, the human understanding possesses two distinct organs, the outward sense, and 'the mind's eye' which is reason: wherever we use that phrase (the mind's eye) in its proper

---

sense, and not as a mere synonyme of the memory or the fancy. In this way we reconcile the promise of Revelation, that the blessed will see God, with the declaration of St. John, God hath no one seen at any time.[138]

Coleridge anxiously attempts to exploit every consideration by which, at one and the same time, reason is the reason we all mean by that word, and something radically different from 'la raison'. He carefully isolates the use of the term as a groundwork of scientific thought:

If the reader therefore will take the trouble of bearing in mind these and the following explanations, he will have removed before hand every possible difficulty from the Friend's political section. For there is another use of the word, Reason, arising out of the former indeed, but less definite, and more exposed to misconception. In this latter use it means the understanding considered as using the Reason, so far as by the organ of Reason only we possess the ideas of the Necessary and the Universal; and this is the more common use of the word, when it is applied with *any* attempt at clear and distinct conceptions. In this narrower and derivative sense the best definition of Reason, which I can give, will be found in the third member of the following sentence, in which the understanding is described in its three-fold operation, and from each receives an appropriate name. The Sense, (vis sensitiva vel intuitiva) *per*ceives: Vis regulatrix (the understanding, in its own peculiar operation) *con*ceives: Vis rationalis (the Reason or rationalized understanding) *comprehends*. The first is impressed through the organs of sense; the second combines those multifarious impressions into individual *Notions*, and by reducing these notions to Rules, according to the analogy of all its former notices, constitutes *Experience*: the third subordinates both these notions and the rules of Experience to ABSOLUTE PRINCIPLES or necessary LAWS: and thus concerning objects, which our experience has proved to have *real* existence, it demonstrates moreover, in what way they are *possible*, and in doing this constitutes *Science*. Reason therefore, in this secondary sense, and used, *not* as a spiritual *Organ* but as a *Faculty* (namely, the Understanding or Soul *enlightened* by that organ)—Reason, I say, or the *scientific* Faculty, is the Intellection of the *possibility* or *essential* properties of things by means of the Laws that constitute them. Thus the *rational* idea of a Circle is that of a figure constituted by the circumvolution of a straight line with its one end fixed.[139]

The tightly drawn threads in the foregoing fabric of discourse are of a fineness and complexity worthy of Isfahan or Tabriz. Their configuration is especially rewarding in that its touch reveals a palpable difference in texture from the neighbouring textures of Kant and Jacobi.

As Coleridge is careful to delineate the domain of scientific reason, he is equally careful in attempting to specify the relation of reason to other

[138] *Friend*, i. 156–7.　　　　　[139] Ibid. 157–8.

concerns. His discussion of the relation of reason to conscience is notable for its nuance as well as for its care:

This reason applied to the *motives* of our conduct, and combined with the sense of our moral responsibility, is the conditional cause of *Conscience*, which is a spiritual sense or testifying state of the coincidence or discordance of the FREE WILL with the REASON. But as the Reasoning consists wholly in a man's power of seeing, whether any two ideas, which happen to be in his mind, are, or are not in contradiction with each other, it follows of necessity, not only that all men have reason, but that every man has it in the same degree. For Reasoning (or Reason, in this its *secondary* sense) does not consist in the Ideas, or in their clearness, but simply, when they *are* in the mind, in seeing whether they contradict each other or no.[140]

Coleridge continues, in measured discussion, difficult to follow but compelling in its acuteness and consequence. Careful reading brings its rewards:

And again, as in the determinations of Conscience the only knowledge required is that of my own *intention*—whether in doing such a thing, instead of leaving it undone, I did what I should think right if any other person had done it; it follows that in the mere question of guilt or innocence, all men have not only Reason equally, but likewise all the materials on which the reason, considered as *Conscience*, is to work. But when we pass out of ourselves, and speak, not exclusively of the *agent as meaning* well or ill, but of the action in its consequences, then of course experience is required, judgment in making use of it, and all those other qualities of the mind which are so differently dispensed to different persons, both by nature and education. And though *the reason* itself is the same in all men, yet the means of exercising it, and the materials (i.e. the facts and ideas) on which it is exercised, being possessed in very different degrees by different persons, the *practical Result* is, of course, equally different—and the whole ground work of Rousseau's Philosophy ends in a mere Nothingism.[141]

It is interesting to note that Coleridge's coinage, 'Nothingism', lost out historically to Jacobi's term 'Nihilism'; but both terms urge the same awareness.

Coleridge's animus against Rousseau, which is co-ordinate with that ultimate rejection of the French Revolution discussed in Chapter 3 above, is here only elliptically presented. Later on in *The Friend* he discusses Rousseau, at length, in an essay entitled 'On the Grounds of Government as Laid Exclusively in the Pure Reason: or a Statement and Critique of the Third System of Political Philosophy, viz. the Theory of Rousseau and the French Economists.' In that chapter appears a notable apostrophe, one

---

[140] Ibid. 159.   [141] Ibid.

that illustrates strikingly that reason in the Romantic era was not allowed to remain in the circumscribed confines of Enlightenment emphasis:

REASON! best and holiest gift of Heaven and bond of union with the Giver! The high title by which the majesty of man claims precedence above all other living creatures! Mysterious faculty, the mother of conscience, of language, of tears, and of smiles! Calm and incorruptible legislator of the soul, without whom all its other powers would 'meet in mere oppugnancy.' Sole principle of permanence amid endless change! in a world of discordant appetites and imagined self-interests the only common measure![142]

The magnificent apostrophe continues, with scarcely diminished flow and pertinence, towards the lodestone of Rousseau:

Thrice blessed faculty of Reason! all other gifts, though goodly and of celestial origin, health, strength, talents, all the powers and all the means of enjoyment, seem dispensed by chance or sullen caprice—thou alone, more than even the sunshine, more than the common air, art given to all men, and to every man alike!

The hailing of reason merges into a consideration of its indispensability to that community called a country, and thence to consideration of Rousseau's political theory:

To thee, who being one art the same in all, we owe the privilege, that of all we can become one, a living *whole*! that we have a COUNTRY! Who then shall dare prescribe a law of moral action for any rational Being, which does not flow immediately from that Reason, which is the fountain of all morality? Or how without breach of conscience can we limit or coerce the powers of a free agent, except by coincidence with that law in his own mind, which is at once the cause, the condition, and the measure, of his free agency? Man must be *free*; or to what purpose was he made a Spirit of Reason, and not a Machine of Instinct? Man must *obey*; or wherefore has he a conscience. The powers, which create this difficulty, contain its solution likewise: for *their* service is perfect freedom. And whatever law or system of law compels any other service, disennobles our nature, leagues itself with the animal against the godlike, kills in us the very principle of joyous well-doing, and fights against humanity.

By the application of these principles to the social state there arises the following system, which as far as respects its first grounds is developed most fully by J. J. Rousseau in his work *Du Contrat social*.[143]

Coleridge concedes that Rousseau saw that all laws obligatory on the conscience arise from reason, but he argues that a fateful discrimination in Rousseau led to the perversion of reason's role in the Revolution, and in

---

[142] *Friend*, i. 190.   [143] Ibid. 191.

the Napoleonic succession to that Revolution. He claims that Rousseau did not properly assess the relation of expedience to reason:

But which of these results is the more probable [in the mitigations and neutralizations of parliamentary debate], the correction or the contagion of evil, must depend on circumstances and grounds of expediency: and thus we already find ourselves beyond the magic circle of the pure Reason, and within the sphere of the understanding and the prudence. Of this important fact Rousseau was by no means unaware in his theory, though with gross inconsistency he takes no notice of it in his application of the theory to practice. He admits the possibility, he is compelled by History to allow even the *probability*, that the most numerous popular assemblies, nay even whole nations, may at times be hurried away by the same passions, and under the dominion of a common error. This will of all is *then* of no more value, than the humours of any one individual: and must therefore be sacredly distinguished from the pure will which flows from universal Reason. To this point then I entreat the Reader's particular attention: for in this distinction, established by Rousseau himself, betweeen the *Volonté de Tous* and the *Volonté generale*, (i.e. between the collective will, and a casual over-balance of wills) the falsehood or nothingness of the whole system becomes manifest.[144]

This, then, the fateful distinction between two forms of communal will, leads Coleridge to his recurrent charge of 'mere Nothingism' for Rousseau's political philosophy. The point is elaborated with political finality:

For hence it follows, as an inevitable consequence, that all which is said in the *contrat social* of that sovereign will, to which the right of universal legislation appertains, applies to no one Human Being, to no Society or assemblage of Human Beings, and least of all to the mixed multitude that makes up the PEOPLE: but entirely and exclusively to REASON itelf, which, it is true, dwells in every man *potentially*, but actually and in perfect purity is found in no man and in no body of men. This distinction the latter disciples of Rousseau chose completely to forget and, (a far more melancholy case!) the constituent legislators of France forgot it likewise. With a wretched *parrotry* they wrote and harangued without ceasing of the *Volonté generale*—the *inalienable sovereignty* of the people: and by these high-sounding phrases led on the vain, ignorant, and intoxicated populace to wild excesses and wilder expectations, which entailing on them the bitterness of disappointment cleared the way for military despotism, for the satanic Government of Horror under the Jacobins, and of Terror under the Corsican.[145]

So that is enough. This rather lengthy presentation of the interrelations of Coleridge's conception of reason, his attitude towards the political thought of Rousseau, and his rejection of 'the satanic Government of

---

[144] Ibid. 193.   [145] Ibid. 193–4.

Horror under the Jacobins', has been adduced in illustration of the interconnectedness of Coleridge's intellectual commitments. The interconnectedness constitutes an interweaving of concerns that results in a distinctive texture of Romanticism.

Though much more could be said about reason in Coleridge, and reason in the Romantic era as such, further discussion must give way to the emphasizing of two large truths about the matters taken up in this and the preceding chapter. First of all, it is evident that Coleridge, Jacobi, and Kant, though utilizing the same distinction of reason and understanding, all present idiosyncratic and differently woven textures of discourse. Though both Coleridge and Jacobi follow Kant's division of reason and understanding, Kant himself followed that established by Tetens, so priority is not really an issue. Each thinker contributed much more from his own intellectual need and cast of mind than he borrowed from another. Of the three, Coleridge elaborates in much greater ramification than do the other two.

Secondly, though reason would, on the surface, seem to be the peculiar concern of seventeenth- and eighteenth-century thought, it is revealed as not an exclusive emphasis; for the Romantic era also contemplated deeply the nature and function of reason. For instance, in a high Romantic work of 1806, Steffens begins with the words:

There is only one true knowledge, and this is the absolute knowledge of the reason [*Vernunft*].

What in the reason becomes known is nothing except the reason itself; and knowledge too, on the other hand, is merely reason.[146]

Indeed, the highest architectonics of pure reason, transcendental mathematics ('Mathematics', said Kant, 'presents the most splendid example of the successful extension of pure reason, without the help of experience'[147]), were as richly achieved in the Romantic era as in the preceding 'Age of Reason'. The greatest algorist of the eighteenth century—Leonhard Euler—could hardly be said to be a more supreme mathematician than the gigantic figure of mathematics in the Romantic era, Johann Friedrich Gauss.

This truth becomes all the more resonant when juxtaposed against a prophecy by Diderot, the chief sponsor of the claims of Enlightenment 'raison'. In 1753, Diderot predicted than in another hundred years there would not be three great geometricians left in the whole of Europe—that geometry would have stopped short at the point where men such as Euler

---

[146] Steffens, 1.   [147] *Kant*, iii. 468.

had left it; that Euler and his fellows would have erected the Pillars of Hercules, which no one would go beyond:

j'oserais presque assurer qu'avant qu'il soit cent ans, on ne comptera pas trois grand géomètres en Europe. Cette science s'arrêtera tout court, où l'auront laissée les Bernoulli, les Euler, les Maupertuis, les Clairaut, les Fontaine et les d'Alembert. Ils auront posé les colonnes d'Hercules. On n'ira point au-dela. Leurs ouvrages subsisteront dans les siècles à venir, comme ces pyramides d'Egypte, dont les masses chargées d'hiéroglyphes réveillent en nous une idée effrayante de la puissance et des ressources des hommes qui les ont élevées.[148]

But reason, and its crown of glory, mathematics, in utter disregard of Diderot's prophecy, maintained themselves in undiminished and ever-renewed splendour, though in different configurations, into and beyond the age of Romanticism. The same situation obtains, with priorities reversed, in the concern with imagination noted in the preceding chapter. Imagination was supposedly an emphasis peculiar to Romanticism—'the quintessence of Romanticism'. On examination, however, though it is revealed to be without doubt an extremely important emphasis in Romanticism, it is revealed as not a topic entirely limited to Romanticism. The Romantic conception, though idiosyncratic, was intertwined with earlier considerations.

These facts point to an important truth about Romanticism, and about other sensibilities as well. The Romantic sensibility had few elements absolutely confined to itself. It was rather characterized by a differing valorization of elements present throughout a continuum of human awareness. Indeed, Romanticism would have been superficial, instead of the profoundly significant intellectual movement it is, had it not been based on existential bedrock. Historical considerations change and vary; existential realities—birth, death, childhood, age, love, hate, hope, anxiety, aspiration—are a constant (*pace* the claims of Ariès). It is on those realities that everything of ultimate interest must be based. The sonatas of Romanticism, so to speak, like the differing compositions of the so-called neo-classic and Baroque sensibilities, were all played on keys of the same keyboard. To change the metaphor to the realm of weaving, Romanticism used existential threads always present, but wove them into configurations and densities distinctive to itself.

[148] Diderot, 180–1.

The Realm of the Vague

THE foregoing chapters have attempted to present widely separated textures of the text called Romanticism, all palpably connected despite their separation. The touching of such textures, each woven with threads inhering in the Romantic tapestry, could proceed indefinitely. But the six heretofore isolated, along with the one to be descried in the present chapter, make up, so to speak, a quorum—or perhaps better, a critical mass—for the consideration of the characteristics of the fabric called Romanticism. Fewer textures would not attain the necessary plurality; more would doubtless be interesting in themselves, but would be redundant for the task of this book, which is to document not only the variety, but the complexity and richness, of the text called Romanticism. To that end, some of the previous chapters are lengthier and more detailed than a purely schematic presentation might have necessitated; their length and convolution are dictated by the intent of presenting, as fully as possible, what is implied by that metaphorical complexity called texture.

The discussions contained in the previous chapters, it is hoped, might seem interesting each in itself. But that is not the chief reason for the presentations of this book, nor for the development of the discrete topics of its discourse. That controlling reason, on the contrary, is polemical. The introduction and first chapter of the book are overtly polemical; the third chapter and the present one are as well. But the remaining chapters, on the surface, might not seem to be. Yet, underlying every discussion there is an insistent polemical intent: to rebut, or at least qualify, those new approaches to Romanticism—New Historicism, deconstruction, the viewpoint of Jerome McGann, the viewpoint of Marilyn Butler, the opinion of E. P. Thompson—that dominate the scene in these last decades of the twentieth century. It is the implicit standpoint of this book that all those approaches, in their current implementations, tend, in different ways and in varying degrees, to obscure the true nature of Romantic achievement, and its quality as well.

That is not to say, however, that those approaches are in themselves without value. It would be idle to dispute the enormous impact of deconstructive theory, or to deny the specific instances in which deconstructive analysis results in illumination. Indeed, those who have troubled themselves to attend to the texture of this book's touching of texture will realize that, at various times, it too invokes deconstructive procedures. The same may be said for the relation of its arguments to New Historicism. The book is not unremittingly hostile to Marx—however hostile it may seem to be to Marxist critics. At various places the argument takes note of the permanent importance of the Marxist analysis of culture, history, and human activity. The book also presents, more than once, though it does not signal that fact, concatenations that happily illustrate the chief contentions of McGann.

To cite only one, in Chapter 3 it was noted that Schiller's initial enthusiasm for the French Revolution gave way to despair over its realities, and that by the advent of the nineteenth century he had retreated to a purely ideal affirmation: 'Freedom exists only in the realm of dream | And beauty blooms only in song':

> In des Herzens heilig stille Räume
> Musst du fliehen aus der Lebens Drang,
> Freiheit ist nur in dem Reich der Träume,
> Und das Schöne blüht nur im Gesang.[1]

So why then, one asks, is the book so antipathetic to McGann's agenda? Because, throughout, and at best, it substitutes a minor part for a major whole. Of course, the nature of the symbol is also to substitute a part for the whole; but the part emphasized by McGann contradicts the whole, which a true symbol cannot do. McGann's procedure is, on the contrary, Procrustean; it affirms a part and lops off all the rest. Moreover, the truths the agenda does affirm are not, despite their author's claim, definitive of Romanticism; they are, on the contrary, true for all cultural formation whatever. For instance, McGann urges that the 'Romantic Movement, from its earliest to its latest transformations, is marked by extreme forms of displacement and poetic conceptualization whereby the actual human issues with which the poetry is concerned are resituated and deflected in various ways'.[2] But such resituation and deflection are endemic to all imaginative construction.

To be sure, the relation of mankind's efforts in the real world (whatever that may be—certainly one should heed Barry Stroud's John Locke lectures on 'reality') to his capacity for constructing ideals and ideal worlds, is a constant in human activities, and in Romanticism as well. Simply to stay with Schiller, one may point to his poem 'Das Ideal und das Leben'. And in his 'Rousseau' of 1782, Schiller tries to ameliorate the

---

[1] *Schiller*, ii. 823.   [2] McGann, 138.

sorrows of the real Rousseau in the real world by an invocation of ideal transformation:

> Nicht für diese Welt warst du—zu bieder
> Warst du ihr, zu hoch—vielleicht zu nieder
> Rousseau, doch du warst ein Christ.
> Mag der Wahnwitz diese Erde gängeln!
> Geh du heim zu deinen Brüdern Engeln,
> Denen du entlaufen bist.[3]

But to try to set up, as McGann does, a supposedly complete, and intrinsically mistaken, conception of Romanticism—'the Romantic ideology'—supposedly endorsed and shared by the Romantics themselves ('Today the scholarship and interpretation of Romantic works is dominated by an uncritical absorption in Romanticism's own self-representations'[4]), and contrast it to a correct and Marx-controlled understanding of that protean sensibility, is to do violence to the depth, complexity, and variety of Romantic commitments. In truth, it is to attempt to restore the sense of depth, complexity, and variety, that this book was undertaken.

The book seeks, above all, to rescue the qualitative understanding of Romanticism from what it sees as the obscurations of the dominant approaches today, all of which, to greater or lesser extent, seem subtly to patronize Romantic experience. McGann well says that 'the critical literature on Romanticism has begun to lose its grip on the historical and structural peculiarities of Romantic works'.[5] But his chief illustration for his own agenda seems to be Marjorie Levinson's approach to 'Tintern Abbey'; and that approach has been stigmatized by several scholars as precisely losing its critical, if not its historical, grip on Wordsworth's poem. Her discussion of the poem (which was not published until after McGann's volume appeared) has been attacked by M. H. Abrams, savagely attacked by Helen Vendler, attacked as far away as Australia by Simon Haines, and attacked by the present author: 'In Levinson's discussion, "Tintern Abbey" becomes simply a document of sociological bad faith. Far from seeming a great poem, her transformed understanding makes it seem not even a good one.'[6]

But McGann puts forward Levinson's elucidation of the poem as a paradigmatic example of what his agenda urges. He thinks of 'The Ruined Cottage' as an exemplary illustration for displacement:

[3] *Schiller*, i. 43.   [4] McGann, 137.
[5] Ibid. 20.   [6] McFarland, *Wordsworth*, 16–17.

'The Ruined Cottage' is an exemplary case of what commentators mean when they speak of the 'displacement' that occurs in a Romantic poem. An Enlightenment mind like Diderot's or Godwin's or Crabbe's would study this poem's events in social and economic terms, but Wordsworth is precisely interested in preventing—in actively countering—such a focus of concentration.[7]

True. But neither Diderot, nor Godwin, nor Crabbe, none of them, in his wildest imaginings, could have produced a poem remotely comparable in quality to 'The Ruined Cottage'. Not one of them, even if his life hung in the balance, could have produced the poem, or, in any mode chosen, could have produced an alternative poem that in any way challenged the heights of 'The Ruined Cottage'—which Coleridge called 'the finest Poem in our Language',[8] which Leavis called 'the finest thing that Wordsworth wrote . . . certainly the most disturbingly poignant'.[9] Take Diderot, Godwin, and Crabbe, add to them the mightiest intellectual efforts of Voltaire and the whole French Enlightenment, and no poem of the quality of 'The Ruined Cottage' could result. To change what Wordsworth actually did would be to destroy a supreme poem. And to understand the quality of what Wordsworth actually did is by the same token the most urgent, and ultimately the only, task of criticism.

McGann, however, moves calmly from the revealing statement above to an even stronger statement, this one about 'Tintern Abbey': 'Yet the character and extent of the displacement in "The Ruined Cottage" is quite different—is far less extreme—from what we may observe in "Tintern Abbey".'[10] McGann observes that

In the course of the poem not a word is said about the French Revolution, or about the impoverished and dislocated country poor, or—least of all—that this event and these conditions might be structurally related to each other. All these are matters which had been touched upon, however briefly, in 'The Ruined Cottage,' but in 'Tintern Abbey' they are further displaced out of the narrative.[11]

McGann suggests that nevertheless those subjects 'are present in the early parts of the poem, only to be completely erased after line 23'.[12] But their presence is 'maintained in such an oblique way that readers—especially later scholars and interpreters—have passed them by almost without notice'.[13] At this point he invokes Levinson's still-unpublished, but 'brilliantly researched and highly controversial polemic', and sketches her argument.

Levinson does indeed take extensive notice of what the poem does not

[7] McGann, 84.   [8] *Collected Letters*, iv. 564.   [9] Leavis, 179.
[10] McGann, 85.   [11] Ibid.   [12] Ibid.   [13] Ibid. 85–6.

mention, 'the French Revolution' and 'the impoverished and dislocated country poor'. She concludes that 'we are bound to see that Wordsworth's pastoral prospect is a fragile affair, artfully assembled by acts of exclusion'.[14] She concludes that 'Given the sort of issues raised by "Tintern Abbey" 's occasion, it follows that the primary poetic action is the suppression of the social'.[15] Such identification of 'the primary poetic action' is apparently the kind of judgement McGann's agenda is happy to espouse; and it is the kind of judgement that this book is obliged to reject.

If McGann's Procrustean subjection of all phenomena to a single mechanism wreaks havoc in our understanding of what Romanticism in fact is, and most especially of the quality of its activity, Marilyn Butler's denial of any unmistakable and defining linkage between and among the phenomena does as much damage in a different way. A true awareness of Romanticism, on the contrary, must remain suspended, though perpetually maintained by contemplation, between the Scylla of too rigid a definition, and the Charybdis of no definition at all. That is, of course, a difficult and sometimes unrewarding endeavour; but it is nevertheless what a scholar and critic of Romanticism must seek to do. He or she must constantly, and with ever-renewed effort, seek to recapture the plangency of a unique and decisive moment in the cultural history of the world. If that plangency is restored to our hearing, then questions of value and quality answer themselves.

This book has concerned itself overridingly with the attempt to hear the plangency of Romanticism, which is metaphorically identical to touching the texture of Romanticism. It has accordingly neglected almost entirely the obligation of providing a unitary view of Romanticism's nature. It is, of course, not necessary, in the cultural exploration of Romanticism, constantly to have such a view before one's eyes. So long as the plangency of Romanticism is not muffled, so long as the texture is felt, the critic may move at will among Romantic phenomena. At some theoretical point, however, real but not defined *a priori*, the question of unitary conception does arise; and if it cannot be answered, by at least a schematic, if not necessarily total, answer, all understandings are compromised. It is not McGann's commitment to unitary conceiving that this book rejects, but rather that his unitary formulation forfeits much of the plangency, slides untouchingly over much of the texture, of Romanticism.

Hoxie Neale Fairchild, more than sixty years ago, provided a unitary conception of Romanticism that, in its moving between supposed reality

[14] Levinson, 32.　　　　[15] Ibid. 37.

and ideational construct, has something in common with McGann's. Fairchild's definition is that Romanticism is 'the endeavor, in the face of growing factual obstacles, to achieve, to retain, or to justify' what he called an 'illusioned view of the universe and of human life'.[16] Leaving aside the important question of whether all views of human life are not, always and at all times, illusioned, one may comment that this definition, though open to some of the same objections as McGann's, is spared some of its reproaches by maintaining slack, as it were, in the depending network of phenomena. The definition may not account for everything about Romanticism, but it is not formulated, as is McGann's iron mechanism, in a way that leaves no room for variety and complexity.

The present author's unitary view of Romanticism, although not until now invoked in this book, also, whatever its theoretical insufficiencies, allows a large amount of room for complexity, contradiction, depth, and contrary awarenesses—in a word, for diversity among phenomena:

Romanticism was a complex of realizations and denials set in motion by the fear that man 'had no reason why'. And underlying its three main sources of political-social, economic, and spiritual pressure was the single great transformation: the demise of substance and the rise of process.[17]

No one, of course, is obliged to invest in such a definition; but, strictly in its form as definition, it is implied by, first, varied experience of the phenomena supposed to constitute Romanticism, and secondly, tactile awareness of the actual texture of Romantic cultural events. Phenomena and definition mutually require one another, for without at least implicit definition how can phenomena be recognized as subsumed under the category, Romanticism, which in its turn ineluctably calls for delineation in its generality?

The two previous chapters have attempted to touch the texture of Romantic imagination, and the texture of Romantic reason. This concluding chapter will now attempt to descry a third Romantic emphasis, that associated with the concept of *symbol*. In line with the mode characterizing this book, this discussion too will take place in a polemical matrix. The polemic is here to be directed against what this chapter will see as another instance of the distortion of Romantic awareness, this one inhering in Paul De Man's adjudication of the significance of Romantic symbol.

The adjudication occurs in an article, 'The Rhetoric of Temporality', which might fairly be said to have been one of the most influential articles,

---

[16] Fairchild, 251.   [17] *Romantic Cruxes*, 21.

at least in literary affairs, of the century. De Man's career was unusual in many ways, not least in that he was already a figure of major significance (aside from his journalistic articles on the Continent) before he had published very much. His first book, *Blindness and Insight*, did not appear until 1971, by which time he was already Professor of Comparative Literature and French at Yale, having previously been a professor at Johns Hopkins, and before that at Cornell, where he had also, in a special arrangement, held a chair at Zurich.

To be sure, despite the early absence of published books, De Man had never been an idle man. His academic career was delayed by the exigencies of wartime, but once he landed at Harvard as a student, his reputation rose rapidly, fuelled by word of mouth reports of great things to come. In 1989 the University of Minnesota Press published a posthumous collection of twenty-five of his essays, edited by Lindsay Waters, and called *Critical Writings 1953–1978*. These essays, many of them reviews, not only reveal the sophistication that was always one of De Man's trade marks, but testify as well to his intense intellectual activity prior to *Blindness and Insight*. Still further, they reveal that his favourite vehicle of publication was the article. *Blindness and Insight* itself is a collection of articles, as is the important later volume called *The Rhetoric of Romanticism*. Even the book of 1979 called *Allegories of Reading: Figural Language in Rousseau, Nietzsche, Rilke, and Proust*, is in its structure a loose collection of articles.

That an article, 'The Rhetoric of Temporality', should have borne so much of the early fame of De Man is therefore not unfitting. It was published in 1969, in a volume containing distinguished work by figures such as Gombrich, and it made De Man widely known to the international intellectual public as a thinker of deep culture and dazzling sophistication. It remains fully capable of bearing the weight of severe attack.

The article treats of allegory and symbol, with a reversal of the traditional preference for symbol. Allegory is now raised to the theoretical heights. As to why De Man so much preferred allegory, the answer is perhaps to be gleaned from a consideration of his personal history. Since the revelation of his tarnished past as a Nazi sympathizer, commentators have frequently—and one thinks, justifiably—sought in that past explanations for some of his theoretical emphases, not least his theoretical assertion of the impossibility of final and decided meaning. Certainly, his emphasis on Nietzsche's apotheosis of the role of forgetting in human life seems to relate to such matters also. Likewise, the epigraph from Proust that appears at the beginning of *Blindness and Insight* takes on added poignancy in the context of De Man's Nazi past: 'Cette perpétuelle erreur, qui est précisément la "vie" . . .'.

So too with De Man's emphasis on allegory. For allegory above all witnesses a disjunction. One line of meaning or statement is already in existence, and a parallel line of meaning supervenes, with a darkening of the first line, a making it absent in the statement at hand, and a focusing of overt attention on the sole presence of the second. In the double allegories of *The Faerie Queene*, Gloriana, in the poem, stands for glory, outside of and prior to the poem, and allegorizes as well Queen Elizabeth, also outside of and prior to the poem. But only Gloriana is spoken of. To extrapolate allegorical considerations for De Man's life, his Nazi period was outside of and prior to his American academic career. Only the academic career was present to others, and presumably uppermost in De Man's own mind. But the earlier reality was always there, though absent, and indissolubly connected with the meaning of the present reality.

Of course, allegory reigns not just in De Man's theoretical pantheon, but at other times than the Romantic era was considered an urgent intellectual form. It dominated in the medieval world. Saying that 'Symbolism is a mode of thought, but allegory is a mode of expression',[18] C. S. Lewis, in *The Allegory of Love*, notes that

Whatever the causal order may be, it is plain that to fight against 'Temptation' is also to explore the inner world; and it is scarcely less plain that to do so is to be already on the verge of allegory. We cannot speak, perhaps we can hardly think, of an 'inner conflict' without a metaphor; and every metaphor is an allegory in little.[19]

Elsewhere Lewis urges that allegory was less mechanical and rigid in its Spenserian usages than later conceivings would have it. He says:

The allegory or 'inner meaning' of *The Faerie Queene* is generally regarded as twofold: a 'moral' or 'philosophical' allegory, and a 'historical' or 'political' allegory. The first is clear, certain, essential; the second obscure, often doubtful, and poetically of little importance. Spenser himself in his prefatory 'Letter' to Raleigh has told us that Gloriana, the Faerie Queene, means (in a certain sense) Queen Elizabeth; James I complained that Duessa was obviously Mary Queen of Scots. . . . After Spenser allegory became, till quite modern times, merely a sort of literary toy, as it is in Addison's or Johnson's essays. Spenser was the last poet who could use the old language seriously and who had an audience that understood it.

They understood it because they had been brought up to it. We shall understand it best (though this may seem paradoxical) by not trying too hard to understand it. Many things—such as loving, going to sleep, or behaving unaffectedly—are done worst when we try hardest to do them. Allegory is not a puzzle.[20]

Lewis also notes that 'the poetry of symbolism does not find its greatest expression in the Middle Ages at all, but rather in the time of the

---

[18] Lewis, *Allegory*, 48. [19] Ibid. 60. [20] Lewis, 98–9.

romantics; and this, again is significant of the profound difference that separates it from allegory'.[21]

But De Man, notwithstanding, boldly enters into the sanctum of symbolism—'the time of the romantics'—and, as it were, harrows it forth. 'The symbol', he says, 'in the post-romantic sense of the terms, appears more and more as a special case of figural language in general, a special case that can lay no claim to historical or philosophical priority over other figures.'[22] His statement, however, in demoting symbol, does not heed Lewis's distinction whereby only allegory is a mode of expression—or 'figural language'. Symbol, on the contrary, said Lewis, is 'a mode of thought'. The difference, as will presently appear, has fateful consequences for the validity of De Man's position.

Certainly his view is radically divergent from what the most theoretically-minded of the Romantics themselves believed. As counterpart to his distinctions between imagination and fancy, between reason and understanding, Coleridge produced an almost equally well known 'desynonymization' of symbol and allegory:

Now an Allegory is but a translation of abstract notions into a picture-language which is itself nothing but an abstraction from objects of the senses; the principal being more worthless even than its phantom proxy, both alike unsubstantial, and the former shapeless to boot. On the other hand a Symbol . . . is characterized by a translucence of the Special in the Individual or of the General in the Especial or of the Universal in the General. Above all by the translucence of the Eternal through and in the Temporal. It always partakes of the Reality which it renders intelligible, and while it enunciates the whole, abides itself as a living part in that Unity, of which it is the representative.[23]

Elsewhere Coleridge specifically indicates the structural difference between symbol and allegory. 'The Symbolical', he says in a note,

cannot perhaps be better defined, in distinction from the Allegorical, than that it is always itself a *part* of that of the whole of which it is representative—Here comes a *Sail*—that is, a Ship, is a symbolical Expression—Behold our Lion, when we speak of some gallant Soldier, is allegorical—of most importance to our own present subject, that the latter cannot be other than spoken consciously, while in the former it is very possible that *the general truth* represented may be working unconsciously in the Poet's mind during the construction of the symbol—yet proves itself by being produced out of his own mind, as the Don Quixote out of the perfectly sane mind of Cervantes.[24]

[21] Lewis, *Allegory*, 46.   [22] De Man, 176.
[23] *Lay Sermons*, 30.   [24] *Notebooks*, iii. 4503.

It was stressed above that allegory always witnesses a disjunction, but symbol, by being a part of the whole that it represents, does not. As Coleridge says at the conclusion of the note just presented, 'The advantage of symbolical writing over allegory' is 'that it presumes no disjunction of Faculty—simple *predomination*.' That distinction will be important for what follows in this chapter, as will also Coleridge's insistence on the role of the unconscious mind in the formation of symbol.

In Germany similar differentiations were current, and there too symbol was elevated high above allegory. Both Schelling and Creuzer, even Wilhelm von Humboldt, subscribed to such a differentiation, but it was perhaps Goethe who was most influential in its enunciation. Late in life he formulated a final definition:

Symbol transfers the appearance into the idea, the idea into an image, in such a way that the idea remains always infinitely active and unattainable, and, even if expressed in all languages, remains in fact inexpressible.

Allegory transforms the appearance into the concept, the concept into an image, in such a way that the concept is forever delineated in the image and completely fixed and expressed there.[25]

De Man, on the contrary, argues that symbol, rather than being superior to allegory, is lower than allegory and is, in fact, a conception of little value at all:

After such otherwise divergent studies as those of E. R. Curtius, of Erich Auerbach, of Walter Benjamin, and of H.-G. Gadamer, we can no longer consider the supremacy of the symbol as a 'solution' to the problem of metaphorical diction.[26]

But 'the problem' exists only in De Man's postulates, as does the necessity of its 'solution', and indeed both problem and solution are characteristic of De Man's way throughout his work, where nodes and crises elsewhere not troublesome are repeatedly addressed.

To be sure, De Man's is a sophisticated intelligence, and his views warrant serious attention. Yet a large part of his position on the relative status of allegory and symbol seems, as partly indicated in the passage above, to rest on three twentieth-century sources: one the historical discussion of symbol and allegory in Gadamer's *Wahrheit und Methode*, another, the book on German tragic drama by Walter Benjamin, and the third, Angus Fletcher's work on allegory. Gadamer is in part summarized:

---

[25] Goethe, ix. 532.   [26] De Man, 176.

The subjectivity of experience is preserved when it is translated into language; the world is then no longer seen as a configuration of entities that designate a plurality of distinct and isolated meanings, but as a configuration of symbols ultimately leading to a total, single, and universal meaning. This appeal to the infinity of a totality constitutes the main attraction of the symbol as opposed to allegory, a sign that refers to one specific meaning and thus exhausts its suggestive potentialities once it has been deciphered.[27]

Fletcher is not summarized, but if one looks into his book, the following passage presents itself early:

The word 'symbol' in particular has become a banner for confusion, since it lends itself to a falsely evaluative function whenever it is used to mean 'good' ('symbolic') poetry as opposed to 'bad' ('allegorical') poetry. . . . A critic may say of *The Castle* or *The Trial* . . . that they are 'mythic', and then proceed to read them . . . as the purest sort of allegory.[28]

Though that passage is not cited by De Man, one may perhaps be justified in assuming that it underlies his position. Not only did Fletcher's *Allegory: The Theory of a Symbolic Mode*, which was published five years before De Man's article, substantially broaden the reference of the term 'allegory', and enhance its prestige as well, but also De Man quotes Coleridge on symbol not from a Coleridgean context but from Fletcher's book.[29]

In any event, in the interests of 'temporality' (that is, that allegory is always found in narrative sequences that indicate movement in time) De Man decisively raises allegory above symbol: 'The prevalence of allegory always corresponds to the unveiling of an authentic temporal destiny.'[30] If De Man's own two sequences of life do in fact stand behind his views on allegory, then his great prestige as a theorist of literature in the United States might reasonably be thought of as 'the unveiling of an authentic temporal destiny'. He continues his emphasis on temporality as the realm of allegory (another commentator says succinctly: 'Allegory is successive, the symbol simultaneous'[31]):

In the world of the symbol it would be possible for the image to coincide with the substance, since the substance and its representation do not differ in their being but only in their extension: they are part and whole of the same set of categories. Their relationship is one of simultaneity, which, in truth, is spatial in kind, and in which the intervention of time is merely a matter of contingency, whereas, in the world of allegory, time is the ordinary constitutive category.[32]

[27] De Man, 174.   [28] Fletcher, 14.   [29] De Man, 177, nn. 9–11.
[30] Ibid. 190.   [31] Todorov, 218.   [32] De Man, 190.

What De Man here says about the simultaneity of symbol as contrasted to the temporality of allegory is co-ordinate with what others have seen about symbol as well. As a commentator on Coleridge's use of symbol asks:

What is there in his view of reality that allows him to see 'one Life within us and abroad,' to assert implicitly that a given reality, whether material or spiritual, is essentially linked with all other reality—that we live in a world of symbols, and therefore of symbolic knowledge? The answer lies in what we may call his principle of the 'consubstantiality' of all being.[33]

But where, for De Man, allegory is summoned in conjunction with the Heideggerian up-market term 'authentic', symbol is invoked in conjunction with the denigrative Sartrean formula of 'bad faith': 'we tried to show that the term "symbol" had in fact been substituted for that of "allegory" in an act of ontological bad faith.'[34]

De Man may here specifically be speaking of Friedrich Schlegel, whom he has summoned to buttress his historical contention (he concedes the need to deal 'in a historical manner before actual theorization can start'[35]):

When the term 'allegory' continues to appear in the writers of the period, such as Friedrich Schlegel, or later in Solger or E. T. H. Hoffmann, one should not assume that its use is merely a matter of habit, devoid of deeper meaning. Between 1800 and 1832, under the influence of Creuzer and Schelling, Friedrich Schlegel substitutes the word 'symbolic' for 'allegorical' in the oft-quoted passage of the 'Gespräch über die Poesie': 'alle Schönheit ist Allegorie. Das Höchste kann man eben weil es unaussprechlich ist, nur allegorisch sagen.' But can we deduce from this, with Schlegel's editor Hans Eichner, that Schlegel 'simply uses allegory where we would nowadays say symbol'? It could be shown that, precisely because it suggests a disjunction between the way in which the world appears in reality and the way it appears in language, the word 'allegory' fits the general problematic of the 'Gespräch', whereas the word 'symbol' becomes an alien presence in the later version.[36]

But against this contention of De Man, one can point to a consideration grounded more deeply in comparative texts. Schlegel explicitly says that 'the highest thing can be said only allegorically, precisely because it is inexpressible (*unaussprechlich*)'. Clearly the word 'inexpressible' is a key term; it is also the very word that Goethe, in the passage quoted above, uses to describe the necessary fate of the idea conveyed by a symbol: the symbolic idea must remain 'inexpressible' (*unaussprechlich*). That being

---

[33] Barth, 5.   [34] De Man, 194.
[35] Ibid.   [36] Ibid. 175–6.

so, how then can Schlegel's substitution of 'symbol' for 'allegory' in his own central passage be seen as anything other than a bringing of his own insistence into alignment with the distinction established by Goethe? That distinction was vigorously proselytized by Goethe, as we can see by his introducing a man named Martin Wagner to Schelling in 1803, with the statement that 'if you can make clear to him the difference between allegorical and symbolical treatment, you will be his benefactor, because so much turns on that axis'.[37]

Such a conclusion is bulwarked by the fact that Kant, who really was the first to focus authoritative attention on symbol, had said that 'all our knowledge of God is purely symbolic',[38] and that Schlegel says the very same thing, using the—for him— interchangeable word 'allegory'. As a commentator, siding very much with Eichner's view as to Schlegel's use of the term, and not at all with De Man's understanding of the issue, says of Schlegel's formula:

An unpublished note goes so far as to establish mutual solidarity between the indirect or allegorical mode of expression and the divine tenor of such a message: the meaning of allegory necessarily participates in the divine (here we must remember that for Friedrich Schlegel the term 'allegory' has a generic meaning and is not opposed to 'symbol,' as it is for the other romantics). 'Every allegory signifies God, and one cannot speak of God save allegorically'.[39]

Indeed, other things about De Man's passage just quoted and elsewhere in his discourse suggest that, though both his intelligence and his sophistication are noteworthy, his actual knowledge of Romanticism may not go so deep as surface considerations might indicate. For instance, he refers to Hoffmann as 'E. T. H. Hoffmann'. The name, of course, is E. T. A. Hoffmann; but to make the correction is not entirely the niggling matter it may seem to be. One supposes, at first, that the substitution of the H. for the A. is merely a misprint. But no, later in the essay De Man invokes Hoffmann again, and the mistake persists: 'We mentioned Hamann; in Germany alone, the names of Friedrich Schlegel, Friedrich Solger, E. T. H. Hoffmann, and Kierkegaard would be obvious additions to the list.'[40]

So the substitution of H. for A. in Hoffmann's initials is a palpable error. But more than that, it is an error of the surface that masks misapprehension of matters farther down. For Hoffmann's initials in his given name were actually not E. T. A. but E. T. W. The W. stood for

---

[37] Fuhrmans, 32.   [38] *Kant*, v. 353.
[39] Todorov, 193–4.   [40] De Man, 192.

'Wilhelm'. What happened is that Hoffmann, a man of deep musical culture, decided to offer homage to his beloved Mozart by changing his name. So he changed the 'Wilhelm' to 'Amadeus', and henceforth his name was presented to the world not as E. T. W. Hoffmann but as E. T. A. Hoffmann.

If the depth of De Man's knowledge of Romanticism is somewhat suspect, so is his understanding of symbol. The ontological bad faith charged in a substitution of symbol for allegory, indeed, seems rather to inhere in his own identification of symbol with 'metaphorical diction'. On the contrary, symbol has historically been a conception in the service of theological concerns, and only secondarily in the service of literary concerns. Coleridge, for instance, in the famous distinction between symbol and allegory quoted above, is referring not to literary theory, as a non-contextual reading might suggest, but to religious faith: 'Faith is either to be buried in the dead letter, or its name and honors usurped by a counterfeit product of the mechanical understanding, which in the blindness of self-complacency confounds SYMBOLS with ALLEGORIES.'[41] To understand how entirely Coleridge knew what he was doing, one may simply look at some titles from the bibliography of a modern work on early Christianity:

B. Capelle, *Le symbole romain au second siècle* . . .
B. Capelle, *Les origines du symbole romain* . . .
F. T. Dölger, *Die Eingliederung des Taufsymbols in den Taufvollzug* . . .
G. L. Dossetti, *Il simbolo di Nicea e di Constantinopoli* . . .
A. Harnack, *Apostolisches Symbolum* . . .
A. Harnack, *Konstantinopolitanisches Symbol* . . .
J. Lebon, *Les anciens symboles à Chalcédoine* . . .
H. Lietzmann, *Symbolstudien* . . .
A. M. Ritter, *Das Konzil von Konstantinopel und sein Symbol* . . .
I. Ortiz de Urbina, *El simbolo Niceno* . . .[42]

In view of Coleridge's overriding interest in theological matters ('If there be any two subjects which have in the very depth of my Nature interested me, it has been the Hebrew & Christian Theology, & the Theology of Plato'[43]), it may be hardly surprising that for him the theological use of symbol always took higher place than the literary use; but for us, as literary critics, frequent reminders of this fact may be necessary:

[41] *Lay Sermons*, 30.
[42] Kelly, p. x.
[43] *Collected Letters*, ii. 866.

There is, believe me! a wide difference between *symbolical* and *allegorical*. If I say, that the Flesh and Blood (Corpus *noumenon*) of the Incarnate Word is Power and Life, I say likewise that this mysterious Power and Life are *verily* and *actually* the Flesh and Blood of Christ. *They* are the Allegorizers, who turn the 6th c. of the Gospel according to St. John . . . *they*, I repeat, are the Allegorizers who moralize these hard sayings, these high words of Mystery, into an hyperbolical Metaphor *per Catachresin*.[44]

Such defining attachment of symbol to theology dictates two effects for its use in literary matters. First, it ensures that symbol has an ontological, not a critical function. Symbol, as Lewis said, is a 'mode of thought', and the object of that thought is a mode of being. Only allegory is 'a mode of expression'. Symbol cannot be pressed into service as a tool of criticism: allegory is unravelled by criticism, symbol is not. As Gadamer points out:

Allegory originally belonged to the sphere of talk, of the logos, and is therefore a rhetorical or hermeneutical figure. Instead of what is actually meant, something else, more tangible, is said, but in such a way as to suggest the other. Symbol, however is not limited to the sphere of the logos, for a symbol is not related by its meaning to another meaning, but its own sensuous nature has 'meaning'.[45]

Judging by the number and variety of critical efforts to interpret their meaning, there may be no more palpably symbolic poems in all of English literature than 'Kubla Khan' and 'The Ancient Mariner'. And yet none of the multitudinous readings supplants the pregnant statement of either poem, or is even necessary to it; both poems generate their urgency from hidden sources, despite all the critical ingenuity lavished on them; both glow gorgeously and mysteriously, and their light does not fade (and it is intriguing that for both poems the most nearly persuasive interpretive readings tend to be theological and unspecific, rather than literary and tightly verbal).

Accordingly, when Angus Fletcher, in the passage quoted above, points out that in the act of critical analysis only allegory comes into play, he does not impeach the validity of symbol. The critic who reads '*The Castle* or *The Trial* . . . as the purest sort of allegory' is doing just that; he is not, however, dismissing the possible symbolic meaning of his texts, which is presented to the mind through a combination of intuition and logic, not through criticism.

Secondly, the theological primacy of symbol dictates, against De Man, that symbol does not reside in the realm of 'metaphorical diction'. The 'Symbolical', as Coleridge on the contrary insists, is 'distinguished *toto genere* from the Allegoric and the Metaphorical'.[46] Coleridge's linking of the allegorical and the metaphorical is here co-ordinate with Lewis's observation, quoted above, that 'every metaphor is an allegory in little'. Again, Coleridge speaks against apprehensions by which 'in the mysterious Appurtenants and Symbols of Redemption (Regeneration, Grace, the Eucharist, and Spiritual Communion) the realities will be evaporated into metaphors'.[47]

The key word there is 'realities'. The 'purpose of a Metaphor', says Coleridge, 'is to illustrate a something less known by a partial identification of it with some other thing better understood';[48] but a symbol 'partakes of the Reality which it renders intelligible; and while it enunciates the whole, abides itself as a living part in that Unity, of which it is the representative'.[49] In no event is symbol coincident with metaphor; it is rather a 'medium between *Literal* and *Metaphorical*'.[50] Furthermore, it, as well as allegory, participates in the temporal, despite De Man's efforts to relegate it to the spatial alone. Symbol is characterized 'above all by the translucence of the Eternal through and in the Temporal'.[51]

In general, it might be said that the unsatisfactoriness of De Man's analysis arises from a confusion of symbol with 'rhetoric' and 'figural language'. Though in its literary appearances symbol is compatible with the rhetorical figure of synecdoche, it stems from different roots and is an entity of a different kind. The symbol was in its origins a physical thing, a *symbolon*, not a rhetorical trope. It was a fragment or part broken off from a larger physical whole in order to accredit the bearer when the part was recognized as belonging to that whole.[52]

Coleridge was well aware of this breaking of the physical thing as the origin of symbol. As he says:

Συμβολον. First & simplest, as used by Plato, Symposium, Cap. XVI. ad initium, one composed of two. To break a tablet in two Halves, as our Sweethearts the crooked Sixpence, was an ancient custom of the Greeks—The Half was Tessera. & συμβολον, tessera hospitalis. Thence, whatever in the progress of refinement was substituted for the tessera—and thus, a contract, commercial Treaty, Law of Alliance &c.—Thence, any Pledge as in buying & selling. Thence, eminently, a Ring: that being the Pledge or Ticket given in pledge of the Money contributed by each Guest in a Picnic or Common Feast. . . . Lastly, by progressive Generalization συμβολον was used as σημειον—and as a sign is antithetic to the essence or

---

[46] *Aids to Reflection*, 254 n. [47] Ibid. 294.
[48] Ibid. 312. [49] *Lay Sermons*, 30.
[50] Ibid. [51] Ibid.
[52] See e.g. Max Schlesinger, 'Die Geschichte des Symbolbegriffs in der Philosophie', *Archiv für Geschichte der Philosophie*, 22 (1909), 72.

thing itself, συμβολον became = a *word*, or words; & a representative Image—
Finally, the highest sense of συμβολον rests on the two first senses of
συμβαλλειν—viz. unexpected Co-incidence, & conjectural Deciphering.[53]

That evolving spectrum of pertinences for the conception of *symbolon* is
the reason why the term *symbol* can with propriety refer to the deepest of
Christian mysteries, on the one hand, and, secondarily, to liminal usages of
literary language on the other.

The originating physicality of *symbolon* pointed to by Coleridge has
never left the literarily developed conception of symbol, and even where
nothing physical seems present, physicality always lurks beneath the
surface. As a recent commentator has said:

Since the use of the word 'symbolism' in literary applications dates only from the
end of the eighteenth century, the biblical language concerned would have been
described before then as allegorical or anagogical and the word 'symbol' would
have meant a *thing* standing for something else, like a cross or crescent or
alphabetical letter.[54]

Indeed, the symbol has never been restricted to structures of language. To
take an example from the quotidian, the advertising line, 'a diamond is
forever', is a symbolic statement. The 'translucence of the Eternal' shines
in the word 'forever', as does the idea of unchanging fidelity in a spiritual
relationship that the diamond itself—a physical object, not a figure of
rhetoric—symbolizes by its own permanence and purity. Furthermore,
the symbolizing function made explicit by the slogan occurs without the
slogan; when the diamond is presented as a ring, the whole meaning of
permanence and purity is indicated by the part, that is, by the diamond
itself, without the mediation of language.

The point must be emphasized. Symbol has no necessary connection
with the realm of rhetoric. For instance, the present author not long ago
was driving to a dinner party and noticed a large lighted billboard virtually
empty except for a single representation: a three-pointed silver star
enclosed in a circle. Without any mediation of language whatever, an
entire story was told. The representation was of a physical object: the
symbol by which the Mercedes-Benz company represents itself. The
symbol is commonly seen as the hood ornament on a Mercedes
automobile; it is a physical object that is part of a larger physical object,
and when present totally implies that larger object—a true *pars pro toto*.
Furthermore, not only does the symbol of the three-pointed star invoke

[53] *Notebooks*, iv. 4831.
[54] Piper, 15.

the large physical reality of the automobile itself, but it invokes, as well, an even larger entity—all the intangible and non-physical attributes of that automobile, and of other automobiles by the same company: quality, reliability, luxury, durability, prestige. All those matters were ineluctably invoked by the single representation of the three-pointed star, which, in truth, was why it could be so starkly successful as an advertisement.

In thus bridging the cleft between material thing and intangible idea, and between part and whole, the symbol from its inception has been a unit of meaning (not a figure of language) with an integrative charge directed towards the whole of reality. As Goethe put it in largest compass: 'Everything that happens is symbol, and while it perfectly represents itself, points to other matters [*das übrige*].'[55] A modern commentator makes the same point about the ultimate largeness of symbol: 'it is clear that symbol potentially encompasses the depth of man himself and the height and breadth of all the world, in and out of time. Symbolic knowledge reaches out to all that man can know.'[56]

The specific symbol, in contrast with symbolic knowledge, always suggests a larger whole of which it is either a physical part or a compelling indicator. What empowers the symbolic process is what Coleridge calls 'the great law of the imagination, that a likeness in part tends to become a likeness of the whole'.[57] So anxious was he to bulwark the point that he sometimes supplies incongruous examples, which aside from dramatizing the relation of part to whole, seem almost bizarre:

Must not of necessity the FIRST MAN be a SYMBOL of Mankind, in the fullest force of the word, Symbol, rightly defined—viz. *A Symbol is a sign included in the Idea, which it represents*: ex gr. an actual *part* chosen to represent the *whole*, as a lip with a chin prominent is a Symbol of Man.[58]

However unsufficing the example, the definition itself is elegant.

It is, to reiterate, always the nature of the symbol both to represent itself and to point to other matters. The three-pointed star presents itself, but it also 'enunciates the whole' of the Mercedes automobile and the Mercedes reputation; it 'abides itself as a living part in that Unity, of which it is the representative'. It is 'a sign included in the Idea, which it represents'.

Such necessary and always-present intertwinement points to a crucial truth about symbol. The symbol is fated by its ontological structure always to inhabit the realm of the vague. That noetic location arises from the eternal duplicity of its halfness. Thus, even when the symbolic object

[55] Goethe, xxi. 286.   [56] Barth, 7.
[57] *Friend*, i. 146.   [58] *Aids to Reflection*, 254 n.

is clear and distinct, its complementary extension of meaning can never be so, and a miasmic indistinctness consequently settles over the symbol in its total meaning. The three-pointed star, for example, is clear and demarcated in its physical structure; when it functions as a symbol, however, that clarity is made tenebrous by the vague and imprecise extensions into the prestige, reliability, performance, and luxury of the Mercedes products that are symbolized. The symbol can never escape the realm of the vague.

What is conveyed immediately and totally by the physical object of the three-pointed star, or its representation on a billboard, is described discursively by Gadamer's formulation:

A symbol is the coincidence of sensible appearance and supra-sensible meaning, and this coincidence is, like the original significance of the Greek symbolon and its continuance in terminological usage of the various religious denominations, not a subsequent coordination, as in the use of signs, but the union of two things that belong to each other.... The possibility of the instantaneous and total coincidence of the appearance with the infinite in a religious ceremony on the basis of this tension assumes that it is an inner harmony between the finite and the infinite that fills the symbol with meaning. Thus the religious form of the symbol corresponds exactly to its original nature, the dividing of what is one and reuniting it again.[59]

De Man's apparent unawareness of, or at least lack of emphasis on, the secondary nature of literary symbol is not shared by an earlier praiser of allegory and denigrator of symbol. In 1928, in his *Ursprung des deutschen Trauerspiels*, Walter Benjamin in fact used as the very ground of his rejection the charge that literary symbol was an illegitimate substitute for theological symbol:

For over a hundred years the philosophy of art has been subjected to the tyranny of a usurper who came to power in the chaos which followed in the wake of romanticism. The striving on the part of the romantic aestheticians after a resplendent but ultimately non-committal knowledge of an absolute has secured a place in the most elementary theoretical debates about art for a notion of the symbol which has nothing more than the name in common with the genuine notion. The latter, which is the one used in the field of theology, could never shed that sentimental twilight which has become more and more impenetrable since the end of early romanticism.[60]

[59] Gadamer, 69–70.
[60] Benjamin, 159–60.

Benjamin goes on to censure 'this illegitimate talk of the symbolic'[61] and notes that though its concept 'insists on the indivisible unity of form and content', actually it 'fails to do justice to content in formal analysis and to form in the aesthetics of content':[62]

For this always occurs whenever in the work of art the 'manifestation' of an 'idea' is declared a symbol. The unity of the material and the transcendental object, which constitutes the paradox of the theological symbol, is distorted into a relationship between appearance and essence. The introduction of this distorted conception of the symbol into aesthetics was a romantic and destructive extravagance which preceded the desolation of modern art criticism. As a symbolic construct the beautiful is supposed with the divine in an unbroken whole.[63]

Benjamin urges that allegory, in the context of a distinction between symbol and allegory, serves merely as a foil for symbol and therefore cannot reveal its own structure:

Simultaneously with its profane concept of the symbol, classicism develops its speculative counterpart, that of the allegorical. A genuine theory of the allegory did not, it is true, arise at that time, nor had there been one previously. It is nevertheless legitimate to describe the new concept of the allegorical as speculative because it was in fact adapted so as to provide the dark background against which the bright world of the symbol might stand out. . . . The symbolizing mode of thought around 1800 was so foreign to allegorical expression in its original form that the extremely isolated attempts at theoretical discussion are of no value as far as the investigation of allegory is concerned—although they are all the more symptomatic of the depth of the antagonism.[64]

But whereas Benjamin is undoubtedly right in saying that, for the Romantics, the conceiving of allegory was 'adapted so as to provide the dark background against which the bright world of the symbol might stand out'—we see illustrations of that truth in the paradigmatic passages from Coleridge and Goethe with which the present discussion commenced—it must also be said that not all the objection to allegory was simply to enhance symbol, but rather actually identified deficiencies in allegory itself. Thus Karl Philipp Moritz, in the 1780s, pointed out that it was an ineradicable characteristic of allegory always to diminish the refulgence of the actual statement under consideration:

If a work of art were to exist *only* to indicate something outside itself, it would become by that very token an *accessory thing*—whereas the work of art must always, where beauty is concerned, itself be the principal thing.—If allegory

[61] Benjamin, 160.   [62] Ibid.
[63] Ibid.   [64] Ibid. 161.

appears, it must therefore always remain subordinate, and come as if by chance; it never constitutes the essential or the proper value of a work of art.[65]

Allegory, as noted previously, always exists as a disjunction. There must be a leap from the presented temporal line to the absent temporal line. Symbol, too, indicates something more than its presented object; but symbol, as the definitions of Coleridge show, by being a *part* of the absence invoked, never abandons its centrality as the object of attention. It does in truth constitute 'the essential or the proper value of a work of art'.

But where Coleridge had said that 'Allegory is but a translation of abstract notions into a picture-language which is itself nothing but an abstraction from objects of the senses', and where Goethe had said that 'allegory transforms the appearance into the concept, the concept into an image, in such a way that the concept is forever delimited in the image and completely fixed and expressed there', Benjamin on the contrary says that 'In the context of allegory, the image is only a signature, only the monogram of essence, not the essence itself in a mask'.[66] According to Benjamin, the German tragic drama of the baroque is peculiarly suited to allegory:

Whereas in the symbol destruction is idealized and the transfigured face of nature is fleetingly revealed in the light of redemption, in allegory the observer is confronted with the *facies hippocratica* of history as a petrified, primordial landscape. Everything about history that, from the very beginning, has been untimely, sorrowful, unsuccessful, is expressed in a face—or rather in a death's head. And although such a thing lacks all 'symbolic' freedom of expression, all classical proportion, all humanity—nevertheless, this is the form in which man's subjection to nature is most obvious and it significantly gives rise not only to the enigmatic question of the nature of human existence as such, but also of the biographical historicity of the individual. This is the heart of the allegorical way of seeing, of the baroque, secular explanation of history as the Passion of the world: its importance resides solely in the stations of its decline. The greater the significance, the greater the subjection to death, because death digs most deeply the jagged line of demarcation between physical nature and significance. But if nature has always been subject to the power of death, it is also true that it has always been allegorical.[67]

There is much in that passage to connect matters. Benjamin's insistence that nature 'has always been allegorical' is not structurally at odds with Coleridge's insistence that allegory is 'an abstraction from objects of the

[65] Todorov, 162.
[66] Benjamin, 214.
[67] Ibid. 166.

senses', though the evaluation of the concession is entirely different in the two thinkers. De Man's formula, that 'the prevalence of allegory always corresponds to . . . an authentically temporal destiny',[68] seems to find its strong precursor in Benjamin's 'question of the nature of human existence as such, but also of the biographical historicity of the individual'.

And yet neither Benjamin, nor his successor De Man, seems really to grasp the cognitive structure of symbol. It is interesting to note that neither gives adequate recognition to its context in the defining cluster of Romantic criteria. Benjamin finds no place for symbol in German baroque tragedy, and therefore can for the most part simply abandon its Romantic connections. De Man explicitly tries to divorce it from its place in the Romantic context, even going so far as to make the extraordinary and untenable claim that

We are led, in conclusion, to a historical scheme that differs entirely from the customary picture. The dialectical relationship between subject and object is no longer the central statement of romantic thought, but this dialectic is now located entirely in the temporal relationships that exist within a system of allegorical signs.[69]

De Man does take note of 'the tendency shared by all commentators to define the romantic image as a relationship between mind and nature, between subject and object'.[70] But he argues that 'if the dialectic between subject and object does not designate the main romantic experience, but only one passing moment in a dialectic, and a negative moment at that, since it represents a temptation that has to be overcome, then the entire historical and philosophical pattern changes a great deal'.[71]

No better example could be summoned as text for the present discussion, or indeed for the present book, both of which are concerned with the qualitative distortions introduced even by the most subtle recent commentators. The dialectic of subject and object is intrinsic to human awareness and therefore cannot be restricted to Romantic thought. William James, late in the nineteenth century, takes it simply as a given: 'The dualism of Object and Subject and their pre-established harmony are what the psychologist as such must assume, whatever ulterior monistic philosophy he may, as an indidivual who has the right also to be a metaphysician, have in reserve. I hope that this general point is now made clear, so that we may leave it, and descend to some distinctions of detail.'[72]

[68] De Man, 190. [69] Ibid. 191.
[70] Ibid. 178. [71] Ibid. 188.
[72] James, 216.

Nevertheless, and unequivocally against De Man, the dialectic of subject
and object does figure in Romantic thought importantly and specifically.
It figures in many forms. Robert Langbaum has seen it as defining the very
nature of Romantic poetry: 'The romantic lyric or poem of experience . . .
is both subjective and and objective. The poet talks about himself by
talking about an object; and he talks about an object by talking about
himself.'[73]

Philosophically, an abstract dialectic of subject and object, arising from
Kant's first *Kritik*, totally dominated German systematic thought, and it is
intensely presented in the writings of Fichte, of Schelling, and of Hegel.
But the dialectic of subject and object was ubiquitous. For a single locus as
hilarious as it is pregnant, consider Carlyle's description of Coleridge: 'I
still recollect his "object" and "subject", terms of continual recurrence in
the Kantean province; and how he sang and snuffled them into "om-m-m-
ject" and "sum-m-mject," with a kind of solemn shake or quaver, as he
rolled along.'[74] Again:

His talk, alas, was distinguished, like himself, by irresolution: it disliked to be
troubled with conditions, abstinences, definite fulfilments;—loved to wander at its
own sweet will, and make its auditor and his claims and humble wishes a mere
passive bucket for itself! He had knowledge about many things and topics, much
curious reading; but generally all topics led him, after a pass or two, into the high
seas of theosophic philosophy, the hazy infinitude of Kantean transcendentalism,
with its 'sum-m-mjects' and 'om-m-mjects.'[75]

Divorced from such anecdotal humour, the dialectic of subject and object,
in the form of the interplay of 'I am' and 'it is', occupied the largest portion
of Coleridge's thought for almost forty years.[76] It was also to be the chief
topic of Wordsworth's great philosophical poem, which was to chant 'the
spousal verse | Of this great consummation'.[77] Wordsworth's poetic voice
was to proclaim

> How exquisitely the individual Mind
> (And the progressive powers perhaps no less
> Of the whole species) to the external World
> Is fitted;—and how exquisitely, too—
> Theme this but little heard of among men—
> The external World is fitted to the Mind.[78]

But the distinction is everywhere. Schelling, for an example quite at

---

[73] Langbaum, 53.   [74] *Carlyle*, xi. 55.
[75] Ibid. 56.   [76] See CPT, chs. 2 and 3.
[77] Wordsworth, *Poems*, v. 4–5.   [78] Ibid. 5.

random, said that 'The absolute identity cannot infinitely perceive itself
without infinitely positing itself as subject and object. This proposition is
self evident.'[79] Again, and equally at random, Coleridge, in meditating on
the difference between ground and condition, says:

> The *ground* of Consciousness, i.e. that which every act of Consciousness supposes,
> is the Identity (or Indifference) of Object and Subject; but the indispensable
> Condition of becoming conscious is the Division or Differencing of the *Subject* and
> *Object*—.[80]

And for still a third example to demonstrate how completely De Man's
opinion misses the mark, Steffens, in his *Grundzüge der philosophischen
Naturwissenschaft* of 1806, says: 'Perception itself is posited as a
subjective, and since it is an identity of subjective and objective, posited
simultaneously as a not-subjective.'[81] He says, yet again, that

> Mit dem Gegensatz von Subjekt und Objekt ist die erste Richtung, mit dieser die
> entgegengesetzte, und der Entgegensetzung der Gegensätze ihre wechselseitige
> Relativität, mit dieser Relativität aber so fort die Absolutheit der Einheit gesetzt.[82]

There is no need to draw more examples from the ocean available, for
the point is clear. In attempting to supply 'a historical scheme that differs
entirely from the customary picture', De Man does violence to the simple
truth of the situation. Furthermore, not only is the dialectic of subject and
object a corner-stone of the Romantic way of looking at the world, but it
and the other Romantic emphases are intertwined, a fact not satisfactorily
noticed by either De Man or Benjamin. Coleridge speaks of 'living *educts*
of the Imagination; of that reconciling and mediatory power, which
incorporating the Reason in Images of the Sense, and organizing (as it
were) the flux of the Senses by the permanence and self-circling energies
of the Reason, gives birth to a system of symbols, harmonious in
themselves, and consubstantial with the truths, of which they are the
conductors.'[83]

The intertwinement of imagination and symbol is taken up into the title
of J. Robert Barth's study of 1977, *The Symbolic Imagination: Coleridge
and the Romantic Tradition*, where it is pointed out that the imagination 'is
always for Coleridge the symbol-making and symbol-perceiving faculty'.[84]
Other intertwinements exist also. For a single instance, a Continental
commentator notes that

[79] *Schelling*, iv. 123.   [80] *Notebooks*, iv. 5276.
[81] *Steffens*, 2.   [82] Ibid. 24.
[83] *Lay Sermons*, 29.   [84] Barth, 6, 12.

The organic is therefore for Schelling an essential characteristic of symbol, which thereby fundamentally distinguishes itself from allegory. The symbol remains, in contrast to allegory, intimately bound up with the realm of organic nature. Where this reference to nature is not present, the true 'symbolic' character of an art work, according to Schelling, is lost.[85]

Allied with De Man's and Benjamin's unsatisfactory grasp of the dynamics of symbol's intertwinement with the other criteria of the Romantic complex is their dismissive understanding of symbol's cognitive structure. It is no accident that De Man repeatedly uses the word 'mystification' when his argument veers towards an assessment of the symbolic. 'It becomes a conflict between a conception of the self seen in its authentically temporal predicament and a defensive strategy that tries to hide from this negative self-knowledge. On the level of language the asserted superiority of the symbol over allegory, so frequent during the nineteenth century, is one of the forms taken by this tenacious self-mystification.'[86] Further, De Man says that

the lucidity of the pre-romantic writers does not persist. It does not take long for a symbolic conception of metaphorical language to establish itself everywhere, despite the ambiguities that persist in aesthetic theory and poetic practice. But this symbolical style will never be allowed to exist in serenity; since it is a veil thrown over a light one no longer wishes to perceive, it will never be able to gain an entirely good poetic conscience.[87]

Thus in calling for 'a historical de-mystification' of symbol, De Man reverts to a preference for 'the lucidity' of pre-romantic writers that in rejecting symbol is also rejecting the deep structure of Romanticism itself. Romanticism was profoundly involved with dreams, reveries, twilight states of consciousness[88]—all those 'petites perceptions' summoned by Leibniz against Locke.[89] Behind Locke there lay the criterion of the 'clear and distinct' enunciated by Descartes,[90] even though Locke in accepting

---

[85] Sørensen, 252.

[86] De Man, 191.

[87] Ibid.

[88] For a standard treatment of this important fact, see Albert Béguin, *L'Âme romantique et le rêve* (Paris: Librairie José Corti, 1939).

[89] *Leibniz*, v. 46–8.

[90] It is specifically against 'vn art confus & obscur, qui embarrasse l'esprit, au lieu d'vne science qui le cultiue' that Descartes formulates his four precepts of method: 'Le premier estoit de ne receuoir iamais aucune chose pour vraye, que ie ne la connusse euidemment estre telle: c'est a dire ... de ne comprendre rien de plus en mes iugemens, que ce qui se presenteroit si clairement & si distinctement a mon esprit, que ie n'eusse aucune occasion de le mettre en doute.' The 'clairement' and 'distinctement' criterion, as noted earlier in this book, was idiosyncratically and personally important to Descartes. It is invoked repeatedly in

the criterion testily refused to accept the phrase itself.[91]

It is that criterion, one realizes on re-perusing the passage from Angus Fletcher quoted above, that underlies the preference for allegory over symbol of which De Man is a late formulator. De Man is committed to 'lucidity', to clear and distinct ideas; by that controlling fact he can *a priori* have no sympathy for or understanding of the importance of symbol, which is thought's most distinctive offering to the realm of the vague. But a true Romantic such as Coleridge could ask: 'Whether or no the too great definiteness of Terms in any language may not consume too much of the vital & idea-creating force in distinct, clear, full made Images.'[92] Indeed, the Romantic poets and theorists, conditioned by Leibniz's *Nouveaux essais* and Rousseau's *Rêveries d'un promeneur solitaire*, felt at home, to utilize another concatenation by Coleridge, in states of 'shadowy half-being', of 'nascent Existence in the Twilight of Imagination, and just on the vestibule of Consciousness'.[93] De Quincey, too, formulates the Romantic tropism towards shadowy half-being: 'The machinery for dreaming planted in the human brain was not planted for nothing. That faculty, in alliance with the mystery of darkness, is the one great tube through which man communicates with the shadowy.'[94]

The obscurity and vagueness of symbol were, therefore, not seen by the Romantics as defects, even though, as Coleridge said, it might be 'hard to express that sense of the analogy or likeness of a Thing which enables a Symbol to represent it, so that we think of the Thing itself—& yet knowing that the Thing is not present to us'.[95] Far from trying to make lucid the indistinct aura of symbol, the Romantics cherished that indistinct aura. 'The more incommensurable and incomprehensible for the understanding a poetic product may be,' insisted Goethe, 'the better.'[96]

---

his work, and is invoked specifically in conjunction with the starting point of his thought, the cogito: 'Et ayant remarqué qu'il n'y a rien du tout en cecy: *ie pense, donc ie suis*, qui m'assure que ie dis la verité, sinon que ie voy tres clairement que, pour penser, il faut estre: ie iugay que ie pouuois prendre pour reigle generale, que les choses que nous conceuons fort clairement & fort distinctement sont toutes vrayes' (Descartes, *Œuvres*, 18, 33).

[91] '*Clear and distinct Ideas* are terms, which though familiar and frequent in Men's Mouths, I have reason to think every one, who uses, does not perfectly understand. . . . I have therefore in most places chose to put *determinate* or *determined*, instead of *clear* and *distinct*, as more likely to direct Men's thoughts to my meaning in this matter' (Locke, 12–13).

[92] *Notebooks*, i. 1016.   [93] *Collected Letters*, ii. 814.
[94] *De Quincey*, xiii. 335.   [95] *Notebooks*, ii. 2275.
[96] Goethe, xxiv. 636.

The clear and distinct is not favoured in nature over the realm of the vague; and as the present author has elsewhere observed:

It has been frequently pointed out, especially in recent years, that an actual critical process recognizes only allegory in its analyses, and that accordingly in the distinction between symbol and allegory so much favored by Romantic writers, the higher status accorded symbol would appear to be something of a mystification. In terms of what we have been saying about the numinous transfer of the predicates of soul, however, the seeming contradiction disappears. The whole point of symbol is not to open itself to critical analysis but precisely to defy such analysis: symbol strives to maintain, not dissipate, the aura of soul. 'True symbolism,' as Goethe says, is a 'living and momentary revelation of the impenetrable [*des Unerforschlichen*].' Symbolism, says Kant again, transfers 'our reflection upon an object of intuition to quite a new concept, and one with which perhaps no intuition can ever directly correspond. . . . All our knowledge of God is purely symbolic.' As Friedrich Creuzer noted in 1810, in the third chapter of the first book of the first part of his *Symbolik und Mythologie des alten Völker, besonders der Griechen*, 'If it is true, as the ancients understood, that the nature of symbol is precisely the dark and twilit, how can symbol deny its nature and be clear?' Allegory, he says, is like 'the luxuriantly spreading branches of a climbing plant,' but 'symbol is more like the half-closed bud, which locks in its calyx, undeveloped, the highest beauty.'[97]

In cherishing an aura of indistinctness, symbol protected a teleological function that moved towards the apprehension of a great and incomprehensible whole. This both De Man and Benjamin concede. De Man, summarizing Gadamer, says that 'the world is then no longer seen as a configuration of entitites that designate a plurality of distinct and isolated meanings, but as a configuration of symbols ultimately leading to a total, simple, and universal meaning. This appeal to the infinity of a totality constitutes the main attraction of the symbol as opposed to allegory.'[98] Benjamin, for his part, says that 'As a symbolic construct, the beautiful is supposed with the divine in an unbroken whole.'[99]

But for the Romantics, the way the symbol, despite its obscurity, indicates the whole is ultimately a cognitive structure of reason, not a rhetorical structure of mystification. Thus Coleridge, significantly, identifies as reason itself the symbolic progression from part to whole: 'The Reason first manifests itself in man by the *tendency* to the comprehension of all as one. We can neither rest in an infinite that is not at the same time a whole, nor in a whole that is not infinite.'[100] As the movement towards the whole is the hallmark of reason, so is the

---

[97] *Originality*, 186–7.   [98] De Man, 174.
[99] Benjamin, 160.   [100] *Lay Sermons*, 60.

apprehension of that whole the final task of reason. Coleridge speaks of 'that ultimate end of human Thought, and human Feeling, Unity and thereby the reduction of the Spirit to its Principle & Fountain, who alone is truly *one*'.[101] This end underlies all reason's efforts: 'Reason is the knowlege of the laws of the WHOLE considered as ONE.'[102]

If concern with the whole is the very nature of reason, then symbol's concern with the whole reveals itself as wholly participating in reason itself. Symbol cannot be a mystification. Rather it partakes of the highest cognitive efforts of the mind; its structure is one of cognitive synecdoche, not one of rhetorical mystification: 'It always partakes of the Reality which it renders intelligible; and while it enunciates the whole, abides itself as a living part in that Unity, of which it is the representative.'[103] Coleridge was undeviating in this insistence. In 1815, for instance, he applied a phrase from Phineas Fletcher's *Purple Island* to his concept of symbol: 'Symbols = "the whole, yet of the whole a part"'.[104] Again, in 1825, he speaks of 'Symbol, rightly defined—viz. *A Symbol is a sign included in the Idea, which it represents*: ex. gr. an actual *part* chosen to represent the *whole*'.[105]

But neither Benjamin nor De Man, nor for that matter, Gadamer, treats the involvement of symbol with wholeness as anything that might have cognitive validity. For De Man, especially, it remains simply 'mystification'. Indeed, in repeatedly identifying symbol as 'mystification', De Man is not making a casual comment, but rather aligning symbol in the telescopic sight of his cherished weapon of deconstruction. As he says in his *Allegories of Reading*, 'we are saying that criticism is the deconstruction of literature, the reduction to the rigors of grammar of rhetorical mystifications'.[106] But that De Man's criticism of symbol signally fails in such a reduction can itself be rigorously elucidated.

For symbol is not a mystification. On the contrary, the fragmentary nature of our intuitions, as the present author has elsewhere undertaken to demonstrate in detailed argument, demands the idea of a whole that can only be approached by symbol. No other approach to this idea is possible. Of the German *Trauerspiel* Benjamin concludes that 'in the spirit of allegory it is conceived from the outset as a ruin, a fragment'.[107] Precisely. Hence, in the phenomenological analysis of ruin and fragment, the need for a conception other than allegory. In *Romanticism and the Forms of*

[101] *Notebooks*, iii. 3247.
[102] *Lay Sermons*, 59.
[103] Ibid. 30.
[104] *Notebooks*, iii. 4253.
[105] *Aids to Reflection*, 254 n.
[106] De Man, *Allegories*, 17.
[107] Benjamin, 235.

Ruin: Wordsworth, Coleridge and Modalities of Fragmentation, the present author attempts to show that the phenomenology of fragmentation expressed in the formula 'incompleteness, fragmentation, and ruin' is at the heart of Romanticism. Then, in a concluding chapter called 'The Place Beyond the Heavens: True Being, Transcendence, and the Symbolic Indication of Wholeness', the book tries to demonstrate that incompletion, fragmentation, and ruin logically involve the symbolic indication of wholeness.

To rehearse the phenomenological arguments presented in that chapter, however, is not the task of the present discussion. Rather, the task here is to show that the structure of symbol, considered not merely as an indicator of wholeness, but as a response to the experience of reality, has a rationally cognitive validity. Symbol, far from being a mystification, is a direct accounting of human perception.[108] Indeed, 'Our Images are Usually Vague', a rubric in the great psychological work of William James, subsumes an argument that shows, against Hume's *a priori* confidence in the clear and distinct, that in actual experience the clear and distinct are in short supply.[109]

But in order to elucidate in more detail symbol's relation to actuality, a Romantic formulation of symbolic function divorced from the dialectic of symbol and allegory must be summoned. Its author is De Quincey. Using not even the name symbol, but rather the unique term 'involute'[110]—which serves to locate his conception outside an existing critical tradition and centre it rather on personal experience—the

---

[108] The establishment of this truth seems especially germane in view of De Man's position, both express and implied, that allegory alone responsibly renders reality. 'Whereas the symbol postulates the possibility of an identity or identification, allegory designates primarily a distance in relation to its own origin, and, renouncing the nostalgia and the desire to coincide, it establishes its language in the void of this temporal difference. In so doing, it prevents the self from an illusory identification with the non-self, which is now fully, though painfully, recognized as a non-self. It is this painful knowledge that we perceive at the moments when early romantic literature finds its true voice' (De Man, 191). Again: 'Allegory and irony are thus linked in their common discovery of a truly temporal predicament. They are also linked in their common de-mystification of an organic world postulated in a symbolical mode of analogical correspondences or in a mimetic mode of representation in which fiction and reality could coincide' (pp. 203–4).

[109] James, 691.

[110] The present focus on De Quincey's involute germinated from a paper by Robert Morrison, 'The Autobiographical Art of De Quincey', delivered at the Wordsworth Summer Conference at Dove Cottage, 13 August 1986. For further discussion of 'involute', see Hugh Sykes Davies, 'Involutes and the Process of Involution', *Wordsworth and the Worth of Words*, ed. John Kerrigan and Jonathan Wordsworth (Cambridge: Cambridge University Press, 1986), 121–85; Jonathan Wordsworth, *William Wordsworth: The Borders of Vision* (Oxford: Clarendon Press, 1982), 61.

Romantic essayist provides a framework of considerations that introduces this chapter's final arguments against De Man. De Quincey broaches the term to describe an aspect of his reaction to death:

Let me pause for one instant in approaching a remembrance so affecting for my own mind, to mention that, in the 'Opium Confessions,' I endeavoured to explain why death, other conditions remaining the same, is more profoundly affecting in summer than in other parts of the year—so far, at least, as it is liable to any modification at all from accidents of scenery or season. The reason, as I there suggested, lies in the antagonism between the tropical redundancy of life in the summer, and the frozen sterilities of the grave. The summer we see, the grave we haunt with our thoughts; the glory is around us, the darkness is within us; and, the two coming into collision, each exalts the other into stronger relief. But, in my case, there was even a subtler reason why the summer had this intense power of vivifying the spectacle or the thoughts of death. And, recollecting it, I am struck with the truth, that far more of our deepest thoughts and feelings pass to us through perplexed combinations of *concrete* objects, pass to us as *involutes* (if I may coin that word) in compound experiences incapable of being disentangled, than ever reach us *directly*, and in their own abstract shapes.[111]

In declaring the perceptual inadequacy of experiences that 'reach us *directly*, and in their own abstract shapes', De Quincey is also declaring the inadequacy of the 'clear and distinct' as a criterion. And yet he is adhering strictly to the nature not only of his own experience, but of the experience we all share. For 'compound experiences', not 'clear and distinct ideas', are the true stuff not only of life but of significant literature as well. Not the 'lucidity of the pre-romantic writers', but the 'perplexed combinations' of De Quincey's involutes are the materials of experience, and the art that mirrors it. As Coleridge said, in rejecting the 'lucidity' of his 'pre-romantic' predecessor, Hume:

How opposite to nature & the fact to talk of the one *moment* of Hume; of our whole being an aggregate of successive single sensations. Who ever *felt* a *single* sensation? Is not every one at the same moment conscious that there co-exist a thousand others in a darker shade, or less light; even as when I fix my attention on a white House on a grey bare Hill or rather long ridge that runs out of sight each way . . . the pretended single sensation is it any thing more than the *Light*-point in every picture either of nature or of a good painter; & again subordinately in every component part of the picture? And what is a moment? Succession with *interspace*? Absurdity! It is evidently only the Licht-punct, the *Sparkle* in the indivisible undivided Duration.[112]

---

[111] *De Quincey*, i. 38–9.
[112] *Notebooks*, ii. 2370. Christmas Day, 1804.

In arguing that no one 'ever *felt* a *single* sensation', but rather that every sensation co-exists with 'a thousand others in a darker shade', Coleridge precisely declares for the 'compound experiences incapable of being disentangled' and the 'perplexed combinations of *concrete* objects' that De Quincey later made the characteristic of his involutes. Both insistences are based on an examination of the experience we actually have, not on that 'rhetoric' or 'figural language' that so totally occupies the attention of De Man. Both reject the criterion of the 'clear and distinct', as they reject De Man's 'lucidity of the pre-romantic writers', which indeed they reveal, to use another phrasing of De Man, as being actually itself a form of 'ontological bad faith'. The perceptual insistences of Coleridge and De Quincey, moreover, supply a cognitive justification for the indistinct and vague reference of symbol.

The fact that reality is perceived in the way that De Quincey and Coleridge assert was demonstrated by William James in 1890, in his monumental *Principles of Psychology*, a work that mounts a continuing scientific polemic against the 'lucidity' of 'pre-romantic' theorists of perception. Where Coleridge insists that no one 'ever *felt* a *single* sensation', James in total agreement extensively argues that

No one ever had a simple sensation by itself. Consciousness, from our natal day, is of a teeming multiplicity of objects and relations, and what we call simple sensations are results of discriminative attention, pushed often to a very high degree. It is astonishing what havoc is wrought in psychology by admitting at the outset apparently innocent suppositions, that nevertheless contain a flaw. The bad consequences develop themselves later on, and are irremediable, being woven through the whole texture of the work. The notion that sensations, being the simplest things, are the first things to take up in psychology is one of these suppositions. The only thing which psychology has a right to postulate at the outset is the fact of thinking itself, and that must first be taken up and analyzed.[113]

After subtle and fine-grained argument, James concludes that consciousness is not formed of clear and distinct parts, but rather that

Consciousness, then, does not appear to itself chopped up in bits. Such words as 'chain' or 'train' do not describe it fitly as it presents itself in the first instance. It is nothing jointed; it flows. A 'river' or a 'stream' are the metaphors by which it is most naturally described. *In talking of it hereafter, let us call it the stream of thought, or consciousness, or of subjective life.*[114]

---

[113] James, 219.
[114] Ibid. 233.

In thus broaching that conception of the 'stream of consciousness' that has had such vast subsequent effect in twentieth-century literature and thought, James was developing ideas set in motion by his Romantic predecessors. James's 'stream of thought' flows in the same bed as Wordsworth's 'river of my mind':

> But who shall parcel out
> His intellect by geometric rules,
> Split like a province into round and square?
> Who knows the individual hour in which
> His habits were first sown, even as a seed?
> Who that shall point as with a wand and say
> 'This portion of the river of my mind
> Came from yon fountain?'[115]

With such Romantic lineage, it is hardly surprising that the conception of consciousness as a stream wholly invalidates eighteenth-century psychological postulates based on the 'clear and distinct'. Where Coleridge finds Hume's theory of perception an 'absurdity', James finds it 'ridiculous'. He rejects the criterion of the clear and distinct:

Now what I contend for, and accumulate examples to show, is that 'tendencies' are not only descriptions from without, but that they are among the *objects* of the stream, which is thus aware of them from within, and must be described as in very large measure constituted of *feelings* of *tendency*, often so vague that we are unable to name them at all. It is, in short, the re-instatement of the vague to its proper place in our mental life which I am so anxious to press on the attention.[116]

The Romantic feeling for the world, and especially its talisman, the conception of symbol, above all emphasized what James in his theoretical argumentation attempted to accomplish: 'the re-instatement of the vague to its proper place in our mental life'. James presses home his attack on the 'lucidity' of his 'pre-romantic' forebears:

Mr. Galton and Prof. Huxley have, as we shall see in Chapter XVIII, made one step in advance in exploding the ridiculous theory of Hume and Berkeley that we can have no images but of perfectly definite things. Another is made in the overthrow of the equally ridiculous notion that, whilst simple objective qualities are revealed to our knowledge in subjective feelings, relations are not. But these reforms are not half sweeping and radical enough. What must be admitted is that the definite images of traditional psychology form but the very smallest part of our minds as they actually live. The traditional psychology talks like one who should

---

[115] Wordsworth, *Prelude*, 76 (bk. ii (1805), lines 208–15).
[116] James, 246.

say a river consists of nothing but pailsful, spoonsful, quartpotsful, barrelsful, and other moulded forms of water. Even were the pails and pots all actually standing in the stream, still between them the free water would continue to flow. It is just this free water of consciousness that psychologists resolutely overlook.[117]

But if pre-romantic psychologists mired in the 'clear and distinct'—mired in De Man's 'lucidity'—resolutely overlooked it, Romantic proponents of symbol did not. Romantic symbol, to use the terms of James's metaphor, took the pails and pots standing in the stream and insisted on the inseparability of the water they contained with 'the free water of consciousness' that flowed around them. Romantic symbol witnesses the ineluctable truth established by James's epoch-making treatise:

Every definite image in the mind is steeped and dyed in the free water that flows round it. With it goes the sense of its relations, near and remote, the dying echo of whence it came to us, the dawning sense of whither it is to lead. The significance, the value, of the image is all in this halo or penumbra that surrounds and escorts it,—or rather that is fused into one with it and has become bone of its bone and flesh of its flesh; leaving it, it is true, an image of the same *thing* it was before, but making it an image of that thing newly taken and freshly understood.[118]

It would be difficult to formulate a more complete description of the imagistic structure of the Romantic symbol. In truth, leaving aside its reaching after unity, Romantic symbol is just that indication of the 'halo or penumbra' that in cognitive experience, as demonstrated by James, actually accompanies every lucidly defined object of consciousness. When, as noted above, Goethe said that 'everything that happens is symbol, and, while it perfectly represents itself, points to other matters [*das übrige*]',[119] the *das übrige* is exactly the 'free water' surrounding a defined object of attention, the 'sense of its relations, near and remote', the coincidence of 'supra-sensible meaning' with 'sensible appearance'. Conversely, the defined object is only 'the *Sparkle* in the indivisible undivided duration', or the result 'of discriminative attention, pushed often to a very high degree'.

All this other material—*das übrige*—justifies the key term used by Goethe and Schlegel: the 'inexpressible'. To them the symbol, along with its imagistic presentation, conveys that which is 'inexpressible' (*unaussprechlich*). It evokes, in other words, the truth that 'Every definite image

---

[117] James, 246.
[118] Ibid.
[119] Goethe, xxi. 286.

in the mind is steeped and dyed in the free water that flows round it'. The symbol is an assertion of relationships more, not less, responsible to actual experience than is the allegory of De Man and Benjamin: 'With it goes the sense of its relations, near and remote, the dying echo of whence it came to us, the dawning sense of whither it is to lead. The significance, the value, of the image is all in this halo or penumbra that surrounds and escorts it.'

Just as every seemingly 'definite image' has other relations 'fused' into it, so that it is 'an image of the same *thing* it was before', yet after taking these fused relationships into account, now 'an image of that thing newly taken and freshly understood', so too, definingly, for symbol. Speaking in 1797 of the objects of the plastic arts, Goethe said that

The objects will be determined by a deep feeling which, when it is pure and natural, will coincide with the best and loftiest objects and will ultimately render them symbolic. The objects represented in this way appear to exist for themselves alone and are nevertheless significant at the deepest level, because of the ideal that always draws a certain generality along with it. If the symbolic points to something else beyond representation, it will always do so indirectly. . . . Today there are also works of art that sparkle by virtue of reason, wit, gallantry, and we include in this category all allegorical works as well; of these latter we expect the least, because they likewise destroy our interest in representation itelf, and shove the spirit back upon itself, so to speak, and remove from its field of vision all that is truly represented. The allegorical differs from the symbolic in that what the symbolic designates indirectly, the allegorical designates directly.[120]

As a modern commentator concisely says, 'Allegory signifies directly; that is, its perceptible face has no reason for being save to transmit a meaning. Symbols signify only indirectly, in a secondary fashion: a symbol is present first of all for itself, and only in a secondary phase do we discover what it signifies.'[121]

Sometimes a symbolic process does not isolate a single physical thing or image of that thing, but, in a secondary derivation, inheres in a complex of activity. Answering Eckermann's question as to how a drama must be composed to be 'theatrical', Goethe invoked the symbol:

'It must be symbolic', answered Goethe. 'That means, each activity must be meaningful in itself and eventuate [*hinzielen*] in one still more important. The Tartuffe of Molière is in this regard a great pattern. Think only of the first scene, what an exposition that is! From the beginning everything here is in the highest significant, and encloses something yet more important which will come.'[122]

[120] *Goethes Werke*, xxxiii. 94.
[121] Todorov, 201.
[122] Goethe, xxiv. 179.

Constantly attempting to convey the specific though indistinct nature of
symbol, as it pertains to the difference between symbolic and allegoric
treatment, Goethe elsewhere says that

There is a great difference according to whether the poet is seeking access to the
general through the particular or sees the general in the particular. From the first of
these approaches allegory is born; in this the particular has value solely as an
example of the general. The second approach is nevertheless properly the nature of
poetry: it states a particular without thinking on the basis of the general and
indicating it. But the reader who immediately grasps this particular receives the
general at the same time, without realizing it, or realizing it only later.[123]

In sum, the symbol is what it appears to be, but it is also more than it
appears to be: 'by a symbol', said Coleridge, 'I mean, not a metaphor or
allegory or any other figure of speech or form of fancy, but an actual and
essential part of that, the whole of which it represents.'[124]

Indeed, Benjamin himself, despite the blinkered vision of his *Ursprung
des deutschen Trauerspiels*, elsewhere arrives precisely at Coleridge's
awareness of the coexistence of perceptions, and De Quincey's insistence
on 'perplexed combinations' and 'compound experiences' as the stuff of
perception. In an essay called 'On Language as Such and on the Language
of Man', posthumously published twenty-seven years after the work on
the German tragic drama, Benjamin shows himself finally aware that in
any deep statement the expressible always involves the 'inexpressible',
which for Goethe and Schlegel had been the common and defining factor
in the conception of symbol. Benjamin says, in words that take their place
beside those of De Quincey and of Coleridge, that

within all linguistic formation a conflict is waged between what is expressed and
expressible and what is inexpressible and unexpressed. On considering this
conflict one sees, in the perspective of the inexpressible, at the same time the last
mental entity.[125]

For the Romantics, the symbol, which signified the coincidence and
fusion of the expressed and the inexpressible, was indeed the last mental
entity.[126] It was deeply intertwined with their emphasis on nature, with
their emphasis on imagination, with their emphasis on the infinite, and
with their emphasis on reason. It was not, as De Man would have it, a

[123] *Goethes Werke*, xxxviii. 261.
[124] *Lay Sermons*, 79.
[125] Benjamin, *Reflections*, 320.
[126] Compare Gadamer's succinct formulation of the difference between symbol and
allegory: 'The symbol is the coincidence of the sensible and the non-sensible, allegory the
meaningful relation of the sensible to the non-sensible' (Gadamer, 67).

'mystification'. Nor, as he also would have it, was it, either then or now, merely 'a special case of figural language in general, a special case that can lay no claim to historical or philosophical priority over other figures'. It was rather a necessary form of human thought. It was, further, a token for the idea of unity that became increasingly fragmented in the cultural experience of the Romantics. It was ultimately an assertion of meaning summoned against the nihilism that Nietzsche was to forecast as the inevitable form of future thought, and that even then loomed menacingly on the horizon towards which the Romantics were drifting.

And so this volume reaches its end. The foregoing arguments, in their polemical dimension, have focused themselves mainly against six scholars, Marilyn Butler, Paul De Man, Marjorie Levinson, Alan Liu, Jerome McGann, and E. P. Thompson. In opposition to the varying contentions of these figures, the book has maintained a consistently conservative standpoint with respect to the nature and meaning of Romanticism. Yet conservatism, one must never allow oneself to forget, is an attitude that makes sense only where there is something of value to conserve.

What of value is there to conserve in the understandings denominated by the cultural term Romanticism? The answer urged here is that the term Romanticism represents the primary and necessary sorting of data that must occur before cultural manifestations from approximately 1770 to 1850 can be rewardingly addressed. Leibniz, the most complete intellectual of the last half millennium, stressed that intractable problems yield solutions only where multitudinous data have been sorted into groups based on likeness in structure and contiguity in meaning. *Mutatis mutandis*, the term Romanticism asserts such a controlling similarity in the data it subsumes. The recognition of that similarity is indispensable for all subsequent awarenesses of relationship.

Romanticism was a term settled upon only after contributions from a wide and committed variety of participants, thinking and writing over successive decades. It remains a term that signifies the distillation of the insight and reflection, the perception and understanding, of many different thinkers. It should not lightly be compromised or cast aside in favour of the momentary lucubrations of a few modern scholars noticeably concerned—with all due respect—with having something new to say. It should rather be experienced more closely and attuned more finely as it is brought to renewed life by the study of each new generation of literary and historical thought.

A few years ago there arose the temporary fashion of denying the existence of the Renaissance, on the grounds that it was a word brought to the fore by Michelet and Burckhardt, and not known to the intellects of the period so designated. But one need only recall, as random indicators, that in England, Bacon, in his *Novum Organum*, and earlier, in the projections for *Temporis Partus Maximus*, emphatically specified the difference between his age and those that came before; or, in Italy, in references quite different, that Leonardo Bruni had still earlier, in *Rerum Suo Tempore Gestarum Commentarius*, vividly depicted the bypassing of medieval scholastic models and concerns in the new enthusiasm for the Greek language and Greek models; or that Rabelais, in France, saluted powerfully the sense of a new intellectual world. As with the Renaissance, so with Romanticism. Call it what one will, the sorting known as Romanticism refers to realities, and one ignores these realities at the peril of grievous error in understanding.

In the preface to this book, an intent was set forth to shake the foundations of the new orthodoxy in Romantic studies. Whether or not those foundations are judged to have been shaken, it is hoped that the book will seem a counterpoise to the various approaches it challenges. For as the world continues to metamorphose with increasing rapidity—careering towards 'Zooropa', as it were—Romanticism becomes ever more important to comprehend. It linked the world of the past, before technology accelerated, to the new world in which we are living. It was the last great continental shift in the awareness of reality; for what is called Victorianism is merely an unmistakable extension of Romantic awareness, and what was called the Modern is also a working out of the implications of the Romantic vision.

The new world, that which supervened in the sixties of this century—the Civil Rights Act of 1964 is perhaps as good a hypothetical date for its emergence as any, though perhaps a date connected with the rise of computers could contest for the honour, or still again that of the landing of men on the moon, or the emergence of satellite television, or even the symbolic date of the aircraft *Concorde*—that new world is at present still changing too rapidly to be assessed with confidence. As measure of the baffling enormity of the changes that are upon us, one may ponder a paradox that arises just at the moment when Marxism, which provided the fullest panoply of analysis directed towards the actual world of the nineteenth century, seems to have thunderously collapsed. For the emerging homogenization of world economic markets reveals itself as precisely the condition that Marx posited as the necessary prelude to the establishment of a mature communism. Yet as Hazlitt realized, the future is in very fact, however disturbing or enticing its portents in the present, opaque to us: 'The future is like a dead wall or a thick mist hiding all objects from our view.'[127]

But Romanticism, where process first established its hegemony, is there to be understood, if only we have eyes to see it, and ears to hear it. As Hazlitt also realized, in a continuation of the statement just quoted, 'the past is alive and stirring with objects, bright or solemn, and of unfading interest.'[128] As instance of how the living past can illuminate aspects of futurity, after that futurity comes but before it is defined, the 'hippiedom' that flourished in, and in a sense inaugurated, the new world of the sixties was itself a most pure and unmistakable Romanticism; and certain of the stresses that defined Romanticism are present today in alarming and even augmented force.

By understanding what Romanticism was, and what it meant, we can better understand both what should be valued, and what should be feared, on the horizons of our own experience. But to understand what Romanticism was, it must be attended to very closely; it must be touched, palpably touched, in all the richness of its varied and intertwined textures. That touching is what this book has attempted to supply.

[127] *Hazlitt*, viii. 25.
[128] Ibid.

Index

Abrams, M. H. 14, 78; attacks
    Levinson 268; sees and does not see
    text called Romanticism 15
absence 14, 25, 42, 45; new discourses of
    forfeit relevance 32; receding ocean
    of 44
activity, intellectual engagement an 12;
    ideational 22
Acton, John Emerich Edward Dalberg,
    Baron 138
actuality 153, 154; did not rank highly in
    Shelley's scale of values 153; Leavis
    charges Shelley with weak grasp
    upon the actual 153; Shelley
    insulates himself from 173; Shelley's
    need to deaden himself to 175; stress
    of 174, 175; *see also* reality
Addison, Joseph 217, 224, 273; does not
    distinguish imagination from
    fancy 214; foreshadows Coleridge's
    division of imaginative function 215;
    heralds Romantic apotheosis of
    imagination 216; witnesses turn from
    distrust of imagination 214
Adonais 140, 152, 160, 168, 171, 174, 189,
    198, 199; grief in especially
    plangent 162; its exhortation to
    die 166; restructures Shelley's inner
    desolation 169; Shelley's greatest
    poem 151; suffused by wish for
    death 161
Aeschylus 143
Age of Reason 210, 213, 224, 235, 238,
    264; really inaugurated by
    Descartes 258
Alexander the Great 198
Alfieri, Vittorio, Conte 143
allegorical, difference from symbolical 280
allegory 299; always subordinate 285–6;
    Benjamin on 292; described by
    Coleridge and Goethe 286; described
    by Creuzer 292; difference from
    symbol in Goethe 275; distinguished
    from symbol 274; dominated in
    medieval world 273; as foil for
    symbol 285; a mode of

expression 273, 274, 280; never
    constitutes essential value of a
    work 285–6; origin of 300; originally
    belonged to sphere of talk 280;
    praised by Benjamin 284; raised
    above symbol by De Man 272, 276;
    successive, symbol simultaneous 276;
    and symbol 272; temporality of 276,
    277; witnesses a disjunction 273,
    275, 286
Allegra (Clara Allegra Byron) 184, 186,
    187, 188
Allsop, Thomas 147
Alps, crossing the 39, 40, 46
Althusser, Louis 31
America, Coleridge's plan to emigrate
    to 90; role in French Revolution 99,
    126
American Revolution, defended by
    Burke 99, 100; Hazlitt's view of 87;
    not a true revolution 87
anti-Christianity, Jacobin led to doctrinal
    atheism of Marx 125
Antony, Mark (Marcus Antonius) 55
Apollonius of Tyana 237
apostasy, apostate 80, 93, 101, 102, 112,
    145; E. P. Thompson on 79
Apuleius 143
Ariès, Philippe 265
Ariosto, Ludovico 143
Aristotle, on sight 4, 214; his *De Anima*
    subsumed imagination 208
Arnold, Matthew, can talk of what is
    important in Wordsworth 44;
    denigrator of Shelley 140; his
    judgement of Wordsworth 26–7
Arnold, Thomas 229
Arrian (Flavius Arrianus) 143
art 11; judgement of not matter of
    opinion 30; textual formation known
    as 5, 6
atheism, atheist 157, 232; of Hume and
    Voltaire 245; of Marx 125; as
    pantheism 147; respected by
    Coleridge 146–7; of Shelley 148
Auden, W. H. 79

Thelwall 116; goal of intellectual agenda to free mind from 'it is' 244; argues government based on property 88; gravitates from Kant to Jacobi 249; on great law of imagination 283; greatest talker of the age 115; on Hannibal and Napoleon 47; on history 34; honorific use of imagination 212; hopes for advancement of humanity only from the individual 93–4; his humanitarianism 134; on identity of reason and faith 248–9; idiosyncrasy of his mental activity 83; importance of distinction between reason and understanding 231; intellectual attitudes conservative 123; intent of establishing rational ground of belief in God 246, 248; interconnectedness of his intellectual commitments 264; intertwinement with Jacobi 256; says Jacobin a term of abuse 104; judgement of 'The Ruined Cottage' 269; judgement of Wordsworth 27; and 'Kubla Khan' as dream 61; his learning stupendous 143; link between early and later political attitudes a continuing concern for the human 94; wants life to be as continuous as possible 94; his little world described revolution in an orbit of its own 90; lukewarm admirer of Rousseau 64; called man of blood by Thelwall 113; McGann on Coleridge's theory of poetry 19; mirrored interests of his friends 115, 116, 117, 118, 119; more complex illustrations of reason than Kant or Jacobi 258; need to counter Locke and Newton 244; need for Redeemer 256, 258; needed to elevate prestige of reason 240; needs not satisfied by Kant 248; neither Whig nor Tory 121; no documentation for Jacobin commitment of 89; on nothingism of Rousseau 261, 263; nothing in writings reveals him as man of blood 114; not a Jacobin 80, 114, 127, 128, 138; not a Tory 120; on not repudiating early self 80–1; on nowness and evanescence in

poetry 196; one heart for humanity 256; opposed adherences in politics 121; his opinion of Cobbett 104; opinions on reason parallel those on French Revolution 229; sees political health as product of opposed adherences 84; opposed to Locke, Hume, Helvetius, Condillac 236, 243; opposed to Shelley on Christianity 144; opposed to Enlightenment 236; his opposition to Jacobin spirit 134; opposition to slave trade 134; on originating physicality of *symbolon* 282; overriding interest in theology 279; partial parallelism to Jacobinism 90; permanence and progression in politics 123; on perversion of reason in French Revolution 262; says his philosophy based on distinction between reason and understanding 230; plan to edit Homeric Hymns 147; says Plato and Bacon in agreement 147; on Plotinian One 189; political attitudes of 78; political development consistent with his mental procedures on all topics of thought 83; political essays 42; political hope based on Gospel 93; political role of property 126; politically different from Wordsworth and Southey 120; politics based on opposites 127; portrait of in 'Letter to Maria Gisborne' 144; portrait of in 'Peter Bell the Third' 144–5; his portrait of Robespierre 139; praised for goodness of heart 114; presages position of Aulard 129; and the primacy of self 254; says his principles opposite to Jacobinism 92; programmatic Jacobinism alien to him 135; projected own values into Shelley 145; his proleptic psychoanalytical acumen 10, 11; on Prometheus 147; reads *The Robbers* of Schiller 108; on reality of ultimate ideas 247; reason most potent term in his thought 229; on reason and understanding 259–60; on reason and the whole 254; his reconciling and humane political vision 113;

318 *Index*

Kant, Immanuel (*cont.*)
  WORKS CITED (*cont.*)
  Kritik der Urteilskraft 242
  Metaphysische Anfangsgründe der Naturwissenschaft 242
  Religion innerhalb der Grenzen der bloßen Vernunft 242
Keats, John 20, 163, 164, 167, 168, 222; emotional invocation of imagination 223; judgement of Wordsworth 27; pantheistic dispersal of his elements in *Adonais* 165; Shelley's understanding of merits of 143
Kelley, Donald R. 46
Kellgren, Johan Henrik 109
Kelly, J. N. D. 279
Kennedy, Michael L. 95
Kerr, Wilfred B. 109
Kerrigan, John 294
Kierkegaard, Søren 278
Kitson, Peter 88
Klopstock, Friedrich Gottlieb 108
Knight, G. Wilson 29
Knitch 115
know, in the sense of ultimate touching 5
Kolakowski, Leszek 31, 32
Körner, Christian Gottfried 110
Korngold, Ralph 100
Kurtz, Benjamin P. 119

Lafayette, Marie-Joseph-Paul, Marquis de 126, 127
Lamartine, Alphonse de 101
Lamb, Charles 51; found Coleridge a jokester 118; praises Coleridge's conversation about poetry 118
Langbaum, Robert 228
Leavis, F. R. 140, 169; charges Shelley with weak grasp upon the actual 153; his judgement of 'The Ruined Cottage' 269; on Shelley's ardours, ecstasies, and despairs 153
Lebon, J. 279
Lefebvre, Georges 124, 125, 127, 128, 135
Leibniz, Gottfried Wilhelm 15, 51, 250, 291; against Locke 254; on necessary sorting of data 301; and *petites perceptions* 290; on primacy of mind 254
Lemon, Lee T. 197
Lenin, Vladimir Ilich Ulyanov, called 32, 131, 132

Le Peletier de Saint-Fargeau, Louis-Michel 124
Levinson, Marjorie 22, 26, 32, 33, 301; her argument invoked by McGann 269; attacked by Abrams, Vendler, Haines, and McFarland 268; as illustration of McGann's agenda 268; says primary poetic action of 'Tintern Abbey' is the suppression of the social 70
Lewis, C. S. 273, 274, 280, 281
Lietzmann, H. 279
Liu, Alan 32, 40, 200, 301; accumulating contextual self-indulgence of 43; admirable learning of 46; affirms history 34; cannot allow contextual intrusion of Hannibal 47-8; cannot illuminate fact of genius 44; cannot talk of what is important in Wordsworth 44; his discourse on Napoleon 39-40; his discourse sometimes irrelevant 45; discursiveness of 41; enrols among proponents of new approach 33; identifies imagination with Napoleon 42; occluded vision in 35; point of view of 38, 49; provides a 'mediocre Wordsworth' 49; radical denials of 34; reconfigures Hartman's argument 42; redirects focus from poetry to history 43; on Simplon Pass episode 37, 41; sometimes seems to play games 45; sweeps Hannibal into note 48; substitutes denied history for nature, mind and imagination 34
Livy (Titus Livius) 143
Lloyd-Jones, Hugh, on comparative knowledge of Greek by Coleridge and Shelley 141
Locke, John 93, 236; his claim to understanding conceded by Coleridge 243; Coleridge says *Recluse* should refute 245; Condillac and Hartley his epigones 217, 236; and the criterion of the clear and distinct 290, 291; criticized by Leibniz 254; Kant steeped in tradition of 241; read by Shelley 143; ties liberty to ownership of property 126; his tradition of psychology opposed by Coleridge 123, 236